D0821046

Anarchism
and Cultural Politics in
Fin de Siècle France

Richard D. Sonn

Anarchism

and Cultural Politics
in Fin de Siècle France

WITHDRAWN
UTSA LIBRARIES

University of Nebraska Press
Lincoln and London

Copyright © 1989 by the
University of Nebraska Press
All rights reserved
Manufactured in the United States
of America

The paper in this book meets the
minimum requirements
of American National Standard for
Information Sciences –
Permanence of Paper for Printed
Library Materials,
ANSI Z39.48–1984.

Library of Congress
Cataloging-in-Publication Data

Sonn, Richard David.
Anarchism and cultural politics
in fin de siècle France /
Richard D. Sonn
p.   cm.
A revision of the author's thesis
(doctoral – University
of California, Berkeley)
Bibliography: p.
Includes index.
ISBN 0-8032-4175-5 (alk. paper)
1. Anarchism – France – History –
19th century.   2. Politics and
culture – France – History –
19th century.   I. Title.
HX893.S58 1989
320.5'7'0944–dc19   88-10622 CIP

Library
University of Texas
at San Antonio

For Julia and Alexander,
harbingers of the New Dawn,
perpetrators of an old form of anarchy,
l'anarchie domestique.

Contents

Illustrations

Acknowledgments

This book began as my doctoral dissertation at the University of California at Berkeley. The research was undertaken in Paris in 1977–78, while I was an Ehrman Fellow in European Studies. I wish to thank the helpful staffs of the Bibliothèque Nationale, the Bibliothèque Jacques Doucet, the Bibliothèque d'Histoire de la Ville de Paris, the Institut Français d'Histoire Sociale, the Archives Nationales, and the Archives de la Préfecture de Police. The benefits of availing oneself of a variety of the innumerable libraries and archives in Paris derive in part from the familiarity they afford of different *quartiers*. The materials I uncovered within these research facilities proved invaluable for this study, but the discovery of Paris itself was also important in transforming an overly abstract conception of a thesis into a work bearing the imprint of some measure of experience and delight with the city where anarchist culture evolved.

I am grateful for all the help and stimulation I received from Martin Malia and Martin Jay of the University of California at Berkeley, Department of History, and Georges Longrée of the Departments of French and Comparative Literature. Lynn Hunt read and commented upon the material in chapter 4, which was published in substantially the same form as appears here in *Historical Reflections* 11, no. 3 (Fall 1984). That journal's editors have kindly allowed me to reprint that material here. My mentors are of course absolved of any responsibility for the content and conclusions of this book, which in any case diverges considerably from the dissertation they directed.

A very different sort of inspiration, analogical rather than theoretical, was provided by Bruce "Utah" Phillips. More than anyone else in contemporary America, he embodies the spirit of the anarchist singer and *trimardeur* that I have tried to convey, as he transmutes his own experiences and his knowledge of his "Wobbly" forebears into stories and songs.

I have done most of the work of writing this book while serving as assistant professor of history at Gustavus Adolphus College in St. Peter, Minnesota. I would particularly like to thank the staff of the Computer Center for providing the technical facilities with which to edit the book. Larry Bodin and Tracy Turner helped me do much of the necessary keyboarding.

I owe both personal and intellectual debts of gratitude to my wife, Mary, for her help, stimulation, and patience over the years, for putting up with the privations of an unheated Montreuil apartment while I studied in warm Parisian libraries, and for sharing the longer-term uncertainties and dislocations that commitment to academia so often entails. She has helped me edit the manuscript through successive phases of its life, and helped to overcome my resistance to the computer age. I am grateful too to my parents, Raymond and Ann Sonn, for their long-term support and encouragement.

Introduction

Parisian cafés, churches, the homes of judges, and the seats of power rocked by explosions; heads of state felled by the knives of assailants; anarchist heads fallen to the guillotine; the glitter and charm of Belle Epoque society disturbed by rumblings from the lower depths: such is the melodramatic impression left by the anarchist movement at the end of the nineteenth century. Portrayed as an insidious destroyer of civilization by novelists of the era—Conrad, James, Chesterton, Zola—the anarchist was easily stereotyped, widely feared, and seldom understood.[1] Anarchy commonly suggested disorder, and by most political standards anarchism was indeed anarchic—rebellious, chaotic, and often violent. By character and principle anarchists tended to be resolutely individualistic and therefore refractory to such notions as party discipline and organizational hierarchy. Most anarchists were impatient activists who sought immediate, radical change, even while they harbored utopian dreams of a better future.

These generalizations may help to explain the movement's ultimate failure to achieve its goals, but they do little to clarify its very real successes in creating a mass movement with broad appeal. In evaluating the remarkable vitality of anarchism in its heyday at the turn of the century, one must ask how a philosophy of radical individualism could generate a movement. How did such a movement function with only the most rudimentary organizational framework? Could anarchist hatred of state power and authority produce a coherent alternative view of social order, or were the anarchists true to their stereotype as nihilistic destroyers vengefully clutching a bomb or a dagger beneath their shabby coats?

Beneath the apparent disorder inherent in French anarchism in the 1890s lay a remarkable sense of solidarity, bolstered by the institutions and customs that distinguished a unique anarchist subculture within the environs of Paris. Moral, social, intellectual, and aesthetic bonds—in short, culture—made French anarchism in the 1890s something more than the expression of utopian dreams or terrorist violence. This culture became institutionalized in the anarchist press, in anarchist cabarets featuring anarchist singers, in libraries, schools, and eventually in the unions and the Bourses du Travail where workers sought work and found revolutionary propaganda. The solidarity and devotion fostered by this culture compensated for the movement's very real weaknesses, while manifesting anarchistic values in contemporary life rather than awaiting their realization in the postrevolutionary millennium. It was precisely anarchism's shortcomings as a political movement that increased the centrality of more broadly cultural sources of identity and coherence. This was especially true of anarchism in the 1890s, when the movement's emphasis on propaganda placed a high premium on whatever media were available to them.

As the cultural context is vital for comprehending anarchist politics, understanding anarchist culture requires that one relate it to the lower-class Parisian mentality, or *mentalité,* of the late nineteenth century—the way that ordinary people made sense of the world.[2] It includes "not merely what people thought but how they thought—how they construed the world, invested it with meaning, and infused it with emotion."[3] Those aesthetic images, linguistic codes, religious rituals, and social customs which structured this mental activity offer the best access into this mentality. Anarchist and popular culture were not coterminous, but the former was derived selectively from the latter, and the movement owed its appeal largely to the degree to which its ideology corresponded to prevailing lower-class values. The movement's vitality was due to the anarchists' ability to rephrase the popular mentality in the desired ideological terms, and in so doing to encourage a distinctive anarchist culture. This culture reflected such fundamental structures of discourse as lower-class speech or argot (see chapter 4), which predisposed its speakers to accept anarchist interpretations of social reality. Such mental structures helped compensate the anarchists for their lack of more overt structures of political organization.

Anarchist politics was thus undergirded by anarchist culture, which was in turn based upon particular kinds of thought and perception existing within the popular mentality. The anarchists could utilize popular cultural forms to appeal to the people, but they had to rely on fundamental correspondences between their ideology and the popular mentality of which they were necessarily less conscious. A good example of such a correspondence was the anarchists' valuation of analogic forms of information, that is, "systems of codification which have a real and intrinsic relationship to what they signify."[4] A work of art, the example of a saintly personal life, the terrorist's bomb, the martyr's altruistic self-sacrifice, were analogs either of the revolution or of the anarchist ideal. They all demanded a fundamentally different kind of response from the didactic, expository, abstract message of the socialists, or for that matter, of Jean Grave's organ of anarchist orthodoxy, *La Révolte.* Grave's journal lacked the immediacy and emotional impact of *La Père Peinard,* not to mention of an explosion in the Chamber of Deputies; even the police informers frequently derided *La Révolte* for being overly staid and out of touch with the majority of anarchists. The preference for analogic over abstract modes of information to communicate the anarchist message explains much of anarchism's appeal to artists, tenderers of images rather than ideas.

Anarchism's affinity for analogic information also enhanced the quasi-religious status of the movement. Both artistic images and powerful experiences such as a martyr's death were received as metaphoric wholes; they commanded an immediacy that engendered an essentially emotional rather than analytical response. This is not to say that the anarchists disdained more complex and ideological thought, but that a large place in the movement was reserved for the kind of communication that led to belief rather than knowledge, that valued immediate experience rather than critical reflection.[5] The feeling of total rather than relative comprehension afforded by these modes of communication easily led to the total faith demanded by religious movements, the revolution thereby assuming apocalyptic overtones; social change would be as total and immediate as the metaphoric change in consciousness provided by the propagandistic medium.

Anarchist culture was not simply grafted onto a political movement. Anarchism, at least in the form it took in this period, can not be understood on solely political terms, but must be interpreted as a wide-ranging cultural rebellion, a *critique des moeurs* (to use the title of an

1893 collection of anarchist essays by Paul Adam) that attacked bourgeois morality as much as it did the institutions of state power. Critics at the time remarked that the propagandists by the deed were guilty of social rather than political crimes, because they wished to bring down all of society, not just the polity.[6] The terrorists' highly symbolic targets demonstrated this antagonism to contemporary social life, as explosions shook cafés as well as police stations, the Bourse as well as the Chamber of Deputies. One terrorist was even killed trying to destroy the Church of the Madeleine, and feelings against Sacré-Coeur, then rising on Montmartre's slopes, ran high. The anarchists negatively defined their objective as opposition to all authority. Although this was manifested most dramatically as opposition to the government and its military, law enforcement, and judicial institutions, it also meant opposition to the bourgeois institution of marriage as a symptom of paternal authority, to the orthodoxies of art and learning as embodied in the Academies, to the educational system, to formal culture, to formal language, to all hierarchical structures. Anarchists could not content themselves with a political or even a social critique of existing conditions; only a cultural critique of the competitive and dominative values underlying that system would suffice. Such a total critique led ineluctably to the total alternative of the anarchist utopian ideal, which ranged from the Naturists' primitivist rejection of modernity and longing to return to a hunting and gathering society, to Paul Adam's ambiguous dream of an advanced technocracy whose citizens' lives would integrate productive labor and self-fulfilling creativity.

If anarchism is to be understood as a political movement, then it can only be in the broadest sense of the term *politics*, as the public unfolding and goal directing of the cultural structure of meaning.[7] And yet paradoxically anarchism was an antipolitical political movement, which rejected the partisan struggle for power that characterized parliamentary politics. Anarchists even disavowed revolution insofar as it was a political act that would eventually install new authorities in positions of power. The German anarchist philosopher Max Stirner preferred instead to locate the anarchist spirit of revolt in insurrection, which implied a spontaneous mass uprising that would somehow avoid creating new institutions in place of the old.[8] The anarchists rejected politics per se, that is, any organized means of control vested in some authority. As anarchist utopias functioned harmoniously, with no one compelled to submit to another's dictates, so anarchist practice was also supposed to operate on strictly libertarian principles, which made all attempts to regularize an organizational apparatus anathema. Means and ends were not clearly distinguished. Even revolutionary necessity could not make the anarchists violate the principle of individual autonomy; rather, their fierce individualism made them inherently distrust any political movement, even their own. Both libertarian hyperindividualism and the rejection of authority and organizational hierarchies encouraged a cultural approach to radicalism. While guaranteeing a wide-ranging critique of society, this approach tended to disperse the movement's energy in many directions without ever getting to the business of how that society was to be overturned. The intrinsic tension in the politics of radical individualism surpassed that of laissez-faire individualism, though the adage that "the government governs best which governs least" bore a superficial resemblance to anarchist thought. For the anarchists it was not a question of more or less but of none at all, yet they had to come to grips with the problem of building a revolutionary movement. Their answer in the 1880s and early 1890s was the doctrine of propaganda by the deed; after 1895 the motto became "direct action." Both phrases characteristically stressed activism, yet the former emphasized that communication must precede collective action.

In the 1850s, the Realist painter and revolutionary Gustave Courbet allied himself with the anarchist philosopher Pierre-Joseph Proudhon, constituting what seemed to him the natural alliance of the dual avant-gardes of art and politics. A recent, nineteenth-century conception, the idea of the avant-garde signified that artists perceived themselves as standing in the forefront, in the "advance guard" of change. The belief that artists and revolutionaries pursued parallel routes took firm hold in the 1890s among such Symbolist writers as Stuart Merrill and Rémy de Gourmont.[9] The participation of formerly apolitical artists in 1890s anarchism was the most conspicuous part of the overall culture of anarchism, and historians of the movement have not failed to allude to the fact that even Stéphane Mallarmé and Leconte de Lisle subscribed to La Révolte.[10] The politicization of aesthetes, that is, the impact of anarchism on them, was certainly significant, but it is only a basis for understanding what impact, if any, the artists had on the anarchist movement and culture in these years. Were they willing to function as anarchist propagandists, or did they limit their political role to appreciating the aesthetic or spiritual qualities of violent political acts? Were they anarchist artists, or only artistic anarchists? Were the dual avant-gardes considered to be one coherent movement, or only parallel tendencies?

Historians have minimized the Symbolists' actual contribution to anarchism.[11] Although the involvement of artistic luminaries whose commitment was sometimes ephemeral and often romanticized should not be overstated, the mutual interaction of artists and anarchists was far more fruitful than the production of a few didactic works of anarchist art would indicate. On the artistic side, the Symbolists pursued the notion that a work could be radical within its aesthetic context without manifesting an overt political content—that form more than content determined whether a work was anarchistic. Free verse, the preference for "natural" rhythm over "artificial" rhyme and carefully scanned meters, the Romantic sense of poetry as a wholly different mode of communication from prose rather than as prosaic ideas dressed up in poetic form, were all metalinguistic preferences that challenged artistic codes. Anarchism made the poets more aware of the necessity of challenging prevailing rules of prosody; the poets hoped that such radical art would embody the order of a liberated society. The freedom and creativity of their lives and careers also embodied liberation from repressive regimentation and deadening routine. Painters and poets had no monopoly over signification and communication, but they did affect the conception of such practices as terrorism, conspiracy, and insurrection, and, most fundamentally, of liberation itself. Artists abetted anarchism not directly but dialectically, perceiving in anarchism the justification for the very aesthetic autonomy that had earlier been expressed as "art for art's sake." Anarchist art stood simultaneously for aesthetic autonomy and political *engagement*. The weary pose of the aesthete no longer sufficed in the 1890s, as artists and intellectuals engaged in a continuing debate on their social role both in anarchism and during the Dreyfus Affair, when France split over the guilt or innocence of a Jewish army captain convicted by a military tribunal of passing military secrets to the Germans.

Anarchist discourse suffused the avant-garde literary milieu so thoroughly in the early 1890s that, just as it is not possible to divorce anarchism from its cultural context, Symbolism can not be fully understood without being aware of this political context. The Symbolists tended to extend their aesthetic aspirations beyond the production of works of poetry or prose, to seek correspondences with other realms of experience as well as between the different senses and art forms. Anarchism shared this urge to totality, and encouraged the Symbolists' quest for a broader range of signification. This does not mean that all writers who were affected by anarchist ideas were politically active; chapter 7 will examine the varying degrees of political involvement. As there existed strong affinities between popular culture and anarchism, which the anarchists consciously exploited, so at the elite cultural level correspondences were perceived and developed from both sides. Registering the impact of both elite and popular culture on the movement is necessary to comprehend fully fin de siècle anarchism. To expose these relations is the primary goal of this book, more than to determine conclusively whether so-and-so was "really" an anarchist. It may be admitted from the outset that the search for these relations will lead to what are at times speculative hypotheses concerning the sources of anarchist culture.

The avant-garde writers and painters of the time enriched the culture of fin de siècle anarchism, but they did not create that culture. Aesthetes were attracted not merely to anarchist politics but also to the various elements of popular and anarchist culture. The two cultures, the popular and the elite, met under the anarchist aegis. Elite or "high" culture was certainly less important as a force unifying the anarchist movement. The terrorist François-Claudius Ravachol was supposedly turned toward anarchism by a reading of Eugène Sue's Le Juif errant (The Wandering Jew, 1845), and Emile Henry, who both wrote poetry and threw bombs, referred to Emile Zola's Germinal at his trial.[12] The terrorists displayed no such familiarity with the Symbolist poets who were attracted to anarchism in the 1890s, however. Even among those few writers who sought to broaden their readership base, none succeeded in making a dent in the popular imagination. Anarchism was not yet the strictly working-class movement toward which it would evolve as anarcho-syndicalism, but was rather a collection of marginal and déclassé elements of the population that could easily incorporate bohemian artists as well as tradespeople, intellectual as well as manual workers.

A central link between elite and popular culture was the milieu in which the anarchists interacted. Many of the writers involved in Symbolism lived in the Latin Quarter of Paris, on the Left Bank; others, in the company of the majority of painters and illustrators, lived in Montmartre. A disproportionate amount of anarchist cultural life revolved around the northern Parisian neighborhood of Montmartre, which was not only the home of bohemian artists but of many anarchist leaders and much of the anarchist press, with the notable exception of Jean Grave's *La Révolte*. Montmartre was as vital to the anarchist cultural milieu as the Latin Quarter was to the development of Symbolism. More than just the neighborhood in which many artists and anarchists lived, Montmartre epitomized the anarchist ideal of a harmonious balance between nature and culture, between urban modernity and rustic conviviality. Montmartre embodied both the sin and corruption of boulevard cabarets and the pastoralism of narrow, winding streets and windmills, all coexisting in a libertarian milieu devoted to art and scornful of convention. Focusing on Paris and especially on one key neighborhood—Montmartre—at a particular historical juncture—the period between Boulangism (see chapter 2) and the Dreyfus Affair, from 1889 to 1898—will help to portray concretely a unique era of anarchist cultural efflorescence.

One

The century following the French Revolution gave birth to most of the political ideologies that have shaped the modern world. Attached to conservatism, liberalism, and socialism are the names of some of the great political thinkers of the late eighteenth and the nineteenth centuries: Edmund Burke, John Stuart Mill, Alexis de Tocqueville, Karl Marx, and Friedrich Engels. At the end of the nineteenth century, most commentators would have included Michael Bakunin, Peter Kropotkin, and Pierre-Joseph Proudhon in the list of influential political thinkers. Yet today's history textbooks accord the anarchist movement scarcely a paragraph at the end of their discussion of socialism, with perhaps another brief citation when they mention the Spanish Civil War. In a world divided between capitalism and communism, with socialist and communist parties active in many parliamentary democracies, anarchism appears as a dead-end movement; in a complex, technocratic world of centralized nation-states so powerful that the term "totalitarian" has been coined for some of them, the ideal of a stateless society appears to be a utopian dream fit only for the most out-of-touch visionaries. Without arguing about anarchism's relevance to our own time, this sense of anarchism as a failed movement with no presence in the contemporary world makes it all the more important to reconstruct the vibrant, active movement of a century ago, which seriously challenged the social order and vied with socialism for the allegiance of the lower classes.

Anarchism in the 1890s was nearing the end of its first phase of activity as a more or less organized revolutionary movement. Modern, secular philosophies calling for a stateless, nonauthoritarian society date back to the late eighteenth century, to such thinkers as the English radical William Godwin. Antistatist thought received the most cogent

French expression with Pierre-Joseph Proudhon, who created a voluminous socialist-anarchist literature from the time of his disillusionment with the failure of the 1848 revolution until his death in 1865. The revolutionary debacle of 1848 and the rise of a new Napoleon disabused Proudhon of any belief in a progressive, beneficent state, and his already-advanced socialist contempt for capitalism (his famous statement "property is theft" appeared in 1840) took an increasingly anarchistic turn. Proudhon idealized work in a small-scale peasant or artisanal setting, with small groups freely exchanging goods and services and leading simple and austere lives. The workshop, not the legislature, bank, or industrial mill, would be the basis of society, morally as well as economically. Natural, affective units of family and co-workers would replace impersonal and bureaucratic structures. The polity would be local and decentralized; Proudhon opposed not only the highly centralized French state but also the Italian national unification movement for imposing an artificial unity on diverse peoples, and he favored the South in the American Civil War.[1] Proudhonian ideals of federalism and small-scale production by independent workers would have an enduring impact on the anarchist movement.

The other major influence on the emerging anarchist movement was Michael Bakunin, who was less of a theorist and more of a revolutionary than Proudhon. From his experience at the barricades in 1848–49 to that of Russian prisons in the 1850s, his escape from Siberia in 1861, and his continuous embroilment in subversive sects and conspiracies until his death in 1876, the towering, leonine figure of Bakunin embodied the spirit and passion of revolt. The anarchists inspired by Proudhon and Bakunin were becoming numerous by the 1860s, yet were not yet clearly distinguished from other socialists; Bakunin himself joined Karl Marx's International Working Men's Association in 1864. The struggle between Marx and Bakunin for control of the First International would precipitate a definitive split between socialists and anarchists by 1871, when Marx had banished the anarchists from his organization. Well before, in 1868, Bakunin had clearly stated the differences between himself and Marx:

I detest communism because it is the negation of liberty and because I can conceive nothing human without liberty. I am not a communist

because communism concentrates and absorbs all the powers of society into the state; because it necessarily ends in the centralization of property in the hands of the state, while I want the abolition of the state—the radical extirpation of the principle of authority and the tutelage of the state, which, on the pretext of making men moral and civilized, has up to now enslaved, oppressed, exploited and depraved them.[2]

Among Bakunin's most devoted followers were some skilled artisans, the watchmakers of the Swiss Jura. Such relatively well-educated, independent workers as watchmakers and printers would form one basis of anarchist support à la Proudhon; Bakunin also reached out to the downtrodden elements that Marx sneered at as *Lumpenproletariat*. Thieves, beggars, and others with nothing to lose and little affection for the state seemed to Bakunin to constitute an excellent revolutionary base. To these and to all others who would listen, Bakunin counseled revolt: "The brigand in Russia is the true and only revolutionary, without phrase-making, without bookish rhetoric. Popular revolution is born from the merging of the revolt of the brigand with that of the peasant."[3] Socialists and anarchists clearly envisioned different bases of support, and Italy and Spain did experience widespread peasant anarchist movements which were in fact directly inspired by Bakunin and his protégés. Whereas Marx prophesied class struggle between industrial capitalists and the proletariat, fated to come into conflict due to deterministic laws of history, Bakunin called freely for conspiracies and insurrection, for a revolutionary will among all who felt oppressed in body or spirit. With such profound differences separating them, Marxian socialists and Bakuninist, Proudhonian anarchists would emerge as the principal contending revolutionary forces troubling capitalist, nationalist, and increasingly imperialist European nations in the last third of the nineteenth century. By the turn of the century, anarchism was evolving into the more industrialized movement called anarcho-syndicalism.

The fin de siècle did not witness any final consensus concerning anarchist methods or beliefs. On the contrary, it was due precisely to its fluid and volatile nature that this era was so fertile in elaborating new cultural forms and new intellectual approaches. Replete with such dichotomies as that between pacifism and violence, the paradox of anarchism was not simply resolved by such maxims as Bakunin's "the passion to destroy is a creative passion." In a movement that considered means and ends to be inseparable, could violence engender utopia, apocalypse the era of harmony? Although most anarchists welcomed the prospect of a violent revolution, they were far from united on how it should be brought about. Some favored a carefully planned insurrection in the Blanquist tradition (Auguste Blanqui [1805–81] was the archetypal professional revolutionary, forever fomenting uprisings and spending much of his long life in jail), others idealized a spontaneous mass outburst. Anarchism was equated with avant-garde art as the scourge of bourgeois morality and was simultaneously seen as epitomizing moral responsibility and self-sacrifice. Anarchism was furiously anticlerical and atheistic and at the same time likened to the primitive church before it became institutionalized in Rome, with terrorists playing the role of "anarchrist"; it was both individual and collective, though wary of urban mass society; it was apocalyptically future-oriented and nostalgic for a simpler past; it was both political and antipolitical. It was, in short, a movement full of contradictions whose ambivalent expression revealed the dialectical structure at the base of anarchist culture. These contradictions were essential to the anarchist goal of reconciling nature and culture, self and society.

Because they questioned not only the political power structure but the very basis of legitimate authority, the anarchists necessarily questioned the nature of order itself, in the natural as well as the social order. Anarchist philosophers such as Peter Kropotkin attempted to undermine peoples' cognized models of social order by demonstrating as unnatural those norms and practices assumed to be rooted in the natural order of things. Kropotkin tried to dethrone the late nineteenth-century ideology of Social Darwinism, which justified capitalism and imperialism on biological grounds, and presented a countermythology that demonstrated how far humans had strayed from the natural order. He saw a continuum from natural to human history, from the *Mutual Aid* of ants and bees to that of the medieval town. Contemporary society was neither natural, organic, nor free, but the model of nature could be harmonized with urban culture, as it had been in the past. Parallel to this desire to establish a more natural social order was a more radical primitivism that repudiated technology, modernity, and urban civilization. *L'Etat Naturel* (The Natural State) was literally identified with life in nature, with living directly off the land. Though the Montmartre publication by this name was the product of urban fantasies, several anarchist communes did seek the simple life on the land, the most notable experiment perhaps being that of Fortuné Henry, the elder brother of the terrorist Emile Henry. Their father had participated in the Paris Commune of March to May 1871, the abortive attempt by an assortment of radical Jacobins, Blanquists, and socialists to secede from France and create their own social democracy. The different routes taken by these two sons of an exiled Communard, one creative and pastoral, the other destructive and urban, illustrate the radical alternatives that men with similar ideas could pursue.

The cultural ferment within the French anarchist movement in the 1890s existed in inverse relation to the capacity of the anarchists to generate political or economic institutions capable of organizing and promoting their aims. Unlike the socialists, the anarchists had no party organization; their few attempts at holding international anarchist congresses fell victim to their antiorganizational mania; before 1894 there were only tentative anarchist forays in organizing workers, most leaders being skeptical of the meliorist tendencies of unions. The highly individualistic doctrine of propaganda by the deed, adopted by such leading revolutionaries as Errico Malatesta and Peter Kropotkin at the 1881 anarchist Congress of London as the best means of emancipating the workers, held sway over a truly anarchic movement composed of small autonomous groups.[4] To spread the message, the anarchists therefore availed themselves of a broad range of propagandistic media, extending to highly publicized acts of violence, but also including cabaret songs, posters and leaflets, lectures, and the anarchist press. Lacking elaborated bureaucratic networks, this culture and its means of expression took on disproportionate importance within the movement.

The most visible propagandistic medium, the one most responsible for filling the organizational vacuum inherent in anarchy, the anarchist press was made politically and economically feasible by the liberalized French press laws of 1881. After granting amnesty to the Communards in 1880, the republicans in the Chamber of Deputies decided to abolish the strict laws controlling the press it had inherited from the Second Empire. The law of July 29, 1881, lifted all preventative measures and administrative formalities governing the publication, sales, and distribution of all newspapers, journals, and posters. Article 5 stipulated that periodicals did not need to post the security money that had greatly restricted the founding of new journals.[5] With printing costs minimal, it now became easy to attempt a publishing venture. It was also safer, for the new law held neither the editor, publisher, nor printer responsible for libel, but rather the director. This position was required of all papers, and only if a responsible director could not be found did liability then extend from editor to publisher to printer. Only statements that encouraged a particular act of violence could be prosecuted, though after a year the law was amended to place greater restrictions on the moral latitude allowed the press.[6]

The law of Waldeck-Rousseau which legalized unions and strike activity on May 21, 1884, also had far-reaching consequences. French anarchism and anarcho-syndicalism were both made possible by the liberal tenets of the Third Republic, although the 1884 law specifically prohibited unions from engaging in political activity.[7] The climate favorable to anarchist propaganda in the 1890s was due in large part precisely to the combination of relative political tolerance and social conservatism that characterized Radical and Opportunist parliamentary politics, creating or maintaining deep-seated social grievances while allowing for the expression of discontent. The scandals of corruption in high places that peaked in the Panama Affair of 1892–93 catalyzed this volatile mix, increasing hostility toward the government.

The French press experienced tremendous growth in the years following passage of the new press laws. The anarchist press grew more slowly and did not experience a great "boom" until the early 1890s (there were of course tremendous scales of magnitude between the impoverished anarchist press, which typically appeared once a week, and such daily newspapers as *Le Figaro* and *L'Echo de Paris*). During the 1880s, the field was dominated by Jean Grave's *La Révolté* (The Militant), founded by Kropotkin in 1879, which moved from Geneva to Paris in 1885, changed its name to *Le Révolte* (Revolution) in 1887 (in order to avoid paying a fine for having sponsored an unauthorized lottery), and remained such until it was closed and its editor jailed in the winter of repression of 1894. In 1885, Grave wrote: "We do not believe . . . in long term associations, federations, etc. For us, a grouping . . . must only be established on a well-determined point for immediate action; the actions accomplished, the group re-forms itself on new bases, either among the same elements or with new ones."[8] One wonders whether Grave ever reflected that his own permanent position of power as anarchist editor might be a possible source of hierarchical entrenchment, running counter to the ad hoc spirit propounded in his newspaper. The anarchist *compagnons* referred to him jestingly as "the pope of the rue Mouffetard" (the Left Bank street where Grave maintained his garret office) to point out his ideological domination over the movement. Called the "pope" rather than the "king," Grave relied on the mantle of orthodoxy conferred on him by the anarchist elders Kropotkin and Elisée Reclus. His authority necessarily rested on doctrinal controls rather than on the eschewed power relations derived from political legitimacy. Yet ideological orthodoxy was also a tenuous authority base in a movement as rebellious and youth-oriented as was anarchism in the 1890s.[9]

The police informers were not slow in noting the erosion of *La Révolte*'s once-dominant position by more innovative anarchist papers such as *Le Père Peinard* and *L'Endehors* in the early 1890s. Grave's refusal to champion the propagandists by the deed (though he had editorially supported violence a decade earlier) may have been pragmatic, but it also may have resulted from the threat that charismatic figures such as Ravachol posed for his continuing leadership. Outlaws and martyrs were unlikely to inspire faith in legitimate spokesmen, and the authority of the pope was challenged by that of the saints. In this context, it is likely that Grave's own arrest and imprisonment in 1894 reaffirmed his legitimacy within the embattled movement and helped ensure his twenty further years of journalistic activity as editor of *Les Temps Nouveaux*.

Grave's sympathy for the literary fellow travelers of anarchy was attenuated by suspicion of their sincerity and their bourgeois origins. The high point of literary comradeship came at Grave's trial in February 1894 for the second edition of *La Société mourante et l'anarchie,* when Grave's lawyer called Paul Adam, Octave Mirbeau, and Bernard Lazare, as well as Elisée Reclus, as character witnesses. Despite the support of such poets as Stuart Merrill and Adolphe Retté, such painters as Paul Signac, Camille Pissarro, and Maximilien Luce, a gulf remained between art and politics that Grave was not prepared to bridge with his weekly literary supplements. As the organ of anarchist orthodoxy, *La Révolte* did not represent the most advanced positions either in art or in politics, and Grave generally preferred to publish didactic works by Tolstoy or Herbert Spencer to esoteric Symbolist poetry. As it was surpassed in circulation, so it was outmaneuvered on the left by Pouget's *Le Père Peinard*, while the Montmartrois journal of literary anarchism, *L'Endehors*, was more hospitable to bohemian writers.

Like Jean Grave, Emile Pouget was no newcomer to anarchism when he founded *Le Père Peinard* in 1889. Younger than Grave by six years, he was born into the petit bourgeoisie, the son of a provincial notary, and was sent to a lycée until the death of his stepfather in 1875 sent him out in the world at the age of fifteen. He worked as a store clerk until he was fired for having founded a clerks' union in 1879, and spent time in prison in the 1880s after having been unjustly accused of fomenting a violent demonstration.[10] Whereas Jean Grave was the model of the self-educated worker, Pouget was a *déclassé* who had the benefit of some formal education before being thrown in the lower-class *argotique* milieu. He shared this downward social trajectory, as well as the Montmartre he came to inhabit, with the bohemian artists. He produced *Le Père Peinard* almost single-handedly, writing articles in the colorful popular slang that ensured his paper's widespread appeal. Police estimates of *Le Père Peinard*'s circulation varied, but all agreed on its success. The comprehensive assessment of the movement, made by the police in November 1891, said that circulation was nearing 14,000 and would hit 20,000 in four or five months, a figure that they estimated represented at least 100,000 readers. It was distributed nationally and was especially popular in the industrial districts of the Loire, Saint-Etienne, Le Creusot, and the mining country, and from the miners it began to spread to the peasantry.[11]

L'Endehors (The Outsider) fell somewhere in between *Le Père Peinard* and the Left Bank literary reviews, sharing the former's Montmartre bohemian location and the latter's personnel. Despite his close association with many prominent left-wing writers, editor Zo d'Axa was reluctant to call himself an anarchist, and for ideological rather than strategic reasons.[12] He specifically denied adherence to any political doctrine and claimed that if he were brought to the scaffold, he would shout no courageous last words to the crowd: "I know no formula in which one can enthusiastically take refuge. *Vive la Révolution! Vive*

Dieu? Vive le Roy! Vive l'Anarchie! Why? Because, in sum, I am sure of nothing save that one must live for Oneself: to live in joy, to live in battle, to give oneself to the present so completely that the future no longer matters."[13] A true anarchist would even refuse to march behind the movement's black flag. Glorying in his *déclassé* status as the "outsider," Zo d'Axa felt that the true individual was beyond classes, parties, laws, states. The purest expression of the cultural anarchism of that era, *L'Endehors*'s antipolitics suggested that the style of one's life and one's art took precedence over their content, the act of rebellion over the cause. Despite his literary supplements, Grave's *La Révolte* remained the ideological organ, while Pouget spoke for popular, social anarchism, and Zo d'Axa for its literary variant.

Abetting the propagandistic activities of the militant anarchist press were the numerous "young reviews" published by the Symbolist writers to create a forum for their works, as access to the traditional literary reviews was frequently denied them. The editors of these combative reviews were hostile to the large-scale press and to their literary elders and justified their existence by the public's antagonism to their enterprise.[14] The simultaneous boom in the anarchist and literary avant-garde press led to considerable sympathies and some direct relations between them. The principle literary journals inclined toward anarchism, all founded around 1890, included *La Revue Blanche, La Plume,* and *Les Entretiens Politiques et Littéraires* (Political and Literary Conversations); *Le Mercure de France* and *L'Hermitage* were somewhat less politicized.

Les Entretiens Politiques et Littéraires was the most polemical review, reflecting the political activism of editors Paul Adam and Bernard Lazare. In April 1891, the journal published extracts from the *Communist Manifesto,* and in the following year summaries or extracts of Stirner, Bakunin, and Proudhon.[15] Jean Grave requested permission to reprint articles from *Les Entretiens,* and in turn he contributed an article to the May 1893 issue, a year after Elisée Reclus had his "Dear Comrades of *Les Entretiens*" letter published in the review. Paul Adam published one of the most notorious pieces of literary anarchist propaganda in the July 1892 issue. In his "Eulogy for Ravachol," written upon the execution of the terrorist, he declared that "the murder of Ravachol will open an era."

La Plume was more eclectic and less serious in tone than *Les Entre-*

tiens and featured special issues on the cultural vogues of the day, anarchism taking its place alongside issues devoted to *japonisme,* the vogue for Japanese culture, and the popular cabaret singer Aristide Bruant. Nevertheless, the "L'Anarchie" issue appearing on May Day, 1893, was impressively serious and combined artwork by Camille and Lucien Pissarro and by Maximilien Luce with drawings by Henri Gabriel Ibels, Adolphe Willette, articles by Walter Crane, André Veidaux, and a host of anarchist luminaries, and poems by Léon Cladel, Jean Richepin, Jean Carrère, and Théodore Jean. The editor, Léon Deschamps, wrote to Grave in prison in November 1894, requesting philosophical articles for *La Plume,* and Adolphe Retté became closely associated with *La Plume* during his anarchist-Naturist period.[16] Retté reported on Sebastien Faure's public lectures on anarchism in *La Plume* in 1895, contributed his attacks on Stéphane Mallarmé in 1896, and had his most radically political poetry published by *La Plume* in book form. Anarchism did not fade out of *La Plume* or of *La Revue Blanche* with the end of the era of *attentats* (roughly translated, "attacks" or "outrages") in 1894, but rather fed directly into the *littérateurs'* Dreyfusard involvement.

The most important journal to defend simultaneously the causes of Symbolism, free verse, and anarchy was *La Revue Blanche.* The fashionable, Right Bank location of its editorial offices was due to its wealthy patrons, the Natanson family; Thadée Natanson served as director and art critic for the review and was the most sympathetic toward anarchism of the three Natanson brothers. His editor in chief in the early 1890s was Lucien Muhlfeld, who wrote to Jean Grave at one point, "All thanks from *La Revue Blanche* for sending your excellent publications. Believe in all our sympathies, of head and of heart."[17] Thadée Natanson sat in the audience during the *Procès de Trente* of August 1894 and took notes on the proceedings. He was so impressed by Félix Fénéon's performance at this trial of anarchist intellectuals and militants, as well as by his earlier art criticism, that he hired him for the *Revue Blanche* staff after the trial, and Fénéon soon became its editor in chief, a position he retained until the journal ceased publication in 1903.[18]

The anarchist press sufficiently appreciated the social direction taken by the editors of *La Revue Blanche* to advertise it in company with their own periodicals. On the final page of the *Almanach du Père Peinard* for 1896 were three subscription coupons: for Pouget's *La Sociale,* Grave's

Les Temps Nouveaux, and for *La Revue Blanche,* whose editorial staff was listed as including "Paul Adam, Zo d'Axa, Victor Barrucand, Léon Blum, Félix Fénéon, Bernard Lazare, Lucien Muhlfeld, Thadée Natanson, Elie Reclus, Emile Verhaeren, etc."[19] Pouget perhaps exaggerated in placing all these writers on the editorial staff, but even as contributors they formed a significant anarchist contingent. In the course of the Dreyfus Affair, Pouget sought to unite all "avant-garde papers" through a common subscription service. Again he included *La Revue Blanche* with *Les Temps Nouveaux, Le Père Peinard,* and *Le Libertaire.* Pouget's acceptance of *La Revue Blanche* as a fellow organ of revolt was all the more remarkable considering his distrust of intellectuals and salon anarchists, a distrust that might have been exacerbated by the fact that a wealthy Jewish family supported the journal.[20] His personal acquaintance with members of the staff, such as Fénéon, probably assuaged his distrust. Different as they were in style, substance, and readership, *Le Père Peinard* and *La Revue Blanche* were both products of the new trends in anarchism that surfaced in the 1890s.

The close contact between artists and anarchists that was so striking throughout the early 1890s did not cease in 1894, but the meeting of elite and popular anarchist cultural elements diminished, the anarchists became more distrustful of their bourgeois colleagues and, most important, anarchism became more overtly oriented toward the working class with the promotion of anarcho-syndicalism by Fernard Pelloutier. Anarchism after 1894 gradually turned away from its propagandistic and extreme individualist orientation to concentrate instead on the realities of union organizing, in part because of disillusionment with the inadequacy of the doctrine of propaganda by the deed, but also out of necessity because of the government's repressive measures.[21] Pelloutier's Bourses du Travail and the Confédération Générale du Travail supplied the organizational framework and ideological focus formerly provided by the anarchist press.

This transition was not precipitated by the anarchists themselves, but rather by the efforts of the government to crush the anarchist movement and the anarchist press in particular. The excuse for this wave of repression was Auguste Vaillant's bombing of the Chamber of Deputies on December 9, 1893. No one was killed by the bomb tossed from the gallery, though several deputies were slightly injured, and it was said that "the only victim was the liberty of the press."[22] The nonlethal bombing could scarcely have been better calculated to give the government an excuse to redouble its antianarchist campaign than if it had been planned by the government itself, and accusations to that effect were not long in coming. Premier Casimir-Périer responded to anarchist terrorism by ramming *les lois scélérates,* "the scoundrelly laws," through both legislative houses in a matter of days after Vaillant's *attentat.*

Whereas the 1881 press laws limited prosecution to direct incitements to violence, the new laws extended culpability to indirect provocations, which included apologizing for such acts after the fact. The glorification of acts of violence was viewed as essential to the chain-reactive effect that one *attentat* had on another, and in the first months of 1894, the anarchist press was virtually shut down or sent into exile. The police halted *Le Père Peinard*'s publication on February 21, 1894, *La Révolte*'s on March 10. By this time Grave was already in prison and Pouget had fled to England, where he continued to publish his paper.

The anarchist communicative network was further encumbered by the second *loi scélérate* to be ratified by the senators and deputies in December 1893, which tried to hinder the relations among anarchist intellectuals and between leaders and the rank and file by inculpating any conspiracy to commit an act of violence, even if that act was never carried out. The wording of this law was kept purposely vague, so that merely the intent to commit a crime was sufficient to define a conspiratorial group. Here too the lack of any real organized conspiracy was implicitly recognized in laws designed to be as all-inclusive as possible.

Confronted by the wave of urban terrorism and armed with new laws, the police visited a wave of terror of their own upon the anarchists in the winter of 1894. The raids opened on January 1, 1894, and by the end of June, 426 people had been arraigned for engaging in a criminal conspiracy, after thousands of searches and arrests.[23] At the legislative session of January 27, 1894, the socialist deputy Clovis Hugues expressed his fears that the authoritarian principles of the Second Empire were returning. Since Vaillant's bombing, he claimed, 2,000 searches and more than 60 arrests had been made, "as if you held in your hands the thread of an abominable universal plot." He especially bemoaned the rifling of Elisée Reclus's papers, and accused the police of blurring the distinction between a theoretician such as Reclus and a militant (*révolté*).[24] The

police informers circulating among the anarchists found far fewer conspirators than the large number of searches and arrests would suggest.

From January to July 1894, the mood among the literary anarchists
changed from one of resentment toward *les lois scélérates* and the
repression the laws made possible, to one of outright fear that they
would share the fate of Grave, Pouget, and Faure, and be forced to
choose between prison and exile. Informers seemed eager to note a new
attitude of circumspection on the part of the anarchist intelligentsia.
"M. Paul Adam closes his door [to reporters], and has it said that he is
away in the country. M. Hamon maintains a profound silence. M. Bernard Lazare only opens up before familiar reporters. MM. Dubois, Natanson, etc. of *La Revue Blanche* are maintaining an extreme prudence."
Even the irrepressible Octave Mirbeau had become more cautious. In
July, an informer commented that such anarchist-tinted journals as *La
Revue Blanche* refrained from printing material touching on President
Sadi Carnot's death, and specified that Thadée Natanson had refused an
article by Saint-Pol Roux concerning the assassination. Also in July, an
informer code-named "Bouchon" told of a discussion with the anarchist
Paterne Berrichon, who revealed that his literary friends were especially
anxious about what would happen after the new *lois scélérates* being
debated in the Chamber were adopted. (After the assassination of Carnot, new laws were voted by the Chamber of Deputies on July 26, 1894,
which inculpated private as well as public incitements to violence, and
graphic as well as written anarchist propaganda; judicial jurisdiction
over such cases was transferred to the Correctional Tribunal, and even
public reproductions of courtroom debates were authorized to be suppressed if they were deemed to endanger public order.) The authors who
feared being linked to anarchist militants were Adolphe Retté, Georges
Darien, Bernard Lazare, Lucien Descaves, Paul Adam, Augustin Hamon,
and A. Ferdinand Hérold. The informer suspected that many anarchist
brochures and placards had actually been composed by these young
writers.[25]

The intellectuals' fears were not unfounded. Diatribes against the
anarchist press and anarchism's literary and bourgeois admirers surged
in the daily press. The police rounded up artists as well as theoreticians
and journalists of the movement. The anarchist painter Maximilien
Luce, who had contributed numerous drawings to *La Révolte*, was

arrested, as was a young Swedish painter named Gustave Aguelli, who was eventually tried alongside his friend Charles Chatel. Adolphe Retté was briefly arrested and released, leaving Félix Fénéon as the most notable literary figure to be tried for his anarchist activities. The writer who suffered the most for his convictions was undoubtedly Laurent Tailhade, who lost an eye in an explosion in 1894 and spent a year in prison seven years later for inciting violence against the czar on his visit to Paris. The general attitude toward anarchist intellectuals was summarized by a professor of criminal law at Lyon, who reviewed *les lois scélérates* in a book published in 1895:

There exists a group of keen minds who gravitate around anarchy and constitute its brain. Not content to intoxicate the simple ones by the literary exposure of doctrines, some intellectuals provoke anarchist acts either directly in inciting to commit them or indirectly in publishing formulas for explosives, in poeticizing the authors of outrages, in surrounding them with a false and lying halo, in presenting them as martyrs of the idea, in seeking to create sinister imitators of them. Thus is formed, under our eyes, a whole anarchist literature, serving as vehicle to the guiltiest excitations, and establishing a continuous link between the theoreticians and practitioners of the sect.

The anarchist crimes have in effect created a considerable confusion, for the intellectuals, between the abstract speculations and the acts of odious monomaniacs who listen to such speculations. Some of these writers accept the epithet "anarchist"; others deny it; all merit it.[26]

Echoing Emile Henry's terrible refrain to justify his bombing of the Café Terminus, "There are no innocent bourgeois," the jurist responded, in effect, that there were no innocent intellectuals either.

The combined application of these two laws resulted in the Procès de Trente of August 1894, in which nineteen anarchist writers, artists, and theoreticians were tried alongside eleven suspected thieves in a grand *association des malfaiteurs*. The *littérateurs* Félix Fénéon and Charles Chatel sat in the dock beside the painter Gustave Aguelli and publicists such as Jean Grave and Sebastien Faure; such intellectual luminaries as Stéphane Mallarmé appeared as character witnesses. This trial, not the assassination of President Carnot, was the real culmination of the "era of *attentats.*" The government's contrived attempt to link anarchist leaders and intellectuals in a conspiracy with common thieves was a strategic political decision. Despite an almost total lack of evidence, the government wanted to justify the hundreds of arrests made that year, to prove that the vast anarchist plot so often spoken of in the official press had indeed been uncovered, and to prove the necessity of the new laws against the press and conspiracies.[27]

The era was not distinguished chiefly by violence but by the range of propagandistic tools that included terrorist deeds. To focus simply on the *attentat* or even on the series of terrorist bombings oversimplifies the nature of the anarchist movement in those years, which was marked more by the call to revolution than by the actual fomenting of one. *Les lois scélérates* and more specifically the Procès de Trente made manifest the symbolic and propagandistic nature of the anarchist threat to authority by broadening the government's range of repressive activities to allow for the suppression of the cultural and intellectual structure that supported individual acts of violence. That the government failed to convict the multifaceted intellectual movement underlying anarchism in August 1894 attested to the difficulty of attaching clear-cut political motives to a movement of social and cultural regeneration.

While the testimony of Jean Grave and Sebastien Faure was given behind closed doors, that of the literary figures was widely reported in the press. Félix Fénéon and Charles Chatel, both aesthetes and Montmartrois, represented to perfection the mode of artistic anarchism. Chatel wore the long hair and expressive dress of a bohemian à la Henry Murger's literary sketches, while the enigmatic Fénéon was more the dandy who, in Baudelaire's celebrated phrase, delighted in astonishing others while never appearing astonished himself. Fénéon managed to contribute both to Symbolist and anarchist journals while maintaining a job as principal clerk at the Ministry of War, a position he lost as a result of his arrest and trial. In 1884 he founded *La Revue Indépendante* with a friend, published the works of Mallarmé, Paul Verlaine, and Tailhade, and became an important Post-Impressionist critic. In 1892, when Zo d'Axa fled to England, Fénéon discreetly assumed the direction of the review and, in company with André Antoine of the Théâtre-Libre, visited Zo d'Axa in London. At the time of his arrest in April 1894, Fénéon was receiving correspondence from several literary anarchist friends in exile abroad.[28] It clearly appealed to Fénéon's spirit of *fumisterie* or mockery to pose as the model employee at the Ministry of War who polished his memos to the point of self-parody, all the while participating in the dual avant-gardes of art and politics. One of the pieces of evidence used against him at the trial was a flask of mercury that he kept in the safe at the ministry; fulminate of mercury was an important ingredient in the manufacture of detonators. The prosecution believed he had received the flask from an anarchist named Matha, suspected of being Emile Henry's accomplice. Fénéon claimed he found it while going through his father's possessions after his death, and that his father had claimed he had found it in the street. When the prosecutor scoffingly demanded why he had not thrown it away rather than compromising himself with it in his possession, Fénéon replied, "You see, then it would be possible to find it in the street." When asked whether he knew about mercury's use in constructing bombs, he replied that it could also be used in thermometers. Fénéon's cross-examination was one of the high points of a sensational trial and aptly revealed both his wit and his capacity for deception. He managed to obfuscate all his dealings with fellow anarchists while making the prosecutor's efforts at establishing a conspiracy look ridiculous.[29] Chatel protested that his artistic individualism precluded the possibility of engaging in any sort of conspiracy; Fénéon merely professed intellectual curiosity about the new state of spirit represented by anarchism, just as he might about some new movement of art. This may have been disingenuous, as he in fact remained a lifelong leftist, but it was also true that Fénéon was attracted to anarchism because it allowed him to test the moral and political boundaries of bourgeois life, just as bohemia did. In the Procès de Trente, Montmartre bohemian anarchism triumphed over the government, individuality and life-style (*genre de vie*) over conspiracy and organization. Yet this victory came at a time when the anarchists were already reassessing their movement and the role that the bohemian model of individual creativity and liberation from bourgeois constraints was to play in the future of anarchism.

Ironically, the jury's decision to acquit all the defendants except for those accused of actual criminal acts did more to end the era of *attentats* than any conviction could have, closing the cycle of retribution that Ravachol had begun two years earlier. Despite the mass searches and

Paul Signac's *Portrait of Félix Fénéon* (1890) shows the anarchist as dandy. Both Signac and Fénéon were japonistes; the artist adapted the unusual background from Japanese textile designs. (Courtesy of Françoise Cachin.)

arrests that had anarchist intellectuals such as Paul Adam ready to flee the country, the police were unable to prevent the revenge bombing of Emile Henry at the Café Terminus or the assassination of President Carnot in Lyon. Executed a week after the conclusion of the Procès de Trente, Caserio Santo was the last anarchist martyr of the era.[30] In 1895, Emile Pouget brought back anarcho-syndicalist ideas from his English exile, which he expounded in a new series of Le Père Peinard. Released from prison in the February 1895 amnesty declared by President Félix Faure, Jean Grave signaled the changed times by the title of his new paper, Les Temps Nouveaux. As firmly opposed to the ballot box and to parliamentary politics as ever, the anarchists shifted from a predominantly cultural to an economic orientation, from a movement attracting déclassés to one appealing to workers.

At the very end of the century, then, the anarchists were making the critical shift toward the movement that would become known as anarcho-syndicalism. As early as 1892, the international group of anarchists in exile in London, who called themselves the Avant-Garde Group and whose principal members were the Italian Errico Malatesta, the Russian Peter Kropotkin, and the French Charles Malato and Louise Michel, called for anarchist penetration of or creation of unions.[31] When Emile Pouget returned from exile in London in 1895, he brought these ideas back with him, although in the late 1870s he had already attempted to organize his fellow department store clerks (and lost his job in the process). Pouget eventually became the chief propagandist for anarcho-syndicalism as editor of La Voix du Peuple in the first decade of the twentieth century. At the same time, other French anarchists were realizing the need to bridge the gap between libertarian ideals and organizational necessity. Fernand Pelloutier was the key figure in leading the anarchists to recognize the unions and the municipal labor exchanges (the Bourses du Travail) as crucial sources of future anarchist recruitment. In so doing, Pelloutier helped shift anarchism from the tactics of terrorism and insurrection to labor organizing and confrontational strikes. In theory, while awaiting the great general strike to bring down the state, the unions and labor exchanges would develop as alternative worker-run bodies that would eventually replace the political structure. Pelloutier died at age thirty-three in 1901, and the years from 1895 to 1902 were really transitional ones between anarchism and syndicalism. The federation of labor unions, the Confédération Générale du Travail (CGT), had been founded in 1895, but until Pelloutier's death it remained a weak rival to Pelloutier's own Federation of the Bourses du Travail. In 1902, the two bodies united, with the CGT under the vigorous leadership of the anarchist Victor Griffuelhes, and the era of anarcho-syndicalism was born.[32]

Although syndicalism would dominate the anarchist left until the First World War, individualistic anarchism did not suddenly cease to exist. Between 1895 and 1899, militants such as Sebastien Faure argued against the new tendencies. In his paper *Le Libertaire,* Faure argued for the orthodox anarchist doctrines of individualism and revolutionary spontaneity. This antisyndicalist tone would be maintained in the journal *L'Anarchie* from 1905 to 1914, which condemned the unions as an "adaptation of capitalist organization" and which colluded with the anarchist band of thieves called the Bonnot Gang, who were captured and tried in 1913. Even aesthetic anarchism continued in the journal *L'Action d'art* of 1913, which also acclaimed the thieves in an article entitled "De Bergson à Bonnot: Aux sources de l'heroïsme individualiste," which linked Bergson's intuitionist philosophy to the anarchist sense of self. The journal's manifesto declared that "to live our life in beauty we know we must struggle. . . . Revolt, for us, is the action of art." *L'Action d'art* was read by such young writers as André Breton, thereby influencing the surrealist movement of the 1920s (although Breton and many other surrealists affiliated themselves with the French Communist party rather than with the anarchists). Several of the Italian Futurists were also anarchists in the years before the Great War.[33] Anarchism clearly retained its appeal for avant-garde artists throughout the Belle Epoque; anarcho-syndicalism by and large did not, and tended to separate the working classes from the artists and intellectuals to a greater degree than was the case in the early 1890s.

As the illegalist and terrorist side of anarchism was displaced by the syndicalist, the culture of bohemian individualism was supplanted by that of proletarian solidarity. Increasingly too the workshop was being supplanted by the factory in the economic boom lasting from 1896 to 1914. The radicalism of the Parisian faubourgs was supplemented by that of industrial suburbs, Saint-Ouen and Saint-Denis to the north, Ivry to the south. Even in the working-class faubourgs of Paris such as

Belleville, by 1915 militants were being drawn primarily from the building and especially from the metal trades rather than from the older artisanal occupations such as furniture making and shoemaking that had played such an important role in revolutionary activity throughout the nineteenth century.[34] As the suburbs saw new industries such as automobile manufacture draw workers out of the workshops and into factories of over a thousand employees, in Paris itself traditionally skilled craftsmen such as furniture makers were being deskilled as workers in factory settings did one specialized task. A growing number of shop clerks, restaurant workers and cooks, and transport workers all signaled the gradual displacement of the traditional manufacturing trades by the service sector by the early twentieth century.[35] Discontent and exploitation remained, but the syndicalists were better positioned to adapt to the changing nature of French economic life than were the old anarchist individualists. The theorists of the revolutionary general strike may have been no less quixotic than were those of propaganda by the deed, and they remained as suspicious of parliamentary politics as ever, but the movement that evolved in the decade after 1895 differed in tactics, social base, and cultural tone from the bohemian and artisanal anarchism of the fin de siècle. The nineteenth century was over.

To what should one attribute the major change in orientation taken by the anarchists in about 1895? How important a factor was government repression? Clearly the government crackdown gave the anarchists an opportunity to rethink their doctrines, and this applied especially to those in prison or exile. Among the literary fellow travelers of anarchism there has been noted a certain amount of fear amid the repression of 1894, and it seems likely that a number of the more faint-hearted writers were frightened away from the movement—this at any rate was Adolphe Retté's conclusion.[36] Yet the failure to convict the anarchists in the Procès de Trente and the amnesty of the following year might have been seen as encouraging signs for pursuing the old ways. It seems clear that, given the syndicalist ideas already in the air, the anarchists reevaluated the meager fruits of a decade or more of propaganda by the deed and found the doctrine wanting. The shift from that slogan to the dominant catch-phrase of the next two decades, direct action, says much about this change. Anarchism from 1881 to 1894 had been a movement dependent upon publicity. Through oral and written propaganda and through dramatic deeds, the anarchists hoped to spread their revolutionary message. The propaganda continued after 1895, but it ceded its central place to the recruitment and organization of workers, whose numbers and militancy would, it was hoped, lead to revolutionary confrontation. "Direct action" suggested that the anarchists were tired of relying primarily on media-focused deeds and craved instead the immediacy of mass action. Along with the syndicalists' related emphasis on working class autonomy from all bourgeois spokesmen, this rejection of the central role of media sundered the alliance with bohemian and literary anarchists and decreased the importance of cultural forms of revolt in general.

The anarchists were continually engaged in a sometimes purposeful, sometimes unconscious search for structure to counter the anarchic tendencies inherent in their movement. Pelloutier's emphasis on the role of the Bourses du Travail and the anarchist penetration of the CGT after 1900 were coherent strategies designed to redress this characteristic problem. In organizing workers, the anarchists organized themselves. Before anarcho-syndicalism, anarchism in its purer form sought order in a less organized fashion from two rich sources: nature and culture. Peter Kropotkin was the main advocate for emulating the cooperative social patterns of animals such as ants and bees, and the power of primitivist and pastoral imagery to serve as an alternative to exploitive urban and industrial society was deep and wide-ranging.[37] More important and even less consciously formulated were attempts to identify with the structures of everyday life among the Parisian lower classes, to penetrate and assimilate the popular culture which was the mental environment of Parisian anarchism. This too had its limitations, because identifying with traditional popular culture bound the anarchists to regressive models of social revolt, but overall it increased their identification with the community. Such culture sources of order and identity not only provided the anarchists with lower-class followers but with many artistic adherents as well, for two reasons: the artists perceived that they were welcome and needed in the movement, and they were enticed by the popular cultural aura that pervaded anarchism. They could be *engagé,* earthy, and outrageous.

The anarchist need for structure within cultural forms, and their more overt search for media to spread their beliefs, led to a movement in which elite and popular culture briefly coalesced. This syncretic style fit the era well. As Samuel Bing and Henry van de Velde sought to unify art, design, and everyday life in the all-embracing style of Art Nouveau, so anarchist songs, newspapers, poems, posters, speech, and celebrations formed a coherent culture of anarchism. The linguistic and oral, the visual, the poetic, and other literary forms of anarchist expression can be analyzed as discrete elements of anarchist culture. Suffusing this culture was the violence which some considered to be an art form in its own right, and which certainly enhanced the movement's reknown, and the religious aura which transformed terrorists into martyred "anarchrists." Order and disorder, poems and dreams and bombs: in failing to attain its goals, French anarchism demonstrated the limitations of cultural politics.

The Context of Extremist Politics:
Les Extrêmes Se Touchent

Anarchism was only one of a variety of extremist movements that violently opposed the parliamentary regime of the Third French Republic during the fin de siècle. To the traditional monarchist or Bonapartist right that had never reconciled itself to the Republic, and the socialist left that opposed the prevailing economic order but which was gradually being drawn into the political system and relied more on votes than violence, were added a host of opposition groups that sought new bases of support and new issues upon which to focus popular discontent against the regime. In the late 1880s, this opposition unified around the figure of the dashing General Georges Boulanger, the popular minister of war. Blanquists, independent socialists based more on the indigenous French tradition dating from Charles Fourier and Proudhon than on Marx and Engels, Paul Déroulède's *revanchiste* (advocating a war of revenge against Germany after France's defeat in 1871 in the Franco-Prussian War) Ligue de la Patrie Française, the anti-Semites stimulated by the astounding recent success of Edouard Drumont's sensationalist *La France juive* (Jewish France, 1886), and everyone else who saw in Boulangism an opportunity to overturn the Republic and create the conditions for their own seizure of power, united behind the man on horseback. Fortunately for the Republic, the chosen hero was not up to the task of leading a revolution or even a coup d'état, and did not share the opinions of many of his supporters (for instance the anti-Semites). Boulanger himself was far less significant than the passions to which the movement in his name gave rise. Especially among his more radical followers, the strident authoritarianism and nationalism, when combined with demands for an end to capitalist exploitation and mixed with the new wave of anti-Semitism, struck a popular chord. Progressive nationalism, after all, followed in the heroic century-old Jacobin tradition, leavened with the memory of Napoleonic glory. Though the general did not conquer the Republic, thirty Boulangist deputies did enter the Chamber in 1889, at least twenty of whom considered themselves socialists of some sort.

Historians have noted the protofascist elements in this mixture of nationalism, socialism, and racism; some have considered Boulangism a precursor to similar twentieth-century syntheses that strove to unify disparate dissatisfied groups around xenophobic issues and which joined a moral or spiritual to an economic critique of society.[1] Considerable insight may be gained by reading later developments back to their point of origin and interpreting these early rumblings as essentially fascist, but the danger in such historical hindsight lies in imputing more ideological sophistication and self-consciousness of the import of this new synthesis than the participants themselves possessed. Certainly until the Dreyfus Affair catalyzed tensions and clarified positions, one can scarcely exaggerate the frenzied groping of political position taking in this period. The generation of the 1890s was consciously seeking new political syntheses, but its determination to transcend old antagonisms in a new and higher union led to only tentative results in an era of transition. One may be justified in calling Maurice Barrès a fascist based on common qualities he shared with individuals of a generation or two later who welcomed that appellation, but one must not let the "ism" obscure the developmental nature of Barrès's political *engagement* or the terminology he himself used to describe his position. The nationalistic element only dominated the socialistic after 1898; between the Boulanger and Dreyfus affairs, Barrès would have described himself as a socialist, perhaps appending "independent" or "Proudhonian" or "decentralist" to distinguish his socialism from that of Jules Guesde and Jean Jaurès.

After the failure of the Boulangists and the comic opera flight of their leader to Belgium and into the arms of the woman for whom he killed himself two years later, the most notable and active revolutionary force to shake French society of the fin de siècle was anarchism. Though the anarchist leadership had resisted the attraction of the military hero, no one doubted that many of the rank and file had grabbed his horse by the tail, as Emile Pouget put it. Parisian Boulangism and anarchism were strongest in exactly the same areas, among the lower and lower-middle classes of the north and east sectors of the city extending in a crescent shape from Batignolles to the Bastille. Boulanger himself was elected to Montmartre's Clignancourt seat in the Chamber in July 1889 (though his election was invalidated), and the eighteenth arrondissement had more Boulangist committees than any other region of Paris.[2]

The *classes populaires* could readily switch their allegiance from Boulangism to anarchism, and the same held true of antiparliamentary writers and intellectuals. The best example of this particular transition is Paul Adam, who joined Barrès in campaigning for a position in the Chamber as Boulangist deputy from Nancy. That Barrès won and Adam lost was no doubt important in the latter's further radicalization, so that he became first a convinced anarchist and later an ardent Dreyfusard, both positions influenced by his close literary colleague Bernard Lazare. Yet in Adam as in Barrès the cults of militarism and nationalism were never fully extinguished even during his anarchist militancy, and in the first decade of the twentieth century Adam tried to accommodate his nationalist and even imperialist sentiment to his peculiar vision of socialism. By the late 1890s Adam was one of many writers who had moved away from their earlier anarchist faith. Among those who returned to purely literary involvements, some were open to the accusation of political dilettantism—of a primarily aesthetic interest in anarchism as a corollary to their literary theories, a commitment that was never serious or compelling. Although it was certainly true that anarchism was in part a cultural vogue that swept many young Symbolists along in an undifferentiated enthusiasm for Henrik Ibsen, revolution, and free verse, much of the apparent ambivalence and political wavering of writers such as Adam and Barrès can be traced to ambiguities within the anarchist movement, and beyond that to the general confusion of traditional political patterns and allegiances. French anarchism was a dialectical movement caught in a balancing act between the claims of the individual and the collectivity, between spontaneity and conspiracy, between nostalgia for a simpler past and the expectation of future social regeneration. Anarchism embodied the paradox of a social and cultural movement that deeply distrusted state and civilization and based itself instead on the promptings of natural law, or rather natural forces.[3]

Much as Boulangism united a wide range of people disenchanted with the current system of government, so anarchism represented a political and cultural complex irreducible to a single outlook. As a constellation of groups united around the anarchist dilemma of how to preserve individual liberty within a mass and mercantile society, anarchism defined one moment of a continuing quest to find a just political system capable of grappling with the pressures generated by the industrial and urban society emerging in France as elsewhere. Its intellectual as well as artisanal adherents were being bypassed by these technological changes. It was a revolt not of the have-nots but of the left-outs, a factor that created inherent ambivalence toward what the future would bring. They expressed their indignation in a radical refusal of the contemporary social order that denied them the place they thought they deserved, but they frequently looked backward as well as forward for the model of the well-ordered society. Though the anarchists' solutions differed from those of the Blanquists or Boulangists or Déroulède's *ligueurs* (members of the League of Patriots), their shared antipathies and common social background traced a continuum that transcended apparent right-left conflicts across the political spectrum. Anarchism's single greatest ideological touchstone, hatred of the authority of the state, may not have been universally shared, but all the extremist groups of the era at least opposed, and opposed violently, the particular form that state took in the Third Republic. That was enough to encourage ideological cross-overs, as well as to occasion numerous attempts at *rapprochements* between the various contesting groups.

Some leading Boulangists would only turn to anarchism several years later; meanwhile a variety of radical leftist and rightist groups were already involved in intrigues with the anarchists in the early 1890s.[4] Assorted Boulangists, royalists, anti-Semites, and representatives of the church were all involved in secret as well as open contact with important anarchists of both militant and literary orientations. The overall effect of these intrigues does not appear to have been profound, and an anarchist leadership jealous of its autonomy limited rightist aid to offers of financial support by well-connected opponents of the regime such as the marquis de Morès. As potential conspiracies they nevertheless aroused considerable interest among the authorities, and not without good reason. The internal contradictions of an anarchist revolutionary movement prevented the anarchists from creating any serious threat to the regime. If this appeal was mixed with the rising tide of anti-Semitism directed against the plutocrats who supposedly pulled the strings of government while exploiting the working class, and with Blanquist patriotic insurrectionism in the image of the Commune, perhaps a true revolutionary union could be forged that would be greater than any of its parts. Ideologies were fluid enough for such unions to be far from unthinkable, at least until the Dreyfus Affair made nationalism, anti-Semitism, and xenophobia banners to be waved by the right.

The anarchists never paid serious attention to attempts at coconspiracy from the right, and though not immune to anti-Semitism they were hardly able to countenance royalists, priests, or ultranationalists. What they did have in common with groups somewhere to their right was the plebeian origin of most of their supporters and an antipathy for traditional electoral politics. Déroulède's *ligueurs,* de Morès's lower-class followers, the butchers of the La Villette district of Paris, Blanquists, and anarchists were all willing to take to the streets. Activism was not only a means to a political end, but an affirmation of youth and vitality, an existential alternative to parliamentary talk. Zo d'Axa, Maurice Barrès, Georges Sorel, and Pierre Drieu la Rochelle, the French fascist of the 1930s, were all prey to the appeal of activism as a means of regenerating one's existence.[5] The political thought of Sorel, who wavered from anarcho-syndicalism to monarchism, and from Lenin to Mussolini, was at least as ambiguous as that of Barrès and Adam, and the fascists' appreciation of Sorel is well known. Disdain for legality and the parliamentary process, and the cult of violence and existential activism all mark a protofascist mentality which certainly existed in 1890s France, though less among the anarchist militants than in the literary milieu.

To understand the efforts of the marquis de Morès to enroll the anarchists in a union of the left, and Maurice Barrès's more literary attempt to find an ideological common ground, their positions must be placed against a background of continual endeavors by a wide variety of political groups to affiliate the anarchists to their cause, or at least to capitalize on the notoriety achieved by the propagandists of the deed. Some of the more unlikely liaisons, especially those of the royalists on the extreme right, provide evidence of behind-the-scenes conspiracies that may have justified government worries about a concerted, organized attempt to topple the Republic. At the same time a note of caution must be inserted as to the veracity of these reports of conspiratorial efforts, as most of the evidence of secret meetings between anarchists and royalists, Boulangists, and so on comes from police informers who were overly inclined to see conspirators behind every lamp-post. A purely spontaneous revolutionary movement left little room for informers to insinuate themselves, whereas a conspiratorial movement made the use of informers imperative for police intelligence gathering. Conspiracy theory was self-serving. Furthermore, since most of the reputed conspiracies involved subsidies paid to the anarchists, and the anarchists were not overly scrupulous about whom they accepted money from, these liaisons were more likely to shed light on the motives of whoever was tendering the aid than on the anarchist recipients. Even if such conspiracies were only of marginal importance, the likelihood that some conspiratorial attempts did indeed transpire suggests that one can not study 1890s anarchism, especially its cultural manifestations, in isolation from other opposition movements of the period.

The best-documented example of collusion between the anarchists and other opponents of the Third Republic was the Boulangist episode. This was also the least conspiratorial and most mass-based example of revolutionary convergence, as anarchists along with everyone else who were disenchanted with the opportunistic Republic were swept along in the Boulangist fever. The strongholds of Boulangist and Blanquist support, the areas where Paul Déroulède recruited most of his Ligue des Patriotes, were the same *quartiers populaires* where the anarchists were most active.[6] At an anarchist meeting in January 1889 at which 150 people were present, the anti-Boulangists were initially in control, but new arrivals swung the majority over to the Boulangists. Neither Boulangist spokesmen nor their opponents could be heard above the din. After calm was established, the candidacy of Boulanger and two Boulangist-anarchists was passed as the order of the day. A leaflet entitled "Les Anarchistes au peuple de Paris" violently attacked Boulanger as one more "governmental incarnation" and characteristically linked the movement with the socialists, republicans, monarchists, and imperialists; to the anarchists, all "authoritarian" parties were fundamentally the same. Only the anarchists could oppose this new false messiah, as they proclaimed themselves the "negators of authority under all forms: religious or scientific, capitalist or proprietory, familial or statist."[7] Later that month Pouget and Constant Martin noted that another anarchist,

Sourdey, was working for Henri de Rochefort (one of Boulanger's lieutenants) and favored Boulanger, and was therefore a traitor to the
anarchist movement, but elsewhere a police agent remarked that if the
anarchists publicly proclaimed Boulanger a massacrer of the people, they
were secretly enchanted by his followers' tactics, which seemed to
portend a revolution from which they could only benefit.[8]

Later that year, after several ballots had sent various Boulangist
deputies to the Chamber but had not toppled the government, agent
"Jean" was able to make an in-depth analysis of the situation on the left.
Anarchist press circulation and attendance at meetings were down as
attention was focused on electoral politics. The anarchist movement had
been sufficiently distracted by Boulangism that it could not maintain any
coherent policy of its own; rather, all revolutionary activities awaited the
outcome of the Boulangists' assault upon the Republic. The informer
indicated that despite a considerable number of grass-roots sympathizers, the anarchists had been least compromised by Boulangism
(compared with the Blanquists, independent socialists, and various
rightist groups), and their leaders confidently awaited the aftermath of
the affair when they might take the lead among the revolutionary
factions. The anarchists intended to profit from the political upheaval
either by exploiting the revolutionary situation created by the Boulangists or by succeeding them as the chief opponents of the regime.[9] Only
after the failure of Boulangism did the anarchists begin to strike.

The anarchists were also in contact with the anti-Semitic wing of
Boulangism represented by Drumont and de Morès, with whom their
relations extended into the 1890s. The newspaper *Le Nation* reported on
the eve of the first May Day celebrations of 1890 that among the anarchists seized by the police in an effort to dampen the festivities were
P. Martinet, Malato, and de Morès; the latter was called an instigator and
subsidizer of revolutionary maneuvers who had been detained just before fleeing the country.[10] The relations between the marquis and the
anarchists were hardly secret, since he openly announced to the large
rally held on April 15, 1890, that the government was taking measures to
abort the demonstration, a prediction with which Malato agreed. This
was the mass meeting where Maurice Barrès, Boulangist deputy from
Nancy, briefly advised the audience to demonstrate as peacefully as
possible.[11] In 1892, during the Ravachol furor, a socialist deputy named

Lavy declared in the Chamber that the anarchists battled the socialists far more fiercely than they did the extreme right, and cited the Boulangist episodes, at which point Paul Déroulède rose and angrily denied such infamous connections.[12] Yet later that same year, an agent claimed that 150 Boulangists and 20 anarchists together disrupted a large Possibilist (moderate socialists, followers of Dr. Paul Brousse) meeting at the Salle Wagram. If cooperation was minimal, at least they shared common goals. The anarchists' collusion with the Boulangists was primarily tactical rather than ideological. Unlike Adam and Barrès, most of them mistrusted the nationalist, militarist, and Caesarist tendencies of the Boulangists, but they were flexible enough to take advantage of all proffered aid, financial or otherwise.

Boulangism played an important role in delimiting the era of cultural anarchism, which can be dated from 1890 when disappointed Boulangists such as Paul Adam and, to a lesser degree, Barrès, turned to anarchism and founded the literary reviews that championed the dual libertarian avant-gardes of Symbolism and anarchism. The Boulangists' disillusionment increased with the publication in 1890 of a book by Mermeix (pseudonym of Gabriel Terrail), *Les Coulisses de Boulangisme,* which revealed the general's monarchist financial backing.[13] No sooner had the anarchists assumed center stage from the discredited Boulangists than they too were suspected of entering into the same conspiratorial relations with the parties of the extreme right. The duchesse d'Uzès's offer to adopt Auguste Vaillant's daughter could be attributed to a stylish *anarchie au salon,* and aristocratic donations to known literary anarchists might be written off as insurance against violent reprisals. Nevertheless, between 1890 and 1894 the police amassed evidence linking royalist opponents of the Third Republic with the anarchists in more than sentimental or self-serving ways. Although the evidence suggests that the parties of the right were not as deeply involved with anarchism as they had been with the Boulangists or would be with the anti-Dreyfusards, the fact that some such collusion did exist makes the transition of a Barrès from Boulangism to anarchism to anti-Dreyfusism easier to understand. As revealed in the *L'Ermitage* referendum of the political views of writers of 1893 (see chapter 7), more than one writer wavered between supporting aristocracy or anarchy, and Charles Maurras recognized that even the Jewish-run, cosmopolitan *Revue Blanche* and the anti-Semitic and nationalist *La Cocarde* shared a common federalist and decentralist ideology. If police allegations of Orléanist (royalist) funding of *La Revue Blanche* are to be believed, there was more similarity between the two journals than Maurras realized. Though one must accept the evidence of informers with caution, there was in fact an aristocratic and elitist species of anarchism in the fin de siècle that may have enticed the royalist reactionaries of the faubourg Saint-Germain.

A report by the "Contrôle Générale" dated May 1, 1890, set the stage for royalist-anarchist relations. Conversations overheard the day before indicated that

Boulangism was to be definitively abandoned and that on the other hand, concerning agitation, funds were presently to be furnished to the anarchists.

One has even heard M. Siehon, secretary of Lambert Ste. Croix, declare that the red specter of anarchy [*sic*], which had effaced itself for lack of subsidies when Boulangism had been supported by royalist money, had only reappeared in the last revolutionary demonstrations thanks to the action of the Orléanists.[14]

This would tally with other informers' statements that anarchist activity had been retarded in 1889, although attributing this paralysis solely to lack of funding was clearly insufficient. (To give one example, 1889 saw the birth of *Le Père Peinard,* whose humble origins may therefore be assumed to have been free of the taint of rightist support. Later on we know that Pouget rejected the offers of collaboration from de Morès.) After the "Contrôle Générale" report, there was little talk of royalist-anarchist relations until 1894, when police surveillance of anarchist activities and suspicion of conspiracies greatly increased. In the interim, the major link between left and right was embodied in the person of the marquis de Morès. A report of January 6, 1893, affirmed that anarchist support for de Morès extended even to his placing the exiled pretender the comte de Paris on the throne, which would at least have had the merit of ending the Republic.[15]

In the first months of police activity following passage of *les lois scélérates,* some vague references were made to royalist relations with the anarchists; beginning in May 1894, more precise information regarding such collusion began to appear. A royalist named Dufeuille claimed he knew more about the anarchist party than the police did, for whereas the police were compelled to search everywhere for evidence of anarchist plots, the anarchists came to his door in search of aid. He claimed he had not responded to their inquiries, but in any case he was certain that the police would not uncover any compromising bits of evidence such as the letters from priests found on the person of the recently arrested Marius Tournadre (see chapter 10), for neither he nor other royalists would be so imprudent.[16] Apparently some anarchists would be. A provincial prefect wrote to the minister of the interior quoting correspondence from an anarchist to one M. Passama, head of the local conservative party. The unnamed anarchist suggested that numerous sympathizers for reaction and monarchism existed within the revolutionary milieu. He cited Boulangism as an example of such co-operation between the left and right in the common interest of over-throwing the government and suggested future meetings to discuss such a reconciliation.[17] These were mere hints compared with the allegations leveled at literary anarchism in the spring of 1894. In the report on "L'Anarchie Lettrée," probably issued in March 1894, an informer reported that before his arrest, Charles Chatel was nearly ready to reissue his *Revue Libertaire,* thanks to funds received from the duchesse d'Uzès (whom Mermeix had portrayed as a former Boulangist supporter). The duc de Bellume was also named as a source of aid for "anarchist bohemians."[18]

By far the most detailed information linking royalists and anarchists concerned *La Revue Blanche,* probably the most important remaining source of literary anarchism since the demise of *Les Entretiens Politiques et Littéraires* the preceding year. Despite the personal fortune of the Natanson family, the police informer who made the lengthy report on *La Revue Blanche*'s political connections implied that some secret revelation was needed to explain how the journal could afford to main-tain relatively lavish offices at a prestigious Right Bank location and support numerous employees. "The truth," affirmed the informer, "is that *La Revue Blanche* lives on Orléanist funds. One speaks of the comte de Fitzjames, the great friend of the comte d'Haussonville. Other names are also indicated from the same milieu."[19] The crucial connection was the administrator of the journal, Marcel Barrière, who before taking his current post had been a secretary to the duc d'Orléans and had accompanied him on his Asian travels. Barrière was described as a very capable man thirty-eight years of age, whose polished speech and bearing inspired confidence in those around him. Thadée Natanson and Barrière presumably found funds "among the concealed Orléanists who stir up socialist ideas in their salons and thirst for the new and unexpected. They . . . are the agitated and neurotic." Lest it be supposed that literary rather than political interests predominated in this nexus between salon and journal, the informer specified the political goals of "Barrière and his *littérateurs,* the Bernard Lazares, Paul Adams, Saint-Pol Roux, etc." Along with support from the aristocracy, they wished the nobles to "accept a special socialist program absorbing all the schools—collectivists and anarchists included—as was Boulangism, allying intelligence and fortune and addressing itself to all the oppressed classes. This grouping will choose its leader, its 'socialist Boulanger,' and counts on an enormous mass of voters following. This great dream agitates 1 rue Laffitte [office of *La Revue Blanche*], and one must avow that it is in the hands of men of energy."[20] The informer described the aid that Barrière offered to impoverished anarchists as arising out of his sincerely democratic sentiments, as he dressed in worker's smock and visited them in their *quartiers.*

Although unusually detailed in its analysis of the situation, the police report of May 21, 1894, was not the only one to link *La Revue Blanche* with Orléanist intrigues. Three weeks later, another report insinuated that several aristocrats favored "subsidizing a publication of combat." Renard and Millet, seeking to profit from this interest, were communicating with the Orléanists about the possibility of publishing such a paper at a time when the curtailed anarchist press badly needed whatever support it could muster. Renard believed that Thadée Natanson, "who is in close contact with the amateur aristocracy of painting" (and the aristocratic professional painter Toulouse-Lautrec as well—one wonders whether he was involved at all in anarchist-royalist intrigues), would be among those who would sponsor such a publication.[21] Finally, on September 10, 1894, after the acquittal of the Procès de Trente defendants further encouraged the publicists to revive the anarchist press, the police noted increased activity among anarchists seeking the necessary funds. With Pouget in exile and Grave in prison, the journalistic field was left open to bohemian anarchists such as Charles Chatel, who were not adverse to accepting royalist backing. The death of the comte de Paris, exiled pretender to the French throne, which received considerable attention in *La Cocarde,* was reportedly much discussed among the anarchists because of their relations with the duc d'Orléans. According to the informer, Orléans as well as the comte de Chavilly and the marquis de Breteuil were aiding the anarchists. "Finally, *La Revue Blanche* has always been friendly to anarchy, and one knows that its administrator, M. Marcel Barrière, is a former undersecretary to the duc d'Orléans." Although the leftist sympathies of the journal's staff were not in doubt, this informer implied that the Orléanists encouraged anarchist agitation so as to discredit the republic and provoke a reaction that would lead to the restoration of the monarchy.[22]

However the royalist motives in forging this unlikely alliance may have diverged from those of the literary anarchists, there evidently were such relations and they seem to have peaked at the moment when the anarchists were most in need of aid to recover from the fierce repression visited on them by the authorities. On the other hand, the years of Boulangist and anarchist fervor also marked the centenary of the French Revolution, and the authorities may simply have been casting long historical glances back to the role of the duc d'Orléans in fomenting sedition against the Bourbons in 1789. Revolutions created by liberal dukes and by freemasons would be easier to forestall than those fomented by popular discontent.

The most suggestive aspect of these reports was the motive that the informer attributed to *La Revue Blanche*'s directors in enlisting Orléanist aid. Their efforts bore close parallels to Maurice Barrès's attempts later that year to effect the same sort of broad-based alliance of rightists and leftists around socialist and anarchist principles. Whereas *La Cocarde* attracted the anti-Semitic wing of the Boulangist party, *La Revue Blanche* was the center of the progressive Jewish intelligentsia. Paul Adam, whom Sternhell has labeled an anti-Semite for an 1889 article he contributed to the Boulangist *Courrier de l'Est,* published numerous articles in *La Revue Blanche* between 1893 and 1895, a few years before he sealed the bond with marriage to Lucien Muhlfeld's sister-in-law (Muhlfeld preceded Fénéon as editor in chief of the journal).[23] As ready as Barrès to find a new synthesis among the parties of the left, Adam avowed himself a decentralist and altruist collectivist. He protested

Barrès's Caesarism but apparently was not adverse to calling on the old French nobility to whom he was related to take a hand in toppling the Republic. He doubtless would have justified this commingling of royalism and socialism as the merging of tradition and innovation in a uniquely French approach to revolution. Neither *équipe* considered itself counterrevolutionary, yet both groups seemingly compromised their leftist integrity by appealing to royalists or to nationalists and anti-Semites. After the failure of Boulangism and the dead-end of anarchist terrorism, when the 1893 elections had demonstrated the socialist electoral potential, the need for a new approach to the "social problem" was evident. What distinguished these two attempts of 1894, Barrière's and Barrès's, was their willingness to cross class barriers and unite aristocrats, artists, intellectuals, and the workers in an antiparliamentary front. Whereas Benjamin Disraeli had championed Tory democracy, a patrician-worker alliance, by extending the suffrage and buttressing parliamentarianism, these far more radical fin de siècle activists were less sanguine about the promise of democracy.

That the socialists and anarchists of *La Revue Blanche* were also seeking alternatives to the republican status quo in a class-transcending union may serve to caution one about applying the term "protofascist" to this transitional era. Many of Barrès's *équipe* turned to the right in later years; nevertheless, the *La Revue Blanche* group included the future socialist statesman Léon Blum, the Dreyfusard activist Bernard Lazare, and Julien Benda, who ironically would be remembered for defending the values of intellectual detachment. Anarchist attempts to coalesce the different classes in a revolutionary union failed, as the principal extraparliamentary movement on the left after 1895, anarchosyndicalism, abjured all nonproletarian interference (though it continued to attract the admiration of intellectuals who, moreover, were not immune to the attractions of the right as well). After 1898, the "bourgeois revolution" would indeed be a creature of the right, whereas Dreyfusard socialists of all classes defended the Republic and became increasingly identified with parliamentary politics.[24]

Reviewing the criminal and judicial events of 1892, Albert Bataille noted that year that anarchist and anti-Semitic violence appeared to be the outstanding and conjoined events of the season. Along with the bombs of Ravachol there appeared pamphlets distributed by the marquis de Morès and his henchmen at the wedding of Mlle. de Rothschild, which read "Rothschild et Ravachol." That year, in a duel witnessed by his friend Major Esterhazy, the marquis fought and killed a Jewish army captain named Joseph Alexander Mayer. At the trial that followed, the prosecution asked for Morès's condemnation in order to stop Drumont's anti-Semitic campaign, yet the jury acquitted the noble duelist. Bataille saw anti-Semitic violence as being essentially anti-capitalist, mentioning Baron Jacques de Reinach, Arton, Hugo Oberndorfer, Lévy-Crémieux, and Cornélius Herz as rich Jews recently emerged from the German ghetto, now involved in political scandal: "Money! it is against the colossus on feet of clay that revolutionary socialism and anti-Semitism are linked, perhaps without knowing it. It is the parallelism of that double explosion that is important to note, as a double symptom of the same social malady."[25] The old religious anti-Semitism was being re-invigorated by a new economic and class antagonism.

In the decade when the anti-Dreyfusards dredged up French xeno-phobia and racism, supplanting anarchism as the most immediate threat to the Republic, the strength of the anti-Semitic appeal can scarcely be overestimated. The Panama Affair of 1892–93, which implicated a num-ber of Jewish financiers and journalists as well as Deputy Georges Clemenceau, engineers Gustave Eiffel and Ferdinand de Lesseps, and others, stirred up both anarchists and anti-Semites, and the radical left was not free of a certain anticapitalist anti-Semitism that identified the Jew as a class enemy.[26] The marquis de Morès was the perfect fin de siècle embodiment of this new force in French politics.

A figure out of a Jules Verne adventure story, the marquis de Morès had all the makings of a great demagogue. He had spent part of the 1880s in North Dakota trying to make his fortune as a cattle baron, and would meet his death in Africa in 1896, not quite forty years old, apparently killed by his own Tuareg bodyguard while on an imperialist venture. In the early 1890s he was among the most active anti-Semitic political organizers and was eager to enroll the masses in his Anti-Semitic League. The pseudonymed journalists Flor O'Squarr, whose *Les Cou-lisses de l'anarchie* (The Corridors of Anarchy, 1892) revealed the same mixture of racism and socialism as motivated de Morès and who claimed personal communication with the marquis, reported that de Morès so admired the aggressive tactics of the anarchists who invaded his meetings that he tried to enroll them in his movement. Early in 1892, around the time that Drumont founded *La Libre Parole,* O'Squarr wrote that Michel Zévaco, former editor of *L'Egalité,* was the intermediary in a meeting between de Morès and Emile Pouget. Pouget was eager to transform his *Père Peinard* from a weekly to a daily publication, but lacked the necessary funds. De Morès proposed that they collaborate on one paper with separate editorial staffs, each independent and signing its own articles. According to O'Squarr, Pouget expressed admiration for Drumont's literary skills but distrusted his clericalism and refused to compromise his independence by any arrangement with *La Libre Parole*: "To attain a true, useful, practical socialism, Drumont must first throw Jesus overboard with Judah."[27] According to this interpretation, not anti-Semitism but clericalism was the stumbling block in such a union of the left. In a clarificatory note at the end of the book, O'Squarr wrote that de Morès had not intended to enroll the anarchists in *La Libre Parole* but rather to group all the socialist forces in another newspaper; the same ideal underlay Barrès's *La Cocarde* two years later.

As early as 1890, the police reported similar cordial relations between radical anti-Semites and anarchists. In order to woo anarchist support, the marquis was willing to underwrite the costs of their meetings. Finances were always a problem for the anarchists, and as the marquis seemed genuinely interested in their movement, they were not particularly concerned about his anti-Semitism.[28] Late in 1892, the marquis was still subsidizing anarchists, providing 100 kilos of bread and 10 kilos of meat for the anarchist soup-lecture at the Salle Favié on December 12, and giving an anarchist named Leboucher 40 francs that same month.[29] Leboucher later surfaced as a reporter for *La Cocarde,* supposedly in contact with the anarchists there, which is not surprising considering his continuing hostility to the republic and his old friendship with Louise Michel, which dated back to 1870. At a time when not only the House of Rothschild but the numerous Jewish financiers implicated in the Panama Affair symbolized the corrupt interrelations of capital and government, it was natural that anti-Semitism should spread among the left. Yet aside from providing the anarchists with financial support, no serious or lasting *rapprochement* was concluded between the anti-Semites and the anarchists.

Relations were further complicated by suspicions among anti-

Semites of the extreme right that anarchism was being aided by Jewish money. In May 1894, the police informer "Legrand" told of the vicomte d'Hugues, "the new marquis de Morès of the moment," who sought to discredit the Jews by attributing the anarchist crimes to their malign influence. The vicomte had sent his personal police to England and Belgium to seek the sources of anarchist funding. Rather than pursuing the Natansons or other wealthy and liberal Jews, he stalked the legendary Rothschilds, who he heard were in touch with the anarchist Charles Malato. Some of his information on "the participation of the high Jewish bank in the anarchist *attentats*" came from the abbé Garnier, and he was willing to pay handsomely for all denunciations accompanied by proof.[30] Another report issued that spring noted: "The Rothschilds show themselves very complacent toward the anarchists. They have a secretary who writes to certain anarchists who are in search of funds, under pretext of misery or heavy family burdens." Several received a louis from their Jewish benefactor, according to the informer.[31] Just why the Rothschilds would want to support anarchist efforts to bring down the state was not made clear. In 1889, Paul Adam was among those who blamed Jewish subsidies to the government for contributing to the Boulangist defeat, which was certainly more plausible considering their relative security under the Third Republic. The most obvious reason why the Rothschilds would pay off the anarchists was to insure themselves against bombings. In August 1895, a bomb did explode at the Rothschild residence, injuring their secretary. An informer frequenting the Left Bank Café Procope, where Mécislas Golberg and other contributors to the anarchist journal *Sur le Trimard* gathered, overheard a discussion in which it was theorized that a disgruntled anarchist, perhaps one of those tried in the Procès de Trente, had unsuccessfully solicited funds from Rothschild and had bombed his residence in revenge.[32] Rothschild attributed the bombing to anti-Semites rather than anarchists.

Anti-Semitism did exist among the anarchists, but never as a central issue. There were a considerable number of Jewish anarchists and anarchist sympathizers among the proletariat and the *littérateurs*. Typical of the class antagonism transferred to racial-religious grounds was the caricature of Rothschild hanging from a gallows that adorned Jean Grave's garret editorial office. In *Le Père Peinard* of April 20, 1893, Emile Pouget wrote that the Jew who formerly had been a "pauvre bougre" persecuted for his religion was now the exploiter par excellence. But he added that "of religion, of race, there is no longer a question," thus making it clear that he would not engage in diatribes against the Jews as a people but only as capitalists.[33] This attitude left Pouget cold about Alfred Dreyfus's fate, for he reasoned that the case of the wealthy army officer was being resumed only because his family had the necessary funds to pursue it, while numerous anarchists rotted in prison. Pouget eventually followed Sebastien Faure's lead in allying himself with the Dreyfusards, for he appreciated the harm done to the army by the "Panama militaire."[34]

Far removed from the circles of the Jewish barons of finance were the working-class Jewish anarchists, most of whom were recent immigrants from Eastern Europe, just as were the American anarchists Emma Goldman and Alexander Berkman. One police report of 1892 described a meeting of fifty Russian and Polish Jews at the Salle du Trésor, at which the *compagnon* "Saint-Denis" read his eulogy "Ravachol devant l'histoire." Meetings were held on Saturday evenings at the conclusion of the Jewish sabbath. During the repression of 1894, fear among the anarchists was such that only seven people met at the regular meeting at the Café du Tresor, and the Jewish newspapers *Arbeiterstimme* and *Arbeiterfreund* were not even distributed.[35]

More visible in the anarchist milieu, at least to Barrès, Drumont, and company, were the sophisticated Jewish writers of *La Revue Blanche,* who simultaneously championed the aesthetic and political avant-gardes. Around the Polish-born Natansons who owned the review were gathered several young Jewish writers: Lucien Muhlfeld, Léon Blum, Julien Benda, Pierre Veber, and Romain Coolus. Blum wrote a long article in 1894 called "Nouvelles Conversations de Goethe avec Eckermann," in which he described the true Jewish religion as a passion for justice and claimed Marx and Ferdinand Lassalle as modern secularized Jewish thinkers.[36] That same year, just after the Procès de Trente of August 1894, Pouget wrote to Charles Chatel inquiring about sponsors for a new anarchist paper. The police noted that "Chatel had several rich people in mind when he published the *Revue Libertaire,* rich men of the Natanson milieu, newly arrived Jews who launched *La Revue Blanche.*[37] Anarchist anti-Semitism was neither strong enough to cause the *compagnons* to resist the aid offered by Jewish sympathizers nor to dissuade these writers from supporting them financially and propagandistically. The relations between *La Revue Blanche* and Pouget remained close up to and during the Dreyfus Affair, when Pouget finally allied himself with their cause and *La Revue Blanche* became an active center of Dreyfusard support.

As the Dreyfus Affair polarized formerly ambiguous political positions and clearly separated the radical right from the left, so it apparently made anti-Semitism, if not a monopoly of the right, at least clearly identified with national chauvinism. Ironically, rather than effecting a union of the left as Barrès had hoped, anti-Semitism separated nationalist opponents of the Republic from the socialist and anarchist internationalists, identifying the former as defenders of the army. Nevertheless, such leftist periodicals as Zo d'Axa's 1898 *La Feuille* and *L'Assiette au Beurre* in the next decade would retain an anti-Semitic overtone, even if there was little chance of their uniting with Charles Maurras's royalist rabble-rousers of the Action Française.[38] Not popular anti-Semitism but clericalism, militarism, and national chauvinism separated the various radical opponents of the parliamentary regime.

The Social and Symbolic Space
of Parisian Anarchism

Three

Whether or not Paris was truly the capital of the nineteenth century, as
Walter Benjamin claimed, it was by all measures the expanding, com-
manding center of France.[1] The city's population had quintupled in a
century, and was approaching 3 million in the 1890s, at a time when the
population of France as a whole was growing very slowly. Important as
was the city's political hegemony, its cultural predominance was even
more marked, especially in communications and the arts: literature,
publishing, painting, and the graphic arts. Anarchism in the era of
attentats was before all else a propagandizing and proselytizing movement, and Parisian words and deeds resonated more loudly than provincial ones. Although the anarchists idealized a decentralized society, the
very fact that so much power was centered in the capital meant that
anarchists who wished to attack effectively the symbols of that power
must also come to Paris. Their dependence on a wide variety of media to
spread their message encouraged the growth of a significant anarchist
press in Paris, which led most of the movement's leaders to congregate
there. Anarchist newspapers published from Roubaix to Marseille show
that anarchism was active in the provinces as well, yet after Jean Grave
moved *Le Révolté* from Geneva to Paris in 1885, the capital was the
nerve center of the anarchist movement, the place most in contact with
events happening abroad, especially with the anarchists of Brussels and
London.[2]

The century of the phenomenal growth of Paris was also the century
in which the French capital had become identified with the most radical
political events of a tumultuous era. French history of the century
preceding the era of anarchist *attentats* offered a living tradition of
revolution. With the exception of the first Napoleonic Empire, there had
been a revolution in France every twenty years since 1789, and every

revolution had been centered in Paris. The generation that was coming of age in 1890, raised among the blood-soaked shadows of the Paris Commune of 1871, had every reason to expect that the Third French Republic would be no more immune to revolutionary upheaval than all the previous governments—republics, monarchies, and empires—had been. With Boulangism, the Panama scandal, anarchist terrorism, and the Dreyfus Affair all sharing the crowded political stage of one brief decade, stability was not to be taken for granted. The anarchists could only benefit by capitalizing on this revolutionary heritage.

The Parisian past lived on in the present; history infused the environment with symbolic meaning, and that historical meaning might easily be construed in revolutionary terms. Local patterns of behavior or geographical features functioned symbolically by standing for something transcending their immediate utility. Such symbolism might express itself in the most mundane event, so that a minor altercation between boss and worker may have symbolized the impossibility of maintaining amicable class relations. The Moulin Rouge offered entertainment, but it also came to symbolize the fin de siècle spirit of Paris. Spaces may share utilitarian and symbolic functions, but they do not share them equally. The Eiffel Tower exercised a purely symbolic function, and Sacré-Coeur's symbolic counterrevolutionary function designating the triumph of church and state over the anticlerical Communards outweighed its social utility as a local church, at least in the historical context of the Third Republic. The average foreign tourist, for whom Sacré-Coeur is no more meaningful than any other imposing monument, could possibly confuse it with another white-domed monument, the Pantheon, which symbolizes very different things to the Parisian. Symbolic spaces demand mediating, contextualizing information to render them meaningful. In return, such spaces and places may reinforce political identification by nonliterate means.

The social and cultural geography of fin de siècle Paris, the *quartiers* and faubourgs, boulevards and *impasses,* was so profoundly entwined with the anarchist movement that one can discern the orientation of different factions within the movement simply by describing the particular milieu with which each identified. The impact of this social geography was greatly enhanced by the symbolic geography—the significance of certain buildings, neighborhoods, and sites charged with emotional and historical meaning. Paris provided the anarchists with both social milieu and symbolic space; history and politics cast long shadows over their daily lives. The newest and most affronting shadow was cast by Sacré-Coeur, symbol of the domination of church and state, looming insolently over the place du Tertre in Montmartre. Its planned destruction was the theme of Emile Zola's fictional treatment of anarchism, *Paris,* written between the era of anarchist bombings and the Dreyfus Affair in the mid-1890s. Montmartre had a radical as well as bohemian past, having been the site of the murder of the two Versaillaise generals that inaugurated the Paris Commune of 1871, and Sacré-Coeur explicitly contravened that revolutionary heritage. The most important symbol of leftist resistance was Père Lachaise cemetery, where the Communards had made their last stand. In these centennial years of the great French Revolution, Paris provided a vivid metaphorical landscape to sustain a movement that was devoted to destroying old symbols of the social order and constructing new ones in their place.

Paris was not a unidimensional symbol of political power; it also stood for literature and art, for higher education, for culture in general. Insofar as high culture was institutionalized at the Beaux-Arts, the Comédie Française, or the Sorbonne, it too stood for power. Much like the bohemian artists with whom they commingled, the anarchists rejected all these sources of official, bourgeois values. Paris was too compromised by wealth and power not to be tainted in anarchist eyes. They wished to be in Paris but not fully of Paris. For most anarchists, neither the Sorbonne nor the milieu of salons and literary reviews provided a sufficient sense of an anarchist counterculture; 1890s students did not swell the culture of opposition, though they could riot spontaneously when the need arose (as in the July 1893 Latin Quarter riots against government censorship and prudery).

The likeliest choice for the anarchist homeland in opposition to official Paris would seem to have been the working-class faubourgs, mostly running from the seventeenth arrondissement of Batignolles on the north to the twentieth arrondissement on the east, and consisting of such traditional radical-artisanal bastions as the faubourg Saint-Antoine. This was in fact where the Parisian anarchists drew most of their strength, and numerous meetings took place in this northeast quadrant of Paris. Yet this working-class region was unable to project itself as the symbolic alternative to the powers-that-be. Why? For the same reason that the anarchists were ambivalent about work and work-related values, which signified to them exploitation rather than the nobility of labor envisioned by the Marxists. The east of Paris was dominated by the west; these faubourgs were a fruitful source of adherents to the cause, but their disenchantment with the status quo was not a sufficient basis for establishing an alternative vision of what society should be like. The socialists might imagine their workers' paradise sometime in the distant future; the anarchists wished to embody their utopia in the present, to live rather than plan for the revolution. The faubourgs might stand for revolt, but not for liberation from contemporary society.

Symbolically, and to a surprising extent socially as well, the Parisian anarchists of the fin de siècle gravitated toward bohemia. The artists' colony of Montmartre, rising above Paris on the north and since 1860 incorporated into the capital, allowed just that sense of separation from the metropolis sprawling below its heights that the anarchists needed to preserve the feelings of autonomy and integrity that allowed them both to envision alternatives to the present social order and to actively experiment with such alternative arrangements in their daily lives. The faubourgs stood for work; Montmartre signified pleasure, embodied in its cabarets, and the free play of imagination, typified by its artists. Art and pleasure—sexuality sublimated and released—expressed the ethos of anarchist liberation better than sexuality denied, transmuted into work. The Right Bank centers of commerce stood for freedom abstracted into money (the anarchists would doubtless have agreed with Marx's statement in the *Communist Manifesto* that the bourgeois' true freedom was free trade), whereas the Left Bank's detached intellectuality stifled the free life of impulse. Pleasure and imagination when taken together appeared to the anarchists to negate the dominant bourgeois culture more effectively than did the life-denying qualities of labor, money, and mind.

The areas of greatest anarchist recruitment were not always coterminous with the centers of anarchist activity, and political activity did not determine the anarchists' ideological and cultural universe. The ordinary rank and file failed to project a strong symbolic image onto the anarchist movement; they were the masses in a movement that valued individualism. Anarchist militants were somewhat more influential, and terrorists and certain bohemians, artists, and entertainers influenced cultural norms to a degree out of proportion to their numbers. Terrorists identified the enemy by exploding bombs in highly symbolic locales, nearly all of which lay in the fashionable neighborhoods and boulevards lying to the west of the central Parisian north-south axis defined by the boulevards Sébastopol and Saint-Michel. Bohemian Montmartre epitomized the cultural alternative to the dominant society that the terrorists were attacking, in part because "for the artists and writers, anarchism represented a general attitude of life rather than a specific theory about society."[3] For the purposes of this study, then, Paris may be divided into four parts: bourgeois and aristocratic Paris, the Latin Quarter, the working-class faubourgs, and Montmartre, the last of which came closest to uniting the social and symbolic space of anarchism into a libertarian milieu.

Anarchism exercised a snobbish appeal over wealthy Parisians in the fin de siècle. The anarchists found two means of access to the bustling commercial sector of Paris seated among the fashionable boulevards of the Right Bank and in the aristocratic faubourg Saint-Germain on the Left Bank. They could plant their bombs there, or they could appeal to the Tout-Paris via the *littérateurs* enamored of anarchy who had the proper social connections. The explosions in the boulevard Saint-Germain, at the Church of the Madeleine, at the Restaurant Foyot and the second arrondissement police headquarters were unlikely to gain many converts for anarchism, at least among the rich, although Vaillant's bombing of the Chamber of Deputies did occasion an outpouring of sympathy for his little daughter Sidonie among the chic set. (The duchess d'Uzès offered to adopt her upon the execution of her father, but Vaillant preferred to leave her in the custody of Sebastien Faure, the anarchist orator who lived on the rue Ramey in Montmartre, far from the aristocratic quarter.) A more prevalent form of anarchist sympathizing was *l'anarchie au salon*. One of the writers interested in tapping a lucrative means of support for the generally impoverished movement was Bernard Lazare, the writer and journalist who from 1896 was a central figure in bringing the Dreyfus Affair to light. As an editor of the literary journal *Les Entretiens Politiques et Littéraires,* with Paul Adam and Francis Vielé-Griffin, Lazare was instrumental in turning the Symbolist literary movement toward anarchism in 1892. The police were aware of his political activities and reported in 1894 on his efforts to raise support for anarchism by means of banquets and literary gatherings.[4]

The association between anarchism and the avant-garde was such that by 1893–94 some wealthy men thought that they might protect themselves from terrorist attacks by supporting the writers linked to anarchy. The prince de Sagan and the Rothschilds had received letters suggesting that they contribute, and the marquis de la Rochetulon bought several tickets for Ibsen's *Solness the Builder,* put on by the "Théâtre de l'Oeuvre, which the police informer "Legrand" termed an "anarchist literary society."[5] Another report noted a M. Lebaudy and the duc de Bellume in addition to the duchesse d'Uzès as potential support- ers of anarchism, and expressed the belief that fear of reprisals was motivating them to finance an Octave Mirbeau, a Paul Adam, or a Georges Courteline: "This strange circumstance is today experienced among the aristocracy, that instead of putting the resuscitated bohe- mians of Murger out the door, they open their salons to them and make them gifts."[6] Writers tried to capitalize on the situation by seeking support for literary soirées, subsidies for theater efforts, sometimes a job as secretary. The police may have read anarchist influence into some largely literary endeavors, but whether their suspicion was founded on fact or paranoia, that they equated bohemian *déclassés* with anarchists was significant. Such suspicions also bore witness to the widespread fears of an anarchist conspiracy, especially among members of the police and the government. The informer who produced the report on "L'Anar- chie Lettrée" in 1894 singled out the educated youth surrounding the newspaper *Le Journal,* whose literary critic, Octave Mirbeau, was influ- ential among anarchist writers and planned to provide radical plays for such new theater companies as Gabriel de la Salle's Théâtre de l'Art Social.

The cult of Ibsen and anarchism were parallel vogues among the dilettantes and aesthetes who found rebellion a comfortable pose. In an era when Maurice Barrès could write in *Le Figaro* in 1891 that "the little brochures of Peter Kropotkin . . . display a beautiful generosity and strong logic," it was inevitable that snobbism would mix with anarchism among the Parisian elite.[7] It was easy enough for Jean Rameau of *Le Gaulois* to mock those adornments of the salon—the works of Gabriele

D'Annunzio, Ibsen, an anarchist thinker—beneath which "nietzsche-ries" one was likely to discover the hastily hidden novel of George Sand. In his attempt to appear knowledgeable about the latest developments, especially if they smacked of the exotic, the snob could annex the most antibourgeois ideologies to his set of beliefs. Anarchism not only connoted rebellion and bravado, but also stood for originality and individuality, qualities much admired by snobs. In conjunction with the Nietzschean justification for aristocratic elitism that was also making the radical chic rounds after 1892, anarchism crystallized a series of attributes equally appealing to the artistic avant-garde and to snobbish society, and salon anarchism was central to the snobbism that so characterized the fin de siècle.[8]

While contributing intellectual leadership to anarchism, the Latin Quarter failed to unite the avant-garde of art and politics into a coherent cultural force. With the exception of *La Revue Blanche,* which moved to the fashionable Opéra quarter in 1893, the vast majority of the Symbolist journals found their home on the less exclusive Left Bank in the shadow of the Sorbonne. The rue des Ecoles, where most of the reviews originated, was to the literary avant-garde what Montmartre was to the painters. This literary and student milieu made a natural base for anarchist propaganda, and groups like the Individualistes Anarchistes, which organized lectures at the Salle Octobre, 46 rue Montagne Sainte-Geneviève, appealed precisely to this coterie. One might expect to hear such writers as Paul Adam, Bernard Lazare, and Lucien Descaves, the sociologist Augustin Hamon, or the esteemed anthropology professor Letourneau.[9] *La Plume* held noisy and popular *Soirées de la Plume* every other Saturday night at the Soleil d'Or, place Saint-Michel. According to *La Plume*'s editor, Léon Deschamps, "politics are excluded from these meetings, which are attended by all the intellectual youth of Paris."[10] That prohibition did not prevent Laurent Tailhade from making his famous quip about Vaillant's "beautiful gesture" at one such soirée (see chapter 8) and the magazine itself consecrated special issues to anarchism. Pervasive intellectualism distinguished Latin Quarter anarchism from its Montmartre poorer cousin; nevertheless, this same intellectual youth willingly engaged in street fighting when the occasion arose, as it did after the censorship of the students' Bal des Quat'z'Arts in July 1893. For five days the Latin Quarter witnessed near insurrection, and the police accused anarchists of exploiting a spontaneous revolutionary situation.[11] Budding anarchist poets such as Adolphe Retté and Jean Carrère (who was wounded in the melee) were further politicized by their participation in the revolutionary psychodrama.

The center of Left Bank anarchism was located further up the hill beyond the Sorbonne and the literary cafés, where Jean Grave steadfastly published *La Révolte* on the narrow and ancient rue Mouffetard. It was often pointed out at the time that if Emile Pouget's *Le Père Peinard* represented the popular Montmartre version of anarchism, *La Révolte* was entirely appropriate for its Left Bank locale, printing the words of Kropotkin and Elisée Reclus in sober and scholarly prose. Just as Grave's official organ was surpassed in popularity by Pouget's *canard,* so the Latin Quarter failed to form a coherent culture of anarchism among its mixed population of professors, students, writers, and artisans. Grave never employed culture as a force for popular identification with the movement, as did Pouget, nor did he show much sympathy for the artistic avant-garde. Rather, he maintained a middle course of edifying didacticism that failed to inspire either workers or artists, and which apparently had no cataclysmic effect on the nearby university population. Left Bank anarchism was intellectually active but lacked the social organization maintained by the more enthusiastic *compagnons* across the Seine. It expounded anarchist ideas, but failed to exemplify them.

The working-class faubourgs provided the basis of anarchist support. In 1890, the police compiled a list of 47 anarchist militants, some of whom were additionally termed "dangerous." The stated occupations of 36 of these anarchists give an indication of the relatively humble social position of the vast majority of Parisian anarchists. The largest group represented were the carpenters and joiners, with 6 men falling in this category. The faubourg Saint-Antoine, traditional center of the Parisian furniture industry as well as of revolutionary activity, was known to be an anarchist stronghold, and in 1891 two anarchist-run newspapers catered to the carpenters and cabinet-makers of this quarter. After a schism among the editors of the *Pot à Colle* (The Glue-pot), another corporatist anarchist paper appeared entitled *Le Riflard* (The Carpenter's Plane), published in nearby Montreuil. Also in 1891 and 1892 there appeared an anarchist paper directed at the printers and typesetters and entitled *Le Cri Typographique,* and in 1893 *La Réveil du Tailleur* (The Tailors' Awakening) emerged. Though the anarchists were not involved in labor organizing as their syndicalist successors were shortly to be, the working classes already were active in the movement. Another short-lived journalistic effort, called simply *Le Faubourg*, succinctly identified the locus of anarchist support.[12] One typesetter was listed on the police roster of anarchist militants, as well as 3 hairdressers, 2 tailors, 2 cobblers, 2 café waiters, 2 masons, several clerks, 4 journalists (not including Pouget and Grave, who were listed as store clerk and cobbler, respectively), an illustrator, a man of letters, and an unskilled laborer. Four years later in the newspaper *Le Matin* it was estimated that there were 500 anarchists in Paris, who were divided into propagandists and practitioners. Among the former were cited 10 journalists, 25 printers, and 2 proofreaders; the latter included 17 tailors, 16 cobblers, 20 grocers, 15 sympathizers, and perhaps 8,000 more throughout France.[13] Though the figures are unreliable, the job categories reveal that the anarchists of the 1890s were drawn from a mix of the traditional artisanal trades along with lesser or unskilled workers, excepting those who made their living by the pen. The representation of printers and publicists signifies the centrality of propaganda in the presyndicalist era.

Most of the laboring anarchist populace lived in the northeast quadrant of Paris, in the ninth, tenth, eleventh, twelfth, eighteenth, nineteenth, and twentieth arrondissements. Literary interest in the working-class neighborhoods had been spurred by Emile Zola's *L'Assommoir,* which presented life around a low dive in the rue de la Goutte d'Or, in the eighteenth arrondissement. Almost twenty years after *L'Assommoir*'s publication in 1877, another writer came to the faubourgs to reevaluate Zola's Naturalist portrayal of the seamy life of the "lower depths." Henri Leyret opened a café in the Belleville-Ménilmontant quarter, and played proprietor for five months during the winter of 1893 and 1894, a crucial period for French anarchism. The record of his experiences, published in 1895, revealed a great deal about the popular social milieu in which anarchism flourished. Leyret compared himself to Gauguin, who had recently gone "to live among the primitives in order to approach a primitive art, to create an intimately Tahitian soul." Exploring the alien culture in *En plein faubourg,* Leyret contended that the working-class bar functioned more as a social center than as a sinister asylum of drunken escapism, and he depicted it as a setting in which the whole family would convene on Saturday nights.[14]

According to Leyret, the typical *faubourien* was uninterested in politics. When a worker entered with the news of Vaillant's bombing, rendered in the *argotique* "the aquarium has been blown up," others who wished to continue their conversation answered, "leave us alone with your deputies." Leyret generalized that though he might not vote, the faubourg dweller would fight for his rights: "if disillusioned he be— or because disillusioned, and desperate!—the true *faubourien* will never flee the odor of powder." This combination of deep distrust of bourgeois politics with hot-tempered defensiveness provided fertile soil for anarchist propaganda, and the *faubourien* was most likely to encounter politics at the local level of workers' societies, study circles, and committees of the quarter. Countering his example of the apolitical worker, Leyret described two others who explained their preference for some well-known libertarian journalists with "a surety of judgment that more than one critic would have envied." He spoke of the "crazy laughter" that the anarchists had been reaping for a decade with their caricatures and satire of the *gros legume* (big vegetable) of a bourgeois and cautioned that "one caricature wounds more surely than the most passionate invective. . . . laughing leads to demolishing."[15] The 1880s sowed the seeds of popular radicalism, Boulangism left disgust at deception, and ensuing scandals only strengthened this disgust:

Fifteen years of strikes, fifteen years of disillusions, fifteen years of rot—all that purulent agony of a century had troubled the soul of the faubourg, infinitely weary of hope! *Compagnons* surged, anathematizing these decadent times, preaching the return to the state of nature, in evocation of a terrible cataclysm of which the bomb was a prelude, such as the trumpets of the last judgment.[16]

Seeing this ferment in the faubourgs, the middle classes tended to blame the wine merchants for sowing revolutionary propaganda. Leyret minimized their role, conceding only that "one or two hundred of the thousands are political," but because his book argued for the centrality of cafés in lower-class life, he could not deny their place as centers of communication and propaganda.[17]

Breeder of personal degradation or of social discontent, the working-class bar was practically the sole social institution available to the *faubourien*. The leftist art critic Gustave Geffroy suggested supplementing it with a proletarian cultural center, to be set between the place de la

République and the Bastille, in the heart of the faubourgs. No proletarian Ecole des Beaux-Arts, the Musée du Soir would display workers' own productions, produce pride in their work, and be an integral part of their daily lives. Police spies reported that the most important anarchist group in Paris, the Cercle International, also convened in the heart of *populaire* Paris, at the Salle Horel, 13 rue Aumaire. Smaller meetings were held at the anarchist printer Cabot's on the rue du Marais, where the movement's scanty funds were handled.[18] Despite this activity, the faubourgs of northeastern Paris were not self-sufficient in giving working-class culture a specifically anarchist orientation. In his novel *Paris*, Emile Zola set his story of conspiracy between anarchist workers and ideologues not in Belleville or in the faubourg Saint-Antoine, but on the slopes of Montmartre.

If the anarchism of the elite was centered in the faubourg Saint-Germain and the Right Bank boulevards, and intellectual anarchism matured on the Left Bank, the popular culture and much of the elite culture of anarchism thrived in Montmartre. To understand why Montmartre most closely approximated an anarchist community in the 1890s requires a glance at its history. It social and cultural importance as a bohemian refuge began in the eighteenth century for largely geographic reasons. Lying just north of the customs wall, Montmartre was exempt from the excise tax levied on all wines brought into Paris. Eighteenth-century Parisians came there to drink the *vin de pays* that would have been rendered too costly by the relatively high duty. A 1790 document noted that "the interest of more than a million cultivators is linked to Montmartre."[19] On Sundays and holidays one met the Parisian *petits bourgeois* in Montmartre's cabarets; weekdays found workers from the quarries who had long mined the lime of Montmartre to make the slightly misnamed plaster of Paris. These quarries so undermined the Butte that houses were known to collapse into them. Lower Montmartre was annexed to Paris in 1790 but the Butte remained outside of the city's jurisdiction until 1860, thus managing to maintain its autonomy along with its village appearance well into the nineteenth century. The population, which grew from 2,000 in 1800 to 30,000 in 1860, was one of modest means, and included the prostitutes who even then haunted the boulevard Rochechouart, and a floating population of thieves and smugglers who frequented the wineshops and hid in the quarries until Baron

Haussmann filled them in during his rebuilding efforts in the 1850s, returning the plaster from whence it had come while sparing the Butte from his urban renewal plans.[20]

After becoming a portion of the eighteenth arrondissement in 1859, Montmartre grew meteorically. As the Parisian population surged over the 2 million mark, the exterior boulevards impinged upon the rustic Butte. The quartiers constituted distinct blocs, differentiated by social class and mode of existence to an extent unknown to the older, more heterogeneous urban population.[21] Montmartre owed its specialization as a bohemian and pleasure center to its heritage of political independence and to its altitude that had helped maintain its separation from Paris. The incorporation into the city speeded its growth but did not greatly affect its demographic composition. In 1898, Aurélian Scholl charted the change from windmills to theaters and restaurants, but could still write, "The Butte, the real Montmartre, seems at first view to be one-half country village and one-half large provincial town . . . one would believe himself more than two hundred miles from the metropolis."[22] One year later, a former police inspector reported that prostitution still thrived on the slopes: "Montmartre has replaced, from the standpoint of joy and pleasure, the old Latin Quarter; the students themselves say as much and come in groups when they want to laugh."[23] Those students did more than laugh. He described the 40-sous *gigolette* (whose name derived from the *gigue* or jig she danced in the open air dance halls), closely followed by her *marlou* or pimp. On Sunday afternoons at the Moulin de la Galette, one met everyone from pimps and streetwalkers to great courtesans and dandies; in the evening the pimps began to predominate and the dance hall became "less variegated and more vulgar" (*moins panaché et plus populaire*). "Monsieur Jean" found that the contrast between the chic courtesans lounging in late night restaurants and the low-level prostitutes on the streets gave Montmartre its special charm. The "lower depths" that thrived on Montmartre's heights were an important element in the popular cultural milieu of the Montmartre anarchists.

Besides prostitutes and wine merchants, the other major group to populate Montmartre from the 1830s on were the painters who enjoyed its rustic and precipitous streets and low rents. The painters were joined by numerous writers, composers and *rapins* or aspiring young artists, among the earliest of whom were Berlioz and Gérard de Nerval. Degas and Renoir were the most prominent Impressionist Montmartrois, to be followed by a flood of painters among the Post-Impressionist generation. The styles of Toulouse-Lautrec, Seurat, Signac, Luce, and van Gogh were inseparable from the milieu they represented. They were accompanied by a host of lesser artists and illustrators, among whom Théophile-Alexandre Steinlen and Adolphe Willette were the most well known as well as the most tenacious, maintaining residences in Montmartre until the 1920s. The generation of Picasso also made its aesthetic revolution in Montmartre. The twisting streets witnessed the ferment of generations of artists and revolutionaries; when Montmartre's low-life charms were undermined by commercialism instead of by quarrying, the bohemians migrated to Montparnasse and elsewhere to create and revolt.

The other principal influence on fin de siècle Montmartre's reputation as an artists' colony was due as much to entrepreneurship as to art. A twenty-nine-year-old one-time painter named Rodolphe Salis, often described as half *cabaretier* and half Barnum, planned to open a cabaret in Montmartre. In December 1881 he met the poet and publicist Emile Goudeau, and in January 1882 Goudeau became the editor of the newspaper that Salis published under the sign of the *Chat Noir* (Black Cat). The poets who were lured out of the Latin Quarter to congregate at the Chat Noir cabaret were thereby given an organ in which to publish their works, and their presence at the cabaret was advertised as an inducement for others to rub shoulders with gentlemen of letters. They also consumed considerable quantities of the proprietor's beverages. Though there was nothing novel about writers sojourning at a favorite cafe, Salis's *cabaret artistique* integrated the roles of poet and performer.[24]

One other innovation by Salis that contributed to the unprecedented success of his establishment, the conjoining of cabaret and journal in which the Chat Noir's literary lights could be published while advertising the place, was due directly to the liberalized press laws. The *Chat Noir* appeared less than a year after the July 29, 1881, press laws made it possible to start a newspaper without having sizable capital reserves to post as security money. To gauge the effect of these laws upon the Montmartre cultural efflorescence of the 1880s and 1890s, one may compare the paucity of printed works before the *Chat Noir* with the hundred or more imitators it spawned over the next two decades. Of thirty-four earlier journals published in Montmartre over the preceding forty years, nearly all had appeared courtesy of wars and revolutions, which disrupted the governments' normally close control over the press. Records reveal one Montmartre publication dating from 1840, another from 1846, then suddenly thirteen in 1848 and thirteen more over the next four tumultuous years. After 1852 only one paper was published in Montmartre during the whole two-decade span of the Second Empire, then four more appeared in 1870–71, followed by another long hiatus until the *Chat Noir* opened in 1882. Papers with names such as *Plus de Bourreau* (No More Hangman) and *La Peine de Mort* (The Pain of Death, both 1848) and *Le Nain Rouge* and *Le Monde Nouveau* (The Red Dwarf and The New World, both 1849) were probably radical, but the majority bore innocuous names that did not reveal their orientation.[25] At least nine cabarets issued house publicity organs in the 1880s and 1890s, and being in league with a prosperous cabaret assured the papers of a securer future than most Montmartrois publications. When Aristide Bruant opened his cabaret in 1885, he followed Salis's example by publishing *Le Mirliton*, which featured a song by the proprietor accompanied by a Steinlen or Lautrec drawing. That same year witnessed Maxime Lisbonne's *Gazette du Bagne*, issued from his short-lived and controversial Taverne du Bagne. In all cases the illustrated, licentious, and publicity-conscious Montmartre cabaret press contrasted with the more somber Left Bank literary reviews.

Maxime Lisbonne vied with Salis and Bruant as most colorful *cabaretier* of Montmartre in these years, and what he lacked in taste and discretion he made up for in panache. Whereas Salis was antibourgeois in a bohemian manner, Lisbonne was frankly revolutionary, thereby attracting considerable attention among the police and their informers, one of whom wrote, "Lisbonne was a force for anarchy in Montmartre."[26] Lisbonne was born in 1839, of a Catholic mother and a Portuguese Jewish father. For his participation as a colonel in the Paris Commune, he was transported to New Caledonia, then pardoned in the general amnesty of 1880. The succession of cabarets he opened in Montmartre and Belleville in the next fifteen years were a means of reliving, dramatizing, and capitalizing on his years as a political renegade and prisoner. On November 19, 1885, Paul Lafargue recounted to Friedrich Engels the

The anarchist as bohemian—Maxime Lisbonne, ca. 1885. (From Mariel Oberthur, *Cafés and Cabarets of Montmartre,* trans. Sheila Azoulai [Salt Lake City: Gibbs M. Smith, 1984]. Courtesy of Peregrine Smith Books.)

The *Gazette du Bagne* of Lisbonne's cabaret, 1885. Lisbonne's cabaret published a newspaper of the same name, depicting a waiter dressed as a prisoner. This issue featured Lisbonne's fellow Communard Louise Michel. (From Mariel Oberthur, *Cafés and Cabarets of Montmartre,* trans. Sheila Azoulai [Salt Lake City: Gibbs M. Smith, 1984]. Courtesy of Peregrine Smith Books.)

Théophile-Alexandre Steinlen, "The Four Paws," published in *Le Mirliton*,
1893. Steinlen portrayed a bourgeois examining Toulouse-Lautrec's poster of
Bruant on this cover of the *Mirliton,* Bruant's cabaret journal.

opening of Lisbonne's Taverne du Bagne, 2 boulevard de Clichy, in lower Montmartre:

Lisbonne, professional ham (*cabotin*), has had the genial idea of opening a café where the doors are barred, where the tables are chained, where all the waiters are dressed as galley slaves, dragging chains . . . the success has been crazy; one lines up to go drink a bock in the prison of citizen Lisbonne, who makes you pay double on top of it. The society people go in their carriages, and are happy to hear themselves addressed with *tu* and to be ill-treated by the prison guards, who use the academic language of prison to speak to their clients.[27]

Just as with Bruant's contemporary Mirliton, Lisbonne's (short-lived) success was based on presenting a rude and *argotique* manner that appealed to bourgeois *nostalgie de la boue* (nostalgia for the mud), as slumming was then called. If Montmartre was not the center of a true working-class culture, it nonetheless mediated between the upper and lower classes, with the bohemians acting as go-betweens. Lisbonne's melodramatic style, by which he transformed the political events of his life into stage settings if not works of art, was a typically bohemian posture, parodic rather than either cynical or pedantic.

A bewildering succession of cabarets followed the Taverne du Bagne, all playing upon Lisbonne's antagonism to the Third Republic. After the 1887 Taverne de la Révolution Française came the Brasserie des Frites Révolutionnaires, where he performed the play of Clovis Hugues, bohemian socialist deputy and poet from Marseille, entitled *Le Sommeil de Danton*. With the failure of the 1889 Les Brioches Politiques, Lisbonne was casting about for another site and was being advised in June 1892 by editors of *Le Père Peinard* to install an anarchist cabaret on the site of the infamous Restaurant Véry, where Ravachol had recently been identified and captured and where a bomb of revenge had killed the proprietor Véry during the trial. The police agent noted that the owner was having difficulty renting the place.[28] The year 1893 saw the Casino des Concierges, and finally the Concert Lisbonne opened in October 1893, all in lower Montmartre. This last achieved some fame for the production of a little dramatic scene called "Le Coucher d'Yvette," in which on March 3, 1894, Miss Blanche Cavelli performed the first striptease, removing as many layers of undergarments as the censor would allow in the process of getting ready for bed. The act generated numerous imitators in succeeding months.[29] Lisbonne was continually testing the bounds of "decency" and provoking the censors, and perhaps making a small statement for sexual freedom.

Lisbonne's more overt political activity, which fell into the categories of the humorous and the serious, was recorded mainly by the police informers. His biographer notes only his role in the anti–Jules Ferry manifesto launched by "The Equal Ones of Montmartre" in the 1887 presidential campaign, and his own campaign as a "fantasy candidate" in the legislative elections of 1889.[30] After the Ravachol bombings rocked Paris, Lisbonne announced his "Insurance Company against the Explosion of Dynamite," which he placarded around Montmartre. After a treaty made with four anarchist groups, the Invisibles, Those Without Pity, the Avengers, and the Spiders of Despair, buildings would be sheltered from dynamite by means of a simple insurance policy contracted by the new Company of Public Safety. Widows and unmarried women proprietors could dispense with a policy by marrying an anarchist. *La Patrie* of March 21, 1892, copied this proclamation and published it with a note, "One laughs at everything on the Butte." The following month, Lisbonne organized a benefit at a Montmartre hall which featured his Dynamite Polka. At 1:00 A.M., Lisbonne took the conductor's baton; revolver shots punctuated the music, and the odor of burnt powder filled the room.[31] On a slightly different note, facing the campaign of Senator Bérenger against prostitution in 1895, Lisbonne instituted a campaign called the "Suppression of Prostitution by Marriage." As an alternative to the useless laws and prison terms suggested by Bérenger, Lisbonne offered to sponsor cabaret weddings between prostitutes and philanthropic bourgeois who created the demand for prostitutes in the first place.[32]

Lisbonne was willing to lend his cabaret for serious political meetings as well. In July 1889, a public anarchist meeting composed of 250 people came to hear Louise Michel, the "red virgin" of the Commune, proclaim that they must make more blood flow, as their ancestors had done a century before. The following month the Disabused Group of the Eighteenth Arrondissement attracted between 120 and 200 people. The police informer attributed the remarkable turnouts to the notoriety of Lisbonne's place, though the 1889 elections and the Boulangist fever that had stimulated passions in Montmartre as elsewhere may be cited as more general causes of high political participation.[33] That Lisbonne could host such meetings while running a farcical political campaign conjoining satire and subversive activity was perhaps only natural in the year in which *le brave général* fled to his mistress's side rather than bringing down the Third Republic. Politics too were prone to the fin de siècle love of stage settings and theatricality, in an era when personal acts acquired a highly visible and public character. In his consciousness of acting out a role on the social stage, Lisbonne was typical both of his times and of the anarchist movement which, before 1895, relied mainly upon extremely dramatic propagandistic acts. Lisbonne clearly felt no compunction about exploiting his notoriety as a bohemian or a revolutionary for the sake of his entrepreneurial ventures.[34]

As terrorism reached its peak in 1894, the police informers who kept a close watch on Lisbonne's activities revealed a great deal about his milieu but uncovered no conspiracies. They noted that with the opening of his new café-concert on the site of the former Divan Japonais, a friend of Lisbonne's was charged with breaking up the anarchist clientele when it became too demanding on the proprietor's aid and financial resources. Lisbonne was considering opening a Montmartre newspaper devoted to the anarchist literary movement if he could find some talented youths to aid him (*L'Endehors* closed early in 1893 and *les lois scélérates* had recently brought an end to Charles Chatel's *La Revue Anarchiste*). The money was to come from a rentier friend of one of the Concert Lisbonne's female stars.[35] The times being inauspicious for such an undertaking, the project remained stillborn, and Lisbonne devoted himself to his cabaret. A report of April 30, 1894, by the articulate informer called "Legrand" (informers took care to conceal their real names and identities), entitled "Le Concert Lisbonne, centre anarchiste," drew an informative picture of the Montmartre milieu:

The Concert Lisbonne has always been a socialist-anarchist center. And Lisbonne, while being prudent, preciously tries to conserve his Communard title. His political past is very much in his present fortune, and it is not rare to hear a spectator say: he has been in the Commune, he has been a colonel, he has been deported, etc. This same political past assures him a politico-literary clientele. The anarchists of letters drink many bocks at his place, and Lisbonne does not give credit. One sees

around him also the actors of the *Parti Ouvrier,* of the *Réveil Social,* of the *Réveil du Peuple.* . . . His secretary M. Blavet, a prepossessing and distinguished man, is fully in artistic and political accord with the director of "the sole Concert sheltered from the Bombs." He associates with the former writers of the *Revue Libertaire.* . . . He is entirely devoted to the literary anarchists, and he receives them privately in his secretarial office. . . . The Concert is frequented not only by the anarchists of letters, but by the young women, scarcely opposed to their ideas, who voluntarily speak of blowing things up if one gives them the means. . . . The anarchists of the Concert Lisbonne are journalists, printers, students. One counts some painters and sculptors. Lisbonne awaits the departure of the criminal element from his premises in order to increase his clientele. . . . The anarchists pass the letters of Emile Henry in the bars of the eighteenth arrondissement, at the Concert Lisbonne, in the Grande Imprimerie. Meanwhile, English clubs in Grafton and Wilfield streets are taking up a collection to publish Henry's golden words in several languages.[36]

Some of Lisbonne's performers were known anarchist activists, but with little evidence of any concrete conspiratorial activities the police could do little beyond occasionally closing his cabarets. Despite financial difficulties and temporary closings, a report of October 17, 1894, announced the reopening of the Concert Lisbonne under the motto cited by the informer, "Sole Concert Sheltered from the Bombs."[37] Lisbonne's anarchist clientele appreciated the bravado style that was inseparable from his politics.

It was not easy for the authorities to isolate anarchist political activity in the bohemian atmosphere of Montmartre. Such was the case with another cabaret which, next to the Chat Noir, was most revered by the chroniclers of Old Montmartre. The Cabaret des Assassins was born when a bohemian named Saltz had the macabre idea of placing images on the walls of his establishment illustrating famous crimes such as the Troppman murders. Outside hung an ensign painted by André Gill showing a rabbit dressed as a cook sautéing a comrade in a pot. This cabaret was first transformed into Ma Campagne and then became the Lapin à Gill when it passed into the hands of Frédéric Gérard. "Frédé" had had his first cabaret, Zut, closed by the police for sheltering the anarchists of *Le Libertaire,* Sebastien Faure's weekly located nearby on the rue Collin. His new place, which gradually became known as Le Lapin Agile, remained under the aegis of Frédé and his donkey Lolo until the 1920s and stood for the free spirit of Montmartre to the generation of Pablo Picasso and Max Jacob. As late as 1910, police informers were reporting that Le Lapin Agile was often frequented by anarchists, while its alternative name, Cabaret des Assassins, enhanced its subversive allure. And unlike Lisbonne, Frédé extended almost unlimited credit.[38]

The anarchists had no monopoly in the political economy of the Montmartre cabaret and café scene. In his novel *The Mystery of Crowds,* Paul Adam detailed the interrelationship between leftist political fragmentation and the cabarets of Montmartre. Each sect, such as the Independent Socialists, the Blanquists, and the anarchists, had its own little cabarets. This decentralization was encouraged by the proprietors so as to keep the groups meeting at their café and consuming their wine. At the big meeting where the factions in the novel discussed uniting, they were incited to do so by the owner of the largest café, who alone could accommodate this mass; the Blanquist delegate was secretly sponsored by the small owners to discourage the project. The central figure in the novel, Dessling, was so disgusted by the internecine antagonisms and the commercialization of politics that he left the workers' parties to take up the general's cause, as did Adam himself in Boulangism. The year 1889, the culminating year of Boulangism, was the year the Moulin Rouge opened. In Adam's 1895 novel, the music hall became the symbolic center of a lurid and seditious quarter. Adam despaired that "nothing would change. The people would never attempt the liberating revolution, content to offer up its daughters to the joy of others."[39] The revolving mill blades suggested the endless cycle of poverty and prostitution, rather like the old meaning of the word *revolution,* and justified to Dessling/Adam the search for a Caesar to break the cycle of despair.[40] The noisy stomp of the *quadrille naturaliste* inevitably drowned out some of the rumblings of discontent.

The police also acted to stifle these rumblings. The frequent reversals in fortune of Lisbonne's cabarets may not have been due solely to the fickleness of the public or to the poor business acumen of the proprietor. The Cabinet des Concierges, *direction* Lisbonne, was closed by the police for an unspecified period of time on May 3, 1895. The offense was described only as lacking authorization of the Ministry of Public Instruction and Fine Arts under the decree of December 30, 1852. Such authorization required the daily submission of the cabaret's program of songs to the Office of Theater Inspection and daily approval by the local police commissioner, a practice that made any spontaneity during the performances impossible. Several impresarios protested collectively, but to no avail.[41] Lisbonne's was only one of many cafés-concerts and cabarets cited for punitive measures in the correspondence between the Paris prefecture of police and the minister of public instruction. The origin of the censorship law is revealing, dating as it did from the opening years of the Second Empire and carried on unchanged by the Third Republic. The government was fully inclined to assume the role of arbiter of public morality, and if need be to control the political content of songs and plays as well as of literature, none of which benefited from the recently liberalized press laws. The anarchist and bohemian artists, performers, and writers were vehemently opposed to such government interference in the performing arts, and such repression served to crystallize discontent with the power structure among elements that might otherwise have had little personal cause for complaint (one thinks of Paul Adam's 1885 trial for his first book, a Naturalistic novel about prostitution entitled *Chair Molle,* which was censored for indecency). The very rigorous censorship laws were a major factor in radicalizing artists and were reviled in such anarchist literary publications as *La Revue Rouge.* When the crusading Senator Bérenger raised a campaign for public decency in 1895, no one protested louder against *le père la pudeur* (father decency) than such amoralists as Laurent Tailhade.[42]

It was thus quite common to find one's favorite cabaret closed for a period of several days to several weeks depending on the seriousness of the offense. Merely deviating from the program was sufficient, although political motives were sometimes cited for closing cabarets. Between 1870 and 1900, the census reported explicit political innuendos only for the years 1892 to 1894, the era of greatest anarchist ferment. A typical citation read, "two songs not marked in the program . . . which present an injurious and outrageous character for the agents of authority." That was sufficient to close the Palais des Arts Libéraux on the champs de Mars for two weeks in 1892.[43] At 73 boulevard Montparnasse, a cabaret was closed for two months in 1893 after a policeman was struck and injured there, and late in 1894 the Concert des Décadents was closed indefinitely for seditious libel against the authorities. In the spring of 1892, after Ravachol had terrorized all of Paris, and again two years later in May 1894, at the height of the bombing wave, the prefect of police wrote to the minister to complain of attacks not on individual representatives of authority, but on the institution itself:

The authors of these songs, far from limiting themselves to the mild criticism of some isolated acts of my administration or to some allusions which have the excuse of pertinence, apply themselves on the contrary to give to their productions a mistrustful and odious character for the agents and the institution that they have taken for their theme.

Interpreted in certain milieus such as the concerts of the outer boulevards and cafés of the barriers where the clientele is manifestly hostile to the police, these songs have the effect of exciting and stirring up the listeners against the representatives of my service, who do not miss the occasion to cover with ridicule a guardian of the peace whose duty obliges him to remain at his post.[44]

The prefect cited two songs, "La Ronde des sergots" and "Ou qu'est la police," performed at the Concert du XXe Siècle, 138 boulevard Ménilmontant, which compelled the police to shut down the house, "to repress a scandal which ridiculed the aims of the censors." Two years later he called the minister's attention to a song entitled "Une leçon d'argot," and quoted the line, "in argot, an agent is called a *roussin, sergot, flic*." At the same time in another dispatch he noted a song called "La Ballade des agents," sung by two performers dressed as policemen, and claimed that at both establishments the officer in attendance was made to feel uncomfortable. He requested that henceforth both songs be proscribed by the Office of Theater Inspection. While the Panama scandal rocked the Chamber, while governments fell at an average of one a year and the press of all political hues engaged in the most vituperative assaults on persons and parties, to lampoon verbally the custodians of public order in a cabaret was seen as an affront to the Republic too serious to ignore. The eight cabarets closed between 1892 and 1894 for disrespect to the authorities probably represented an increasingly politically sensitive police force as well as a more politicized repertoire.

Censorship was not practiced uniformly throughout the domain of the Paris prefecture of police. An early example of the differential discretion shown by the authorities took place on May 4, 1886, when the minister of public instruction and fine arts noted that the Café-Concert des Ambassadeurs, on the Champs-Elysées, had announced a *quadrille* executed by the Montmartre dancers La Goulue and Grille d'Egout. Though it had already been performed at the Alcazar d'Hiver and the Folies Bergères, Ambassadeurs was more open to strollers, especially to women and children: "the show is in some sort on the public way. There is no need to conceal that the ladies figuring in the *quadrille* having nothing in common with professional dancers, nor even with acrobats; these are truly scantily clad girls (*filles court-vetues*) coming to exhibit all that which the extreme limit of decency permits them to show. . . . despite the tolerance with which these dances have been the object at the Alcazar d'Hiver, it would not hinder us from examining what decision we should have to take."[45] What was condoned on Montmartre's slopes was deemed inadmissable in the heartland of fashionable, bourgeois Paris.

The double standard of morality with which the authorities regarded Montmartre was not an occasional policy but rather the regular state of affairs. In a very revealing letter received by the minister from the prefect of police in 1897, the etiology of this standard was reviewed. Remarking that the Chat Noir of Salis and Bruant's Mirliton failed to have their works authorized, the police noted: "That situation is not new. The Administration of Fine Arts is not ignorant of its origins [i.e., the freedom from censorship]: it is due especially to the exceptional tolerance to which the first establishment of this genre to open in Paris, the Cabaret du Chat Noir, created by Rodolphe Salis, has received." When the prefecture of police wanted to pursue Salis, "it found itself in the presence of such powerful influences that it had to renounce submitting the Chat Noir Cabaret to the common regimen, sustained energetically by numerous notables in politics, letters, and the arts."[46] No less a personage than the prime minister had telephoned personally on December 20, 1888. The officer commented that though its political allusions would not have passed the censor, it had refrained from real obscenity; shadow plays were less affronting than the can-can. Another police report noted that when Bruant succeeded Salis at 84 rue Roche-chouart, he neither requested authorization to hold a café-concert nor submitted his programs to the fine arts administration. It was difficult to condemn Bruant when Salis was tolerated. Subsequently, other Montmartre and Latin Quarter cabarets did have to have authorization; nevertheless, invoking the Chat Noir precedent, many of them failed to submit their daily programs. When the police heard of such songs being performed, they did not hesitate to close the house. Thus most Latin Quarter cabarets were closed in May 1895, at the height of Senator Bérenger's crusade, and were reopened only upon careful control of the program. The police commented on this crackdown: "It is thought, in effect, that if one could, without too much inconvenience, use a certain tolerance in regard to cabarets situated in a special artist's milieu as that of Montmartre, there were some real dangers to using the same tolerance in regards to those that are frequented by the youth of the schools."[47] The sons of the bourgeoisie required the protection of the vice squad.

Summarizing the situation in the mid-1890s, the police clearly delineated two categories of "cabarets called 'artistic' ": those of Montmartre that did not conform to the rulings but which were said to be no more immoral than the conforming cabarets' repertoires, and those in which the service of guardians of the peace was regularly assured and which generally conformed to the programs. In 1897, the police recommended to the minister that this unequal situation be ended and all made to comply, despite "the numerous protestations which that measure will not fail to raise."[48] The golden age of Montmartre, beginning in the 1880s and lasting until the mid-1890s when Bruant left and Salis died (on March 19, 1897), was encouraged in its bid for artistic freedom and moral license by the complicity of the authorities. Montmartre functioned as a red-light district of the arts, where vice would be tolerated but geographically restricted, rather like the Yoshiwara district of Edo (now Tokyo). Like the Tokugawa Shogunate, the Third Republic was less willing to brook ridicule of the authorities than moral laxity, and cabarets such as Lisbonne's were closed for insulting the police while the innovation of the striptease went unchallenged.

In 1897 the government tried to end Montmartre's privileged status. On April 1, the police sent the director of the Office of Theater Inspection a list of cabarets not submitting their programs for authorization, and each of the proprietors of these cabarets was invited to come to the director's office on April 3. Though the bulk of these cabarets were located in Montmartre, others, such as the Soleil d'Or on place Saint-

Michel or the Café Procope nearby, were Latin Quarter establishments. One surmises that the *cabaretiers* were informed of renewed intent to enforce the old laws, for as of May 1, 1897, a crackdown on Montmartre cabarets went into effect, and all repertoires required state authorization.[49]

Music and song were not Montmartre's only forms of entertainment, but among the lower classes they far outstripped literature, art, or drama as a popular pastime. Along with its (at times) uncensored cabarets, Montmartre boasted two avant-garde theater companies which also managed to circumvent censor and police, though at a high price. Antoine's Théâtre-Libre had been founded in 1887 as the theatrical arm of the Naturalists; Aurélian-Marie Lugné-Pöe's Théâtre de l'Oeuvre celebrated its first season in 1893–94 and was allied with the Symbolists. Their seeming literary rivalry was expressed in the way they performed the works of Henrik Ibsen, the Libre playing him as straight social drama and the Oeuvre as a more metaphysical playwright. What really linked the two theaters was their economic base: both were subscription theaters that played to a select regular audience. At the Oeuvre, one subscribed to a season of eight plays, performed two times each, once a month from November through June. The prices at both theaters were similar and steep: 100 francs for a series seat in the orchestra, 60 francs in the galleries, 40 francs for the least choice seats. Lugné-Pöe was rigorously forbidden to sell seats on an individual basis, and Prefect of Police Louis Lépine still sought to close the theater.[50] By privatizing themselves these theaters were granted relative freedom of censorship, but at the cost of being excluded from the free marketplace of cultural consumption.

"Tenderness and violence, his soul oscillated between these two poles and the whole epoch shared, hesitated in the same manner."[51] Lugné-Pöe's biographer thus felicitously characterizes the theater as its director by the characteristic ambiguity of the epoch. Lugné-Pöe was assisted in his first year by two literary anarchists, Camille Mauclair and Louis Malquin, who served as codirectors. The first season got off to a rousing start with the performance in November 1893 of Ibsen's *Enemy of the People*: the following month G. J. Hauptmann's *Solitary Souls,* whose performance coincided with Vaillant's bombing, was prohibited because it had been translated by Alexandre Cohen, a Dutch anarchist who was deported by the French government. An important feature of each performance was a short lecture introducing the production. For *Enemy of the People*, Laurent Tailhade set the tone for what followed in proclaiming that the play demonstrated "that genius, beauty, virtue are antisocial facts of the first order," for "the superior man is always alone."[52] An enthusiastic seventeen-year-old named Francis Jourdain was in the audience in 1893, and described the scene with a resonating metaphor: "What dynamism and what dynamite! What bombs did we not intend to explode, charged with new explosives, new art . . . bombs that would be fireworks, bouquets of light." He spoke of the imprecise relationship in their minds between art and politics, the "obscure kinship between the Princess Maleine [title of a well-received 1890 play by the Symbolist playwright Maurice Maeterlinck] and Ravachol." He described Tailhade creating an atmosphere of battle: "The violence of that banter, courageous although a little artificial, enchanted us. . . . He spoke little of Ibsen, more of the beneficent anarchy . . . he ridiculed all the idols of the bourgeoisie." Between scenes of *Enemy of the People*, Jourdain and his friends "had to defend the cause of Ibsen, of Liberty, of Lugné-Pöe, of the Individual, of Spirit, of Revolt, in the rooms and in the corridors."[53] While Henry Bauer defended the production in *L'Echo de Paris*, others complained about it being "trop fjord pour moi" or "Oeuvre absolument ibscène." At his trial two months later, Vaillant is supposed to have named Ibsen as one of those inspiring his anarchist terrorist deed.[54]

In the winter of 1893–94 both Maurice Barrès and Paul Adam had plays censored, and their only outlet was to have them performed by the subscription theaters of Montmartre. Barrès's *Une Journée parlémentaire*, an exposé of parliamentary corruption written just after his own electoral defeat, was put on in January 1894 at the Théâtre-Libre. Antoine noted in his diary: "We repeat Barrès. His comedy is a violent pamphlet against the present regime, which makes me ill at ease, for it is linked visibly to political schemings of which I strongly disapprove."[55] Whether these antiparliamentary machinations were of the left or the right Antoine did not say, but he called the event unparalleled in terms of the theater's public impact.

A much greater public impact was registered at the Théâtre de l'Oeuvre in December 1896, upon the presentation of Alfred Jarry's *Ubu*

Roi. The performance has been amply discussed elsewhere, yet the political echoes of this protosurrealist production are worth noting.[56] In May 1894, an informer wrote: "There is a question of launching an anarchist publication in the genre of *La Revue Libertaire*. . . . It is at the Théâtre de l'Oeuvre that there has been a question of that publication, for which one foresees a considerable number of subscribers. They will have as principle editors: Louis Lormel, Alfred Jarry, Leon Paul Fargue, and other literary anarchists of the Latin Quarter."[57] Jarry, who at twenty-one was already in the process of remaking himself into a reflection of his art, was unlikely to have taken politics very seriously. After the performance of *Ubu Roi,* he described the theater audience as "an inert and uncomprehending and passive mass that it is necessary to strike from time to time," though the Oeuvre audience of December 9, 1896, witnessed the outrage of *Ubu Roi* anything but passively.[58] The play resembled an anarchist *attentat* in its violent assault upon the sensibilities of the audience, upsetting their expectations of theatrical decorum and thereby dramatically involving them in the performance. The characters were meant to arouse antagonism rather than believability. The grossly obscene King Ubu, who wreaked havoc in Poland before coming to France to repeat the process in the play, represented as corrupt an image of authority as could be imagined by any anarchist. Though the police informer may have been the first, he was not alone in calling Jarry an anarchist. *Ubu Roi* aroused tremendous controversy in the press. Catulle Mendès saw Père Ubu as a strange mixture "of Monsieur Thiers and the Catholic Torquemada and the Jew Deutz, of a *Sûreté* policeman and the anarchist Vaillant. . . . He will become a popular legend of base instincts, rapacious and violent."[59] The parody of authority had something of the unbridled destructiveness of the anarchist in it. Henri Fouquier of *Le Figaro* described Jarry and company as "anarchists of art," who "are exercising a veritable terror over the public. And it is the imposition of this special, wholly literary terror that public opinion is permitting."[60] *Ubu Roi* breathed anarchy at all levels, from Ubu's discrediting of all authority to Jarry's courting of the "sacred disorder of my spirit," expressed in art that made chaos of social conventions and rationality. In a more philosophical sense, Jarry's entire notion of art and life was anarchistic. His "science" of *'pataphysics* described a world made up of exceptions, and preached the revenge of individual spontaneity against positivistic science. Even latter-day commentators can not help but note the coincidental birthdays, on September 8, 1873, of Jarry and Santo Jeronimo Caserio, the assassin of President Carnot, as if the fault was in their stars.[61]

At ticket prices that were more than a day's wages for most workers, the avant-garde theaters could be assured of a bourgeois and literary clientele. Though the lower classes spent most of their leisure time in cafés, there were some attempts at popular theater. In December 1890, the director of the Théâtre de la Villette issued 300 tickets at reduced prices for a showing of Louise Michel's *La Grève*. Between the acts the anarchists made speeches and sang revolutionary songs. Martinet, a leading Montmartre anarchist, recited a powerful poem entitled "Germinal," which accused the bourgeoisie of making working-class women into prostitutes and looked forward to "Germinal" among images of springtime connoting resurrection and rebirth. After the play, the crowd withdrew singing the "Carmagnole."[62] In 1893, the same year that the Théâtre de l'Oeuvre began productions, the Club de l'Art Social founded the Théâtre de l'Art Social to spread their message to the public, but only lasted for one performance of revolutionary theater.[63] Theater played a significant role in literary anarchist culture, but not in the popular milieu. Ticket prices and production costs may have been one reason, police suppression another, but a more basic reason may have been the people's preference for the unstructured participatory pleasures of the café.

With the important exception of *La Révolte*, every major anarchist journal was edited and published in Montmartre. This included *Le Père Peinard*, *La Revue Libertaire*, *L'Etat Naturel*, *Le Libertaire*, *L'Homme Libre*, *L'Anarchie*, *La Revue Anarchiste*, and *L'Endehors*. Political journalism of a leftist or antiparliamentarian nature peaked in Montmartre between 1889 with the appearance of Pouget's *Le Père Peinard* and 1895. Emile Pouget was a longtime Montmartrois, having come to the Butte after his release from Melun Prison in 1887, and remaining there at least until 1906, when he married and moved to the country.[64] From 1892 to 1895 a spate of anarchist or libertarian revolutionary journals marked the crescendo of the years of anarchist terrorism, though the largest number appeared in 1895 after President Felix Faure declared an amnesty for anarchists convicted under *les lois scélérates* and the police repression eased. Of seventy-four new journals that appeared in the decade from 1885 to 1895, approximately one-third were explicitly radical, and half of those were anarchist.[65] Many more artistic journals, such as Anatole Baju's *Le Décadent* and Henri Mayence's *Montmartre,* sympathized with anarchism, much as did the Symbolist journals published elsewhere in Paris.

The 1885–95 decade that saw the birth of an average of seven newspapers per year for this one Parisian neighborhood was Montmartre's golden age as a cultural focal point. The drop to two or three new journals per year over the next decade reflected the relative loss of cultural prestige suffered by Montmartre, a decline occurring in the mid-1890s that paralleled the end of the heroic era of anarchism and its most profound influence on the artistic milieu that was centered there.[66] The percentage of politically leftist journals dropped from a third of all new Montmartre publications in the 1885–95 period to less than one-sixth in the next decade, as anarchism left the cafés of bohemia for the workplace (see Table 1).

Personal contact by means of public and private discourse was at least as important within the anarchist milieu as the more impersonal communication carried on in the anarchist press. Weekly meetings were held in anarchist strongholds throughout Paris. The anarchist group La Sentinelle de Montmartre, which met Wednesday nights at 19 rue Clignancourt, included Sebastien Faure, Paul Paillette, and the wine merchant Louis Duprat, whose bistro served as a rendezvous point.[67] By 1889, the anarchists of Montmartre were eager to enlist the support of the many artists living on the Butte. In November of that year, the Sentinelle group placarded the walls of Montmartre with posters announcing a meeting specifically addressing the relations between art and politics, to be held at the Brasserie Franco-Russe on boulevard Rochechouart. In bold black print on orange paper one read:

Order of the day
1. On the Principal of Art:
a) Aesthetics; Beauty and Form, b) The Ideal, c) Evolution of Art.
2. Liberty: a) The word Liberty, b) The Future Society.
3. Social Questions.
Writers and Artists are especially invited.[68]

Table 1: Number of New Periodicals Each Year in Montmartre, 1882–1905

	Socialist	Boulangist	Anarchist	Other Politics	Local History or News	Cabaret Organ	Artistic, Literary, Theatrical	Other	Total
1882					1				1
1883			1						1
1884							1		1
1885					2				2
1886		1	1				4		6
1887			1	1	2		1		5
1888			2	1	1	1	3		8
1889		2		1		1	2	3	9
1890	4			2	1		2		9
1891	2			1			2	2	7
1892		1		1	1	1	1	2	7
1893			1	1		1	1	1	5
1894			1		2	1	3	1	8
1895	2		3				1	2	8
1896			1	1			1		3
1897				1		1	1		3
1898				1			2		3
1899			1				1		2
1900								3	3
1901				2				1	3
1902									0
1903									0
1904	1					1		2	4
1905			1				1		2

Based on Maurice Artus, "Essai de bibliographie de la presse montmartroise: Journaux et canards," *Le Vieux Montmarte* 49–50 (July 1905).

The inevitable police informer unfortunately took inadequate notes of the 150-person meeting, at least from an aesthetic standpoint. One learns that the *compagnon* Malescot spoke of the role of art in different epochs, and upbraided young artists for painting outdated subjects. An artist replied that they too were hampered by monetary considerations, but added "we as you are insurgents (*révoltés*)." Other artists made some remarks, then Malescot counseled them to join the newly formed Club de l'Art Social.[69]

The same group sought to affiliate vagabonds as well as artists to the cause. Two days after the successful meeting with the artists, "Jean" noted that a group called the Trimardeurs was none other than the Sentinelle group. They had printed a brochure in Geneva entitled "Aux Trimardeurs" which stated that machine production had created increasing unemployment, so that in addition to the traditional traveling journeymen seeking to perfect their craft were vagabonds who traveled by boxcar while passenger trains rolled by half-empty.[70] Wandering workingmen were in fact a notable means of spreading the anarchist message to the hinterlands. The Montmartre anarchists identified with the hobo who left behind his bohemian existence to *trimarder* (wander) on the great roads at least as much as with the journeyman who found his place within the system of industrial production.

The interests of Montmartre anarchists characteristically diverged from the working-class issues of the faubourg Saint-Antoine. More than one meeting in the first months of 1890 dealt with the roles and relations of the sexes. At a public lecture on February 20, 1890, the Sentinelle member Lucien Weil spoke on free love (*l'amour libre*), and was heard by an audience of sixty of which twenty were women. The next month ten women formed a group to discuss "the free woman." Men were excluded from their group after initial meetings where such orators as Lucien Weil and Sebastien Faure dominated discussions. At another meeting organized by the Sentinelle group in February 1890, the topic was social education. In 1893 a group that felt the need to distinguish itself as "The Workers of the Eighteenth Arrondissement" met at the Salle Baudinot, 96 rue des Martyrs, a popular anarchist meeting place. Some of these workers were typesetters and printers, who following Proudhon's example were active in the movement. Among other local craftsmen attracted to anarchism, the police listed tailors, cobblers, and carpenters.[71]

Most of the meetings took place either in halls or in cafés and wine merchants' bistros, public places that invited police participation. The security problem was recorded by a (probably uncomfortable) informer at a "social studies group" meeting in June 1893. An outspoken Captain Bougogne wanted to attack the clergy by blowing up Sacré-Coeur, an obvious target among the anticlerical Montmartrois (one local leftist paper entitled *The Atheist* published the names of people who consented to civil baptism for their children). The captain asked why they only discussed anarchy rather than plotting propaganda by the deed and said that it was not worth meeting if you could not plot together. "Several *compagnons* . . . remarked to him that among the anarchists, individual actions alone were good and that if each came to recount his agitations to the group, he would be arrested the next day."[72] This was obviously sound advice, though possibly tailored for police ears. Most of the meetings took place at weekly intervals at the same place, making subterfuge impossible. There were very likely secret meetings that evaded police espionage, and which therefore went undocumented in the police archives.

The police records reveal the public Montmartre locales utilized by the anarchists between 1889 and 1897, the density of activity, and the kinds of places frequented. In addition to halls and cafés, these included the local Maison du Peuple, the Bibliothèque Sociale, and the offices of anarchist newspapers. Though one can identify the addresses of some of the leading anarchists, it is not possible to do so for the rank and file, nor can one accurately estimate their numbers except from police estimates of attendance at meetings. These would normally consist of from one to three dozen participants on a weekly basis, but could attract many more for an advertised gathering, such as the one for artists at the Brasserie Franco-Russe, or an abstentionist meeting in November 1890 at which 300 persons proclaimed their disdain for the suffrage.[73] Police records for May 1896 cited meetings two days apart that reportedly drew 200 and 300 people. Meetings with attendance over 100 were fairly common, so it is safe to estimate the base level population of Montmartre anarchist activists and sympathizers as numbering in the hundreds. The map on pp. 84–85 shows Montmartre meeting places over an eight-year period (1889–97). All were not in use simultaneously, but the period is sufficiently limited in time to assume that a relatively stable population attended the various sorts of gatherings.

The most detailed information about Montmartre anarchism concerns activity in 1894 when surveillance was at its height. Whereas attention in 1889 was focused mainly on meetings where discussion alternated with singing, with an occasional family gathering (*soirée familiale*) visited, in 1894 the informers circulated more among the cabarets and bars and even on the sidewalks. Anarchists could no longer meet freely, and their activities were more dispersed within Montmartre nightlife. They still congregated at the anarchist wine merchant Duprat's on New Year's Eve, just before the wave of arrests, where the informer reported a continual coming and going of anarchists, numbering twenty-five or thirty. Afraid to engage in discussion, they sang many revolutionary songs, while a young man sold brochures containing poems on the life and ideas of Vaillant. Duprat had painted a slogan on his wall, "Your happiness has its nest in the common happiness." A week later forty people attended a large family gathering, among whom was Paul Paillette, who was also giving anarchist lunches at 2 rue de la Barre. To assay anarchist opinion on contemporary political events, the informers made the rounds of the familiar cafés. They reported that "the general opinion of anarchists frequenting the bars of rues Lépic and des Abbesses, as those neighboring the cabaret of Lisbonne, is that Emile Henry will be avenged." One day later, "The fall of Minister Casimir-Périer is the object of the attention of the militants of anarchy. They spoke of it yesterday evening at the Café de la Cigale, at the Ermitage, at the Cabaret des Quat'z'Arts where some anarchist singers were gathered who waited to be entertained by their friend Yon Lug, Lyonnais house singer. . . . Outside of the literary milieus . . . the anarchists of the rue Ramey and neighboring streets also believe that anarchy will renew its ascent, its committees and its papers."[74] Later that year, Yon Lug was overheard at the Cabaret des Quat'z'Arts speaking with an anarchist sculptor who had received a violent letter from a soldier stationed at Tonkin in Indochina, who described the vexations to which he submitted and regretted that he had not deserted. The letter finished with "Vive l'Anarchie." Yon Lug thought it wise to use the letter to light his pipe, and thus remove the compromising documents from prying eyes. The same informer spied on the illustrator Wilbem, who claimed to know the Montmartre wine merchants watched by the police. By releasing this information, Wilbem caused a loss of clientele among several establishments on the rues Ramey and du Poteau.[75]

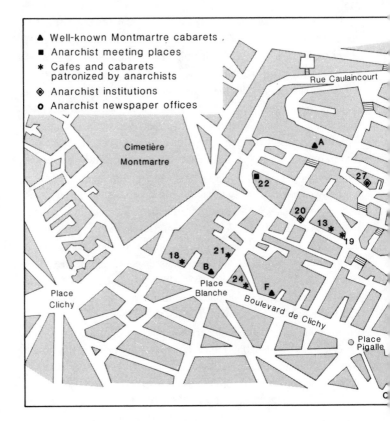

Key		Address	Date of One Informer's Report
	Anarchist Groups		
1	Meeting with Louise Michel, Faure, Pouget, 80 people	Salle du Rocher Suisse 27 rue de la Barre	November 3, 1889
2	La Sentinelle de Montmartre	Salle de la Porte 19 rue de Clignancourt	August 29, 1889
3	Groupe Anarchiste de la Goutte d'Or	18 rue de Chartres	April 20, 1888
4	Ligue Révolutionnaire Abstentioniste	Café Guillaume-Tell 17 rue de Clignancourt	January 11, 1889

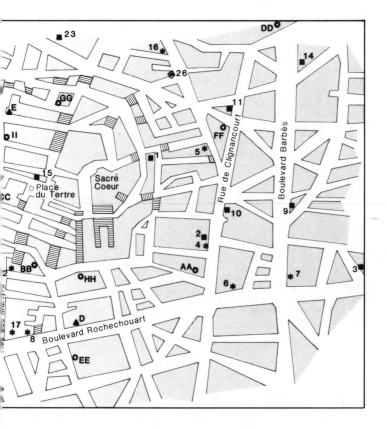

5	—	Salle Barbier 11 rue Ramey	February 14, 1889
6	Les Insurgés	Salle de la Cigogne 26 blvd. Rochechouart	April 7, 1889
7	Soirée familiale	Brasserie Charles 2 blvd. Barbès	October 28, 1889
8	La Sentinelle de Mont- martre	Brasserie Franco-Russe 108 blvd. Rochechouart	November 3, 1889
9	—	41 blvd. Barbès	July 17, 1889
10	La Femme Libre	36 rue de Clignancourt	March 12, 1890
11	Les Anarchistes Absten- tionistes du XVIIIe	63 rue de Clignancourt	November 12, 1890
*	Cercle Libre d'Études Sociales du 18e	13 rue Stephenson	April 27, 1890

continued

Key		Address	Date of One Informer's Report
12	Les Travailleurs Anarchistes du 18e	Salle Baudinot 96 rue des Martyrs	August 5, 1893
13	Les Gars de la Butte	Chez Philippeau 38 rue des Abbesses	November 21, 1893
14	La Sentinelle de Montmartre	88 blvd. Barbès	November 3, 1893
15	—	Salle Catherine 6 place du Tertre	November 3, 1893
16	—	Chez Borgeat 51 rue Ramey	February 21, 1893
17	Collection for Mayence taken at:	Maison Troupel 118 blvd. Rochechouart	July 27, 1894
*	Collection for Mayence taken at:	Treille de Montmartre rue des Martyrs (no street number given)	July 27, 1894
18	Collection for Mayence taken at:	A la Tour Eiffel 104 ave. de Clichy	July 27, 1894
19	—	Les Grands Caves 28 rue des Abbesses	February 11, 1894
5	—	Chez Duprat 11 rue Ramey	February 12, 1894
20	Groupe de l'Art Social	52 rue des Abbesses	May 23, 1896
21	Les Indépendents du 18e	Café des Artistes 11 rue Lépic	April 22, 1896
22	Les Libertaires du 18e	62 rue Lépic	May 10, 1896
23	—	Communal school	May 8, 1896
24	Les Naturiens	Café Warin 80 blvd. de Clichy	November 1, 1896
25	Maxime Lisbonne's	Le Concert Lisbonne 75 rue des Martyrs	1894

	Anarchist Institutions		
26	Maison du Peuple	47 rue Ramey	March 5, 1897
27	Bibliothèque Sociale	2 rue d'Orchampt	May 22, 1897
20	Bibliothèque des Chercheurs	52 rue des Abbesses	February 26, 1897

Key		Address	Years of Publication
	Anarchist Newspapers		
AA	*Le Père Peinard*	4 bis rue d'Orsel	1889–94, 1896–99
BB	*La Sociale*	23 rue des Trois Frères	1895–96
CC	*La Revue Anarchiste*	32 rue Gabrielle	1893
DD	*Le Libertaire*	5 rue Eugène Sue	1895–1914
EE	*L'Endehors*	Rue Bochard de Saron	1891–93
FF	*Le Citoyen de Montmartre*	21 rue Coustine	1892
GG	*L'Etat Naturel*	4 rue Paul Feval	1896–98
HH	*La Vache Enragée*	5 rue Tardieu	1896–97
II	Papers of Mayence and Le Mée	16 rue Cortot	1889–93
	Montmartre Landmarks of the 1890s		
A	Moulin de la Galette	79 rue Lépic	
B	Moulin Rouge	90 blvd. de Clichy	
C	Le Chat Noir	12 rue Victor-Massé	
D	Le Mirliton	84 rue Rochechouart	
E	Le Lapin Agile	2 rue des Saules	
F	Le Cabaret des Quat'z'Arts	62 blvd. de Clichy	

*Not on map.

Fear of repression caused the anarchists to melt into the cabaret milieu; police suspicion now included the artist denizens and performers of these cabarets in the months preceding the government's attempt to link activists and intellectuals in the Procès de Trente. The assassination of Carnot and the upcoming trial increased both paranoia and prudence among the anarchists. In July 1894, an informer wrote: "The arrest of [Maximilien] Luce has thrown a fright in the spirits of illustrators, sculptors, and painters of Montmartre: the most moderate anarchists speak of fleeing—Bernard, 42 rue St.-Vincent, who has often received militants at his home, says he is going to Belgium. Passion is great in the bars of the rue Ramey and rue Clignancourt, at the Café de la Cigale, where the friends of Lisbonne (who has just closed his café 'for repairs') come."[76] At several bars, collections were being taken to aid those comrades wishing to flee to Brussels or London. Anarchists were advised to meet in cells of five and never twice in succession at the same wine merchant's. Others favored the ruse of penetrating the more legitimate socialist committees and "certain literary circles. It was an idea put forth by Gallau and Mayence which is taking shape. Thus, a society called 'La Comète Artistique,' well known in Montmartre, is increasing. . . . Mm. Antoine and Lamontage, founders of that society, have warmly welcomed the literary anarchists."[77]

Though singing formed a part of most anarchist meetings, the participation of the popular cabaret singers was most noticeable at the *fête* or *soirées familiales*. A group called L'Art Libre, founded at the Maison du Peuple, counted a dozen adherents among local singers, including Paul Paillette, Ariana, Buffalo, and Jehan Rictus. The newspaper *Le Libertaire* announced one such evening on its first anniversary of publication in 1896, held at a Montmartre restaurant. The singers included Paul Paillette, the popular Mévesto Senior of the Tréteau du Tabarin, and several singers from the Cabaret du Quat'z'Arts, including Xavier Privas, Gaston Secot, Yon Lug, and Jehan Rictus. Le Père Lapurge was the only performer graced with the title "le chansonnier anarchiste"; Buffalo was called simply a "chanteur populaire." A year later, *Le Libertaire* announced a similar evening to raise funds for the Bibliothèque Sociale on the rue d'Orchampe, with the same organized group of singers.[78] As the anarchist press was served by Montmartre artists and writers, so anarchist festivities drew upon the local resources of cabarets and singers.

These gatherings were social rather than ceremonial functions, "evenings" rather than "festivals." One would expect that anarchists would be receptive to the practice of the *fête* or festival as well. Recent work on the role of festivals in French culture has demonstrated how such celebrations allowed the people to break out of their daily, subservient existence and give their fantasies free rein.[79] Festivals such as the medieval feast of fools reversed notions of reason and order in an unfolding of "exultant subversion," a mode of behavior entirely in accord with the practice of fin de siècle anarchism.[80] As Montmartre offered its inhabitants an alternative social space, festivals provided an other time ritually demarcated from the present.

Montmartre bohemians celebrated their own version of a feast of fools in the Fête de la Vache Enragée, held in 1896 and 1897 as a parody of the official Fête du Boeuf Gras. This "maddened cow" that supplanted the "fat beef" symbolized the bohemian alternative to the bourgeois moral and social order, "maddened cow" being an argot designation for poverty. The Christian motifs of the official festival carried over into the Montmartre celebration, although the Christ paraded through Montmartre's streets was the savior of the humble, the "prolo Jesus." The mixture of a spirit of revolt with a pious air of resignation in the face of poverty distanced this bohemian "Vachalcade" of floats and poetry from anarchism, even though such anarchists as Camille Mauclair contributed to the *Journal de la Vache Enragée*. The tawdry floats wending their way around the Butte fulfilled their purpose of asserting social solidarity within a symbolically demarcated *espace populaire*.[81]

Anarchists were ambivalent toward organized celebrations, feeling that true festivals must issue spontaneously from the people rather than being decreed arbitrarily from above. They were certainly opposed to the bourgeois Fête du 14 juillet. Bastille Day had been established by the Third Republic as a national festival in 1880, and initially had been well received as marking the regime's definitive establishment and the pardoning of the Communards. As the Republic came under attack in the late 1880s, Bastille Day became increasingly routinized, the festival of the triumphant middle classes.[82] An 1892 anarchist leaflet propagandized against the celebration, saying that the taking of the Bastille had not yet delivered them from oppression, and that besides, "We don't want to amuse ourselves any longer with political revolutions, which are only a changing of masters: from Orléans to Bonaparte, Boulanger and Carnot, what does it matter." At an anarchist meeting in Montmartre, some members wished to blow up some monument in protest of July 14, while Brunet argued that each year it had been celebrated with less enthusiasm, and that it would be better to let it die by itself. Zo d'Axa was on the side of the *impulsifs*. An incendiary 1892 article in *L'Endehors* noted that "an act would have great significance and resounding consequences"; with so many soldiers and bourgeois on parade, "one could easily take aim. . . ."[83] Bastille Day symbolized not only the organized power of the state but the ossification of an earlier revolution which it commemorated, and thus seemed to parade bourgeois hypocrisy on the grand boulevards. Its true commemoration, so Zo d'Axa might have argued, would be an anarchist outrage that would recreate the original revolutionary spirit. Not marches and solemn speeches but revolutionary psychodrama was the way to relive the great revolution of a century before.

The anarchists universally scorned Bastille Day, but they were ambivalent about the newly inaugurated workers' holiday—May Day. Celebrated in Europe for centuries as a festival of springtime and regeneration, May Day's modern political connotation dated from the fin de siècle, when the International Socialist Congress of 1889 proclaimed May 1, 1890, an international workers' day. This immediately created dissension among the anarchists, some of whom (Sebastien Faure, for example) condemned it as a sop thrown to the exploited workers by complacent parliamentary socialists, while others wished to make propagandistic use of it. Fearing this first May Day celebration might turn into an actual insurrection, the police made numerous precautionary arrests of radical notables such as Louise Michel and Sebastien Faure, and stationed large numbers of troops in Paris. The day turned out to be quite peaceful. In 1891, however, May Day violence led to the death of ten workers and children at Fourmies, near the Belgian border, and the arrest of several demonstrators, including Guesdists and anarchists. Another clash took place in the Paris suburb of Clichy. Although the immediate results were far less catastrophic than at Fourmies, it would have unexpected consequences, for the chain of terrorist bombings began when Ravachol attacked the homes of the prosecutor and magistrate responsible for jailing some of the demonstrators at Clichy. By 1893, the workers' celebration "had lost many of its apocalyptic connotations," and the anarchists retained mixed feelings about May Day, while the socialists wished to turn it into a national holiday.[84] The anarchists declared, "No festivity! . . . but demonstrations as energetic as circumstances permit! Do not let us forget that the street is the battleground of the people. . . . Rebellion need not wait for a first of May, but if on that day you find a propitious opportunity, then revolt. Individual acts—collective acts—all are good that lead to the same end."[85] May Day as festivity signified to the anarchists the acceptance of the workers' place in the social and political status quo. Therefore, the appropriate working-class response should be demonstrations against the state, just as the proper commemoration of the French Revolution would be to create a new revolutionary situation. The anarchists did not oppose festivities per se, but rather their institutionalization and appropriation by the state. Whereas the socialists wished to adopt a holiday whose content was proletarian but whose structure was indistinguishable from official, bourgeois celebrations (a similarity that has been underlined since 1917, as the Red Army parades its military hardware through Moscow every May Day), the anarchists rejected the whole notion of a standardized festival. Not only eventual government endorsement of May Day but even its serial repetition undermined the possibility of a truly authentic, spontaneous celebration and coopted the instigation of future revolutions. Because the ultimate anarchist celebration was in fact the revolutionary *Grand Soir,* whose breakthrough was conceived as being imminent and spontaneous, the orderly files marching on May Day appeared to them as a perversion of both festival and revolution. The anarchists preferred the vitalist myth of insurrection or general strike to ritual reenactment of past glories.

The spontaneous uprising envisioned by the anonymous group just quoted nearly took place two months after the 1893 May Day celebrations. The first Bal des Quat'z'Arts had been held in 1892 without creating any stir. In the second annual costume party, which was held at the Moulin Rouge, three women who were scantily clad as Cleopatra and her maids were arrested and Senator Bérenger, guardian of public virtue, made sure they came to trial. Each woman was fined 100 francs, and immediately the Latin Quarter exploded in several days of street fighting between students and police. Budding anarchist *littérateurs* such as Adolphe Retté were further politicized by their participation in the melee. One person was killed, the poet and associate of *La Plume* Jean Carrère was wounded, and the resulting furor forced Prefect of Police Lozé to resign shortly afterward.[86] That the disturbances took place in the Latin Quarter demonstrated the student composition of the Ball's participants, but their outrage suggests that they expected that celebrating in Montmartre exempted them from normal standards of public decorum, a reasonable assumption given the relative laxity with which Montmartre was treated by the censors. Though the riots lacked insurrectionary force, they demonstrated the nontraditional grievances and constituency that comprised one part of anarchism of the early 1890s.

Montmartre was as much a symbolic entity as a physical environment for its denizens, and the *château des brouillards* (the castle in the mist; this evocation of a dream-castle served as the title for one of Roland Dorgèles's later histories) was already being cloaked in mythologizing mists by the 1920s, by writers who made a career of their evocation of the good old days when a song would buy dinner *chez* Frédé. One of the central myths, second only to free and easy Bohemia, was that of pastoral Montmartre, where vineyards and gardens covered the slopes, where social relations bore more resemblance to a country village than to an impersonal urban Paris, where nature and culture were balanced in a harmonious whole. Aristide Bruant lived at the heart of this pastoral dream, in a house on the corner of the rues Cortot and Saules surrounded by a large garden where dogs ran free, birds sang, and one could imagine one lived in the country. Every true Montmartrois was thus opposed to any further encroachment upon their village, and at the Chat Noir Jules Jouy already bemoaned Montmartre's transformation by the builders of Sacré-Coeur in the 1890s:

> Depuis qu' d'un temple on l'a chargé,
> Notr' vieux Montmartre est bien changé,
> Grace aux travaux qu'on exécute
> Su' la Butte.
>
> (Since a temple has burdened it,
> Our old Montmartre is much changed
> Thanks to the works that they execute
> On the Butte.)[87]

The most famous music hall of the era constructed an ersatz windmill to capitalize on this pastoral image, then painted it red as if to acknowledge Montmartre's less wholesome traditions of social radicalism and libertinism.

As the rate of urban growth and social change in Montmartre increased, so did the nostalgia for the truly rustic Butte of Berlioz and Gérard de Nerval earlier in the century. This nostalgic note was certainly not muted as Montmartre in the fin de siècle and after turned into the first bohemian tourist center, and nostalgia became a marketable commodity. Despite its growth and commercialization, the old Montmartre survived to a large extent until the eve of World War I, when the maquis, a large wasteland that had long been a shantytown of tin-roofed houses with wattle-and-daub walls, was cleared for urban renewal. Alvan Sanborn, an American visitor at the turn of the century, could still be captivated by Montmartre's "general aspect of a provincial community . . . it has the provincial community's spirit of neighborliness . . . enlived by coquetry and mirth . . . in Paris, but not of it, and yet, by necessity, perpetually conscious of it." Equally impressed by Montmartre's social relations, he described the "genuine solidarity between the workingmen and the artistic colonies of Montmartre, based upon common sufferings, hatreds and hopes. If anywhere there existed an alliance between labor and intellect, it was in Montmartre." Sanborn was highly aware of Montmartre's "present revolutionary spirit," which he described as a fusion of the old Montmartre and the new Bohemia, that is, of the local Communards and the artists. Along with neighboring Belleville, it was regarded as the hotbed of revolution. His utopian conclusion: "Nowhere this side of heaven, probably, is social democracy so real and so devoid of pose."[88]

The mixture of longing for the old Montmartre and bohemian irreverence toward the powers-that-be is evident in the longtime project to establish a free city of Montmartre that would preserve the Butte's charms in an atmosphere of tolerance and humor. From Rodolphe Salis's *fumiste* candidacy to the election of the humorist Jules Dépaquit as first mayor of the free commune of Montmartre in 1920, Montmartre *littérateurs* tried, symbolically if not actually, to reestablish their arrondissement's pre-Haussmannian autonomy. In Salis's campaign, which was sponsored by an election committee composed of such Chat Noir habitués as Jouy, Alphonse Allais, Léon Bloy, and Willette, the *cabaretier* proposed the separation of Montmartre from the state, the nomination by the local citizens of a municipal council and mayor, and the abolition of the custom's duty or *octroi* from which Montmartre had been exempt when it had lain beyond the city walls, and which had been largely responsible for its early prosperity.[89]

After World War I, Montmartre witnessed a series of dada-esque attempts to dissociate itself from Paris and even from France. At a cabaret that bore the name of the Vache Enragée, Jules Dépaquit, who had been briefly held under arrest in 1892 for the anarchist revenge bombing of the Restaurant Véry, where Ravachol had been denounced and captured, was named mayor of the free city of Montmartre. In order to clarify his position vis-à-vis the official mayor of the eighteenth arrondissement, Dépaquit resorted to a distinction entirely characteristic of the Symbolist and anarchist generation: "Montmartre has two mayors, it is true, but they complement each other. My colleague is occupied with the material part. For myself, I am the 'spiritual' mayor."[90] The fantasy element was underlined by Dépaquit's claim to a spiritual mayoralty, yet Montmartre had always represented an ideal to its artist denizens, an alternative society where creativity would be rewarded and eccentricity tolerated, a high-spirited realm where art rather than lucre determined status and social relations. The *vache enragée* reminded these idealists of life's material necessities, but they were more inclined to mock it than to grab it by the horns.

However much Montmartre in its golden age was mythicized by its inhabitants to cover its tawdrier aspects, it remained an ideal that in many ways embodied the anarchist version of utopia, not only in its championing of free creativity or local autonomy, but also in its balancing of the rural and the urban elements, the gardens and the cabarets. The unreality is confirmed by the lack of space given the factory, but then a utopia is not constructed upon the reality principle. Montmartre's attention was perforce directed toward Paris, as Sanborn observed, but it preserved its own sacred space from which to gaze down upon the metropolis, countering its economic dependence with cultural autonomy and radicalism. Montmartrois anarchism rose and fell in conjunction with the changing fortunes of the Montmartre colony, and its seriousness as a political movement was compromised by the compensatory nature of the bohemian revolt, which too often could be summarized as *épater le bourgeois*. That it also surpassed this merely reactive stance is testified by the extent and depth of the anarchist culture that thrived in the tolerant and combative atmosphere of Montmartre.

Language, Crime, and Class

Four

The Parisian lower classes—both artisanal workers and the criminal underclass residing on their margin—spoke a vernacular form of French known as argot that differed greatly from the received standard dialect spoken by the middle and upper classes in the late nineteenth century.[1] The anarchists were particularly cognizant that linguistic cleavages accompanied and magnified the social and political conflicts besetting French society in the 1890s. Couching their political message in terms familiar to the lower classes, they addressed not only these peoples' material interests but identified themselves with the language and popular culture in which the people thought, spoke, and lived. By exploiting popular resentments, the anarchists emphasized the gulf that separated the formal language of the political elites from the subcultural idiom of the Parisian faubourgs in order to reinforce class conflict and promote working-class solidarity. Yet the argot of the Parisian masses was not a neutral medium into which anarchist ideology was injected; rather, it contained traditions and terminology that lent themselves to an anarchist critique of society.

Language conditions cognition as well as communicates ideas. On the metalinguistic level argued by the linguistic relativists following Benjamin Lee Whorf, such grammatical categories as plurality, gender, tenses, and voices are said to influence how we conceive of time, space, matter, and other fundamental aspects of cognition.[2] It is questionable whether the received standard dialect and the vernacular diverge to this extent.[3] Yet as well as containing structural, synchronic elements of grammar, linguistic systems are fundamentally diachronic. Argot and formal language both contain historically embedded cultural attitudes which the speaker may not fully perceive, yet which predispose him or her to favor certain belief-systems that conform to these preconceptions.

Whereas speakers of the standard dialect have knowledge of or at least access to their past via written history, the underclasses maintain contact with their own traditions only in the inchoate, oral form of their language. In a largely oral culture such as that of the lower classes, language is thus an especially powerful cultural medium. I will argue that a congruence of ideology, cognition, and cultural values existed between anarchism and the popular (used in the sense of the French term *populaire*) mentality contained in French argot of the 1890s. This cultural matrix provided a sentiment of solidarity which partially compensated for the anarchists' political and organizational liabilities.

French argot was a particularly suitable vehicle for anarchist propaganda for reasons transcending its use by the lower classes. The anarchists were the heirs of a tradition of illegality attached to argot dating back to the time of François Villon, when roving bands of outlaws such as the Coquillards, formed of the human debris tossed up by the social dislocations of the Hundred Years' War, created secret languages to confuse the king's men. During their trial in Dijon in 1455, this language was partially recorded and records of it thus remain.[4] The late medieval underworld origins of argot continued to haunt late nineteenth-century sociolinguists, who hesitated to refer to the Parisian vernacular as argot because of the term's criminal associations.[5] As well as deceiving the authorities, argot differentiated those members of the closed corporations of beggars and thieves from the rest of society, thus affirming the unique identity of the in-group using the language. Much as a military password, and for the same reasons, the vocabulary of argot evolved in order to retain its secrecy. The more separate and closed that criminal society was, the less the language would need to change.

In the course of the nineteenth century, argot underwent its most fundamental change since the fifteenth century, losing its closed criminal character and becoming generalized as the Parisian lower-class vernacular. Though scholars argue as to how distinct criminal and popular parlance remained, it is agreed that the language spoken by the burgeoning masses of the capital in the nineteenth century originated largely among the criminal elements, and what it lost in secrecy it made up for in popular vitality as it became the language of a class rather than of a narrow caste.[6] It has been suggested that this shift from closed criminal to democratized lower-class speech was hastened by novelists' use of argot to portray the colorful life of the lower depths, but it seems dubious that literature affected language to this degree.[7] More germane to linguistic change was the rapid urbanization of Paris. As the working classes became increasingly separated geographically from the middle classes, inhabiting especially the north and east quadrants of Paris, the criminal elements probably took refuge in these enlarged *quartiers populaires,* where they would be less identifiable to the authorities than in the more fashionable districts.[8] Irrespective of underworld influence, spatial segregation by class would have encouraged the growth of a lower-class vernacular. As the population of Paris swelled from half a million at the beginning of the nineteenth century to nearly 3 million by its end, lower-class speech became increasingly important and recognized as such, achieving reknown in Zola's novel *L'Assommoir* (1876) and in the songs of the café-concert.

Such voyeuristic fascination with the life of the "lower depths" (the *bas-fonds* of society, often simply called "the milieu") did not imply that the middle classes had suddenly become more egalitarian. At the turn of the century, it was often maintained that the lower classes were given to metaphorical modes of expression which, though colorful and even poetic, poorly adapted them to the rigors of modern life.[9] Modern sociolinguists have similarly argued that the speakers of the "public" or "restricted" language lack the ability to make abstract, analytical distinctions and instead overly concretize and personify concepts. This tendency toward concretization supposedly deprives these speakers of adequate critical capacity, especially of the world lying beyond their immediate horizons.[10] The speakers of French argot did indeed concretize abstract ideas by finding analogues in the world of human beings and nature, yet in doing so they usually deprecated the designated idea or institution. To materialize was to demystify, to invert the social order by speaking of the high and mighty in gross and common terms. In the process of retranslating formal concepts into public terminology, argot functioned as the poor people's critical consciousness. Nowhere was this deprecatory spirit better mobilized than in the pages of Emile Pouget's *Le Père Peinard,* where the critical potential of argot was harnessed to serve political ends.

Le Père Peinard was not the first newspaper to rabble-rouse in plebeian tones. A century before, Jacques Hébert had similarly addressed the French revolutionary crowd in *Le Père Duchesne,* and Pouget imitated the phrase *bons bougres* (good fellows) that Hébert had employed in order to evoke a similar conversational tone. Although he consciously appealed to French revolutionary traditions, Pouget found abundant sources of social antagonism in the discourse of his own milieu. Founded in 1889 by the one-time department store clerk who had spent time in prison in the mid-1880s for anarchist activities, *Le Père Peinard* was by 1892 the best-selling French anarchist newspaper. Its circulation of 20,000 copies a week surpassed that of Jean Grave's "official" anarchist organ, *La Révolte.*[11] Pouget's *argotique* style contrasted with Grave's formal layout and ideology in exactly the same way that his Montmartre locale differed from Grave's Left Bank garret office near the Sorbonne. Even the police informers poked fun at Grave's serious, didactic tone which was little calculated to appeal to the anarchist rank and file, and made puns about the *gens graves* for whom the paper apparently was intended.

In an early issue of *Le Père Peinard,* Pouget justified his use of argot to a reader who objected to the paper's violent tone:

Each society, each profession has its special argot. Why should mine, which is that of the great working crowd . . . offend you more than the foulnesses (*saloperies*), of Catulle Mendès? . . .

Listen, the priests (*ratichons*) speak in Latin, the dirty bailiffs write a jargon that no one understands, some funny guys want us to learn Volapük, decadent writers brutalize us with distorted words, and the people should no longer have the right to think and write in their language?[12]

Displaying a high level of linguistic sophistication, Pouget argued that the people's naturally rooted speech contrasted favorably with the hothouse creations of aesthetes and internationalists. Rather than using language as a secret code to mystify others, as he insinuated the bailiffs and priests did, he was clearly employing it to increase working-class identity, as well as to popularize his own newspaper.

Anarchists were not above using secret languages to keep their intentions hidden from the ubiquitous informers who infiltrated the movement. A police informer stationed in the north Parisian industrial suburb of Saint-Denis reported, for instance: "The anarchists come to adopt a conversational language in order to correspond between themselves. The conventional language is expressed entirely differently than the words which they use in the dispatch."[13] The police file entitled "Secret alphabets and codes of correspondence between the anarchists" attests to the anarchists' linguistic creativity.[14]

Yet Pouget favored neither a conspiratorial nor even strictly criminal interpretation of the anarchist use of argot. Distinguishing between the secret and public forms of Parisian slang, Pouget justified his own use of the latter:

But, by God, if one accuses me of *speaking argot* [his emphasis] I strongly deny it, I put my feet on the plate.

Argot? I don't know a traitorous word, dammit, or at least so little that it is not worth speaking of.

I tasted prison, I ate from the bowl at Mazas, even at great Roquette, ah well, I never understood the jabbering of the guys who spoke the *langue verte*.

Eh gossiper, that strikes you as strange? It's nonetheless true!

"But then what gibberish do you speak, Père Peinard, shaver of the devil?" jabber the guys who knock me. . . .

I write as everyone speaks, or at least I try to achieve that. . . . Try it, listen to someone speak, and you'll see that there's a lot of resemblance between your manner of speaking and my speech . . . I conclude that the spoken language has nothing in common with the written language. The written language that one reads in books is an idiotic invention, good for muddling ideas and hindering the people from understanding them. . . . In using that language the scientists and all the group on high only understand themselves. . . . Thanks to this trick, the *populo* remains cut off from progress. . . . If on the contrary books were written simply, with words known to all, everyone would understand!

Yes, by God, everyone would understand! But the first thing the *populo* would understand is that the rich folks and the government steal from them, and don't give a damn about them. Then instead of enduring all that rubbish, they would break their mugs.[15]

The *langue verte* or underworld cant coexisted with argot, as criminals continued to coin secret words in such contexts as prison. Disavowing any desire for secrecy, Pouget preferred to refer to his own parlance as *populaire* rather than *argotique*. This distinction emphasized rather than denied argot's criminal roots, yet clearly differentiated contemporary popular speech from the language of the underworld.

The article's chief significance lies in what it reveals about Pouget's own motives for using what was commonly called argot. Pouget was not trying to assimilate the criminal elements into the brotherhood of anarchy, but rather was appealing to the working-class populace who, he reasoned, would be more willing to read a newspaper written as they spoke rather than one written as the bourgeoisie wrote. This attempt to transliterate the oral discourse of the outer boulevards into print accounts for the frequent interjection of verbal oaths such as *nom de dieu* and *mille bombes*. The use of "Père Peinard" was also a device to personalize the approach, as the readership would presumably feel more comfortable listening to and arguing with a cobbler than with the relatively unfamiliar and impersonal entity "editor." A *compagnon* could write directly to Père Peinard, a fiction that removed the bureaucratic intermediaries interposing themselves between paper and reader. Pouget's excluse use of the *tu* form in *Le Père Peinard* also emphasized a tone of equality and personal relationship.[16]

In protesting that he was not writing in a specialized and secret vocabulary but rather as everyone spoke, Pouget closely approximated what Basil Bernstein has called a "public language," which he defines as "a linguistic form which maximizes the means of production of social rather than individual symbols."[17] The usual way of referring to oneself in argot was by the third-person "Bibi," thereby emphasizing one's commonality rather than one's individuality. Bernstein contrasts this with the "formal language" learned in school, which he contends is more impersonal, deals with processes rather than with things, and allows the speaker to transcend immediate experience while encouraging a more subjective, individuated interaction with the environment. Bernstein considers public language to be an inherently conservatizing medium in that it encourages interest in things rather than in processes and reasoned principles. Pouget recognized as much when he protested that lack of access to formal informational channels helped keep the poor ignorant. Yet the social nature of public language compensated for its limitations by furthering social solidarity (a possibility also recognized by Bernstein), while the anarchists could supply the critical awareness that may have remained latent in the criminal domination of argot.[18] A formal, individuating linguistic code allows for a progressive and liberal conception of society, whereas the public and personal language would appear to be either conservative or radical, depending on how it is channeled and on the traditions it communicates. Since many of the traditions and terms of French argot derived from the criminal milieu and fostered distrust of authority, it became a useful vehicle for anarchist propaganda. By associating the formal language with those most formal of institutions, the church and the legal system, Pouget translated the evident contrast between the public and the formal languages into that of people versus bourgeoisie. In employing the popular idiom he protested against an abstract and formal structure that both signified and defined the legal order of authority. Pouget attempted to inject a political overtone into an existing cultural phenomenon: the people speak differently; they are different; let us stress and increase that differentness and thus increase class consciousness.

Le Père Peinard signifies the importance of popular discourse within the anarchist movement, but is of limited use in revealing the thoughts of Pouget's readership. A more objective record of nineteenth-century speech is provided by dictionaries of argot published at the time. Dictionaries furnishing translations of argot into standard French were not new in the 1890s; samples date back to the *Jargon de l'argot réformé* of 1628. Spurred by the interest of the Romantics in the lower depths of society, especially in its more colorful criminal elements, and later by that of the Naturalists, dictionaries of argot appeared sporadically throughout the century, notably in 1860, 1866, and 1878. According to Lazare Sainéan no new dictionaries appeared until 1894. The increased political and social visibility of the lower classes at the end of the century, coupled with a final burst of popularization by singers such as Bruant and by a new generation of poets and writers, led to the publication of at least seven such dictionaries between 1894 and 1901.[19] As might be expected, these attempts to render the popular idiom intelligible to the newly interested bourgeoisie, if only so they could read Zola, were not edited by members of the working class. One dictionary was compiled by a former head of the political police (*sûreté*); another was issued by Bruant himself after his retirement from the cabaret scene, with the unrewarded assistance of the singer Léon de Bercy; the others were by writers specializing in the contemporary social scene who had become familiar with argot in the course of their researches. The most scholarly dictionary was George Delesalle's *Dictionnaire argot-français et français-argot,* which attempted to include all words of argot from the fifteenth century to the present. Perhaps the most popularized but also the most exhaustive, Aristide Bruant's dictionary devoted 457 pages to argot; the projected second volume translating argot into French never appeared.

In order to reconstruct the social and political universe of the Parisian speaker of argot in the 1890s, I analyzed four of these works in terms of the linguistic specificity they reveal for certain words, the assumption being that the more important a concept, person, group, and so on is to the speakers of a language, the more nuanced will be their vocabulary in defining or categorizing the thing signified, and the larger the place it will assume in their cognitive system. The classic example from sociolinguistics is the incredible subtlety with which Eskimos lexicalize different kinds of snow that we less efficiently designate as fine snow, wet snow, and so forth.[20]

A basic assumption of sociolinguistics is that the speakers of a unique language constitute a distinct group as to geographic location and/or social class. Weighing the relative emphasis of the language on various aspects of the social scene should facilitate a number of tasks: to determine the extent of the change in usage from a specific jargon of thieves and mendicants to a more generalized lower-class speech, to identify the persons and groups who loomed largest in the *argotique* milieu, and to reveal the attitudes of the speakers of argot toward the political, social, and legal hierarchies. Linguistic analysis illumines these groups' culturally cognized significance, not their actual social impact, though the latter obviously bears on the former.

But cognized by whom? How reliable are dictionaries compiled by a policeman, a *cabaretier,* and middle-class social commentators as accurate indicators of the Parisian vernacular? The greatest danger of distortion probably lay in overemphasizing the more lurid aspects of lower-class life such as crime and prostitution, while neglecting more mundane working-class pursuits. One may compare the lexicographer's emphases with the findings of Lazare Sainéan, a distinguished scholarly contemporary, as presented in his magisterial 1920 study *Le Langage parisien au XIXe siècle.* Sainéan separates his discussion of the social factors contributing to Parisian argot into two long chapters, one entitled "legally constituted classes," the other "on the margin of society." In the former group he places soldiers, sailors, and such artisanal craftsmen as printers, cobblers, and butchers as significant contributors to argot. A variety of miscreants and mountebanks are included in the second group and he identifies the underworld as the principal source of the *bas-langage.* The Parisian vernacular was implicitly conceived to be the fusion of laboring classes and dangerous classes.[21] Our lexicographers thus do not seem to have been entirely governed by romantic impulses. Nevertheless, conclusions based upon sources that are at least once removed from the popular culture itself and even more distant from a specifically anarchist subculture must necessarily be speculative.

The linguistic specificity concerning the legal authorities shows a very exact cognizance of the forces of law and order, their deployment, and their means of enforcing their penalties. Magistrates and judges appeared in argot at several levels of authority, with specific terms for the corrupt ones. Lawyers too were represented, but as might be expected, the police attracted the most attention of all representatives of authority. In terms of the relations between the police and the people, the most enlightening terminology comes from words for informer and the act of informing. Of the many terms for *dénoncer* and *dénonciateur,* several referred specifically to police informers. The equivalent term for "stool pigeon," *mouchard,* received considerable attention, with specific terms denoting *agents provocateurs* and for prisoners who spied on each other. Informers played a crucial role in the anarchist movement, as the prefectural records attest. Many of the arguments against conspiratorial tactics and much of the dialogue within the movement up until 1894 dealt with the difficulty or impossibility of retaining secrets, and there was no worse insult nor surer catalyst for violence than to level the charge of *mouchard* at a *compagnon.* In a wider sense, to denounce one's fellows or accomplices in crime or conspiracy to the authorities meant betrayal of group and class solidarity. To closely define the boundaries and betrayers of this solidarity preoccupied both the speakers of argot and the anarchists of this period, as denoted by the attention given specific terms for denouncing falsely or involuntarily, and for denouncing one's accomplice.

No physical location or place occupied as much linguistic attention as did prison in argot. Aside from general terms, each prison in Paris had its own popular name, with the greatest variety reserved for Saint-Lazare, the Paris jail where prostitutes were sent. *Bagne,* the moored prison ships, and infamous overseas prisons such as Devil's Island, figured highly in the people's imagination, but the distant specter of the *bagne* paled before the more proximate terror of the guillotine. The succession of dramatic thefts, bombings, and assassinations carried out by the propagandists of the deed in the 1890s did not fail to affect public opinion, though the more blindly terroristic attacks—as against anonymous restaurant patrons—were widely reviled. The terrorists' expiation for their crimes at the hands of executioner Deibler in front of La Roquette Prison generated far more sympathy for the anarchist cause, and usually inspired another terrorist to avenge his death. Public executions were far less politically astute than was relegation to Devil's Island. The anarchist martyrology that played a major role in the era of *attentats* was mirrored in argot. While Symbolist writers wrote eulogies for Ravachol and spoke reverently of the "Anarchrist" who sacrificed himself for the cause, *argotiers* spoke of the scaffold as the *abbaye de mont à regret* or the *abbaye de cinq pierres* (the abbey of the reluctant climb or of the five stones or steps, presumably those leading up to the scaffold).

The age-old heritage of crime and especially of theft in the *argotique* milieu still cast a long shadow over 1890s parlance. It would appear that to a speaker of argot, illegality and violence were daily occurrences, if not actually then at least rhetorically. The various kinds of thieves and theft were extremely well lexicalized, both as to method and object. Between the two sources that specified kinds of thieves, there appeared seventy-one different categories, from dog-stealers to those who ransacked churches, and from solitary thieves to those in gangs. One category cited by Bruant included those who did not shrink from the prospect of murder, but generally murder was emphasized less than cleverness, manifested in such ploys as substituting false jewels for real ones, mystifying one's victims, or even by simulating epilepsy. The high value placed on ingenuity seems supported by the large number of terms designating an *escroc* or swindler. Functions related to thievery cited were the fencing of stolen goods, counterfeiting, and smuggling. The linguistic specificity attached to the thief's *métier* itself connoted guile in exploiting every possible option open to a prospective criminal in a complex society, and the number of terms for minor crimes, such as Bruant's twelve terms for shoplifting, or the theft of linens off the line, or the theft of bread, suggests misery rather than class antagonism or aggression as underlying motives. Nevertheless, just as the fascination with the guillotine revealed a preoccupation with bloodshed and violence, so did the number of terms designating violent assault, though with much less specificity than terms relating to theft. *Meurtrier* and *meurtrir*, which correspond to the English second-degree murder or assault, got very little mention, but *frapper*, "to strike," more than made up the deficit. *Assassin*, which has a more general application than its English cognate and is equivalent to "murderer," was specified as to techniques of murder (by knife, strangulation, poisoning, by a hard blow, etc.), all means mentioned being fairly rustic, though argot terms for revolver and rifle existed as well as for knife. Argot revealed an atavistic quality in which traditional uses were retained, traditional methods clung to despite technological advances. This dual quality of argot, at once atavistic and innovative, parallels the appeal of anarchism among artisans, skilled craftspeople, and even artists and writers, all tied to old methods of production, and yet looking to future rather than past models of social relations for their salvation.[22]

More familiar categories of crime had the most argot terms describing them in argot. Thus terms such as *bandit* received little attention, *malfaiteur* almost none, *voleur* (thief) or even *réceleur* (fence) a great deal. This was not the case with the French employed by the authorities, where a general term like *malfaiteur* was continuously applied by the police and the judiciary to such intangible anarchist crimes as conspiracy and incitement to violence. The criminal terms with political implications generally received little attention in argot. Not one of the dictionaries mentioned *attentat* or *explosif*. Only Bruant listed a term for *dynamite*, Delesalle alone one for *bombe*. Dynamite had only existed since the 1860s, and bombs played far less a role in the criminal underworld than did the thief's all-purpose crowbar or *pince*. One marginally criminal term that acquired some notoriety in popular anarchist circles did appear in the dictionaries of argot. Three of them referred to *déménagement à la cloche de bois*, or "moving with wooden bells," thus noiselessly, which became an anarchist specialty in the 1880s and 1890s. Several *compagnons* would serve as nocturnal furniture movers, while others would, if necessary, detain the *concierge*. This activity was celebrated in *Le Père Peinard* by "Le Chant des anti-proprios," with music and accompanying illustration. A greater concordance existed between anarchist and argot discourse at the level of popular usage than at the more spectacular one of bombs and *attentats*.

Crime attained a marked social visibility well beyond the *argotique* milieu. Within the anarchist camp, the trial of the avowedly anarchist thief Pini in late 1889 brought the issue of the legitimacy of theft as an anarchist tactic to the surface. Even when the anarchist movement became more clearly working class and syndicalist after 1895 such anarchist criminals as the master thief Marius Jacob and the Bonnot Gang continued to make pre–World War I headlines. The echo of Proudhon's cry "property is theft" was still strong, but the more idealistic anarchist leaders renounced both private property and theft as entwined features of bourgeois society, and strove for a kind of revolutionary purity which had no room for the more *lumpen* social elements. Yet crime with no political overtones was a far more significant threat to social tranquillity. Charles and Louise Tilly note that suicide rates, vagrancy, and criminal convictions all climbed during the nineteenth century, peaking around 1890 at record levels. The year 1894, the high point of anarchist propaganda by the deed (acts of terrorism), was also the zenith of criminal convictions in France during the whole nineteenth century.[23] At the end of a generation-long depression (1873–96), in a society beset by the anomie accompanying rapid urbanization, by class antagonism, unemployment, and low wages, it is scarcely surprising that crime was both common and normatively accepted in the lower-class Parisian milieu. The criminal underworld figured importantly both in argot and in contemporary society, but although the anarchists perceived criminal acts as inchoate condemnations of the authority of the state, they were not willing to reduce anarchism to this prepolitical form of protest. All criminals were potential anarchists; all anarchists were not criminals. Though the popular appeal of criminal defiance remained strong in the twentieth century, the anarchists increasingly looked to organized workers rather than to thieves as their model human being; to strikes, especially the general strike, rather than to crime, in order to justify and exemplify the political use of violence.

The relative paucity of political terms in argot when compared with criminal terms reveals the anarchists' strategic wisdom in couching their political message in familiar terms with which the populace could identify. Politics itself was not a valued activity among speakers of argot, being perceived either as remote to their interests or as a tool for ever-changing and always-the-same authorities. Discourse about power was cast in more traditional terms in argot, in terms of criminality, as the anarchists sought to mobilize the latent political content of long-existing popular attitudes. The 1890s witnessed a great upsurge in socialist as well as anarchist activities, but whereas Bruant listed three words in argot denoting *anarchiste*, Lermina one and Delesalle four, not one of the dictionaries mentioned *socialiste*. Some of the words, such as *anarcho*, were coined by the anarchists themselves; others, such as *compagnon* were appropriated by them as a fraternal mode of address. The anarchist term for bomb, *marmite*, was not picked up by any of the compilers, but in his section of argot-français, Delesalle defined the word *crever*, which in standard French means "to split" or "to burst," as meaning "to kill," as in *crever un bourgeois*, and cited testimony from the trial of the anarchist Léon-Jules Léauthier, convicted in 1894 for attempting to assassinate a foreign diplomat, as an example of this usage.[24] Bruant cited a term taken from *Le Père Peinard, le chambard*, as one of two terms for *bouleversement* (overthrow), which was his unsophisticated way of referring to social revolution. *Révolution* itself did not appear in the dictionaries, nor did *saboteur* or *sabotage*. As well as offering eight terms for *bonapartiste*, Bruant listed one term each for *député* in general and for *député de droite, de gauche, de centre, de l'extrême droite*, and *de province*. One might surmise that antiparliamentary movements of the right and left had more popular support among the speakers of argot in the 1890s than did socialism, radicalism, or other parliamentary groups. Because anarchist strength in the north and east quadrants of Paris directly followed that of the Boulangists, often among identical elements of the population, the mixture of authoritarian and libertarian sentiments in the slang is not too surprising. Indeed, the one political party that received more attention than the anarchists were the Bonapartists. This focus might have reflected the inclusion of argot terms from earlier decades, although the same charismatic magic that ensured Louis-Napoléon Bonaparte's electoral and plebiscitary successes would have made likely his representation in the vocabulary of argot.

Sociolinguists' contention that speakers of argot translate abstract into concrete terms is generally borne out by the evidence gleaned from these dictionaries. If political parties and ideologies were little specified in argot, social and class terminology tended to be more lexicalized the more concretely it related to the speakers of argot. Thus *bourgeois* was more specified than political terms, but somewhat less so than *patron,* boss. Delesalle cited eleven general terms for *bourgeois,* and one term each for *bourgeois riche, banal et sententieux,* and *imbécile. Patron, Patronne* (female boss), and *fils de patron* (boss's son), as well as *voilà le patron* (here comes the boss) were all richly and deprecatingly specified by such terms as *singe* (monkey) and *singeresse.* The difference between frequency of abstract and concrete referents was greatest when the speakers of argot referred to themselves. Thus *peuple* had almost no place in argot, although *misérables* and *miséreux* were very important terms. Bruant listed fifty-two such terms, nine referring solely to *misérable sans domicile* (without lodging). *Misère* and *pauvreté* were also well-recognized conditions. *Paysan* and *campagnard* had their place, but were less important than *vagabond.* (*Peuple* and *paysan* were meaningful social categories to a demographer, neither very specific nor highly emotion-laden. The morally neutral tone that commended them to scientists discouraged their use by the *argotiers.*) Conveying stronger impressions, *misérable* and *vagabond* also said more about the social relations of the individuals who fell under such categories. Not given to euphemisms, argot was more apt to express the self-pity of society's outcasts.

Social and class awareness generally outweighed national awareness, despite the frequent calls for *la revanche* (revenge) by rightist politicians. No words were cited for *français,* though several existed at the more specific level of *parisien. Etranger* was also too general to stimulate argot creation. *Anglais* and *allemand* produced roughly equal numbers of terms, owing to long and dramatic contact and conflict, whereas *russe* stimulated no words despite all the political fanfare accompanying the Franco-Russian alliance, which culminated in the czar's visit to Paris in 1896. This lack of popular resonance may be contrasted with the sixteen words that Bruant listed for *juif,* more than for any national group that might signify "other." In the early 1890s, the anarchists' greatest competitor for the allegiance of this *argotique* milieu was the marquis de Morès, whose program of radical anti-Semitism received an enthusiastic response from the butchers of La Villette before the adventurous marquis was killed in Africa in 1896.

Le Père Peinard (whose title was itself a term taken from argot signifying "taking it easy," proceeding in an unhurried manner) had for its frontispiece the image of a cobbler, and was directed at a working-class readership. As this title indicated, work and work-related values were treated ambiguously by the anarchists, many of whom associated work with exploitation, or else with the current system of production which would largely be done away with in the anarchist utopia to come. The argot reveals a similar ambivalence about work and workers. Each of the three dictionaries (excluding Rossignol's brief work) listed approximately twenty terms signifying "worker." Over half the terms for *travailler* signified forced work, careless work, or the least possible work, betraying some doubt as to the value of labor. Terms for *travail* increase this sense of ambivalence: of Bruant's nine general terms, five referred specifically to prostitution and were cited again in the category *travail pour prostitution.* Four terms indicated difficult work and one hurried work, again indicating some distaste for laborious effort. When contrasted with words related to values directly opposed to "honest labor" and the professions most clearly signifying "those who do not work," the numerical significance of the terms for work and working appear in greater relief. Terms for *fainéant* and *flâneur* (idler) and for *paresseux* (one who is lazy), and for the verbs describing such lack of activity, were roughly equivalent in number to those signifying work and workers.

Among the lower classes, the vocation of prostitution was the clearest alternative for a woman who did not wish to seek "honest" work, who came from the provinces seeking work and found that profession instead, or who had been led astray by male friends or employers. Of her inevitable accomplice, the *souteneur* or pimp became synonymous in the world of argot for those who, in avoiding work at all costs, profited from the labor of others. Terms for *prostituée* in argot were only rivaled, though not equaled, by those for thief, Bruant being able to summon nearly 300 words for this timeworn occupation. One questions whether all of them were current, but many categories clearly referred to the contemporary sociolegal situation of prostitutes, differentiating between carded and noncarded or unauthorized prostitutes, girls in houses versus those on the streets, those practicing their profession in the Bois de Boulogne, in trains, and so forth. *Souteneur* was far less distinguished by type, yet Lermina cited 31, Delesalle 41 general terms, and Bruant specified 53 different terms for a vocation that was not even legally defined until 1903. Bruant and Delesalle also cited many words for *bordel*, though terms for *prostitution* itself were few.

As with argot terms related to crime, so with prostitution one must question whether the high degree of lexicalization recorded in the dictionaries reflected the importance that streetwalkers exercised over the popular imagination and in the social milieu, or whether it merely reflected the sexual imagination of the lexicographers. Historical evidence seems to justify accepting the dictionaries as legitimate sources. Though the laws governing prostitution remained fairly constant during the latter of the nineteenth century, the practice of prostitution changed considerably. From 1870 to 1892, the so-called *maisons de tolérance* or licensed brothels declined from 145 houses to only 59, as their proprietors found it increasingly difficult to compete with less-regulated alternatives, such as bars served by women. Less-regulated establishments incurred fewer expenses, and their clandestine status itself increased their attraction to customers. As the number of prostitutes domiciled in houses dropped by two-thirds, the number on the street doubled from 1872 to 1903.[25] As streetwalkers, both those inscribed on police dossiers and those *insoumises* who practiced prostitution clandestinely, became more numerous, so did the number of pimps supported by them. Most prostitutes were of working-class origin and were often forced into the profession by the inadequate salaries paid to seamstresses and domestics (who together accounted for 60 percent of the women who later became prostitutes).[26] Most prostitutes came from the same northeastern quadrant of Paris to which the anarchists appealed and where anarchist activity was concentrated. The government seemed powerless to regulate streetwalking, despite such attempts as the Bérenger law of 1895 prohibiting the renting of hotel rooms to minors.

Does the prostitute's prominence in argot reflect her increasingly important place in that portion of the society in which argot was spoken? Is there in fact a direct correlation between lexicalization and social role, so that the prostitutes should be considered more central to working-class culture than cobblers or printers? The prostitute clearly was central to argot, but not necessarily to society. It was in fact precisely her peripheral role in the lower-class milieu that made her such a potent symbol, for she existed not at the center but at the boundaries of that society, at the interface between classes. Her very marginality defined the perimeters of the lower class far more effectively than could those members located firmly within that class. Although the various terms designated highly specific categories of prostitutes, taken together they signified not the women's social function but rather their cognitive role in defining a critical relationship between the classes. Behind each term for prostitute lay an intimation of a relationship, either between the prostitute and her pimp or her customer. The pimp was portrayed typically as being a tough scion of the lower classes; the "john" was seen as being middle or upper class (for an analysis of the imagery of prostitution in the songs of Aristide Bruant and Paul Paillette, see chapter 5). Abstract class relations were transformed into illicit sexual relations, thereby familiarizing and naturalizing the exploitive social interchange.

The relation between anarchism and prostitution is less immediately evident than is that between anarchism and crime. Anarchists often praised "individual repossession" as a means of redistributing the bourgeois' ill-gotten gains, yet they did not similarly encourage sexual commerce. Prostitutes and pimps, evidently important and perhaps central to argot, were linked to anarchism symbolically rather than directly. Thieves and prostitutes might both feel victimized by society, but the thief might take satisfaction in getting his revenge through theft, whereas the streetwalker's only hope of improving her status was to integrate herself into society either through marriage or by becoming a highly paid courtesan in the manner of Zola's *Nana*. Either of these options— wife or *demi-mondaine*—was rejected by the anarchists as simply substituting one form of exploitation for another. The thief's relation to society was symmetrical and symbolized vengeance; the prostitute's was submissive or complementary and stood for exploitation. Both *métiers* amplified the reality of class differentiation in bourgeois society, and thereby supported the anarchists' contention that only revolution could end this state of affairs. Prostitution provided the anarchists with a symbol of bourgeois exploitation of the daughters of the working class, and more generally of a decadent society's perversion of natural passions for purposes of gain. The image of the exploited prostitute thus served the anarchists as a dual symbol of bourgeois domination of nature and of culture. The thief, the pimp, the whore served as culture symbols for many in the working class while remaining at the boundaries of that class, respected for their hostility toward the dominant classes, sentimentalized for their suffering, and reviled when they betrayed their fellows for personal gain.

Both Emile Pouget, editor of the principal *argotique* newspaper, and sociolinguists of the era were uncertain whether lower-class language merited the name argot, which they understood to designate a secret language created in order to hide criminal intentions from the authorities. This was clearly no longer the raison d'être of 1890s argot. Can the use of argot in the 1890s be understood as a functional response to social and political pressures weighing upon many members of the lower classes? The creation of new terms was now less a matter of immediate individual need than of registering the corporate demands of the social group. Argot still had a function to perform, but it was the indirect, cognitive function of creating in-group solidarity and of defining the boundary between the group and outsiders. This solidarity function was not new, but whereas before it had been a by-product of a more direct secretive function, it was now its primary role. As the group defined by argot grew larger and more diffuse, the need to express this feeling of solidarity became more pressing.

Argot appealed to the anarchists not because they needed a secret language in which to conspire, but because it served as an extension of their propaganda, which was again primarily a cognitive function. As a linguistic code, argot structured a supraindividual consciousness, helping to organize changing lower-class experience by defining categories such as that of the informer or the prostitute who symbolized particular forms of social interaction, in these cases transgressing certain norms. The informer violated lower-class norms of solidarity and was expelled from the body politic; the prostitute's position confused work and sex, and stood not only for exploitation but for the hypocrisy of bourgeois morality. Not bombs and deputies, not even pimps and thieves, but ultimately social relationships were mediated by argot; the vocations symbolizing critical relationships were therefore deemed important. If the figures chosen to represent these relationships appear less than praiseworthy, that is because argot tended to be demystifying and derogatory, thus operating on a kind of negative logic whereby that which was last came first, that which was most marginal and disreputable was accorded pride of place.

Anarchist theory and practice corresponded to the "negative logic" of argot in a number of ways. The central anarchist values of revolutionary spontaneity and direct action were paralleled linguistically in argot by the dominance of the concrete over the abstract, of the particular and local over the general and distant. The culture of argot had little use for delayed gratification, as exemplified either by the bourgeois work ethic or by the socialist faith in historical determinism. Neither could it become inspired by the prospect of parliamentary democracy; what politics it did profess were direct and participatory rather than representative. The bomb thrown by an anarchist into the Chamber of Deputies on December 9, 1893, expressed most graphically the disdain for mere words compared with the heroism of the deed. The pervasive terrorism of this "heroic" era of anarchism, which seems to have arisen spontaneously from below rather than conspiratorially from above as the police suspected, was the most overt form of anarchism's negative logic—the direct, purifying, and avenging act of violence. The bomb, called a *marmite* in argot after the iron pot that it resembled (although the commoner meaning of *marmite* was a prostitute who provided well for her pimp—his "pot" or meal ticket), spoke for the inarticulate masses more directly than the deputies' voices temporarily silenced by its crudely irrational impact.

Anarchism was not the only political movement to eschew the parliamentary forum for a more confrontational style, and the Sorelian cult of activism and violence, of means over ends, could feed into the radical anti-Semitism expressed during the Dreyfus Affair as well as into anarchism and anarcho-syndicalism. Both extreme right and left expressed their disenchantment with the Third Republic in an archaic vocabulary that appealed to traditional sectors of the artisanal and underclasses while looking forward to the new styles of mass demogoguery of the twentieth century. Insofar as style rather than ideological substance determined popular political preferences, anarchism's appeal was more akin to contemporary protofascist movements than to socialism. Anarchists moved reluctantly into the modern industrial world, casting a nostalgic glance back toward prepolitical figures of rebellion such as the criminal. This does not mean that anarchism was in fact a preindustrial movement existing anachronistically in modern Paris, any more than contemporary truck drivers who see themselves as cowboys and listen to country-western music are not entirely at home in industrial America. Just as the criminal and prostitute were important to the popular culture of anarchism because of their social marginality, so the anarchists' atavistic biases, their longing for a simpler, preindustrial age, were temporally marginal. In rejecting the urban present so totally, it was inevitable that they would envision the unknown future in terms of the familiar past. Argot provided them with familiar terms and themes drawn both from the past and from the underclass, both marginal relative to the social and political realities of the present.

To surpass the traditional mentality in envisioning a liberated social order required a transcendence of the archaic biases ensconced in argot. These biases were less libertarian than sullenly rebellious and, as argot's ambivalence toward figures of authority showed, could be evidence of sympathy for Caesarism on the right as well as for anarchism on the left. Charismatic figures, whether generals or terrorists, mobilized people more effectively than party programs, which explains why the anarchists prized terrorists such as Ravachol, the criminal-turned-anarchist-turned-martyr. Symbolic figures had more impact than did ideologues in the concretizing world of argot. It was Pouget's genius to realize that the high degree of in-group solidarity fostered by argot, its deprecatory and irreverent spirit, its illegalistic origins and biases, and its clarification of class distinctions and inequalities all made it a useful medium for anarchist propaganda against the social and political status quo. Yet finally, to consider argot as simply a useful tool misses its symbolic resonance for anarchists such as Emile Pouget or Félix Fénéon, the aesthete who sometimes contributed argot pieces on art to Pouget's paper. Argot itself metalinguistically signified the collective oral culture of the people, whose raucous voice was harsh but true, contemporaneous but rooted in the deepest folk traditions. Anarchism of the fin de siècle appealed profoundly to artists who saw in it the same message of resolute individualism and nonconformity that they imbibed from Nietzsche and Ibsen. Stéphane Mallarmé was one of a number of Symbolist writers who subscribed to *La Révolte* and contributed modest sums to anarchist causes. As opposed to this late Romantic *culte du moi,* Pouget sought the voice of the people (in the first decade of the twentieth century, Pouget edited an anarcho-syndicalist organ called *La Voix du Peuple*) as the authentic language of protest against the spirit and power of bougeois liberalism.

Five

When Emile Pouget declared that his goal was to write his anarchist newspaper *Le Père Peinard* in the language that the people spoke rather than that which the bourgeoisie wrote, he was acknowledging that the popular culture was essentially oral, not written. Pouget addressed his *canard* not to an illiterate class but to an oral culture; that is, he recognized that the lower classes did not simply lack certain middle-class linguistic skills, but possessed instead their own style of communication, which was direct, personal, and oral. To some extent, radical populism rather than anarchism made Pouget inclined to foster this indigenous style; after all, Hébert had similarly addressed the masses a century before in the *Père Duchesne*, and a paper with the same name and a similar format appeared during the Paris Commune. Yet anarchists were particularly sensitive to popular culture as an emblem of solidarity in the 1890s, and anarchists were much more likely than socialists to emphasize such cultural distinctions as that between orality and literacy rather than encouraging the workers to ape bourgeois speech and style. Pouget was not addressing a submerged, "underprivileged" class but a vital culture that possessed its own functional and expressive standards and that rejected the dominant prescriptive and aesthetic standards as politically and culturally alien. Formal grammar and vocabulary were the paradigm of bourgeois repressiveness; the *argotique* popular song was the expression of rebellious insouciance.

To say that the popular culture was primarily oral does not mean that the majority of French working-class people were illiterate, but that such literacy as did exist did not greatly affect working-class culture in general and popular artistic forms of expression in particular. The printed word, encountered by the workingpeople much more commonly in newspapers than in relatively costly books, expanded their horizons and politicized their culture. Frequently read aloud in one's favorite café, which often subscribed to the reading matter favored by its clientele, newspapers served primarily to provoke discussion rather than silent contemplation.[1] The popular press was a preeminently public medium reinforcing traditional patterns of sociability. Although the anarchists mastered the use of the press as a means of spreading revolutionary propaganda, they remained suspicious of literacy as a mode fostering habits of obedience and uniformity.[2] Orality reinforced class-based solidarity; literacy led to the age of the masses, homogeneous and isolated, controlled from above. The age of mass literacy led to what Flaubert with characteristic cynicism called "the age of received ideas," in which people mouthed the clichés fed to them by the appropriate authorities. Anarchists were never comfortable with the centralized control and conformity implicit in mass culture.

Ostensible literacy rates probably overstate the degree to which lower-class people could read with relative ease and, equally important, such statistics say little about how much they actually read. The rate of illiteracy declined markedly in the second half of the nineteenth century, from an estimated 40–45 percent in 1850 to 31 percent in 1872, down to 17 percent for French people aged ten or over in 1901. In 1890, the army found that 10 percent of conscripts were illiterate; by 1901, 12 percent of industrial workers and 14 percent of unemployed workers were said to be illiterate. A more encouraging figure yet emerges for Paris, where only 4 percent of the total adult population was illiterate in 1901. On the other hand, out of more than 6 million army recruits tested between 1881 and 1900, 8 percent could neither read nor write, 2 percent could read but not write, 87 percent could read and write but had not finished elementary school, and 3 percent possessed the *brévet de l'enseignement primaire* certifying that they had completed the requirements for a basic education. This suggests that between the 3 percent of the totally literate and the 8 percent of the illiterate lay a very large gray area of 89 percent semiliterates or quasi illiterates.[3]

In this situation in which widespread literacy was a recent phenomenon, in which the test for literacy often amounted to whether the husband and wife could sign their names to the marriage certificate, and in which the great majority of the lower classes still had minimal formal education, it appears likely that despite nominal literacy the oral culture persisted as the dominant means of expression and communication. It has been argued that reading remained a collective act annexed to the traditional culture for a very long time in France, and that the distinction between oral communication and reading became truly marked only with the spread of writing, which shifted the context of literacy decisively from the public sphere to that of private expression. This underscores the argument that newspapers read aloud and discussed in a café extended rather than departed from traditional oral culture. Even more suggestive is the same authors' suggestion that oral communication binds the immediate group, whereas written culture extends identification out to the market and the state as embodied in contracts and laws.[4] Anarchists willingly rejected the abstract, "written" state and market economy in favor of the more proximate solidarity of the community.

One would expect that the very fact of their politicization meant that most anarchist militants were in fact literate, and that their rate of literacy was higher than that of their lower-class brethren. The perfect model of the anarchist autodidact was Jean Grave, who began life as a cobbler, a trade common to many anarchists, and became editor of *La Révolte*. Among his readership there were doubtless other self-educated workers who struggled through the selections by Tolstoy and Kropotkin that Grave included in his weekly Literary Supplement. Pouget, on the other hand, though not of proletarian origins, set out to bridge the gap between the literate culture of the anarchist ideologues and the oral culture of the lower classes. Cabaret singers such as Aristide Bruant similarly bridged the oral and literate cultures, as Montmartre bohemia as a whole allowed the different classes to rub shoulders in its tolerant *déclassé* milieu. Anarchism can not be described solely as either an oral or literate culture, but contained elements of each.

Though it is difficult to separate out the respective influences of oral and literate cultures on anarchism, it is nonetheless critical to be aware of biases registered in the kinds of media available to the movement. The cultural distinction between orality and literacy is essentially one of class; lower-class anarchists lived in a culture of residual orality, middle- and upper-class anarchists were highly literate. As anarchism was also a movement in transition, the shift from oral to literate forms of communication may help to explain changes in its political and tactical orientation. Finally, anarchism had far more impact on the Latin cultures of Europe and South America than on Germanic and Anglo-Saxon countries. If Andalusian peasants were more open to anarchist influence than were German workers, part of the reason may be that anarchism inherently appealed to members of a less technologically developed oral culture. As with argot, so in a broader sense orality fundamentally structured the consciousness of many of the adherents of anarchism.

Considering lower-class anarchist culture as an oral culture may clarify one of the most perplexing problems with the movement in its presyndicalist phase: the seeming utter utopianism of its revolutionary project. The anarchists were never able to articulate how the policy of propaganda by the deed, known today as terrorism, would ever lead to a mass insurrection that could topple the state. Though Bakunin and Kropotkin had both authorized terrorism in earlier decades, by the 1890s many of the militant leaders had decided that propaganda by the deed was ineffective, and it was carried out in France primarily by the most *lumpen* elements of the lower class.[5] The terrorist acts thus percolated up from below rather than being orchestrated from above, as conspiracy-minded police agents and novelists liked to imagine.

If anarchist propaganda by the word and the deed was not instrumentally effective, it might instead attain a "magical" efficacy. In oral cultures, words and names are not just tags attached to the thing designated, but are intrinsically related to them. Uttering a name is seen to materially affect the person or object named, and thus one's name is often carefully guarded for fear of the power it can bestow on he who utters it. Name-calling and vituperation play a major part in oral or residually oral cultures, as does fulsome praise. Both define a "highly polarized, agonistic oral world of good and evil, virtue and vice, villains and heroes."[6] Oral cultures bestow power on words which effaces our literate distinction between causal and symbolic acts. Among the Zulus of southern Africa, for example, battles were sometimes decided by having each side choose a poet to represent them; he who best declaimed his verse won, thus demonstrating that the word was mightier than the sword.[7] Though words were clearly accorded a position of great importance, their effective power in this case depended on both sides agreeing to accept poetic arbitration. The words themselves were not powerful; their decisive role simply reflected the values of the culture in which they were spoken.

It seems plausible to assume that lower-class anarchists similarly confused semantically logical categories. Anarchism provided them with a polarized world view, leading them to believe that the resolution of the conflict between classes, or between authority and the people, was within their reach. Henri Leyret used the metaphor of "trumpets of the last judgment" in 1895 to describe the anarchists' attitude toward the bombs rocking Paris and elsewhere; when the walls of the city collapsed, the new anarchist Jerusalem could rise from the rubble.[8] The confusion between the prelude to revolution and the cause of one reveals the lack of a clear separation between two classic semiotic categories: an index pointing to something, and a symbol standing for something. The bomb was understood both as a sign indicating that the revolution was coming soon (an index) and a sign that indicated that that revolution would be similar to this prefigurative event (a symbol). Bombings were indeed symbolic events, but were of dubious indexical value, especially as it was easy to assume a causal link between merely contiguous events. This semiotic confusion between various kinds of signs and between signs and their referents was necessary to the spontaneity theory of revolution, by which the anarchists supposed that the people would rise up when aroused by some sufficiently stirring deed.

This attitude of apocalyptic expectation, brought on by some cosmic omen, is common to many cultures, and may be heightened by an oral culture's limited sense of linear historical time. Lacking written records of the past, members of oral cultures necessarily possess a radically different sense of time from that which we take for granted. The long-awaited event is always perceived as being just over the horizon, about to break through to the ever-expectant present. Such expectation is heightened tremendously by a portentous event such as a political assassination, when the symbol becomes an index, and the index is propelled by hope into the agent of change. This sense of "absolute presentness," which fostered the illusion that the revolution must come soon, shattering the continuity of historical time, was the single dominant feature by which Karl Mannheim characterized the chiliastic mentality, of which he saw the anarchists as the perfect modern exemplars.[9] Though the sense of temporality played a key role for Mannheim in distinguishing between various forms of what he termed the utopian mentality, he did not relate these ideal types to the distinction between oral and literate cultures. If the mentality of socialists and anarchists differed as much as

Mannheim suggested, this would have affected their respective ideologies profoundly. Bakuninist insurrectionism reflected the ahistorical, chiliastic mind-set of an oral culture; Marxist historical determinism was the ideology of more literate classes (bourgeois parliamentary socialists and their industrial working-class followers). Mannheim believed that the anarchistic mentality was waning, having been surpassed by socialist historicism just as Bakunin had lost control of the First International and as industrial workers had supplanted peasants and artisans in the modern economy. Mannheim wrote half a century ago, yet since then peasants have played a central role in the revolutions of the Third World, while the culture of literacy may well have declined in the media-saturated West. The importance of such mentalities can be maintained more confidently than the definitive triumph of one or the other.

In the ahistorical mental universe of orality, great events play an especially important mnemonic role, epitomizing in a single act a complex ideology, and thereby enduring in people's memories long after speeches have been forgotten. Action speaks louder than words, though even words directly experienced have a physical component. Parliamentary speeches would clearly have minimal impact on an argot-speaking dweller of the Parisian faubourgs, certainly less than a personal anarchist harangue or word of a violent deed. Furthermore, epics and other oral genres typically feature high levels of physical violence—the *Iliad* of Homer is an outstanding example.[10] Literate civilization is not more peaceful than orally based traditional cultures, but it is more impersonal; members of oral cultures respond to the personal confrontational style inherent in oral communication, rhetorically and physically. Oral cultures have need of *terribles simplificateurs*.

Whereas the faubourg dwellers would hear about terrorist acts by word-of-mouth or, if they were literate, read about them in the newspaper, they might witness personally the public execution of the terrorist. For the individual whose culture is primarily oral, public rituals satisfy the need for unmediated experience, memorialize notable events, and evoke events in the past that might otherwise be forgotten. The great guillotine set up in the place de la Roquette, in the heart of the faubourgs; executioner Deibler in his black stovepipe hat; the condemned anarchist's awareness of the importance of maintaining his *sang-froid* in the face of death; perhaps especially his final words, declaimed so well by Emile Henry on the scaffold—*"Courage camarades, Vive l'anarchie"*: all heightened the dramatic impact of this most poignant of public events. The repetition of this scene gave to the terrorists' words the authority of supraindividual ritual and accentuated the nobility of their self-sacrifice, which in turn increased anarchism's quasi-religious status. In this oral culture, deeds preceded and gave added weight to words, whose impact was strengthened by their public and ritual character. As each terrorist sacrificed his life for the cause, so his individuality was subsumed into a type, making both his own deed and anarchism in general appear less contingent and more as an implacable natural force.

All oral communication must involve some social interaction, unlike literate communication which normally occurs silently and privately. Oral culture is therefore more demandingly public than literate culture and places more emphasis on rhetorical skill. The trial of accused anarchists thus became a showplace of anarchist bravado and resolution, with the accused frequently making speeches justifying whatever deed they had committed. The terrorist Emile Henry used his trial to justify rather than mitigate his acts, even confessing to *attentats* that had not been attributed to him (possibly to forestall the arrest of his accomplices). Ravachol likewise claimed sole responsibility for his deeds and argued that they had been carried out to serve the cause, while the judge tried to show that his murders and robberies were only self-serving. The most brilliant display of verbal repartee was undoubtedly that of the art critic Félix Fénéon, whose witty rejoinders to the prosecutor in the Procès de Trente were widely reported in the Parisian press. At the same trial, the government feared that the anarchist orator Sebastien Faure would use the courtroom to his own advantage, and therefore conducted his examination and that of Jean Grave behind closed doors. Of course, what the government really feared was not their words per se but the reporting of them in the press; their discourses depended on the written word for their propagation.

Whatever the public impact of propaganda by the deed, it never replaced the more mundane dissemination of the anarchist message by speeches and word of mouth. Anarchists proselytized tirelessly, and whether they were gifted and famous orators or simple *compagnons*, many traveled widely to promote their violent gospel. Wandering *tri-mardeurs* went from town to town spreading the word and passing out leaflets. Often they were journeymen who propagandized while making the traditional *tour de France,* seeking sympathetic ears among their fellow tradesmen. Among the well-known anarchist militants was the "traveling salesman" of anarchy, Sebastien Faure, who on a typical tour in the fall of 1891 covered the greater part of France, especially the region between Lyon and Marseille, Bordeaux, the Loire, and the industrial north around Lille where anarchism was most active. In the Lyon region alone Faure made forty speeches, averaging an impressive 683 listeners per speech for a total audience of over 27,000. He also sold 2,000 of his own brochures and distributed 134,000 leaflets. An even more famous anarchist orator was Louise Michel, the "red virgin of the Commune," who died in 1905 in the course of one of these tours. Her body was brought by train from Marseille to Paris, where 100,000 people accompanied it to the cemetery.[11] At a time when the government feared large open-air gatherings and consequently restricted public speech more than freedom of the press, the anarchists were notable for pursuing oral discourse. As a sympathetic observer noted in 1904, "the section of society which is freest from this [governmental] intolerance, and readiest to tolerate diversity of opinion in discussion, is the Anarchist section, who are, also, practically the only people who attempt to establish publicly the right of free meetings."[12]

Music and singing, the preeminent artistic expressions of Parisian popular culture, also formed an integral part of the anarchists' own gatherings. The act of collective singing blurred the distinction between meetings and social gatherings. At one such meeting of anarchists in October 1889, which the police informer "Jean" said was typical of the genre, speeches were followed by a lengthy session of communal singing. The anarchist orator Sebastien Faure being absent, the piano was badly played, "Jean" reported wryly. He concluded his report, "The meeting, or rather the concert, ended at midnight." The *compagnons* sang "Les Pieds plats" (The Flat Feet—undoubtedly a reference to the police), "Le Père Lapurge," "La Mort d'un brave," and similar songs. Brunet, composer of "Faut plus de gouvernement" (No More Need of the Government), terminated the series with a crude new song: "Bourgeois, you constipate us / With your great principles / Your laws and your virtues."[13] These songs were more concerned with venting the anarchists' anger at the dominant order than with vague references to future harmony. As anarchism diverged from socialism in its concern for direct action, these songs differed from the cabaret offerings of the socially realistic singers by their violence and activism. They simultaneously painted a picture of despair amid a rotten society and the means of vengeance if not of social change. "La Mort d'un brave" described the situation of an old man who, poor and shivering on New Year's Day, was roused to fury by the mere sight of a haughty bourgeois, as if the holiday made social inequities all the starker. As he planted his knife in the rich man's throat, he said softly to himself, "in the ecstasy of a last dream / It is thus that a vagabond dies." Quoted in *L'Eclair* on December 18, 1893, the song was compared to the remarkably similar statement of Léauthier, an anarchist who attacked the Serbian ambassador: "I was at the end of my resources. I did not want to live submissively; I spotted a bourgeois of haughty and ornate appearance, and I planted my dagger in his throat." A song by Pierre Dupont called "Pain" (Bread) affirmed that "Everything goes, to steal, to kill / When our bellies are hungry."[14]

Not all anarchist productions dealt with violent deeds; most of Paul Paillette's repertoire sketched a happy future of free love and harmony with nature. What the songs like the movement most lacked was a way of bridging the gap between reactive means and utopian ends. The songs did contain a political prescription, defining what was wrong with society and what was to be done, but generally lacked the perception of present-day reality so sharply etched in the works of Bruant or Jouy or Yvette Guilbert. In a sense, the violent and utopian songs were linked by their shared element of fantasy, by their desire to negative immediate reality either by destruction or transcendence. Activists and idealists who had little grasp of pragmatic solutions were seemingly inspired with a mystical faith in their ultimate triumph by the collective art of singing. Oral culture was not sufficient to guarantee a utopian mentality, but rather reinforced utopian habits of thinking among the politicized members of that culture.

At least twenty songs praised the anarchist *attentats* as vengeance for all of the working class. They generally did not record specific deeds, but rather ridiculed the daily fear of the bourgeoisie, as in the song which recounted the discovery of a little spherical object in the street ("La

Bombe à renversement," 1893). "Le Faubourg St.-Germain" (1892) did celebrate the bombing of that aristocratic quarter, but "La Frousse" (1892) was more characteristic with such lines as "Everyone is afraid / Of a blast of dynamite." Two songs censored for their anarchist content, "Les Libertaires" (1892) and "Comment on devient anarchiste" (How One Becomes an Anarchist, 1893), instead of glorifying terrorists evoked hypersensitive artistic types who wished to live intensely.[15]

Not all anarchist songs were contemporary ones. They also tapped such traditional sources of protest as the "Père Duchesne," the revolutionary song whose first four stanzas dated from the Directory, the fifth and sixth from the bloody June Days of 1848. On his walk to the scaffold, Ravachol loudly intoned the blasphemous verse that suggested cutting the priests in two, razing the churches and dethroning God, and hanging the landlord.[16] Ravachol's name was applied to an updated version of the French Revolutionary "Carmagnole," whose old refrain "Vive le son de l'explosion" seemed newly relevant in the era of dynamite, and emphasized the explosive's auditory effect. Pouget printed words and music of "La Ravachole" alongside Charles Maurin's woodcut of the terrorist martyr in his *Almanach du Père Peinard* of 1894. ("Ravacholiser" also enjoyed some success as a verb meaning "to blow up.") In a collection of songs published by Jean Grave's *Les Temps Nouveaux* sometime in the late 1890s, the "Marseillaise" was labeled the bourgeois theme, and the "Carmagnole" was claimed by the lower classes. In printing the song, the anarchist editor apologized for having to delete the more recent stanzas that were deemed an incitement to violence and forbidden under *les lois scélérates*.[17]

On Saturday and Sunday evenings the workers too gathered together in cafés to drink and sing songs that were occasionally patriotic but, when allowed, also revolutionary. On New Year's Eve, 1894, Henri Leyret's cafe could remain open all night long, and despite police warnings he did not ban political songs. Later that year he recalled how

socialist songs, anarchist songs, all the revolutionary repertoire was performed, to the joy of all. I note that there were about fifty people there. . . . In the midst of thunderous applause a voice had sung [a revolutionary song] that sufficed to awaken the revolutionary instinct. [Applause] was to he who would sing the most violent and emphatic refrain of the Carmagnole. . . . That lasted from ten in the evening till

six in the morning: not once was the Marseillaise requested, no one dreamed of singing it. On the other hand, some declaimed a socialist Marseillaise, another launched some couplets which, if the new laws of general security had then existed, would have sent him to prison . . . and me with him. Among other things, I believe it recommended the use of dynamite. . . . But there was no cry of protest, no less applause. That happened twenty days after Vaillant's *attentat*.[18]

On requesting a permit to stay open late two weeks later, he was turned away peremptorily at the police commissariat. Spontaneous outbursts in a café were generally free of censorship, but at the height of police suspicion of anarchist activity, such bravado in public suggested at least disdain of the authorities, if not outright hostility. The social context of group singing was an important stimulus to class identification whatever the ideological content of the songs sung there.

The neighborhood café occupied the heart of lower-class culture; one step up was the cabaret, which retailed popular culture to anyone willing to listen, pay, and drink. Whereas cafés and bars were distributed throughout the working-class *quartiers,* cabarets tended to locate in special entertainment centers. Zola portrayed the working-class bar as a daily haunt in *L'Assommoir*; Gervaise and Coupeau sought entertainment at the circus or cabaret only on special occasions, though their wayward daughter Nana willingly displayed her charms at Montmartre's dance halls. The suggestive atmosphere of the dance hall and cabaret offered her a way out of the working class and into the *demi-monde,* though for Zola this was a morally equivocal step. Lower-class people did frequent dance halls such as the famous Moulin de la Galette on the slopes of Montmartre, and sometimes watched the can-can dancers do the *quadrille naturaliste* at the Moulin Rouge. They sipped their drinks in a cabaret and listened to a singer such as Jules Jouy or Yvette Guilbert intone ballads about people like themselves, in that era of socially realistic songs. Because professional entertainment cost more than the participatory pleasures of the café or dance hall, the percentage of lower to middle classes in the audience went down at the café-concert, and dropped nearly out of sight at the theater and concert hall.

The cabaret was a way up for the performers as well, and some became quite wealthy. Compared to artists in literary genres, cabaret singers were more likely to issue from the lower social strata.[19] Some singers had turned toward the cabarets after failing to find a space for themselves in an overcrowded and unremunerative poetic market. While these suffered from a sense of *déclassement,* others tried to use their popularity as a springboard for political office. Though Aristide Bruant failed in his legislative bid, Maurice Boukay (pseudonym for Charles Couyba) managed to enter the Chamber of Deputies in 1896 after performing at the Chat Noir and the Quat'z'Arts. Boukay had the advantage of a university background and had taught at the Lycée Arago before embarking on his Montmartre career. He later became a senator and finally a minister, apparently of imprecise political tendency despite his early stance as a militant leftist, as recorded in his collection of *Chansons Rouges,* illustrated by Steinlen and published in 1897.[20]

Boukay's popular "Moulin Rouge" exemplifies the integration of social criticism and popular sentiment. Despite the role of the miller in the song, the real Moulin Rouge was only a mock-up of once-functioning windmills such as the Moulin de la Galette, yet it clearly symbolized Montmartre's role as leaven of a better social order, as well as a place where the poor could forget their suffering amid the joys of drink and the flesh. The sensory stimuli of this surrogate paradise sometimes impeded the social critique that its singers intoned. The miller sings the first stanza and the chorus to his mill, which replies:

> Sur la hauteur, tout près des cieux
> Quand la nuit descend sur la terre,
> On voit s'allumer les grands yeux
> Du bruyant moulin de Cythère . . .
> Dis-nous pour qui tu mouds ton grain
> Moulin, pour qui tournent tes ailes?
> Mouds-tu la joie ou le chagrin?
> Mouds-tu pour eux, mouds-tu pour elles?
>
> Moulin Rouge,
> Moulin Rouge,
> Pour qui mouds-tu, Moulin Rouge?
> Pour la Mort ou pour l'Amour?
> Pour qui mouds-tu, jusqu'à jour?
>
> Je mouds pour que les nains, les fous,
> Les désherités, les malades

Aient, moyennant quarante sous,
Leur part d'amour et des ballades . . .

Je mouds pour que les meurt-de-faim,
Oubliant que leur ventre gronde,
S'enivrent des rhythmes sans fin
Et des visions de chair blonde . . .
Sur la montagne des Martyrs
Je mouds le Rêve et l''Harmonie . . .
Je mouds un avenir meilleur
Par la croix rouge des mes ailes!

(On the heights, close to the heavens
When night falls on the earth
One sees light up the large eyes
Of the noisy mill of Venus . . .
Tell us for whom you mill your grain
Mill, for whom turn your blades?
Do you mill joy or sorrow?
Do you mill for men or for women?

Moulin Rouge,
Moulin Rouge,
For whom do you mill, Moulin Rouge?
For Death or for Love?
For whom do you mill till dawn?

I mill so that the dwarves, the madmen,
The disinherited, the sick,
Can have, by means of forty sous,
Their share of love and ballads . . .

I mill so that those dying of hunger,
Forgetting that their bellies growl,
Get drunk on the endless rhythms
And visions of pale flesh . . .
On the mountain of Martyrs
I mill the Dream and Harmony
I mill a better future
By the red cross of my blades!)[21]

Typifying the popular leftism current in the Montmartre cabarets, the apotheosis of the dream and of harmony of "Moulin Rouge" displayed familiarity with anarchist rhetoric, but the deputy was more of a "Chat-noiriste" than an anarchist. His fellow singer Jehan Rictus was possibly thinking of Boukay when he wrote, "tout les genr's de révoltés / Qui finniss'nt par et' . . . députés!" (all the types of insurgents / Who end up as deputies!).[22]

More radical in argotique style and political content was "Les Lanternes" of the colorful bohemian Yon Lug, who paraded in the 1896 Vachalcade as a prolo Jesus, leading a tame bear and wearing a copper halo. The song, subtitled "Aventure rouge," portrayed an anarchist whose drink-loosened tongue got him in trouble:

> Une nuit, un anarchiste
> Qu'était ouvrier fumiste
> Avait bu p't'être un peu trop
> C'qui fait qu'il était poivrot.
> Il disait dans sa soûl'rie:
> "Du sang! plus de bourgeoisie!
> "Faut qu'on pend' les proprios
> "Au gaz, qu'éclair' les prolos!"

> (One night, an anarchist
> Who was a half-hearted worker
> Had drunk perhaps a bit too much
> And that made him quite drunk.
> He said in his drunkenness:
> Some blood! no more bourgeoisie!
> We must hang the proprietors from
> The lamp-post which lights the workers!)

The unfortunate worker was hauled into the police station, after which the song sagely concluded:

> La moral' de cett' romance,
> C'est qu'en pareill' circonstance,
> Anarchiste ou pas du tout,
> Faut pas aimer étant saoûl.

    (The moral of this romance
    Is that in such circumstances
    Anarchist or not at all
    One shouldn't like getting drunk.)[23]

The idea of hanging one's landlord was probably suggested by the sixth stanza of the "Père Duchesne." "Les Lanternes" and to a lesser extent "Moulin Rouge" were part of a trend toward increasingly class-conscious songs in the 1890s.[24]

If Aristide Bruant has a claim to immortality beyond that bequeathed him by Toulouse-Lautrec's famous poster of the singer clad in red and black, a street tough loitering ominously in the shadows, it is as the singer of the life of the faubourgs, rendered in the argot of the people of whom he sang. Laurent Tailhade called him the sole true poet of argot since François Villon and contrasted his songs favorably with Jean Richepin's *Chansons des gueux* (Songs of Scondrels), which Tailhade felt lacked sincerity and empathy for their heroes.[25] Many years later the lifelong socialist Alexandre Zévaès (Bourson) wrote a book recalling his youthful memories of Aristide Bruant, in which he admirably pinned down the class of people evoked in Bruant's songs:

It is not the claims of the worker, the proletariat; it is not the revolt of the employees weighed down by the crushing domination of capital: the personages of Bruant ignore the road of the workshop and the factory. It's the lament of the wretched, the trembling, those without clothes and without lodging who don't know where they'll sleep the night, the pariah's cry of sadness. . . . It is the continual deception of those whose inclement lot and economic injustice condemn to vice, that elder son of poverty and social disorder.[26]

Zévaès specified that the dealers in vice were those that the law of March 27, 1885 called "special vagabonds," referring to them by three of their commonest argot names: *dos, dos vert,* and *marlou.* These were the pimps such as Toto Laripette who died at the hands of executioner Deibler; others died in the streets they ruled. Zévaès too noted the similarity with Villon (as did Francis Carco), but ended his book by withdrawing the comparison. He contrasted Bruant's two volumes of *Dans la rue* that appeared in 1889 and 1895 with his later collection of songs entitled *Sur la route,* published in 1899, which showed the singer to be a complacent proprietor who wished his son to inherit his wealth, defend his country and faith, and die a proprietor (his son was to die an officer in World War I).[27]

Bruant did not simply sell out his constituency; rather, his political attitudes evolved in a very telling manner from a vague sort of popular socialism. As early as 1891 the Naturalist writer in argot Oscar Métenier noted that the one institution for which Bruant banned mockery in his cabaret was the army.[28] Nevertheless, "A Biribi," published in volume two of *Dans la rue,* condemned the army's penal camps in Africa, made infamous by the 1889 novel of the same name by Georges Darien. The Montmartre singer Léon de Bercy, who collaborated with Bruant on his dictionary, recounted in 1902 Bruant's legislative election campaign of May 1898. Supported in his campaign by a former anarchist named Michel Morphy, Bruant ran as the people's candidate for Belleville, the lower-class quarter just southeast of Montmartre. He proclaimed himself an enemy of "capitalist feudalism and cosmopolite Jewry, true Union of Treason organized against France." He lost the election to the socialist candidate, but *Sur la route,* which appeared the next year, contained lyrics of a pronounced anti-Semitic and nationalist character.[29]

Bruant's aggressive championship of the most self-assertively masculine and criminal elements of popular culture, his sentimental portrayal of the vagabond at the mercy of economic forces beyond his comprehension, combined with his pandering to the "high life" at his popular cabaret, foreshadowed nationalist socialist leanings in the style of Maurice Barrès's campaign of 1898. As Barrès has been accused of protofascist tendencies for substituting anti-Semitism and xenophobia in place of class struggle as a solution to the problems of French workers and *déclassés,* so Bruant may be termed a protofascist for tendering a similar solution couched in a vague populist rhetoric.[30] All populists were not fascists, but the appeal to the *Lumpenproletariat* that the Nazis exploited so cleverly bore remarkable similarity to the butchers of La Villette who followed the anti-Semitic demagoguery of the marquis de Morès in the 1890s. Theirs was the sort of rebelliousness that Bruant championed in his *cabaret brutal.*

Attitudes toward Bruant's theatrical patronizing of the *Tout-Paris* who flocked to the Mirliton for an evening of slumming varied greatly.

On the one hand, Laurent Tailhade praised him highly even after the election campaign, while throughout his cabaret days the lifelong anarchist Théophile-Alexandre Steinlen illustrated his songs and was considered Bruant's alter ego.[31] Yet Francis Jourdain recalled Bruant as a *poseur* who knew that songs of crime and low-life sold well. He considered his theatrical costume to be facilely picturesque, while his self-professed *cabaret artistique* appeared to be bourgeois-bohemian. Jourdain claimed that Toulouse-Lautrec preferred the less equivocal atmosphere of the café-concert despite the famous posters he made for the singer.[32] Bruant himself loudly proclaimed his disdain for the

pile of idiots who do not understand what I sing to them, who cannot understand, not knowing what it is to die from hunger, those who have come to the world with a silver spoon in their mouths. I revenge myself in insulting them, in treating them worse than dogs. That makes them laugh to tears; they believe that I joke when, often enough, it is a breeze from the past, miseries submitted to, dirtiness seen, which remounts on my lips and makes me speak as I do.[33]

Bruant was nevertheless the single most influential popularizer of the Parisian *déclassé* subculture during the 1890s, the most important exploiter of the argot vein (with the possible exception of Pouget), and a powerful if sentimental voice for the subproletariat. Contrasting the subjects treated in Bruant's songs with those of Paul Paillette's *Tablettes d'un lézard* will clarify the political implications of appealing to this cultural milieu. Paillette's volume appeared in several different editions in the late 1880s and early 1890s and was also written in argot. Paillette was the most resolutely anarchistic singer of the epoch, whereas Bruant displayed the right-wing populism that was becoming increasingly common in the 1890s (see Table 2).

The 1895 edition of *Dans la rue* contained Bruant's most political song, "Pus d'patrons." The protagonist said he was a "socialist republican, Comrade, ultra radical, Revolutionary, anarchist, etc., etc." He admitted that most of what the orators said was beyond him, but "it's of a biblical simplicity. First don't need the government, then the Republic isn't necessary . . . no laws, no army, no church, none of that, none of anything. Then we can be our own masters, be lazy every day and Monday. [Then the worker scratched his head as he uttered the punch

Table 2: Content Analysis of Songs by Aristide Bruant and Paul Paillette

	No. of Songs	
Subject Matter	Bruant	Paillette
Prostitution (both pimps and prostitutes)	4	5
Prostitutes	6	0
Pimps	11	3
Lower-class girls	2	0
Women as artists' ideal	0	1
Male-female relations, marriage, and family	2	4
Idealized love, critique of chastity	0	3
Free love	0	21
Laziness	2	1
Attack on bourgeois morality, hypocrisy	0	3
Prison settings, guillotine	5	0
Thieves	4	0
Army	3	0
Drink and drunks	3	0
Working class	2	1
Class violence, consciousness, revolt	3	9
Poverty and bums	6	0
Pets	1	1
Argot	0	1
Writers and artists	0	2
Natural harmony; evil state, civilization	0	7
Miscellaneous	7	0
Total	61	62

Songs with regions of Paris in the title:

Outer arrondissements	8	1
		(Montmartre)
Inner arrondissements	4	0
Prisons	4	0
Bois de Vincennes, Boulogne	2	0
Paris	0	1

Based on Bruant, *Dans la rue,* 2 vols. (Paris: Aristide Bruant, 1889, 1895), and Paillette, *Tablettes d'un lézard* (Paris: Librairie Nouvelle, 1892).

line] But if there are no more bosses, who will pay us on Saturday?" These last four lines are quoted in Delesalle's 1896 argot dictionary as an example of the word *flemme,* "laziness." Bruant was humorously implying that the real goal of anarchist idealists was to get out of working for a living, yet it is significant that he equated the radical with the idler. Of the sixty-one songs in his two volumes of *Dans la rue,* two others dealt explicitly with the *fainéant* who would do anything to avoid work. Two songs featured working-class settings: one the lament of a gravedigger, the other, entitled "Greviste," about workers on strike. This latter, despite Steinlen's industrial images and drawings of dead workers, was curiously apolitical in its lyrics. It concerned a worker who refused to work in the unsafe conditions of the steam plants; each verse ended "Respect your limbs." There were many more songs about impoverished bums than about the working class.

An analysis of the two volumes of songs demonstrates concerns remarkably similar to those revealed in Bruant's and the other dictionaries of argot. Thieves and crimes were less important in Bruant's songs, whereas sexual matters dominated all other categories. Bruant cited nearly three hundred terms for prostitute and perhaps one-fifth as many for pimp in his dictionary; in *Dans la rue* the emphasis was reversed, with twice as many songs dealing with pimps as with whores and several more detailing their interactions. "A la villette" showed a pimp awaiting the guillotine; the "Marche des dos" portrayed the pimps celebrating their good fortune in having a *marmite,* or a whore who provided well for her man. For one of this happy band luck ran out early, as the song ended with a pimp facing executioner Deibler at the scaffold. "Les Vrais Dos" concerned a class-conscious pimp who called the rich man with the woman in furs the real pimp and said that he would smash him if it was not for the *sergots* (police). In "Les Petits joyeux," a pimp got drafted into the army but "les marlous aim'nt pas l'gouvernement" (the pimps don't like the government). Pimps dealt not only in sex but also in violence, often committing other crimes as well. Bruant portrayed them as rebels who viewed the rich as customers to be exploited or robbed, and the government as something to keep one's distance from. Bruant once confided to an interviewer that the pimps of Montmartre believed he was one of them, an impression he fostered.[34]

The sexual milieu was the street scene of unlicensed prostitutes and pimps. No song described the courtesan or kept woman, few took place in brothels. None contrasted the streetwalker with the courtesan or even dwelt on her fantasies of success. The perspective was rather that of the pimp who wished to keep his woman working for him; her desires were secondary. Not upward mobility into the ranks of the bourgeoisie, but the battle of the sexes formed the major motif of Bruant's songs (over one-third the total number of songs) dealing with prostitution; lesser themes suggested poverty or family troubles as reasons for women becoming prostitutes; others described animosity toward the client or toward each other, as in the song in which the pimp told his woman to take advantage of the customers, for it was "mort aux vaches" (death to the "cows"). Using his women, contributing only protection by the threat of violence, proud of his status as one who did not work, the position of the pimp was equivocal at best. And yet it was the pimp rather than the prostitute, the worker, the soldier, or the thief who dominated the popular Parisian social world as depicted by Bruant. The traits that identified this king of the streets—laziness, violence, exploitiveness, expressive masculinity, and argot-filled speech—made of him a peculiar but revealing culture hero of the lower classes. It was not an image likely to be cultivated by the socialists, and even anarchists who admired his antiauthoritarian temperament would shy away from his exploitation of sexuality. Combining asocial violence with an imitation of bourgeois exploitiveness transposed to the "milieu," Bruant's pimps projected a latently fascist cultural image that reflected the singer's own political tendencies.

Bruant not only identified the social milieu but also located it with geographic specificity. Nearly one-third of the songs in *Dans la rue* referred to particular quarters of Paris in their titles. By far the largest number took place in the northern outer quarters—Montmartre, La Chapelle, La Goutte d'Or, Batignolles, Saint-Ouen, and Belleville-Ménil-montant—and the area appears more predominant if one includes the songs set in prisons, most of which were located in the same area. This was the region with which Bruant, from his Montmartre base, was most familiar. It was also among the heaviest working-class areas of Paris, rivaling the eastern and southern outer arrondissements. Interestingly, the twentieth arrondissement, already part of the eastern "red belt" in terms of political allegiance, was more solidly working class than the northern arrondissements and had about half the number of clerks and office workers as the areas sung about by Bruant.[35] A similar economic makeup characterized Montrouge and Grenelle in the southern quadrant of the city; the latter areas also housed the Ecole Militaire. The older, more central areas were Montparnasse, La Bastille, and the *places* Maubert and La Madeleine. This latter, the only exclusive quarter featured by Bruant, was the locale of a song in which a pimp mused about the possibilities such a rich quarter might afford.

Tracing the voting patterns of Bruant's chosen arrondissements in the elections of 1893 reveals an area that was leftist but less completely so than the eastern red belt. Whereas the entire eastern third of Paris voted more than 60 percent socialist, the northern edge of the city voted 50–60 percent socialist, and the quarter of Montmartre 40–50 percent socialist. Abstentions, a significant factor given the anarchist attitude toward elections, were higher in Batignolles and Montmartre than in the rest of the northern and eastern sector. Perhaps more significant yet were the election results of 1889 when General Boulanger threatened to topple the Third Republic amid popular acclaim. Some 40–50 percent of the northern and northeastern edge of Paris voted for Boulangist candidates compared to 20–30 percent for the twentieth arrondissement.[36] The marginal urban areas in which Bruant situated his songs of poverty, prostitution, and violence were poor but less completely working-class oriented than the eastern region stretching from the faubourg Saint-Antoine to Montreuil. Both their economic makeup, which included sizable petit bourgeois elements, and their voting patterns indicated anarchist and radical rightist as well as socialist support. Certainly Aristide Bruant selected his themes for their sentimental and popular appeal, but he did not misrepresent the cultural disposition of his milieu.

Paul Paillette was far less well known in his own time than Bruant, and his anonymity has kept pace with Bruant's immortality. His birth and death dates have gone unrecorded, though Léon de Bercy estimated that Paillette was "not far from sixty" in 1902. Even twenty years before, de Bercy wrote, "he was already the indomitable anarchist that one knows." He recalled that in 1894, after "the special laws against the anarchists," Paillette was overheard singing "J'm'en-foutiste" (I don't give a damn) in the Ville Japonaise. As a result, the cabaret was closed for several months, and Paillette was not heard in public for some time.

Paillette published his poems and songs progressively in sixteen-page editions under the collective title *Tablettes d'un lézard,* which de Bercy estimated ran to 10,000 verses. The police informer "Jean" wrote that Paillette was perhaps the sole anarchist singer with some talent, and that he played mostly in *soirées familiales.*[37]

The 1892 edition of Paillette's *Tablettes d'un lézard* contained sixty-four songs, virtually the same number as in Bruant's two volumes, and like Bruant's they were written in the popular speech, though fewer words were pure argot (such as *kif-kif*) and more tended toward ideological abstraction (*harmonie, nature, anarchie*). By twisting popular attitudes as expressed in argot terms such as "C'est kif-kif" (it's all the same to me) or "J'm'en-foutiste" to suit an ideological function, Paillette tried to uncover the latent anarchism in the discourse itself. He was less skilled than Bruant at situating this discourse in its Parisian locale.

Sexual motifs abounded in Paillette's songs as in Bruant's. Bruant's sex was bought and sold, combative and exploited—a metaphor for the existing capitalist society—whereas Paillette idealistically devoted one-third of all his songs to the theme of free love. Nor did he ignore the role of sex in contemporary French society; in at least ten other songs he criticized chastity, idealized romance, the institution of marriage and the family, and bourgeois hypocrisy and morality in general. Sex and love were absolutely central to Paillette's notion of nonrepressive anarchist liberation, and songs such as "Amour libre" equated anarchism and the sex drive ("Free love is harmony / The incessant communion / The sane moral blessed / By life in erection"). In "Cupidon l'anarchiste," Cupid claimed he would break up the family, whose sanctity was made possible by the existence of prostitution. The sex drive was the natural ally of anarchism, undermining the hypocrisy of bourgeois morality, family, and private property. His most utopian vision was expressed in "Heureux Temps," where he wrote that "in the time of anarchy / Nature will be a paradise of love / Woman sovereign / Slave of today, tomorrow our queen / We will seek your 'orders of the day.'" As J. J. Bachofen sought his matriarchies in the past, Paillette situated them in a future when humanity and nature would be reconciled. Another song, "Enfant de la nature," concluded in heavy capitals, "Vive l'Anarchie! Vive l'Amour!" Paillette belonged to the Montmartre anarchist group L'Etat Naturel that exaggerated anarchism's Rousseauan tendencies in preaching the abolition of modern technology and the return to a hunting and gathering society. Nature was frequently invoked by the anarchists as a standard with which to contrast the artificiality of contemporary society. Human sexuality would be liberated from the hypocrisy and restraints imposed on humankind's natural drives by civilization.

Paillette condemned prostitution as the exploitation of lower-class women by upper-class men. He presented the prostitute sympathetically but described the pimp as a supporter of the status quo and a worthless idler. Far from condemning idleness, Paillette wrote one song in praise of *flâneurs,* and the title of his whole collection signified laziness, since a lizard in popular parlance was one who lay about in the sun. Not idleness but exploitive maleness was the charge leveled not only at the pimps celebrated by Bruant, but at the whole aggressive and competitive society. Prostitutes were only the clearest example of nature being corrupted by materialism.

Paillette's identification with the sluggish lizard reflected his Rousseauan ambivalence toward modernity. In the powerful prose-poem entitled "Homme" (Man) with which *Tablettes d'un lézard* opened, man was viewed as a being in perpetual motion in a chaotic civilization, all busy-ness. Paillette's persona inquired, "Do you know what the lizard sings in the sun? / Bastille-Madeleine Man! / Steam Man! Electric Man." Modernity's careening course, symbolized especially by the railroad, was cursed by the bohemian who knew that he was being passed by.

Neither Bruant nor Paillette suggested the worker as the alternate model to the *déclassé*; neither perceived labor to be an inherently ennobling activity, the fount of all real value in the Marxian sense. Paillette was deeply distrustful of technology; Bruant, a former clerk for the Northern Railway Company, sang of, and in a largely preindustrial environment, maintained the illusion of a country estate at his Montmartre mansion, and retired in 1895 to Courtenay to live as a *châtelain*.[38] Bruant offered much sentiment but little critique of the society he depicted so vividly; Paillette couched his social criticism in natural-sexual terms.

One other poet-singer of Montmartre declared himself against "the very brutalizing myth of Work." Gabriel Randon, who went by the name Jehan Rictus, engaged in anarchist journalistic activity from 1892 to 1894, first published his verses in 1894, but went totally unnoticed until he began to present his *Soliloques du pauvre* on the stage of the Quat'z'Arts cabaret in 1896. He attracted the praise of Laurent Tailhade, who noted that "that anarchist has doubled as chronicler."[39] No one was more taken with him than the radical Catholic writer and perpetual Montmartrois Léon Bloy. Considering Rictus to be the virtual embodiment of the Christ of the poor, with his long, thin face and dolorous expression, Bloy printed a long letter that Rictus had written to him, dated October 4, 1900, in which Rictus justified his social and linguistic position in response to Bloy's earlier protest against the coarseness of his language:

If there is something I've tried to denounce in the popular language it is the Dogma of Work without Love, so dear to the capitalists and to Zola, and the goal that I have proposed for myself . . . to paint, to express the state of servitude and absolute abasement of the modern helot that is the industrial worker, the miserable and mechanical Child of the Tool and of the Machine. . . . Be assured that one day I will have in my hands, with means of action, a terrible popular force, and if that ever happens I will not leave standing a single wall of the bourgeois edifice. All is better, even a return to barbarism, to the primitive cavern, than such a social organization.[40]

Forty years later a highly critical biographer claimed that Rictus, who died in 1934 a member of the Legion of Honor, ended his life aligned with the Action Française.[41]

In 1900 Rictus was still an anarchist who explained that he used popular speech "to provoke horror and terror . . . it matters that the Bourgeois suspect the suffering they cause, the crimes of which their hypocrisy and egoism suffocate the clamor . . . how could I have done so without employing the same words of the crushed?"[42] Rictus used the popular idiom to further identify with the people whose cause he championed. His letter to Bloy identified these people as industrial workers forced to pleasureless labor; in *Les Soliloques du pauvre* he focused instead on the unemployed. In the poem "L'Hiver," Rictus castigated writers and painters who enriched themselves in feeling sorry for the poor, borrowing their language, revealing their customs, doing all but preaching by example. Politicians too profited from the poor, for which he cursed the socialists and their royalist friends in the Chamber. He mentioned some popular and successful names:

Ben, pis Bruant and pis Zola
Y z'ont plaint les Pauvr's dans les livres,
Aussi c'que ça les aide à vivre
De l'une à l'autre Saint-Nicholas!

(Ah, worse Bruant and worse Zola
Who've pleaded for the poor in books,
Which also helps them to live
From one Christmas to the next!)[43]

By the standards of most poets this certainly was colloquial, but Rictus generally restricted himself to reproducing the popular pronunciation, much as Kipling did for the British soldiery, and rarely used any specialized vocabulary. The criminal, the whore, and the pimp did not appear in his monologues, only an abstractly pathetic *pauvre* who spoke a language that sounded authentic, but was more likely the creation of a *littérateur* trying to arouse sympathy, much in the manner that he condemned in "L'Hiver." Rictus was in fact accused of just this sort of exploitation of false pity by his former admirer Tailhade, who wrote in 1901: "The rich have nothing to fear from guys of this temperament. They are domestics and not insurgents."[44]

As with Bruant, who wrote a dictionary of argot, and Paillette, who wrote a song about it, so Rictus was highly conscious of argot as a literary form. In a letter written to the argot scholar Sainéan in 1915, Rictus enumerated three reasons why he chose to write in (what he termed) argot. He liked argot's mixed ironic tone, both happy and sad; because "the populace which speaks that language is a great unconscious artist which has the gift of images as no poet will ever have"; and most important, because a "terror of the raw and popular term has given us, in poetry, a Niagara of inexpressive and colorless alexandrines . . . at least obscenity, the cynicism of an expression applied to a living fact, has the advantage of destroying the conventional expression."[45] The poets of Rictus's generation were in open revolt against traditional poetic forms, attacks against the alexandrine were many, and a few found in "the music of *faubourien* conversations" a model of poetic revolt.

This model of revolt based on the folk idiom had traditional roots. All the Montmartre singer-poets admired the way argot continually evolved yet contained echoes of an earlier way of speaking, more earthy and picturesque than modern French. They heard in argot the echo of the vigorous language of the French Renaissance, before Racine substituted *seins* for *tetons* (breasts for tits), as Rictus put it. This historical preference had definite political implications. Whereas the monarchist Charles Maurras idealized the neoclassical seventeenth century as the conjoined high point of French literary clarity and absolute monarchy, the young anarchist poets found a historical precedent for their own literary ideals in the more tumultuous century from Villon to Rabelais, when the language remained fluid and artists received their inspiration and even their vocabulary directly from the people. Innovative oral discourse, continually evolving according to the demands of the moment, contrasted sharply with the rigidly codified language sanctioned by the Académie Française.

As a system free from formal constraints imposed by academic and governmental authorities, oral culture, epitomized by lower-class argot, stood for anarchist ideals of spontaneity, autonomy, and revolt. Though cheap to produce and distribute, it seems unfortunate in retrospect that Emile Pouget was limited to the newspaper format in order to convey an essentially oral message. That message was largely phatic rather than denotative, in the sense that it was meant to establish a relationship between editor and readers: "we are all *compagnons, bons bougres,* so let's hang together." Perhaps this collective sensibility was preserved if *Le Père Peinard* was read aloud in a neighborhood café, but it is not difficult to imagine Pouget making use of electronic means of communication such as the radio in order to talk directly to the *populo* of the expanded global village of the twentieth century. The modern mass media was in fact already emerging alongside such "traditional" forms of media as *Le Père Peinard*—the Lumière brothers introduced the motion picture to the Parisian public in December 1895. Films remained silent for a generation, yet the coming electric media would reinforce certain patterns of oral culture, and technologically sophisticated cultures are sometimes called cultures of secondary orality.[46] Yet all the new mass media displaced the oral sense of immediate involvement and active participation as people became the passive recipients of sounds and images generated by machines.

Six

It is even more difficult to isolate the visual arts component of anarchist culture than it is to distinguish oral and written cultures. Like the anarchist writers, anarchist painters were part of an elite culture catering mainly to the privileged classes. Only in their graphic arts work, designing posters and illustrations for the popular press, including the anarchist periodicals, did artists succeed in reaching a mass audience. With a few exceptions all of them were of middle- or upper-class origin. The Neo-Impressionists in particular collaborated closely with Symbolist writers, critics, and other intellectuals. Although the painters must be evaluated within the larger context of the repoliticization of the artistic avant-garde after several decades of relatively little interest in political issues, they also deserve to be studied separately. For one thing, visual artists were among the most fervent adherents to anarchist ideals, and many of them maintained close relations with both Jean Grave and Emile Pouget, contributing numerous illustrations to *La Révolte* and *Le Père Peinard*. The main justification for dealing with artists in a separate chapter, though, is to be able to evaluate their political contributions formally as well as substantively, in terms of the new visual language they elaborated in the last two decades of the century. As a self-conscious avant-garde, these artists sought to conjoin aesthetic and political radicalism without hampering the autonomy of either. Anarchism seemed to many of them the only possible avenue for political engagement and artistic freedom.

The political commitment of many of the Neo-Impressionist and Post-Impressionist painters is widely recognized, yet the feeling persists that only purely aesthetic motives for innovation are worthy of consideration. A noted art historian has written, for example:

Thus Signac specifically (but surely wrongly) claimed that the Neo-Impressionists were revolutionaries not only in boldly adopting new techniques which rendered them totally unacceptable to the bourgeois public and critics, but also in choosing to portray can-can dancers, café-concerts, and circuses, in order to show the decadent pleasures of the bourgeoisie and the "vileness of our epoch of transition." In this way Seurat and Signac could claim to be putting back into style those very political implications that had been repudiated by Corot when a journalist asked him in 1848, "How is it that you, M. Corot, who are such a revolutionary in art are not also with us in politics?"[1]

Seurat and Signac are implicitly criticized for returning to an aesthetic position that had been rejected forty years before. Although it is true that a bowl of fruit can be painted in a revolutionary manner, and decadent pleasures can be portrayed by decadent, apolitical, or reactionary artists, it is not irrelevant that Signac and others perceived that their politics followed aesthetic criteria and that their art had political connotations: that the two realms were seen to be mutually reinforcing. The artists themselves sought such correlations not merely on the level of content but in terms of formal principles as well, seeking for instance in the technique of divisionism traces of the radical dialectic of harmony through contrast. Such groping for parallels may have been after-the-fact rationalizations, but since we know that political discussions occurred alongside artistic ones in the studios and cafés of the 1880s where the techniques were born, it seems wiser to consider the political-cultural milieu as a whole, as the artists themselves experienced it, rather than isolating their art for internal analysis.

From the Salon des Réfusés where Napoleon III had consigned all art that diverged from the academic norm, there was a natural progression to the *politique des réfusés* practiced by the anarchists. Art under the Third Republic remained surprisingly dependent not only on patronage by the bourgeoisie but on the state as well. Only fifty-six artists were admitted into the French Academy between 1808 and 1891, and they were not likely to choose unconventional works to be exhibited in the yearly Salons, which remained the chief showplace for contemporary art.[2] The link between officially sanctioned art and institutional power increased the likelihood that the excluded avant-garde artists would defiantly reject both artistic and political norms, and that their alternative Salon des Indépendents would affront bourgeois social as well as aesthetic standards. With the exception of Camille Pissarro, the Impressionists had not become politically involved, but in the 1880s Pissarro allied himself with the younger generation of Neo-Impressionists, followers of Georges Seurat, and he may have influenced their political orientation. In the mid-1880s, Paul Signac hosted a gathering of painters and some Symbolist writers in his spacious studio near the boulevard de Clichy, and most had anarchist sympathies like their host. Among the writers were Paul Adam, Félix Fénéon, and Gustave Kahn; the Neo-Impressionist painters (a term coined by Fénéon) included Pissarro, Seurat, Maximilien Luce, Albert Dubois-Pillet, Henri Edmond Cross, and Théo van Rysselberghe. Pissarro, Seurat, and Signac could also be found discussing aesthetic questions in the office of the Symbolist weekly, *La Revue Indépendante*.[3] The Post-Impressionists were less uniformly radicalized than the Neo-Impressionists; Vincent Van Gogh knew Signac and shared his political views; Charles Maurin was an anarchist; Henri de Toulouse-Lautrec's attitude toward contemporary politics was more complex. Illustrators such as Théophile-Alexandre Steinlen, Henri Gabriel Ibels, and Adolphe Willette, who mainly produced lithographs and engravings published in books and periodicals, freely expressed their political opinions in their art. The outstanding forum for their work and that of other graphic artists, *L'Assiette au Beurre*, which devoted its entire format to such pictorial essays, did not appear until 1901, but the 1890s did not lack publications willing to publish satirical drawings. All of these artists, whether avant-garde or more popular, differed from the Symbolist and Salon painters in finding their subject matter around them in daily life rather than in history or mythology. All were painters of modern life, though some eventually left behind the Parisian urban landscape for more pastoral surroundings.

The artistic avant-garde also diverged from the style of the fashionable Salon artists in preferring to leave the surfaces of their paintings rough and unglazed and details less finely rendered. Their works were both more realistic in subject matter and less in *trompe l'oeil* illusionism and draftsmanlike virtuosity. The academicist tried to make the unreal look real; the avant-gardist moved in the opposite direction, painting from life but keeping the viewer aware that he or she was seeing an unvarnished interpretation of reality. The Neo-Impressionist painting was unfinished in another sense as well, in that the optical effect of the divisionist technique of separate dots had to be resolved in the eye of the viewer. A dramatic change had occurred in the relationship between picture and viewer. Rather than lulling the viewer into unconscious admiration, the painting jarred him or her into a double awareness of the reality being depicted and the representational means chosen by the artist, forcing an interaction with that medium. This peculiar tension between reality and artifice was analogous to that within anarchism— this movement of the people that encouraged the spontaneous rising of the masses but which also accommodated the conspiratorial artificers of revolt. This insistent dialectic between form and content, between signifier and signified, between culture and nature, was to be a continuing problem for the avant-garde to face in these years of reassessment of the heritage of Romanticism and Impressionism.

The first French painter to be influenced by anarchism was Gustave Courbet. At the same time that Charles Baudelaire rebelled against Romanticism and proclaimed the poet's task to be the representation of modernity, more specifically (and radically) the social relations of the urban milieu in which he lived, Courbet was championing the new doctrine of realism in art. After 1848 Baudelaire renounced any political ideals, while Courbet increasingly received the critical and ideological support of the father of French anarchism, Pierre-Joseph Proudhon.[4] Proudhon praised Courbet's painting of contemporary social reality rather than mythological or historical subjects but protested against the appellation "realism." Rather than contrasting realism and idealism (Proudhon considered all art that transcended the photographic reproduction of reality to be idealistic), he preferred the "idealism of the idea to the idealism of form." As he stated in the beginning of his book of aesthetic theory, "the question of content always takes precedence over that of form," and he admired the moral principles underlying Courbet's work over that of inward-turning formalist works that did not stimulate the intelligence. Proudhon preferred to call this highest form of idealism the critical school, and defined it as consisting of a moralizing and revolutionary art that would undertake a *critique des moeurs*. Proudhon's ethic of truth and rationality failed to lay the groundwork for a distinctly anarchist aesthetic. His declaration on the last page of his book, "We must renounce our bohemian habits," however well-meaning, was no more likely to attract members of the future avant-garde than was his rejection of the importance of form.[5]

In fact the artists who most closely approximated Proudhon's aesthetic ideals were not the Impressionists but the Naturalists. In 1880, Joris-Karl Huysmans issued a Naturalist appeal, calling on artists to represent daily, even industrial, life. Perhaps the greatest exponent of epic Naturalism in the plastic arts was Constantin Meunier, who cast heroic bronzes of the toiling ironworkers of Picardy and Flanders. In *La Revue Rouge* of March 1896, Manuel Devaldès began a sixty-year career as an anarchist activist by praising the Meunier exhibition at Bing's new Art Nouveau gallery. The upper-class gallery-goers lauded Meunier's glorification of an abstraction called *Work* and the nobility of labor, while Devaldès saw the pain and degradation of actual social conditions.[6]

In the mid-1890s, the Neo-Impressionist painter Maximilien Luce was directly inspired by Meunier and by the Belgian poet Emile Verhaeren, who rendered scenes similar to Meunier's in verse, to attempt his own evocation of the Black Country. In 1896 Luce published an album of ten drawings, *Les Gueules noires* (The Black Faces), and spent three more months that year painting this industrial inferno. Luce had spent forty-five days in prison for his anarchist activities during the summer of repression of 1894, and after his release he published an album of ten lithographs entitled *Mazas,* in which drawings of his prison experience accompanied a text of the Communard Jules Vallès. Unlike Meunier's conventional casting of epic bas-reliefs, Luce experimented with Neo-Impressionism from 1887 to 1897, after which he retreated to a less experimental Impressionist style. His numerous contributions to anarchist journals were rendered in a more realistic graphic style. In 1890, in the magazine *Hommes d'Aujourd'hui,* Jules Christophe already associated Luce with the anarchist milieu: "This man in the shapeless hat who sits in a modest cafe attentively reading *La Révolte,* an anarchist publication, is of medium height, with a bulging forehead. . . . There is something of Vallès and Zola in his expression, with much of the rancor of a plebeian revolutionary."[7] The representational and humanist art of Meunier and Luce fulfilled Proudhon's desire for moralistic art that raised social relationships over questions of style and form.

In specifying that the real opposition between artistic styles lay not in

Paul Signac, *Luce Reading "La Révolte,"* 1891. (Courtesy of Françoise Cachin.)

the degree of realism but rather of formalism, Proudhon had foretold the coming struggle between aesthetic modernism and socialist realism. Anarchist artists usually joined those who rejected didactic art, yet the more humanistically inclined among them, such as Luce and Steinlen, in devoting themselves to the anarchist cause ironically diminished the distinction between anarchist and socialist art. Didactic, realistic art was moral art, and as such was abhorred by most members of the avant-garde. Anarchism rather than socialism attracted them precisely because the anarchists valued the creative freedom of the artist more than the mass appeal of their artistic creations. To the anarchists, the avant-garde work of art signified freedom; to the socialists, either it had clear social relevance or else was likely to be deemed decadent. Avant-garde anarchist artists of the fin de siècle rejected Proudhon's subordination of form to content. Artists perceived that the harmony of their works' signifiers and signifieds, not the domination of "reality" over creative imagination, best conveyed their message of liberation.

Less attuned to the formal innovations sought by avant-garde painters, illustrators were more willing to endow their work with the moral message desired by Proudhon. The most notable anarchist illustrator was probably Théophile-Alexandre Steinlen (1859–1923), Swiss-born but a lifelong Montmartrois. He maintained a regular correspondence with Jean Grave, as did Camille Pissarro, Signac, Luce, Ibels, and Willette.[8] Besides illustrating the songs of Bruant and Rictus, he collaborated with Zo d'Axa on *La Feuille* (1899), as well as contributing to *La Révolte*. He also designed posters, including advertisements for Zola's novel *Paris* when it appeared in 1897, and a giant multisheet version of Zola's *L'Assommoir*. Steinlen's connections with Zola and Bruant were appropriate for his realistic portraiture of workers, vagabonds, and dogs and cats. When he did diverge from this naturalistic style, as in his 1896 Chat Noir poster in which the black cat was drawn emblematically, he was probably influenced by Toulouse-Lautrec. In his posters, image and text were never integrally related; the text remained a descriptive caption, while the picture generally told another story, as if the visual image could not stand by itself but had to have meanings describing or described by it. The clear subordination of the pictorial to the ideological metaphorically described the role of the protagonist vis-à-vis the politician or ideologue. As early as 1919, a book on Steinlen, "painter of the

Parisian proletariat," was published in the Soviet Union, and he was later to be hailed as an exemplar of socialist realism.[9]

The ideology signified by Steinlen was certainly that of his lifelong anarchism, yet his work for Bruant and Zola suggested a vaguer, humanitarian socialism. In fact the source of Steinlen's inspiration lay not in anarchism but in a late nineteenth-century social humanism that he shared with Jean Grave and the socialist deputy Jean Jaurès among others. They believed that men and women and not blind economic forces shaped history, and that the end of that history was to benefit people's welfare rather than to bequeath to them absolute freedom or communism. Their beliefs were couched largely in moral and sentimental arguments about contemporary misery and injustice. Steinlen was a moralist rather than an ideologue, a satirist or, least of all, an aesthete. The same predominance of the moral over the formal aesthetic sense that appeared in Proudhon, his mistrust of artistic self-absorption, characterized the anarchist illustrators. Despite their commitment to the movement, their Naturalist aesthetic makes it difficult to distinguish what species of leftism they favored; hence the need for descriptive text or ideological context (publication in *La Révolte*).

One must look to such avant-garde anarchist painters as Paul Signac to find political meanings expressed formally. Signac maintained a lengthy correspondence with Jean Grave, though mostly from 1900 to 1914 (in 1914 he expressed disillusionment with Grave's support of the French war effort after thirty years of producing antimilitarist propaganda).[10] As early as 1891, his *Portrait of Maximilien Luce* that appeared in the September 1 issue of *La Plume* showed Signac's artist friend reading a copy of *La Révolte*. The only canvas in which he depicted workers, *Le Démolisseur,* also appeared as a lithograph for Grave's *Les Temps Nouveaux.* He also designed the cover that appeared on *Les Temps Nouveaux* from 1896 to 1900, showing an artist slaying a three-headed capitalist dragon with his brush.[11]

Yet Signac was far from content with the propagandist's role. In a 1902 lecture, Signac explained his conception of the political responsibility of artists:

Justice in sociology, harmony in art: same thing. The anarchist painter is not he who will exhibit anarchist paintings, but he who, without care

for lucre, without desire for recompense, will struggle with all his individuality against bourgeois and official conventions in his personal contribution. The subject is nothing, or at least only one of the parts of the work of art, not more important than the other elements: colors, drawing, composition.[12]

Still politically radical, Signac in 1902 was primarily concerned with recording the play of light and color in the sleepy Mediterranean port of Saint-Tropez. Among the earliest Signac paintings that did contain a social message was *Le Petit Dejeuner* (The Breakfast, 1886–87), which showed a stiflingly bourgeois family at their table, portrayed not only statically in the pointillist manner of Seurat but even facelessly, their individuality reduced to types. This could be interpreted as a critique of what Signac viewed as a real loss of individual identity among the bourgeoisie. Claiming that the Symbolists appreciated this effort to "pass from person to personage," Signac was apparently aiming at a symbolic atemporality that would transcend the immediacy of portraiture. Such parody was certainly not his goal in his most important political painting, the pointillist *Au temps d'harmonie* (In the Time of Harmony), which he wanted to call "Au temps d'anarchie" but which he modified amid the repression of 1894, the year it was painted. This large mural portrayed an idyllic scene resembling a Mediterranean picnic and featuring a young couple in its center who probably suggested free love. The painting was inspired by a phrase of the anarchist Charles Malato that Signac had read in *La Revue Anarchiste* in 1893: "The golden age is not in the past, it is in the future."[13] The painting reveals Signac's admiration for the classicist style of Pierre Puvis de Chavannes in its static, modeled figures, and in its unusual departure into the timeless realm of allegory. Inspired by Malato's phrase, Signac was experimenting with a new genre of futurist rather than archaic escapism. Unfortunately, the utopian vision looks as lifeless as Seurat's pathbreaking satirical look at petit bourgeois pleasures, *Dimanche après-midi sur l'Ile de Grande Jatte,* painted nine years earlier. Signac rarely attempted to paint either portraits or subjects with political content after *Au temps d'harmonie,* restricting his political contributions to illustrations.

Nevertheless, Signac defended the antihumanist aesthetic suggested by the pointillist or divisionist technique in his 1899 book on avant-

Paul Signac, *In the Time of Harmony* (1894), an oil study for Signac's most overtly anarchist painting. A lithograph of the same title and design was issued by Grave's journal *Les Temps Nouveaux* in 1896. (Courtesy of Françoise Cachin.)

garde art. He countered his fellow anarchist artist Pissarro's advice to expand his individuality and reaffirmed his artistic belief in scientific rationality and positivist principles.[14] One commentator has suggested formal similarities between Signac's technique of using "strongly accentuated individual brush strokes" of primary colors that formed a harmonious painting and anarchism's "individualistic yet communal spirit."[15] Signac's denial of individualism does not necessarily contradict that supposition, though his disavowal of the pointillist technique itself in his book casts more doubt on this linkage. Other aspects of his technique were more pertinent politically.

In his important theoretical statement of the principles of Neo-Impressionism, published by *La Revue Blanche* in 1899, Signac characterized his movement as one employing "precise and scientific method," which he contrasted with the Impressionists' instinctive understanding of the rules of optics and color theory. In *D'Eugène Delacroix au néo-impressionisme,* Signac divided recent French painting into the Romantic generation of Delacroix, lasting from 1830 to 1863, followed by the Impressionist movement which lasted till 1890, and finally the Neo-Impressionists whom he dated from 1886. Between these three generations of artists Signac saw a clear dialectic operating, moving from Delacroix's "methodical and scientific technique" to the Impressionists' "technique of instinct and inspiration," on to Neo-Impressionist "reasoned composition and aesthetic language of colors," which still preserved the Impressionists' pure palette of primary colors. All the while he perceived a continuous movement toward nature, represented by a "maximum of light, coloration, and harmony."[16] This particular way of situating his own artistic movement bore a distinct similarity to the essential anarchist goal of attaining spontaneity and naturalness within some sort of organizational framework. Signac's scientific faith surpassed that of most anarchists, yet his interpretation seems implicitly influenced by anarchist reliance upon the natural order in preference to social laws. Signac's desire to manifest conscious order and control in his work, suggesting disillusionment with the mainline anarchist ethic of spontaneity (a value he equated with Impressionism), could turn him either toward the more conspiratorial elements of the movement or, more likely considering his positive desire for discipline, toward the anarcho-syndicalists around Pelloutier. Signac's lifelong devotion to the cause lends credence to this latter supposition. Conversely, the ephemeral participation of so many other artists reflected a romantic revolutionary streak in keeping with their own aesthetic positions (though such was not the case with Pissarro).

Signac derived the term divisionism, which he preferred to pointillism, from the divided stroke (*touche divisée*) which "represents only the colored elements, separated and juxtaposed, reconstitutable by the optical mix." His explanation of divisionist principles strikingly resembles anarchist ideology, though not in terms of atomistic little dots residing individualistically on the canvas: "The separation of elements and the optical melange assures the purity, that is, the luminosity and intensity of tints . . . contrast, ruling the accord of similars and the analogy of contraries, subordinates these elements, powerful but balanced, to the rules of harmony. The basis of division is contrast."[17] Signac welcomed the bright primary pigments employed by the Impressionists, "nearest to those of the solar spectrum," but he accused them of muddying their colors by mixing them on the canvas. If instead all the paints were left pure, an "optical melange" would occur in the mind of the viewer, not according to his or her own preferences but according to the laws of color utilized by the artist, those "rules of contrast, of degradation and irradiation." Thus contrasting red and green surfaces would stimulate each other, whereas red and green dots mixed together formed a gray mass.[18] It was not enough to be arrested by the play of natural light; one had to know how to reproduce its effect. The Neo-Impressionist techniques seeking this effect often fell short of the naturalness and lightness achieved by an Impressionist such as Monet, but if one considers the early twentieth-century Fauves who used just such flat surfaces of vibrant color to be "divisionists," then one can appreciate both the potential and the radicalism of Signac's theory.

Like the title of his one overtly anarchist painting, *Au temps d'harmonie,* the contrast between the juxtaposed areas of color on the canvas was meant to achieve an overall impressionism of harmony. The avowed goal was not verisimilitude but totality, to be attained by three main principles: each color was to remain prismatically pure; contrast rather than mixing defined the colors' interaction; and the system of contrasts had to be scientifically understood. The political corollary was neither egalitarian uniformity nor atomistic social chaos, but a natural harmony in which the autonomy of each element was preserved and intensified. Each work was to receive its strength from its capacity to reproduce a system of relations. Signac's concern for technical rigor may have served as compensation for anarchism's inability to specify how one progressed toward the naturally harmonious state. His impatience with the instinctive and spontaneous Impressionist approach to art (as he termed it) made his theory of 1899 more analogous to contemporary anarcho-syndicalism than to the earlier era of *attentats*. For the aesthetic corollary to the presyndicalist epoch of individualist adventurism, one must look instead to the art of Henri de Toulouse-Lautrec.

Sex was for sale in Gay Nineties' Montmartre, as it is today. While artists dominated the narrow sloping streets of the Butte, cabarets and prostitutes held sway over the boulevards Clichy and Rochechouart. Of the many painters, poets, singers, and writers who found inspiration in this milieu, none personifies the ebullience, the decadence, and the amorality of fin de siècle Montmartre better than Henri de Toulouse-Lautrec. His portrayal of the Moulin Rouge and the brothel echoes the almost licentious concern for sexual freedom that one finds in the writings of Romain Coolus (a close friend of Lautrec's), Paul Adam, Octave Mirbeau, Pierre Loüys, and many others, notwithstanding the crusading zeal of *le père la pudeur,* Senator Bérenger. Leaf through any issue of Jules Roques's Montmartrois *Le Courrier Français* or Georges Darien's short-lived *L'Escarmouche,* and one will find countless drawings by Willette or Jean-Louis Forain as well as by Lautrec that are frankly pornographic. Lautrec was not necessarily the most licentious Montmartrois and he was certainly less involved with anarchism than many of his fellow artists. Nevertheless, on stylistic if not ideological grounds, Lautrec may be characterized as best representing the culture of fin de siècle anarchism in the visual arts.

One reason for focusing attention on Lautrec rather than on artists more obviously committed to anarchism, such as Camille Pissarro or Paul Signac, is that their role in the movement has been much better studied.[19] Despite Lautrec's fame, to my knowledge he has never been adequately situated in the social and political currents of his time. More than *engagé* artists like Steinlen or Luce, Lautrec typified a particular confluence of circles and influences that he frequented first in Montmartre and later among the intellectual elite fascinated by anarchism.

Closely associated, in 1894–95, with the Natanson family who directed *La Revue Blanche,* he contributed humorous sketches to the review and became well acquainted with Fénéon, Muhlfeld, Coolus, and others. A decade earlier, when he had commenced his career by illustrating Aristide Bruant's weekly *Le Mirliton,* his paintings had a recognizably proletarian subject matter. Steinlen took over as Bruant's illustrator when Lautrec moved indoors for inspiration. Unlike Steinlen's sentimentalized Naturalism, Lautrec's very lack of overt ideological reference let him penetrate more deeply into Montmartre's social relationships, into the world of dancers and prostitutes that linked the pleasure-seeking, slumming bourgeoisie with the lower classes, a world of *déclassés* beyond the pale of socialist class consciousness.

Devoid of all class or caste sentiment, Lautrec never boasted of his noble heritage as scion of the house of Toulouse-Lautrec-Monfa that had ruled the Albigeois since Charlemagne's time. His origins alleviated the perils of being a struggling artist, as he left Albi for the slopes of Montmartre to study painting in the studio of the academic artist Léon Bonnat in 1882. He soon left Bonnat for the more tolerant atmosphere that prevailed at Roger Cormon's art studio, where he remained until 1885. Montmartre must have been a strange milieu for the eighteen-year-old art student. In a letter written to his Uncle Charles shortly after he entered Cormon's studio, Lautrec described himself as an outlaw (*hors la loi*), and expressed some discomfort at finding himself in bohemia.[20] An outlaw to the respectable society for which he had been bred, Lautrec was also describing his rebellion against the academic traditions that his masters were teaching him, as he and his friends discovered the Impressionists' stylistic breakthroughs. Accepting his status as an outlaw, Lautrec would spend most of his life in bohemian Montmartre.

Lautrec met Aristide Bruant during his art-student years, around the time that Rodolphe Salis moved his Chat Noir to larger quarters and his former employee Bruant transformed the older cabaret into the Mirliton. The association of the young artist with the boisterous *cabaretier* was not merely an occasional one, as Bruant provided Lautrec with his first employment as an illustrator for the weekly paper *Le Mirliton* that helped spread Bruant's fame by printing one of his songs in conjunction with a drawing and the week's nightlife events. Lautrec illustrated songs

Henri de Toulouse-Lautrec, *At St.-Lazare,* 1885. In the 1880s Lautrec did illustrations for the *Mirliton*; this one accompanied one of Bruant's most famous songs and was signed with the anagram Tréclau. (Courtesy of Musée Toulouse-Lautrec, Albi.)

such as "A Saint-Lazare" and "A Montrouge" in a simple and realistic style, inspired by Bruant's social compassion, by his gifts as an observer, and by his raw, crude language. His painting *A Grenelle* hung over the piano at the Mirliton and remained in Bruant's possession until after Lautrec's death.[21]

Under Bruant's influence the young Lautrec began painting scenes of working-class life. Among the proletarian works of his early years were two works entitled *The Laundress,* produced at about the same time.[22] In the drawing, the scene was set outdoors, with one of the horses he drew so adeptly standing hitched to a cart in the background, his head in a feedbag. The laundress was portrayed nearly full length with a large basket on her arm, and looked troubled and harried. In the painting by the same name Lautrec moved his model indoors, where she stood over a table, leaning heavily on her arms, her torso angled diagonally across the picture. She was portrayed in such immediate foreground that the lower corner of the painting cut her off abruptly above the legs, as if Lautrec was self-conscious about depicting legs due to his own stunted ones. This abruptness, combined with a foreshortening and diagonality that lent to the work a sensation of thrust and motion, was to become a Lautrec trademark. Indeed, whereas the drawing of the laundress bore no strong imprint of the personality of the model nor of Lautrec, and could well be mistaken for a Steinlen, the painting much more distinctly individualized both model and artist by representing the painter's own characteristic force in the belligerent pose of the laundress, and by giving the viewer of the painting the illusion that he is enjoying the same dwarf's-eye view that Lautrec had. Nevertheless this was very much a transitional work that retained some trace of Lautrec's older subject matter with a new aesthetic slant.

Bruant and the urban Montmartre milieu were major influences on Lautrec's early career. The change in his style, and probably in his choice of subject matter as well, between 1888 and 1891, must be attributed to his growing fascination for Japanese art. His friend Vincent Van Gogh was another of the many enthusiasts for the Japanese print, the *ukiyō-e,* and had mounted a small exhibition of prints in the Montmartre restaurant Le Tambourin, near the studio of Paul Signac, in 1887.[23] A huge exhibition of these prints was held at the Ecole des Beaux-Arts' Exposition de la Gravure Japonaise in May 1890, for which such reknowned

Henri de Toulouse-Lautrec, *The Laundress,* drawing, 1888. (From *Paris Illustré,* 1888. Courtesy of the Cleveland Museum of Art, Gift of Hanna Fund.)

Henri de Toulouse-Lautrec, *The Laundress,* painting, 1886–89, a working-class character study. (From a private collection.)

japonistes as Samuel Bing, editor of the periodical *Le Japon Artistique* (1888–91) and future proprietor of the gallery L'Art Nouveau, Théodore Duret, Louis Gonse, Hector Guimet, and Edmond de Goncourt lent works from their personal collections. The "floating world," as Edo's Yoshiwara district of geishas and Kabuki players was called, closely paralleled the Montmartre *demi-monde,* the Butte itself floating above Paris in the contemporary image of *le château des brouillards.* Lautrec was one of a great many artists to be influenced by the Japanese prints that celebrated this milieu of transient pleasures, and any further consideration of his career must take into account what this new influence meant to his style. Most of the anarchist aesthetes were also fervent japonistes, and the aestheticization of politics channeled into anarchism was in part a legacy of the Japanese aesthetic that had preoccupied the French artistic elite since Japan was opened to the West in the 1850s.

The *ukiyō-e* offered such anarchist artists as Signac, Seurat, and Charles Maurin an example of socially responsive art, but, more important, it helped them resolve some of the paradoxes posed by anarchism at a more philosophical level. Anarchism sought a harmonious social order in the apparent disorder of the nonregulated, free, and spontaneous society that was its goal. The anarchists rejected the disorder of the Social Darwinist apology for capitalism as well as the overregulated order of the dominative state and bureaucracy that they feared in the socialist model of the planned society. In searching for a natural and harmonious model of order, many proposed a return to primitivist conditions, but the more influential among them (Kropotkin, Pouget) saw the answer in a higher kind of order than that of external regulation and restriction. These accepted the artifice of culture even while casting a wistful glance at natural systems of order in the animal world (Kropotkin's *Mutual Aid*), and hoped for a collective and minimally structured control over technology that would assure men and women greater returns from their labors. Anarchism was ultimately an extended inquiry into the question of order, seeking to conjoin the cosmological with the social order so as to produce a whole person in a whole society. Nineteenth-century utopian socialists from Fourier to Kropotkin grappled with such problems, but so did artists who mediated on questions of order and artifice, at a time when the retinal realism of the Impressionists offered the visual return to nature. Japanese art revealed to many

Neo- and Post-Impressionist artists a model of aesthetic order that balanced nature and culture, environment and artificer more successfully than did naively empirical Impressionism or overly dreamy Symbolism. This same aesthetic may have characterized high Japanese art as well, but the *ukiyō-e* uniquely encapsulated the ideal relationship between social life and its artistic representation.

The Japanese aesthetic that entranced European artists may be described briefly as sophisticated order, expressed in Japanese love for artful asymmetry, for unfinished but highly sanded wood, for gardens so carefully tended that they were indistinguishable from nature. Rather than haphazard disorder or overly symmetrical uniformity, the ideal was a consciously crafted human environment that harmonized with rather than struggled against the pattern and will of nature. The awareness of sophisticated order underlay Marcel Schwob's admiration for Hokusai's adage that he would only achieve complete naturalness at the age of 110, for nothing took more practice.[24] When Théodore Duret praised Lautrec's rapidity of execution as a Japanese virtue, he was probably thinking of Zen-inspired pen-and-ink drawings. Aesthetes weary of decadent artificiality appreciated an art that sought to efface all traces of artifice. Anarchism and japonisme were parallel and autonomous codes expressing similar cultural values.

How were the *ukiyō-e* artists able to impart naturalistic phenomena with such symbolic richness? The Europeans were excited by stylistic techniques that resembled and deeply influenced the Neo- and Post-Impressionists' own efforts. The *ukiyō-e* masters presented a flattened and stylized space that differed radically from the three-dimensional illusion of space that had dominated Western art since Masaccio. Never having employed the principle of the vanishing point, the Japanese works achieved a floating and unreal quality to Western eyes used to formal perspective. Subjects were presented without naturalistic modeling, and with clear black outlines and pure colors (which attracted Gauguin, as did the woodcut process itself).[25] The popularly depicted Kabuki actors were portrayed almost as static icons, in a manner befitting their theatricality. The momentary act, the temporally bound individual, was frozen in an abstracted and stylized gesture.

With its depiction of the surface of life in nature and in the floating world, japonisme lent itself to a romantic conception of reality, one result of which was its influence on Art Nouveau's swirling vegetative forms. An important means by which the *ukiyō-e* appealed to romanticist notions of subjectivity was the sense of immediacy it gave to the viewer. Rather than setting up the viewer as an idealized observer of a unified, coherent space seen from a distant and objective vantage point, the *ukiyō-e* frequently presented the partial perspective of a participant. Instead of reproducing a two-dimensional version of three-dimensional space, the Japanese print reproduced the retinal image almost photographically, even using techniques of cropping and flattening. By cutting off an unseen portion of the subject, and framing the bottom of the print in the immediate foreground, the Japanese communicated a sense of immediacy, as reflected in the momentary slice of life often seen in the works of Degas (a fervent japoniste). This ability to signify formally both the transitory and the essential, to portray the purely visual image in a heightened or visionary way, appealed to the deeply subjectivist writers and painters who valued romantic qualities of individuality and uniqueness.

The *ukiyō-e* aesthetic also looked forward formalistically to the aesthetic modernism of the early twentieth century as well as to a renewed classicism, in presenting a hard-edged image that abstracted and deconstructed three-dimensionality in much the same way as the Cézanne–Picasso revolution of Cubism. Japonisme was a preparatory phase in the European avant-garde's move away from the realistic depiction of nature, and helped free artists from their position as passive recorders of the objective environment. As an intermediate stage in this process it was never totally removed from representation, though Hokusai at times stylized clouds and water almost to the point of abstraction. As Post-Impressionism and anarchism were incomplete, transitional movements, so japonisme lay at the late nineteenth-century border between the romantic and subjective, and the classic and abstract. By Picasso's time, the more geometric and abstract African art had displaced the formal influence of Japanese art. The appeal of primitivism helped the mask of African ebony replace the white mask of the Nō drama.

In Toulouse-Lautrec's case, the jettisoning of his noble heritage so that he might portray the squalor of Montmartre was especially parallel to the fortunes of Japanese artists. An eighteenth-century *ukiyō-e* artist named Buncho (died 1792), for example, was one of a number of samurai who became so addicted to the pleasures of the floating world that they gave up their high social positions to become artists. For a samurai to become an artist not of the aristocratic styles but of *ukiyō-e* involved a serious loss of social prestige in a highly stratified society. That it was possible at all attests to the seduction of the gay quarters, the entertainment district outside the shogun's capital at Edo that was restricted by edict to the Yoshiwara ("nightless city") quarter. Buncho's change in profession may also have been motivated by the excessive number of samurai in the long period of peace maintained by the Tokugawa shogunate. Whereas many French aristocrats turned their backs on the Third Republic, many samurai showed resourcefulness in turning to the arts and to learning.[26] Geisha houses and Kabuki theaters thrived in Yoshiwara, and their performances and stars were advertised by the public posters printed in several colors from hand-cut wooden blocks. The *ukiyō-e* was a distinctly popular and commercial art that reflected the tastes of the urban social strata and glorified the entertainers who symbolized the passing pleasures of the floating world.

Toulouse-Lautrec may not have suffered quite the same social demotion as Buncho in choosing Montmartre's own nightless city as his social and artistic milieu, but he certainly shared his Japanese counterpart's fascination with the seamier elements of that world in depicting the lesbianism that lay hidden behind the brothel doors. From the opening of the Moulin Rouge in 1889 until 1895 when he left Montmartre, Lautrec devoted most (but not all) of his energies to recording the singers and dance hall girls of Montmartre. When he turned increasingly to depicting prostitutes in 1892 and after, it was to those sequestered in the famous brothels in the Chausée d'Antin and not those walking the streets. From his first years in Montmartre until 1895, Lautrec consistently moved indoors, from the public life of the streets to the still public but artificially lit nightlife in the cabarets and cafés-concerts, finally to the totally enclosed environment of the brothels. Fascinated by the color and surface of life, Lautrec also probed deeper into the mores supporting social values, and he proved himself a relentless revealer of the hypocrisy and egoism upon which society was based. Lautrec passed through the stage of social criticism practiced by Steinlen but apparently felt dissatisfied with the depiction of the people's misery. Certainly he was attracted by the excitement of the music hall atmosphere, but he rarely glamorized it (his posters of Bruant are among the few that might have fed the vanity of the performer portrayed; Yvette Guilbert, for instance, was far less pleased), and though the brutality of depiction for which he was known even then may have expressed personal bitterness, it also registered a pattern of social commentary generally overlooked by critics.[27] The example of *ukiyō-e* probably stimulated Lautrec's focus on the theatrical; it certainly served as a model of the unity of style, subject matter, and technical means of expression that was to become his own contribution to the art of his time.

A fellow student at Cormon's art studio commented many years later upon Lautrec's fondness for things Japanese: "Lautrec considered the Japanese as his brothers in height; beside them he appeared normal. All his life he desired to go to the country of . . . dwarf trees, of which he had a marvelous idea inspired by the prints of Hokusai. For lack of a friend to accompany him, he renounced it."[28] The noted japoniste Théodore Duret recognized Lautrec's debt to the Japanese, remarking that he had proceeded in "true Japanese fashion" in rendering the image of Jane Avril, in the series of lithographs entitled *Le Café-Concert*. Duret saw a similarity in the means of expressing movement, by the aid of a rapid execution and a bold yet light touch. More important, in terms of technical considerations, was Duret's contention that the appearance of color lithography in France was due to the example of the Japanese print.[29] For it was in his thirty-one lithographs that Lautrec came closest to reproducing the Japanese aesthetic, as well as its subject matter and mode of production. The simplified forms were bounded by a firm black outline and lacked chiaroscuro, featured unusual cropping and perspective, and were produced in almost garish colors. His 1895 poster of May Milton, for example, showed her face in three-quarters profile and her mouth in side-profile, a technique of Utamaro's.[30] Lautrec was less ornamental than the Japanese and generally communicated a greater sense of vitality, though the May Milton poster appears as rigidly iconic as an *ukiyō-e* print.

By the time he undertook his first experiment in lithography in 1891, Lautrec appears to have fully absorbed the lessons to be gleaned from the *ukiyō-e*. Jules Cheret, who fathered the multicolor lithographic process in the second half of the nineteenth century, was commissioned to do the first Moulin Rouge poster in 1889. Lautrec's Moulin Rouge of 1891 replaced Cheret's cornucopia of windmills and dance hall girls swirling about a fantasy landscape. Lautrec set his scene inside the music hall, and depicted its current stars, Valentin le Désossé in the immediate foreground framing his partner La Goulue. The highly simplified forms gave a much more striking visual image than did Cheret's wispy little figures and projected the viewers into the very scene they would see if they were watching the performers themselves. Responding to the exigencies of the poster form, which required a quick response by passersby hurrying along amid a great variety of visual stimuli, Lautrec's figures were bold and emblematic yet retained their individuality. Aided by his reliance on a foreign aesthetic designed for the poster medium rather than on an anterior style borrowed from painting, Lautrec conveyed a sense of the immediacy of real life. He managed to translate the momentary and individual into a stylized and iconic image, balancing between the naturalistic subject and its aesthetic rendering in a way that contrasted both with Cheret's impersonal rococo unreality and with Steinlen's crude realism. With the aid of Japanese methods, Lautrec was able to unite a naturalistic concern for social reality with an aesthetic that stressed the artist's role in transforming and abstracting the objective data of nature and society. The milieu depicted and the means of depicting it were important aspects of the influence of the *ukiyō-e,* the poster medium itself satisfying anarchist demands for a socially and popularly directed art.

Lautrec's avid researches into the possibilities of lithography in the early 1890s were matched by those of his friend Charles Maurin. A slightly older (1856–1914) artist, Maurin was known for his application of scientific processes to artistic production. In December 1891, he took out a patent on a lithographic process allowing color printing on a single plate by the use of atomizers filled with the primary colors red, yellow, and blue. This early use of spray paints allowed for rapid execution and bright clear colors. Apparently Maurin also shared Lautrec's taste for Japanese prints, as a contemporary newspaper noted a collection of such prints in his studio. Lautrec's biographer Perruchot describes the two artists as friends during the Moulin Rouge days of 1890, and calls Maurin taciturn and absorbed in technical problems; Thadée Natanson wrote that "the anarchist theories, of which Lautrec had learned the virulence from Charles Maurin, often furnished to Maurin and to [Félix] Valloton subjects of conversation which stirred them. . . . Cynicism too, sometimes pushed too far by him, enormously amused Lautrec," and he added that they were drinking friends.[31] More than passing acquaintances, Lautrec and Maurin did lithographs of each other, and finally exhibited their works jointly at what was Lautrec's first major exhibition, at the Galerie Boussod et Valadon, boulevard Montmartre, early in 1893. Maurin's biographer considered this the culmination of all his prior researches and cited the contemporary critic Arsène Alexandre about Maurin's concern for pictorial simplification, his research with flat tones, and his striking arrangements of lines and colors. The critic of *La Petite République Française* noted Maurin's evolution toward Impressionist processes and the Japanese school.[32]

What Maurin's hometown hagiographer nearly effaced was the artist's anarchist fervor. This was not missed by Félix Fénéon in reviewing the joint exhibition for *L'Endehors*. Fénéon wrote of Maurin, "One of his recent pages, of an apotheosizing and popular sentiment, is a woodengraving: the comrade Ravachol—the head haughty, energetic and calm, the naked torso framed between the guillotine's supports and the triangular knife." This well-known woodcut, reproduced in Pouget's first *Almanach du Père Peinard,* showed Ravachol looking clear-eyed into the future, and was probably the best single work of martyrology to emerge from those years. Of Lautrec, Fénéon reported in the same article, "By a drawing which is not a traced double of reality, but an ensemble of signs which suggests it, he immobilizes life in unexpected emblematic images."[33] He described Lautrec's work as almost hostile but highly original in depiction. Other possible sources of anarchist influence on Lautrec at this time were two other anarchist artists: Camille Pissarro, who probably accompanied Lautrec to London in May 1892, and the lithographer Henri-Gabriel Ibels, who together with Lautrec published a collection of twenty-two lithographs entitled *Le Café-Concert* in 1893.[34] Coinciding with Lautrec's rising interest in japonisme and lithography was at least contact with anarchist ideology.

We can ascertain not only that Lautrec was aware of anarchism, but that the anarchists knew of Lautrec, again through the offices of Fénéon. The article in *Le Père Peinard* of April 30, 1893, entitled "Chez les barbouilleurs, les affiches en couleurs" (Among the Daubers, Posters in

Charles Maurin, *Ravachol before History*, 1893. The anarchist as martyr: Maurin's heroic woodcut of Ravachol. From the *Almanac de Père Peinard* (1893).

Henri de Toulouse-Lautrec, *Charles Maurin,* 1898. (Courtesy of Musée
Toulouse-Lautrec, Albi.)

Color), was unsigned but has been identified as being Fénéon's work. If so, it was a stylistic triumph for this master of the elliptical obscurities of Symbolist prose to be able to write convincingly in argot, and deserves to be reproduced in the original:

Un qui a un nom de Dieu de culot, mille polochons, c'est Lautrec: son dessin ni sa couleur ne font pas des simagrées. Du blanc, du noir, du rouge en grandes plaques et des formes simplifiées, voilà son fourbi. Y'en a pas deux comme lui pour piger la trombine des capitalos gagas attablés avec des filasses à la coule qui leur lechent le museau pour le faire carmer. La Goulue, Reine de Joie, Le Divan Japonais, et deux fois un bistro nommé Bruant, c'est tout ce que Lautrec a manigancé comme affiches—mais c'est épatant de toupet, de volonté, de rosserie, et ça en bouche un coin aux gourdiflots qui voudraient becqueter rien que de la pâte de guimauve!

(One guy who has a lot of guts is Lautrec; neither his drawing nor his colors leave any room for doubt. White, black, and red in large patches and simplified forms, that's his thing. There aren't two like him to catch the face of the decrepit old capitalists with some girls seated on their knees, licking their muzzles to make them shell out. La Goulue, Reine de Joie, Le Divan Japonais, and two times Bruant's bistro, that's all that Lautrec has cooked up as posters—but it's got plenty of guts, of will, of treachery, and will astonish the cretins who want to feed their faces on nothing but mediocre stuff.)[35]

Fénéon extolled the poster as an art of the streets—"and it is art, name of God, and the most far out, mixed with life"—but attacked most of the lithographers, especially the patriotic ones. He praised Cheret for his use of color, which he called "lively as dynamite," but reserved the lion's share of attention for Lautrec. He admired his strong colors and simplified forms, but especially enjoyed Lautrec's flippant sarcasm, saying he was unequaled in exposing the lechery and hypocrisy of the bourgeoisie. Fénéon suggested to the readership that if they wished to have an original Lautrec or Cheret poster, why not (cautiously) remove them from the wall where they were affixed and take them home, which was certainly astute advice for potential collectors.[36]

Fénéon apparently authored another article in *Le Père Peinard* con-

Henri de Toulouse-Lautrec, *Reine de Joie* (Queen of Joy), 1893. This is the poster that Fénéon described in *Le Père Peinard,* portraying the capitalist as gross and lascivious. (Courtesy of Musée Toulouse-Lautrec, Albi.)

cerning the new tendencies in art.[37] Reporting on the 1893 exhibition of independent artists, Fénéon praised the work of Luce, Lucien Pissarro, Signac, and Cross. These artists all happened to be anarchists, but as their works contained little of political relevance, Fénéon limited himself to praising their Impressionist air and light that he said made one feel as if one were outdoors. He admired the machines drawn by Ibels, but showed special enthusiasm for Lautrec's paintings of prostitutes and his biting portrayal of bourgeois celebrants slobbering over "the poor girls [who] work hard on the sidewalk and the bed, exposed to the jibes of the johns, the slaps of the pimps, the deceit of the police."[38] By placing Lautrec among members of the anarchist avant-garde and singling out his works for their social relevance, Fénéon may have overinterpreted the political import of Lautrec's works, but his inclusion among the radical artists of 1893 is nonetheless significant as a contemporary reaction.

Among the posters with which Fénéon was familiar, the one of Bruant at the Ambassadeurs portrayed Lautrec's old mentor in symbolic relation to the *déclassés* whose story he told, rather than in physical relation to his cabaret milieu. A small figure looked menacingly over Bruant's shoulder, but remained in the background, eclipsed by Bruant's presence and bohemian sense of style. The denotative or semantic aspect of the poster was reduced to an absolute minimum, the only written information being the name of the café-concert at which Bruant was performing. All that remained was the aesthetic or connotative element, with even the visual information reduced to the minimum needed to communicate at the mass level.[39] The simplified image and minimal message have since become such advertising commonplaces that it is hard to appreciate how this dominating icon must have appeared to Parisians used to Cheret's Watteau-like images or to verbose announcements.

Not all of Lautrec's posters were of popular performers, nor were they all as stylized as that of Bruant. In an 1892 advertisement for *Le Dépêche de Toulouse,* a newspaper running a series on the famous Calas case in which Voltaire had intervened, Lautrec showed Jean Calas entering the room to find his son hanging from a rafter, his upper body and face luridly lit by the candle in the father's hand. This macabre image was surpassed in terrorist effect by another Lautrec poster advertising a

Henri de Toulouse-Lautrec, *Ambassadeurs: Aristide Bruant,* 1893: "Le Chansonnier Populaire." (Courtesy of Musée Toulouse-Lautrec, Albi.)

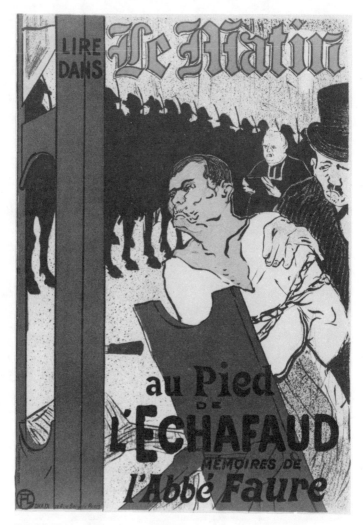

Henri de Toulouse-Lautrec, *At the Foot of the Scaffold,* 1893. Unlike Maurin, Lautrec did not choose to heroicize the person facing the guillotine. (Courtesy of the Musée Toulouse-Lautrec, Albi.)

newspaper serial, this one entitled "Au pied de l'échafaud, mémoires de l'abbé Faure" (At the Foot of the Scaffold, Memoirs of Father Faure), which told the story of the chaplain at the Parisian prison La Roquette, who had accompanied thirty-eight men to the guillotine.[40] In 1893, in the midst of the anarchist *attentats,* Lautrec drew a man awaiting the guillotine, the executioner's hand on his shoulder, priest and horsemen behind him, the scaffold rising in the foreground. One wonders whether Maurin's woodcut of Ravachol inspired Lautrec's poster, but the portrayals were strikingly different. Maurin's noble Ravachol appeared as if he had already risen from the dead and was contemplating his immortality; Lautrec's nameless criminal *in extremis* was clearly facing his last desperate moments on earth. The unremitting honesty of depiction for which he was already known was unlikely to have inspired further anarchist martyrs, as Maurin's illustration has been accused of doing.[41] Whether he was sketching Jane Avril poised on one leg or a condemned man facing the void, Lautrec always drew in the present tense. His subjects' age and vocation reinforced the impression that only the momentary mattered; no old men dreamed of an idealized past, nor young men of a sentimentalized future. Lautrec painted scenes from daily life, not those people whose lives suggested the tedium of endlessly recurring acts, but the performers, prostitutes, and criminals whose vitality signified the immediacy of existence, individuals whom Lautrec apotheosized into the symbols of an epoch whose image remains today. His sense of time was neither the continuous and repeating time of the bourgeois nor the teleological time of the socialists, but the anarchist absolute present, a time of direct and individual action unmediated by theory or organization. Yet neither was the immediacy present in his work apocalyptic, negating time in radical disjunction with the past while posing the possibility of an unknown future looming just beyond the *Grand Soir.* Borrowing Goya's succinct motto for the *Disasters of War* series, "I saw that," Lautrec subsumed any ethical or ideological implications within an aesthetic of absolute visual honesty.[42]

Francis Jourdain called Lautrec a man in love with appearances, who disliked theories and even lacked imagination. "To see the truth. To tell the truth without boasting or prudery. . . . Thus is summed up the ethic and aesthetic of Lautrec. The words ethic and aesthetic would have displeased him."[43] In an era in which sensitivity to graft and hypocrisy greatly swelled anarchist ranks, Lautrec attended the hearings on a suspect financier named Arton whose dealings had compromised members of the government. Whether this involvement was due to a legitimist's joy at smearing the republicans, as Duret contended, or rather to the anarchist influence of his contemporaries, his ethic, or more properly his aesthetic of scrupulous honesty, was accompanied by disdain for the government. Lautrec himself might have admitted a connection between the form of his art and its symbolic implications. Jourdain remembered a conversation with Lautrec:

"Technique of assassination" he told me one day, in sketching the murderous gesture suggested to him by the edge and curve of the blade over whose beauty he was ecstatic, that beauty due only to the perfection of that edge and curve. It would be pleasant to say . . . that the idea of murder was awakened in Lautrec by the sight of a fine-edged knife. That of which I am convinced . . . is his visual intelligence, permitting him to seize certain relations—scarcely mysterious—between the form and its function, between the configuration of the object and its end.[44]

Jourdain's conclusion implied that the "technique of assassination" related the knife to its purpose, but it could also have referred to the artist's technique, his quick, slashing brush strokes and scathing portraitures. The aestheticized violence suggested by Lautrec's ecstasy over the beauty of a well-honed blade betrayed his awareness of the symbolic force of the object portrayed, but also that of his portrayal, as if he could murderously wield his knife/brush in a gesture of disgust and hostility toward social mores. By filling his canvases and posters with those people representing immortality, rendered frankly and shamelessly, Lautrec transvalued the bourgeois order's ethic of modesty and tact, of "don't get caught." If the contrast between his performers' milieu, where illusion and unreality were courted, and his own realistic technique did not adequately convey his attitudes, he included in those portrayals images of corpulent and corrupt bourgeois to remind the viewer that this was the world both scorned and supported by the reigning social order.

"One would not seek altogether in vain under the noble skin—freed from ostentation—the traces of that anarchism toward which so many of his contemporaries were carried in the intellectual domains." The author of these lines on Lautrec, Francis Jourdain, was himself part of the anarchist intelligentsia that fought in the corridors of the Théâtre de l'Oeuvre over *Enemy of the People,* while Laurent Tailhade on stage made sure no one in the audience missed Ibsen's anarchist innuendos.[45] Also a member of this milieu, Lautrec was not only in contact with Montmartre singers and illustrators, but gravitated toward some of the most influential of the literary anarchists. His collaboration and friendship with the literary and theatrical avant-garde in 1893–95 came at the height of these writers' anarchist involvement, and eventually (perhaps paradoxically) led Lautrec away from the Montmartre of his twenties and into Parisian society.

In 1894 Lautrec became close friends with the Natansons who had recently moved the office of *La Revue Blanche* from the rue des Martyrs to the more fashionable address 1 rue Laffitte. Despite the Opéra location, the journal was to grow increasingly anarchistic in 1895 and 1896 under the inspiration of Fénéon and Victor Barrucand, who were perfectly in accord with Thadée Natanson. Lautrec met Fénéon and other literary figures such as Mallarmé at the parties given by the Natansons, where he also met and admired Misia Natanson and had her model for a poster for the journal. He probably heard Fénéon speak of his friend Luce, who had been arrested on July 27, 1894, and was imprisoned for forty-five days under *les lois scélérates.* A secret agent identified only by a Maltese cross wrote: "The arrest of Luce has thrown fright into the minds of the illustrators, sculptors, and painters of Montmartre; the most moderate anarchists speak of fleeing."[46] Lautrec was simultaneously involved in *L'Escarmouche,* a short-lived (November 1893 to January 1894) journal edited by the anarchist illustrator Ibels and by another anarchist named Georges Darien, to which Lautrec contributed twelve drawings. One of these was entitled *L'Union franco-russe* after the much-publicized entente concluded between France and Russia in 1893 that was criticized by the left on account of the czar's autocracy. Lautrec showed a thin worker, in cap and long white smock with "Paris" written on his chest, arm in arm with a much bigger, smiling woman in a contrasting black jumper, looking smug as she towered over him.[47]

In 1895 Lautrec painted his old friend the can-can girl La Goulue at her booth at the Foire du Trone. In the foreground of the large painting he placed two reknowned reprobates, Félix Fénéon and Oscar Wilde.

Fénéon wrote of the painting, "It is me, without having posed, who is seen in a little soft felt hat, shoulder to shoulder with Wilde. . . . We had, one must believe, some analogies that were flattering for neither of the two of us."[48] Fénéon was obliquely referring to the fact that he and Wilde had both been recent victims of infamous trials. Lautrec probably found it against his nature to fill the crowd with anonymous faces, such was his passion for individualized portraiture, and most of his portraits were of friends. Thádee Natanson referred to this painting in discussing Lautrec's accentuation of his models' unique traits and stressed Lautrec's overriding concern for the exceptional, intense, and singular aspects of his subject. An article by Paul Adam in *La Revue Blanche* of May 1895 entitled "L'Assaut malicieux" (The Malicious Assault) defended Oscar Wilde and was accompanied by a drawing of Wilde by Lautrec, who was in London during Wilde's trial. Adam's confused arguments matter less than Lautrec's involvement in the most important public assault on avant-garde sexual mores of the era. After years of portraying hetero- and homosexuality in the frankest manner, the social repercussions against this subcultural amorality were inescapably apparent to Lautrec, and he did not shrink from identification with the victim. The Théâtre de l'Oeuvre performed Wilde's *Salomé* on February 11, 1896, and Lautrec designed the program, seemingly caricaturing a tired, baggy-eyed Wilde with full face and ridiculously tiny, pursed lips.[49]

Lautrec also portrayed Fénéon again in 1895. In a letter to his mother late in 1894, Lautrec wrote that he was beginning a new career as a stage decorator, which he found interesting but not easy.[50] In this characteristically unrevealing letter he was referring to the ancient Indian drama *Le Chariot de terre cuite,* freely adapted to an anarchist interpretation by Victor Barrucand and performed at the Théâtre de l'Oeuvre on January 22, 1895. Lautrec designed the program and painted the sets for the fifth act. Fénéon, friends with both Lautrec and Barrucand, read the invocation as the play opened, and Lautrec painted him with arms outstretched, standing on a balcony supported by an elephant and looking like the prophetic though rather thin Buddha to whom Lautrec loved to compare him. For Antoine's Théâtre-Libre, Lautrec did the program covers for Bjorn Bjornson's *Une faillite* (A Bankruptcy) and Vaucaire's *Le Poète et le financier* for the 1893–94 season.[51]

In his roman à clef of 1898, *Le Soleil des morts,* Camille Mauclair included a well-drawn, thinly veiled characterization of Lautrec which indicated the contemporary opinion of him:

One evening he met . . . the Prince de Lannoy-Talavere, who, not being able to pardon his family and life for having made him a dwarf, painted with genius the prostitutes, the low figures, all the social ignominy, each week throwing his drawings in the face of the public, in the one-sou papers, like so much corrosive spittle, and living ostentatiously in the clandestine houses, as if he wanted to nourish his vengeance and his art on all the dregs of the century. He knew Dessner, the anarchist illustrator, the favorite student of Pierre Peyronny, having left Impressionist painting to sketch the deputies, spectators, the Jews, with a shrewd hatred, son of a concierge he, having trained in Montmartre cabarets to make five minute portraits at ten sous a head.[52]

The "prince" was not called an anarchist; rather, he was associated with them both in milieu and in bitterness against society, though Mauclair ascribed it to personal reasons.[53]

As Mauclair was writing his exposé of the 1890s avant-garde and its revolutionary aspirations, that milieu was already changing. As anarchism faltered and changed after 1894, so Montmartre's star began to fade around 1895. The famous music hall the Elysée-Montmartre was crushed by competition with the Moulin Rouge, while Joseph Oller, proprietor of the latter establishment, installed a new music hall, L'Olympia, on the boulevard des Capucines. Rodolphe Salis sold Le Chat Noir in 1895, and Aristide Bruant left the Mirliton for his new life as a country gentleman at Courtenay.[54] To be sure, enterprises as successful as these were continued and copied by others, but commercialization challenged the spirit and authenticity of the *cabarets artistiques.* New artists and performers would renew the scene around the Bateau Lavoir of Picasso and Max Jacob; others such as Léon Bloy and Steinlen would never desert Montmartre, but the initial efflorescence of the free city of Montmartre initiated by Salis and Emile Goudeau in 1881 was over, having had exactly the same longevity as the first wave of anarchism in France.

These years that witnessed the rise of Montmartre as home and symbol of unbridled creativity were the years in which Lautrec apotheosized the free spirit of the quarter. After 1895 Lautrec left Montmartre to seek inspiration in other regions of the city, perhaps because after living there for over a decade he had outgrown his youthful bohemianism, perhaps because he was aware that its cultural hegemony was ending. After paying a visit to the Art Nouveau theoretician and designer Henry van der Velde in Belgium, Lautrec moved to fancier quarters in 1896 and furnished his rooms in the "modern style" being championed by Samuel Bing. He began frequenting the newly fashionable English and American bars on the boulevards of the Right Bank, and also drank more heavily, to the point of alcoholism (his mother had him increasingly attended and sent him to a sanatorium in 1899). He also drew the fashionable outdoor life of horse riding and bicycling and was a frequent guest at Tristan Bernard's Vélodrome. As his subjects became more diverse and the unity of his style, subject matter, and milieu was broken, his life appeared to be at loose ends. The inward-turning drama that had taken him from the streets of Montmartre to the music halls to the brothels ended with a denouement at the theater, where political, literary, and artistic influences converged most openly at Lugné-Pöe's Théâtre de l'Oeuvre. Political issues were expressed only obliquely in Lautrec's work and were usually mediated through the popular culture he recorded. As an acerbic portrayer of this cultural milieu he was recognized by the anarchist aesthetes to be one of them. Though his involvement was always as an artist rather than as a social reformer, the impression he left was more powerful because of his lack of a potentially distorting ideological filter placed between the artist and his subject. In an era obsessed with untrammeled autonomy and creativity, when Jean Grave is said to have concurred with Oscar Wilde's statement that "art is the supreme manifestation of individualism," Lautrec characteristically exemplified the individual in the form and content of his work rather than through Wilde epigrams or Grave sermons.[55] His aesthetic stance best signified political and moral attitudes when his subject and technique were immersed in his environment, as in the posters plastered on kiosks telling of the performers of the day. For a radical movement founded by one Russian noble and led by another, which extolled both the unique individual and the common people, it was perhaps appropriate that an aristocratic dwarf should best illustrate the enchantments and the disenchantments of its milieu.

Though Paul Signac was more politically *engagé* and more vocal theoretically than Henri de Toulouse-Lautrec, their careers were parallel in several respects. Both artists found their vocation in the studios of Montmartre in the 1880s, where both were heavily influenced by japonisme. The flat planes of pure color employed by *ukiyō-e* artists and by Lautrec also fit into the divisionist scheme of Signac. Their overlapping styles diverged around the spontaneity that Signac clearly renounced as "Impressionist," but this was merely a symptom of a more fundamental difference, founded on the dialectic between naturalness and artifice that was present in both japonisme and anarchism. Signac hoped to achieve an ordered, scientifically rigorous art that approximated the natural order, a conception more appropriate to the Encyclopedists of the Enlightenment than to the Romantics. Signac retained the Impressionist penchant for the outdoors and applied his divisionist theories to the timeless seascapes he executed at Saint-Tropez beginning in 1894. Lautrec preferred painting people in urban, culturally specific settings. His paintings' restless, momentary quality was well served by his fluid brushstroke. As with the artists of Japan's floating world, Lautrec did not eschew careful study and preparation in his studio, yet the final effect brought the artificial world of Montmartre music halls vividly to life. He conveyed the spirit of Romantic criminality and conspiracy together with the vaunted individualism of fin de siècle anarchism. His doctrine of visual honesty, aside from giving his works their immediacy of impact, probably explained his reticence in making political as well as artistic statements except with his brush. In great contrast, Signac's book, replete with clearly outlined distinctions and doctrinal pronouncements, went against the grain of anarchist praxis, as the anarchists disdained laying out blueprints of the revolution.

The anarchist dilemma of how to replace the social order by a natural order was structurally present in the styles and technical approaches of both artists, though their solutions differed. Lautrec's nameless aesthetic appears most congruent with the situation of anarchism in the heroic period of the early 1890s, when his own career reached its apogee. Stylizing the life he saw around him in bold emblematic images, thrusting the viewers into the scene as if they were present at the event, Lautrec's genius lay in transmuting the action-filled life of the dance hall into iconic timelessness. "I saw that" resembles a later motto, "I am a camera"; there was a photographic quality in Lautrec's ability to capture a moment alive.[56] Yet the reality he captured was the artificial life of the stage or the brothel. His own style and the characters he depicted were uniquely personalized. His science of the concrete conveyed the earthy directness of the *argotique* milieu in which he lived. Signac on the other hand decided that fidelity to uniform natural law prevailed over individuality of portraiture or even of artistic style. Equating nature with scientific exactitude, Signac diverged aesthetically from the cultural anarchism of the 1890s. His theory of divisionism instead paralleled anarcho-syndicalism of the two decades following the 1894–95 watershed years, an era marked by cautious organizational advances and fierce maintenance of anarchist autonomy from all political parties.

Literary Anarchism:
The Politicization of Aesthetes

Seven

For the first two decades of the Third French Republic, the leading school of the literary avant-garde was Naturalism. Led by the prolific and combative Emile Zola, these writers devoted themselves to recording the contemporary social scene in all its seamy reality. Despite this interest in their immediate environs, these artists were no more interested in politics than their predecessors under Napoleon III had been. In the years from 1885 to 1895, when Naturalism was becoming passé and the fin de siècle spirit was epitomized by the dreamier currents of late-Romantic Symbolism, writers were much more inclined to seek parallels between their aesthetic vision and radical, especially anarchist, political movements. All demanded unrestrained liberty of expression and they employed political metaphors referring to the insurrection against the rules of syntax and prosody.[1] Writers subscribed to anarchist newspapers, contributed polemical articles to a variety of journals, and looked forward to the end of parliamentary politics and bourgeois society. Nearly all, of course, were of the middle or upper classes. How does one explain this seeming lack of harmony between literary and political styles? At what point did radical politics begin to attract the literary avant-garde, and how did their politics affect their art?

If novelists and poets who considered themselves Symbolists rather than the more socially realistic Naturalists contributed the bulk of support for 1890s anarchism, the critical factor in their politicization clearly could not have been the content of their work. Writing about such themes as strikes, prostitution, and urban poverty did not incline writers to take up their subjects' cause, and as the Naturalists repeatedly emphasized their dispassionate, scientific objectivity, one has only to take them at their word. Nor did class origins correlate in the expected way with allegiance to radical political movements, because the more radical Symbolists generally came from more privileged backgrounds than the Naturalists. Rather than the social content of the work or the social background of the writer, the critical variables determining politicization were the writer's degree of commercial success and commitment to avant-garde values—that writer's place in the "literary field." The popular novelist was more likely to be politically complacent than the esoteric poet. This leads directly to another crucial factor: radical innovations in form were more likely to be associated with adherence to radical political doctrines than were "appropriate" social themes. Stylistic innovation and low status within the literary field both signified one's avant-garde position and predisposed many young writers to embrace anarchism. From 1885 to 1895 the avant-gardes of art and politics came together.

Another important point to underscore in explaining this political resurgence of the 1880s and 1890s is that these *engagés* were members of a new generation. Neo-Impressionism, Post-Impressionism, and the literary movement called Symbolism all coalesced in about 1885–86. Their ranks were mostly filled with young men born during the 1860s who were just entering adulthood, and who were eager to demolish the reigning artistic credos. Some of those born in Paris might have been harboring childhood memories of the Paris Commune of 1871. Such was the case with Maximilien Luce, who witnessed the murderous repression of the Communards at the age of thirteen and would be painting scenes of that event thirty years later. Paul Adam also wrote of his powerful childhood memories of the events of 1870 and 1871.[2] As they attained maturity, many of them experienced obligatory military service, which forced these sons of the bourgeoisie to rub shoulders with the working class and peasants while contending with military discipline. "Barely escaped from the regiment," Paul Adam, Laurent Tailhade, the Rosny brothers, and Adolphe Tabarant were among the writers who laid before their companions "the miseries of the sabre."[3] The last years of the 1880s were also filled with the antiparliamentary rumblings of Boulangism, in which Paul Adam and Maurice Barrès in particular became involved. There were a few exceptions to this Symbolist youth movement who became partisans of anarchism. Laurent Tailhade, born in 1854, started his literary career as a Parnassian poet; Octave Mirbeau, born in 1850, was a realist novelist, though one given to decadent, erotic themes.

If artistic anarchism bore the traces of a youth movement, one might suspect it was merely that—a passing fad to be outgrown like bohemian habits. The writer Camille Mauclair, who wrote a whole anarchist novel in his own youthful enthusiasm, looked back on the era in his later years with a more jaundiced eye, remembering well-fed young writers who thought it chic to be visited by a police commissioner, who had their picture taken with Zo d'Axa and joined in the Latin Quarter riots, but who refrained from contributing money to the anarchist cause. A writer for *Les Entretiens Politiques et Littéraires* (whose title, "Political and Literary Conversations," was itself a sign of the times) noted in 1892 that as once it was stylish to surround oneself with dirty monks or emancipated blacks, now one must dine with workers and young anarchist writers. In style-conscious Paris, where intellectual fashions were shed as readily as sartorial ones, young artists were not the only ones liable to pick up anarchist ideas as a short-lived vogue. An 1893 writer described the ubiquitous specter of social revolution, with cafés filled with talk of German socialism and internationalism, and called the atmosphere saturated with social ideas. He also satirized the student intellectuals whose garbled socialism remained untroubled by sympathy for the suffering poor.[4] Even the conservative newspaper *Le Figaro* noted the stylish socialism of 1892, in an article by the well-known journalist Jules Huret: "Everyone is unanimous in declaring that something must be done. The Pope [Leo XIII, author of the 1891 bull *Rerum Novarum*] is a socialist . . . Maurice Barrès is a socialist, Nini-patte-en-l'air [a popular can-can dancer at the Moulin Rouge] is socialist! And the more income one has, the more one dresses at Redfern's, the more one has one's hair done at Lenthéric, the more one is a socialist!"[5] With such a prevalent mood, in which radical movements garnered the sympathy not only of artists but of a certain number of the more progressive bourgeoisie, it is not surprising that poets would line up behind the left's most violent wing. It is also difficult to separate the vanguard from the *poseurs*.

The police first became aware of this new genre of *compagnon* in 1891. After informers had reported hopefully on a slump in anarchist activity in 1890, one of their number reversed this assessment:

The anarchist idea has made some real progress—is accepted and propagated by a number of men whose past, education, and frequentations seem little destined to such an outcome. It is not among the

working class that one must seek the new anarchists, but among the class of literate youth and even those literati [*lettrées*] of a mature age: M. Octave Mirbeau being a more dangerous anarchist in his articles than the Père Peinard himself! MM. Paul Adam, Georges Darien, and consorts, one could name more than twenty, have become literary anarchists as serious as all the antipatriots of Saint-Denis grouped with those of Clichy. The literary reviews, the published books, are filled with developments of the anarchist idea, developments which will carry their fruit in several years. The working class has hardly swallowed anarchy up to now because it did not understand it, and that which was presented to it made it fearful. . . . one will see the working class come to the anarchism of tomorrow because it will be presented to it by the bourgeois youth.

It is to that period of transition that one owes the momentary halt of anarchist groups, of old-line militants.[6]

The informer exaggerated the influence of young writers on the working classes but correctly foretold that anarchism would evolve in the coming years toward a mounting cultural revolution which would publicize and serve the political struggle. Already, the informer claimed, he could name twenty anarchist writers, though unfortunately he named only three. This report was made before Ravachol's bombs set off two years of terrorist activity. Literary anarchism neither precipitated, nor was caused by, propaganda by the deed. Terrorism served as a dramatic focus for the youth and literati who were attracted to anarchism, and their interaction made the era unique. When Zola wished to portray a terrorist in *Germinal* (1885) he clothed him in Russian nihilist garb and called him Souvarine. By the time he wrote *Paris* in 1897, native French terrorists were entirely credible.

How widespread was the literary fellow-traveling with anarchism? The left-wing writer Séverine, heir to Jules Vallès's radical journalism, mentioned a number of names omitted by the police informer. In "Leur Pitié," dedicated to Laurent Tailhade, she spoke of Mirbeau, the Rosny brothers, Descaves, Tailhade, Adam, Zo d'Axa, Lazare, Darien, Tabarant, Zévaco, Fénéon, Bonnamour, and Conte as belonging to the young generation of writers in love with art but caring also for justice and truth. She counseled future historians to look at the literary supplements to *La Révolte* for the fomenters of the revolution, advice that conflicted with Jean Grave's policy of discouraging avant-garde contributions. Though Mallarmé subscribed, he never penned any of *La Révolte*'s columns. Zo d'Axa was more sympathetic to members of the avant-garde, and when he called for donations to help support the families of imprisoned anarchists, he received a heartening response from more than two dozen painters and writers.[7]

Another popular social charity was the soup-lecture, where the poor were offered free bowls of soup served with generous portions of propaganda. When the police arrested an anarchist named Rousset for conducting one such venture, they thought of implicating all those who had contributed to the operation in an *association des malfaiteurs*. Then they uncovered such supporters as Zola, Sarah Bernhardt, Anatole France, Alphonse Daudet, and various dukes and marquises. One contribution was 10 francs, accompanied by a note that read "gift from a man who is not rich. . . . From the heart for your work, Mallarmé." Fearing to involve such notables, they tried Rousset for abuse of confidence of the subscriptions and sentenced him to six months in prison in 1894.[8]

The police informers described the *compagnons'* eagerness to tap the financial resources of their bourgeois associates. After the Procès de Trente failed to crush intellectual anarchism, there was immediate interest in furnishing the movement with a newspaper to replace those the police had shut down:

The preparation of a paper of Revolt provokes a great movement in the anarchist clan. The title is *L'Au-delà* [The Beyond]; it pleases them very much. Gallo has found some funds. Moitet has designated some friends each of whom will furnish five francs. They think B. Lazare will advance a louis on condition of complete discretion. They have solicited M. Barrès, who has told them to see M. Lagarde Thursday evening, when he escorts the union members and workers' associations.

A few days later, "The idea of asking Paul Adam, Bernard Lazare, Mirbeau, and Zola (well enough liked by the anarchists at this moment) for hundred-franc contributions has been abandoned. They fear to awaken their mistrust. They have been tapped too much. But they know they can count on them for the second number. That, at least, is what Alexander Natanson [an owner of *La Revue Blanche*] has said."[9] In fact it was not until 1895, when President Faure's amnesty released Jean Grave from prison and Emile Pouget from exile, that the anarchist press regained its footing.

A much larger but more perplexing list of anarchist suspects possessed by the minister of the interior in 1894 repeated many of the same names, but the inclusion of other literary celebrities makes one doubt the accuracy, not to say the seriousness, of their sources. The old Parnassian academician Leconte de Lisle and the establishment drama critic Francisque Sarcey shared space on the list with Jules Lemaître and Joris-Karl Huysmans, all of whom were unlikely anarchist sympathizers. Mallarmé, Rémy de Gourmont, Anatole France, and Barrès appeared on the list, as did Edouard Drumont. Along with such likely names as Lazare, Adam, Mirbeau, Tabarant, Pierre Quillard, Retté, Malquin, Séverine, Veidaux, and Hérold appeared the names of the eminent architect Frantz Jourdain, the avant-garde producer Lugné-Pöe, Jean Richepin, and the photographer Nadar. The list of suspects was extended to include periodicals. To *La Revue Anarchiste* and *L'Essai d'Art Libre* were added a number of literary journals and the major Symbolist reviews *La Plume, Le Mercure de France,* and *La Revue Blanche.* They listed 96 agents (*dépositaires*), 67 papers, 3 unions, and 601 assorted other individuals in France, and another 300 people beyond French borders.[10] One possible reason for the unlikely assortment is that they were compiled from the seized subscription lists of *La Révolte*; another is that they were taken from the correspondence carried on by some important anarchist. Such was the case with the names found among Sebastien Faure's possessions when he was arrested in preparation for the Procès de Trente. Other police lists cited Séverine, Veidaux, Fortuné Henry, Pouget, and Paul Paillette, in one case, and a variety of artists and writers including Mirbeau, Malquin, Hamon, Signac, Pissarro, and Ibels in another. If one selects the Symbolist poets, novelists, and critics from these lists, one can easily cite 25 to 30 writers who were at least sympathetic to anarchism, a considerable figure if one takes Ponton's sampling of 57 Symbolists for his literary field studies as a reasonably complete figure.[11] No numerical compilation can adequately portray the pervasive atmosphere of politicization and aestheticism whose peculiar mixture characterized these years.

"The artist will prefer the ideal to the real. The conception of a spontaneous and free organization seems to me to be entirely idealistic, that is, antipolitical. I prefer it." This response of Henry Maubel of Brussels to the "Referendum Artistique et Social" conducted by the journal *L'Ermitage* in the summer of 1893 foretold George Orwell's maxim that the refusal of politics is itself a political position. The referendum asked, "What is the best condition of social well-being, a free and spontaneous organization or a disciplined and methodical one? Toward which of these social conceptions must the preferences of the artist go?" That such an issue should be raised at all in an avant-garde literary magazine was remarkable; that it should be phrased in essentially anarchist terms reveals how deeply anarchism had penetrated the literary milieu by 1893. This is especially impressive considering the fact that none of *L'Ermitage*'s own editors fell under the anarchist, or even the liberal, rubric in the poll. The poll was also pan-European rather than narrowly French, demonstrating the writers' international orientation. Of the ninety-nine artists who responded to the poll, over half agreed with Maubel's libertarian idealism, professing an antipolitics that pushed a smaller number to "group themselves as the partisans of absolute liberty, of anarchy."[12]

The Symbolists accepted parallels between aesthetic and social attitudes as equivalent to overt political partisanship. Thus the *L'Ermitage* staff grouped "the partisans of art for art's sake, doctrine which implies independence," among the "opinions favorable to liberty." Traditional distinctions between left and right, as well as between political and apolitical artists, were replaced by the all-inclusive dichotomy of constraint versus liberty. Among those favoring liberty, most were called "liberals pure and simple" rather than anarchists, as they remained remote from the interests of the lower classes as well as from their own class. Yet judging by the names of Mauclair and Oscar Wilde among the anarchist *littérateurs*, concern for artistic independence outweighed social responsibility among the more extreme advocates of freedom. Mauclair's response to the referendum emphasized the parallel between the aesthetic and political values:

Logic glorifying sensibility, exaltation of the being in harmony with natural laws, valuing others as himself, oppressing neither self nor others—and these two respects coordinating—there is my ethical formula. That is to say I favor all spontaneity. . . .

I say this as artist and as man—same words for me who creates of

my life a parallel work of art. Feel intensely! . . . In life as in art, the event is the product of individual magnetism.[13]

Under "partisans of constraint" were lumped together aristocrats, socialists, and authoritarians. The first category attracted early Nietzscheans such as Hugues Rebell.

The poet Stuart Merrill commented that what was remarkable about the referendum was not that half of the writers interviewed chose libertarian positions while a quarter lined up behind socialism, but that relatively few were apathetic, and that this spirit of commitment seriously affected the artistic production of the fin de siècle. Merrill, a transplanted American writing in French, a supporter of Jean Grave in 1895–96 but classed as a socialist in the poll, wrote of "the conversion of most of the young poets to doctrines of revolt, be they those of Bakunin or of Karl Marx. They will write few poems—I fear and hope—the day the revolution rumbles through Europe."[14] A quarter of the respondents occupied an intermediate position between favoring constraint and liberty, but only eleven were termed "indifferent." Among those hesitating between the two contending forces, *L'Ermitage* grouped A. Ferdinand Hérold and Paul Adam, among the most active of literary anarchists, because they termed themselves communist-anarchists (following Jean Grave's example). Adolphe Retté was also placed in this group for his wavering between liberty and theocracy. Though Retté protested this placement in the next issue and called himself firmly anarchistic, the categorizations of Retté and Adam were prescient considering the underlying religiosity of the one and the militarism of the other, hidden tendencies that would eventually win out.

How many of these writers had been radicalized? Only twenty-one of the ninety-nine respondents were called socialists or anarchists, but the categorization was too arbitrary to be reliable. The editors of *L'Ermitage* emphasized the domination of fifty-two voices for liberty over twenty-three for constraint and twenty-four in the middle. Numerically imprecise, the *L'Ermitage* poll is nonetheless significant for revealing an underlying sense of the breakdown of traditional hierarchies, both social and artistic. One may contrast the response of Richard Dehmel from Berlin with that of Maurice Beaubourg in Paris. Though Dehmel's response correctly placed him among the intermediates, it was still framed in terms of the basic freedom/constraint dichotomy: "The artist, being the spontaneous individual par excellence, will naturally give his preference to all spontaneous efforts of the community, i.e., in times of servitude to spontaneous efforts toward a new liberty, but in times of anarchy toward a new order of public spirit in an effort no less spontaneous." If not anarchistic, Dehmel's artist was at least rebellious. Beaubourg was called an anarchist, and though he placed individualistic values before the community interests stressed by Dehmel, his characterization of the artist was nearly identical: "The artist being an instinctive person, that is to say a force before all else spontaneous and free, he will always go where he can carry out his intransigent individualism, outside of all regimentation and all discipline." Beaubourg continued, "The social well-being will be subordinated in him to his conception of life, and those who want to impose theirs on him will be considered the worst enemies of his art. That is why the words Art and Socialism are exactly at the antipodes."[15] It was evident that in France the *culte du moi* was integral to the artistic variants of anarchism.

Several books appeared discussing the new anarchist vogue among the cultivated classes, beginning in 1892 with Flor O'Squarr's (pseudonym for two journalists) *Les Coulisses de l'anarchie*. The police noted that this book was in high demand in the autumn of 1892, and was to be followed that winter by a sequel called *L'Effondrement* (The Collapse). Another forthcoming work was *Les Gaités de l'anarchie* (The Joys of Anarchy), also inspired by the confluence of literary anarchism and Ravachol's bombings, trial, and execution in the spring of 1892, all of which made good press.[16] In 1895, P. V. Stock published Augustin Hamon's *Psychologie de l'anarchiste-socialiste,* a work pretending to more intellectual rigor than the earlier efforts. In characterizing the psychological tendencies of 170 anarchist informants who responded to his questionnaire, Hamon found a connection between innovation and deviance, the former trait being characteristic of all avant-garde artists, the latter common to artists and anarchists. Hamon did not identify most of his informants, many of whom, one suspects, belonged to the intellectual rather than the working classes, but he did cite the writers Adolphe Retté and Maurice Pujo. Hamon linked the propensity for innovation with that of revolt and noted that "the individual who innovates in Art, Sciences, and Letters evidently possesses the critical mental character" to become an anarchist. Maurice Pujo provided Hamon with just the sort of parallel between aesthetic and political values that he was looking for:

I came late enough to the social question, but if I go through the successive stages of my life, I see developed within me the same principle, I can say the same instinct for liberty that I have recently carried to the social domain. Thus from the aesthetic point of view, I passed to the moral point of view (in the most general sense of the word), and my effort was to conserve in that moral life . . . that absolute liberty that I had found in the aesthetic domain. . . . Liberty in my sense is a living principle, even the essence of life.

Hamon nevertheless refused to conflate avant-garde artists with anarchists. In their distrust of the masses, he wrote, artists "are libertarians . . . for themselves and authoritarians for others," and he derided the proponents of the *culte du moi* for their lack of altruism.[17]

The leading anarchist intellectuals of the era welcomed the adherence of artists to their cause. In his 1885 *Paroles d'un révolté,* collected by Elisée Reclus from Peter Kropotkin's articles in *Le Révolté* from 1879 to 1882, the Russian prince expressed his approval of *l'art social*:

You, poets, painters, sculptors, musicians, if you have understood your true mission and the interest of art itself, come put your pen, brush, engraving tool to the service of the revolution. Recount to us in your style of imagery or in your striking paintings the titanic struggle of peoples against their oppressors: enflame young hearts with the beautiful revolutionary breath that inspired our ancestors . . . show the people that present life is ugly . . . touch the causes of this ugliness.[18]

Strongly influenced by John Ruskin and William Morris, Kropotkin contrasted Raphael's frescoes on city walls with museum-bound art and emphasized art's popular and artisanal usages. He did not sympathize with either the Symbolist or Naturalist literary movements and accused Zola of reducing the technique to a "simple anatomy of society . . . for us . . . realist description must serve an idealist goal."[19] This program resembles the aesthetic credo of the less rarified Symbolists such as Paul Adam. A decade later, Elisée Reclus responded directly to his newfound literary allies. In "To My Comrades of *Entretiens*," he treated the Symbolists in the most cordial terms:

Dear Comrades,

Yesterday we were unknown to each other. Today we are brothers by thought and by will. . . . it is necessary that you have the full and total liberty of comprehension and of personal expression and that you discard all dogmas, along with formulas and prosodies. . . . Painters, engravers, musicians . . . it becomes you to remain yourselves, to reproduce freely that which you perceive in your interior mirror.[20]

Meeting the Symbolists on their own terms, he asked them to help in the creation of anarchist schools and theaters so that the revolution could become a lived reality in the present. He acknowledged the necessity of a cultural revolution to precede and accompany the social and economic one.

Kropotkin and Reclus were members of an older generation who were delighted to enlist the support of activist youth. Demographic and generational factors were important in the adherence of artists to anarchism. *L'Ermitage* recognized this fact when they followed up their initial referendum of artists aged thirty-five and under with a second poll of the older generation. Whereas eleven of the younger group were called partisans of anarchy, only two of their elders, Octave Mirbeau and Edmond Picard, were so classified. Most of the older writers took less clear-cut political stands than the younger ones: Mallarmé spoke vaguely for liberty, Zola for evolution. Verlaine displayed surprising sophistication in admitting "I share the political opinions of Joseph de Maistre, the dream of Bakunin not yet being realizable." By *L'Ermitage*'s reckoning, a young writer was one born since 1858, and most of those polled would have been born during the prosperous years of the Second Empire. The decade from 1856 to 1866 witnessed France's highest birth rate for the second half of the nineteenth century. Symbolism, which was a coherent literary school from 1885–95, was largely a movement of the youth born during the Second Empire who chose as their mentors two figures from the previous generation, Mallarmé and Verlaine. Writers such as Fénéon, Schwob, Saint-Pol Roux, Barrès, and Adam were born in the 1860s, although Camille Mauclair, Alfred Jarry, and Francis Jourdain precociously participated in the literary anarchism of the 1890s while still in their teens. Mauclair especially characterized literary anarchism of the 1890s as "an appendage of youth. It is not a system of social life, but a form of young sensibility," an expansion of the ego which corresponded to youthful idealism.[21]

Mauclair also remembered the July 1893 student riots in the Latin Quarter with Jean Carrère as the student prince leading the melee. Higher education boomed under the Third Republic, with university enrollment doubling from 1875 to 1891, then doubling again by 1908. Barrès viewed this increasing student population as a special constituency worth courting in his newspaper *Le Cocarde,* and he described the plight of the intellectual proletariat of unemployed graduates in *Les Déracinés* (The Uprooted, 1897). In his 1895 psychosocial study of anarchists, Augustin Hamon reported that six-sevenths of the anarchists he polled were under forty.[22]

The Symbolists born between 1855 and 1864 belonged to a large and self-conscious literary generation who were competing for their share of a shrinking literary market. The total number of published writers of fiction in France grew rapidly during the first decades of the Third Republic, with 290 new writers added to the 1890 figure of 592 writers in the final decade of the century. The 1855–64 literary generation was more Parisian-born and less provincial than writers born in the previous decade, and had twice the number of foreign-born writers practicing their vocation in France, which might help explain the frequent accusations that they were alien and cosmopolitan rather than truly French.[23]

The class origins of the literary generation born between 1855 and 1864, though not markedly different from the literary movements of other decades, varied greatly from those of most of their fellow Frenchmen. Though over half of the French population belonged to the lower class, only 7.6 percent of these writers came from the lower social strata. One-quarter issued from the lower-middle classes of schoolteachers, shopkeepers, and employees, one-third from the middle classes, and one-eighth from the upper-middle classes or the aristocracy. Over half of the Realists and Naturalists came from the lower classes or the petite bourgeoisie; only one-fifth of the Symbolists had such lowly class origins. Two-fifths of the Naturalists had middle-class origins or higher; two-thirds of the Symbolists came from the middle or upper classes. Such differential class backgrounds may help explain the common accusation of vulgarity leveled at the Naturalists by the other literary groups, as well as their retort that the others were feeble and anemic dilettantes. The aristocratic literary set appears less elite when compared with the social composition of the Chamber of Deputies, which in 1893 was composed of 23 percent nobles and 34 percent more from the *haute bourgeoisie*.[24]

Many more poets emerged from the 1855–64 generation than in the preceding decade, but less than in the period after 1865. Poets of lower-class origin (12.5 percent) and of aristocratic birth (also 12.5 percent) were overrepresented; poets of middle-class origins were relatively less numerous, dropping from 40 percent in 1845–54 to 15 percent of those born in 1855–64.[25] The poets who would call themselves Symbolists, Decadents, and Naturists became polarized with respect to class origins, and more distinct from the middle class, from which only 15 percent issued. These were among the writers most prone to anarchism, either because they were of lower-class origin and probably disadvantaged in competing in the literary field, or else of upper-class origin and attracted by the individual act of revolt as a symbol of their own *déclassement*. Anarchism found its supporters among the rich as well as the poor, but few among the solid middle classes.

The literary generation of the years 1885–95 faced not only an enlarged number of fellow producers, but also a drop in the number of titles published per year, a decline that was first felt after 1885 and which seriously disrupted the literary market of the 1890s. The novelists' market fell sharply in 1890, and remained at around 400 titles per year for the rest of the decade. Poetic publication declined in 1890–92, then made a slight recovery, hovering at roughly 200 titles per year.[26] As the modest increase did not match the large growth in the number of producers, and the slackening in published titles was matched by a decrease in the number of editions sold, the average share of the market held by each producer diminished markedly. Two-thirds of the books published between 1891 and 1893 lost money, which led to price wars in which a 3.50 franc book was sold for 60 centimes. Thus two-thirds of the novelists of these crisis years reaped nothing from sales, and only six novelists earned more than 10,000 francs per year.

The remaining option for the writer who wished to live by the pen was to move into journalism, but there too the field was overcrowded and the pay was low, about 15 francs per entry in 1903. Lack of access to the mainline press led to the founding of a myriad of what were called young reviews, in explicit reference to the generational conflict inherent in their creation. These literary journals, which appeared at a rate of over sixteen per year in France and Belgium between 1887 and 1894, opposed the venality of the mainline press with dedication to pure art, and true to their disdain for commercial success most folded quickly.[27]

As the literary market contracted in the 1890s and the competition increased among a growing number of writers, their numbers fed by a disenchanted university population (one may cite Marcel Schwob, who entered the literary field after failing to find a place in academia, or the Hellenist scholar and anarchist Pierre Quillard), adherence to radical political doctrines functioned both as an outlet for frustrations and as a strategy for extending one's audience beyond the limited literary readership. "The writer, to save his *raison d'être*, must conquer a social audience at any price," and although writers like Paul Adam contributed many articles to avant-garde journals, others like the poet Adolphe Retté changed the very quality of their output to match their new anarchist creed.[28] Retté's literary retooling did not win him the audience that his Symbolist poetry had failed to find; it was only in turning to Catholic apologetics a decade later that he conquered a whole new readership and began selling books. This is not to say that one turned to anarchism merely for the sake of finding new literary markets, unless one was a sensation-seeking journalist. Rather, economic hardship catalyzed already-powerful literary antagonisms, encouraging the search for a political corollary to those antagonisms that would magnify the difference between groups and dramatize the Symbolists' outsider status. The *déclassement* of an increasingly large body of writers heightened their awareness of their social and economic marginality, leading them to identify with other marginal groups that abetted the anarchist cause. The publishing crisis that coincided with the turn toward anarchist politics by disenchanted artists resulted in a new conception of their role as social critics. The *gens de lettres* became the *intellectuels*.

The "Manifeste des Intellectuels," published in *L'Aurore* on January 14, 1898, gave *intellectuel* the widespread notoriety that would make the term an integral part of the Dreyfus Affair. Later in 1898 the Dreyfusard Emile Durkheim defined intellectuals not as those who possessed a monopoly on intelligence, but as those people engaged in the arts and sciences for whom the extension of knowledge and ideas was both means and ends, whose reason stood sovereign above authority.[29] The manifesto's appearance at the opening of the affair, shortly after Zola's *J'Accuse,* indicates that the term was already in vogue. In the decade preceding the affair, the term was used not to designate an individual but to characterize certain decidedly negative traits. The intelligence was a noble faculty, but the intellectual was a monster devoid of feeling. As applied to the disciples of Hippolyte Taine and Ernest Renan, it was used in conjunction with such loaded terms as dilettante, aesthete, and fin de siècle, and suggested that their intellectualism sapped their vital energy. It was also used pejoratively in reference to anarchists. A speaker in a year-end college address blamed intellectuals for the *attentats,* calling them "these pretended philosophers, false scholars."[30] The bourgeoisie viewed the anarchist writers as subversive *déclassés* who transgressed the bounds of their role and their class. The attack on intellectuals might have garnered additional support if the speaker had known of the anarchist clique that called itself Les Intellectuels, and which in 1894 was composed of Paterne Berrichon (Clement Dufour), Adolphe Retté, and a friend of Verlaine's named F. A. Cazals.[31] An article entitled "L'Anarchie intellectuelle," published in May 1894, blamed Emile Henry's bombings on the writers and their three sins of pride, materialism, and atheism. The critic reproached such writers as Laurent Tailhade and Adolphe Retté for transferring their hatred for their fathers into politics and for irresponsibly propelling ideologically unsophisticated men to their deaths. As with characters in their literary productions, they were seen as engineering men's fates without themselves suffering the consequences of their words.[32]

A figure very much in the fray was Maurice Barrès, a writer and Boulangist deputy from 1889 to 1893, who in his person and in his writing did much to shape the fin de siècle conception of the intellectual. As late as 1894, Barrès surrounded the term *intellectual* with apostrophes, indicating that he considered it to be a neologism. At the end of 1894, Camille Mauclair wrote "Sensibilité du sceptique: À propos de Maurice Barrès," in which he spoke of Barrès's malady of intelligence, of a frigid will in which spontaneity was lost and the oversensitive young intellectual turned cynical and *stendhalien.* Mauclair admired Barrès's flirtations with anarchism as an expression of his individualism but could not help suspect its authenticity.[33] Nevertheless, a bizarre critique of the one-time deputy appeared after his foray in the Dreyfus Affair maintaining that "the spirit of Barrès is anarchy. It has been from the beginning."[34] As Barrès was supporting the army in 1898, this critic evidently feared not his particular position but his very political involvement. If one was not an anarchist, then one was accused of stirring up the forces of doubt and egoism by one's corrosive intellect. The phenomenon of the intellectual frightened many Frenchmen of the 1890s, tainted as it was by the acids of anarchy that dissolved the traditional bonds of the state.

Described by Barrès as *Les Déracinés* (The Uprooted) in an 1897 novel by that name, the intellectuals were defended by one of their number, André Gide, who praised uprooted intellectuals for refusing the desire for faith and certitude that lay in traditional allegiances. Gide's term, *dépaysement,* differed from Barrès's organic metaphor in connoting cosmopolitanism, and is reminiscent of the anarcho-syndicalist Gustave Hervé's self-appellation *le Sans-Patrie. Dépaysement* signified the strength and adaptiveness of the nomad or *trimardeur* rather than the homelessness of the dispossessed peasant.[35] The freedom of the one was the alienation of the other. Like a butterfly on a leaf, Gide's intellectual could alight to favor some political cause, but could not dwell there for long without sacrificing the freedom and, synonymously, the beauty of its flight.

From anarchism to the Dreyfus Affair, the decade of the 1890s registered the discontent of the newly politicized intellectuals whose numbers were swelled by the ranks of the educated unemployed. The intellectuals were made conscious of their new status by the aforementioned social and demographic factors, and by the autonomization of the literary field, those interrelations of writers and literary groups struggling for symbolic domination.[36] Symbolic domination was measured to some degree by financial success, but also by legitimacy in the eyes of peers, public, the press, and the literary establishment. The literary field was progressively autonomized from the economic, political, and religious fields during the last half of the nineteenth century, as writers had less input into extraliterary social relations. Symbolist insistence on the primacy of form over function, and of literary style over subject matter, was the "most specific expression of the demand for the autonomy of the field," as well as compensation for being excluded from the other fields.[37] Outcast and powerless, the autonomy of the literary field increased the likelihood that writers' ideological interests would be conditioned by their place within the literary field rather than by their class origins. When they returned to partisan politics in the 1890s, their participation in the field of power reflected their literary career hopes and institutional relations. By the time of the Dreyfus Affair, writers had regained some of their Romantic predecessors' activist optimism, but in the early 1890s the Symbolist avant-garde whose autonomy was the most extreme and most cherished was still alienated enough from the polity and the economy that the desire to alter the power structure was accompanied by the wish to negate and transcend it through anarchism.

The Symbolists guaranteed their autonomy by their chosen medium of expression. Though Lugné-Pöe attempted to enact Symbolist drama and Paul Adam devoted himself to the creation of the Symbolist novel, most Symbolists writers chose poetry. In a movement that valued introspection, purity of form, and obscurity of syntax, poetry was to the Symbolists what the novel was to the objective and socially oriented Naturalists. It stood for their devotion to art against all material considerations. The vitality of poetry in France after the relative doldrums of the two decades between Baudelaire's death in 1865 and the triumph of Symbolism after 1885 made the Symbolists more conscious of their poetic mission and more bitter toward the poetic establishment known as Parnassus. The elders were attacked for their rigidity and preciosity, for overattention to the rules of prosody and corresponding lack of feeling or spontaneity. Although literary in-fighting is tangential to the study of cultural politics, writers often expressed their political attitudes in their antagonism to other literary groups. Thus in 1893, the young Symbolist Francis Vielé-Griffin announced the publication of a new volume of Parnassian poetry in political terms: "They tell us that the authoritarian Parnassus prepares a blow of force in order to crush the Symbolist anarchy: the attempt is bold and perilous."[38] The Parnassians were the entrenched establishment; the Naturalists represented the mass market: both groups had "made it" either in terms of prestige or in financial and popular success. In opposing them, the Symbolists maintained their identity as the sole writers dedicated to pure art untainted by money or power. They were a self-conscious avant-garde, and felt radical in being so.

The conventional wisdom of the era regarded Naturalism as a style that excelled at depicting crowd scenes but which displayed little sympathy for the individual. Zola's literary mass production was equated with socialist uniformity and regimentation. To Maurice Beaubourg as to most of his fellow Symbolists, "Art and Socialism are exactly at the antipodes," and Octave Mirbeau contrasted the free reign of individualism with socialism, "that imbecilic erasing of the individual, wanting to number, regiment, level the species."[39] In April 1902, Maurice Leblond, writing in *La Revue Socialiste,* contrasted the supposedly socialist novels of Zola with the anarchist ones of Paul Adam and described socialist literature as that which elevated the crowd to center stage.[40] Naturalism was literature of and for the masses. One of the Symbolists' English allies expressed the common attitude toward the public perfectly. In *The Soul of Man Under Socialism,* Oscar Wilde epigrammatized the aesthetes' disdain for the masses:

Now Art should never try to be popular. The public should try to make itself artistic. . . .

In England, the arts that have escaped [interference] best are the arts in which the public take no interest. Poetry is an instance of what I mean. . . . The public like to insult poets because they are individual, but once they have insulted them, they leave them alone. In the case of the novel and the drama, arts in which the public do take an interest, the result of the exercise of popular authority has been absolutely ridiculous. . . .

The public dislike novelty because they are afraid of it. It represents to them a mode of individualism. . . . Art is Individualism, and Individualism is a disturbing and disintegrating force. Therein lies its immense value. For what it seeks to disturb is the monotony of type, slavery of custom, tyranny of habit, and the reduction of man to the level of a machine. . . .

It is impossible for the artist to live with the People . . . the People bribe and brutalize. Who told them to exercise authority?[41]

Despite his misleading title, Wilde's little tract revealed neither social nor socialist consciousness, but it did show why the *L'Ermitage* poll placed Wilde among the literary anarchists. Where the seventeenth-century Puritans respected worldly success as a sign of God's grace, the Symbolists suspected it as signifying an attempt to be popular.

The watchword of individualism that Wilde equated with art became so insistent that literary groupings themselves were called into question and writers denied adherence to any school of artistic doctrine other than their own souls. As early as July 1890, Emile Goudreau described a new antimovement constructed on "the Self (*Moi*), emancipated, audacious, masterless, [which] could found Individualism on the ruins of defunct schools." Two years later statements of this kind had become such a cliché that a critic could mock Adolphe Retté's vaunted paternity of the phrase "there are no schools, there are only individuals," maintaining hyperbolically that "that unsightly phrase has been written no less than 365 times, and by very diverse persons." Rémy de Gourmont put it slightly differently in his celebrated definition of Symbolism as "individualism in art."[42] The endless coteries of the 1880s were rejected as if the anarchist impulse viewed by their contemporaries as being inherent in the Symbolist movement impelled the artists to deny the competitive presence of the literary field itself, to reject its manifestos and self-aggrandizement. Despite their raising of literary politics to the metalevel of challenging the operation of the field itself, at least in regard to their own if not to other literary schools, they could not escape from it. The profession of absolute individualism itself had its political motives. Anarchism had invaded literature.

Was individualism really as subversive as Wilde believed, or was it instead the ideological reflection of bourgeois values, as Bernard Lazare thought? Stéphane Mallarmé, who in welcoming the rebellious individualism of the younger Symbolists proved himself willing to renounce the poetic authority accruing to his position, was aware that poets reflected as well as rejected their society's mores and values. Victor Hugo thought he had determined the course of poetry for a century to come, Mallarmé wrote, but "in a society without stability, without unity, he [the poet] can erect no stable, definitive art. Of that unfinished social organization, which also explains the disquietude of the spirit, is born the inexplicable need for individuality, of which the present literary manifestos are the reflection."[43] Continually driven to renew their art, the poets' belief in progress and unrestrained individualism reflected the dominant social ethos.

The elitist individualism endemic among so many writers like Mauclair and Wilde was contested by others on the left. The social art movement shared the Naturalists' desire to create a popular, mass-oriented art form and shared too its antipathy for the art for art's sake school. In *La Revue Socialiste,* August 1893, the socialists also protested that art for art's sake was a luxury that a society badly in need of transformation could not afford, and that all progressive forces had to struggle for social change.[44] The various groups calling themselves Club or Groupe de l'Art Social were not clearly socialist, their membership being a mixture of socialists and anarchists and, in 1896, including the first syndicalist followers of Fernand Pelloutier. They were more committed to social change than to any specific literary program, but their preference for accessible and didactic works that would stimulate social consciousness appears closest to the form used by radical neo-realists such as Octave Mirbeau, Lucien Descaves, and Georges Darien. Among the members of the first Club de l'Art Social, organized in 1889, were the brothers Rosny, Georges Renard, and Adolphe Tabarant, who proclaimed themselves apolitical and republican and were literarily most akin to the Naturalists. This group lasted only several months and was replaced by the review *L'Art Social* under the aegis of Gabriel de la Salle, which appeared from 1891 to 1894. The journal stood for utilitarian art and social change, and decried the bourgeois individualism of the Symbolists. Nearly all the poetry that appeared in its pages was regularly rhymed and respected the alternation of masculine and feminine lines. Among its collaborators, André Veidaux and Augustin Hamon were anarchists, Alexandre Bourson (Zévaès) and de la Salle were socialists, and only one writer named Diamandy recognized Marxist class distinctions, the rest referring simply to "the people" against the bourgeoisie.[45] Mistakenly thinking all these writers anarchists, the police dissolved the journal early in 1894 and arrested de la Salle in the general anarchist crackdown.

In 1896, such anarchists as Bernard Lazare, Pelloutier, Jean Grave, Charles Albert, and Paul Delesalle reorganized *L'Art Social* to provide a basis for a revolutionary literature. Grave had never been very sympathetic toward Symbolism, and Lazare had become disillusioned with the Symbolists' elitism and with the radical veneer of salon anarchism. As early as 1893, he had debated Pierre Quillard's defense of the "perfect uselessness" of a book and had argued for the higher utility of an ideal toward which all art must strive. A critic rather than a poet or novelist,

Lazare was less responsive to arguments based upon literary form than to the ideas being expressed. In a lecture given in April 1896, later published as "The Writer and Social Art," Lazare called art for art's sake the reflection of bourgeois egotism and referred to the Symbolists as the "rot of the bourgeoisie" who were soon to be surpassed by more progressive classes.[46] Yet Lazare was still aesthetically closer to his old friend Paul Adam, former fellow editor of *Les Entretiens Politiques et Littéraires*, than to Zola. He expressed his belief in a future-oriented art (such as Adam's *Lettres de malaisie*) that would show how society could be transformed rather than dwelling on its present ugliness. Pelloutier, who had been converted from socialism to anarchism by Hamon but had never sympathized with the propagandists by the deed, also delivered a lecture on "Art and Revolt" in 1896, in which he declared that art's role was to make revolutions and invited artists to join the movement as auxiliaries of the syndicalist combat. He did not approve of the Symbolists' cherished autonomy and wished to subjugate art to propagandistic purposes.[47] As the poets' sympathy for anarchism decreased so likewise did the anarchists' toleration of the avant-garde. The demand for aesthetic autonomy, the rejection of didactic and moralistic art, the scorn for the marketplace and the insouciance toward the public that had distinguished Symbolism from Naturalism and made anarchism rather than socialism the Symbolists' political ally became unacceptable to the anarchists as they turned more resolutely working class and trade unionist. The primacy of form over content that was the hallmark of aesthetic modernism became to anarchists and socialists alike a mark of bourgeois decadence, as it had been to Proudhon forty years before.

Many young poets of the generation coming to maturity around 1895 rejected the anarchic individualism of the preceding years. Parnassian aloof detachment had inspired the Symbolists to champion a highly subjective poetic language; the Symbolists' own extremes of hermeticism and aesthetic refinement engendered a reaction of simplification of diction and popularization of themes. As the name Symbolism connoted a spiritual and transcendent idealism, *Naturism* (a short-lived movement distinct from Naturalism) suggested the pantheistic appreciation of the commonplace, the return from artifice to the celebration of the natural world. There was a broad consensus in favor of a more socially directed art in the mid-1890s which was fostered primarily by the socialist and anarchist artists. In a 1907 volume called *La Littérature sociale,* a critic singled out Adolphe Retté's diatribe against Mallarmé in 1896 as the turning point away from the excessive egoism, the taste for the rare and abnormal that he claimed typified Symbolism. The critic associated this literary change with a corresponding political one: "The avant-garde reviews proclaimed the necessity of reacting against literary neurosis and gloom. Most of the Symbolists tended politically toward anarchism, and it was natural following their intense individualism. The newcomers and those from the preceding period who had become more sober turned toward the altruist doctrine of socialism."[48]

Among the writers reevaluating both their poetry and their politics in the mid-1890s, Adolphe Retté exemplifies the correlation between aesthetic and political attitudes. Not only were his political choices influenced by his place in the literary field; they were also a strategic way of dramatizing conflicts, increasing his audience, gaining notoriety and sometimes respect. For writers like Barrès, Lazare, and Retté, art and politics were no longer at the antipodes, nor were they limited to being analogous forms of rebellion; they were functionally entwined in that complex pattern of career choices controlled by monetary and other forms of reinforcement that constituted the literary field. Anarchism, interposed between his Symbolist and Naturist moments, served to redefine Retté's relatively weak position in the literary field, justifying a break and a new aesthetic philosophy.

Born in 1863 and falling squarely into the second generation of Symbolists, Adolphe Retté was a minor poet who published a very esoteric volume of verse called *Thulé des brumes* (Thulé of the mists) in 1892 that was moderately well received but considered derivative of Poe and Baudelaire; Bernard Lazare called him a *haschischin* (hashish taker) who transferred his smoke-filled visions to paper, and recommended, ironically it would appear in hindsight, that Retté follow "his own forces and the power of his own spirit" instead of relying on the inspiration of Mendès and Maeterlinck.[49] In January 1893, Retté published an article in *L'Ermitage* in which he proclaimed his devotion to Stéphane Mallarmé. He had only praise for "the love of the absolute Dream," and although he dared to suggest that "Mallarmé's art seems a bit cold. One feels that the poet lives on Parnassus," he forgave that too because it expressed the poet's personal sentiment. He concluded in calling him "one of the rare thinkers of our time, a prince of the Word that one must admire but refrain from following."[50] Retté's belief in artistic individualism predated his conversion to anarchism.

The year 1893 was the biggest turning point in Retté's life until his 1906 conversion to Catholicism. Three events in the coming year would help politicize him: the Victor Hugo banquet, in which Retté protested against having a table of honor; the July student riots against Bérenger's censorship of the Quat'z'Arts Ball and in protest against the closing of the Bourse du Travail; and the strike of the Pas-de-Calais miners.[51] Retté himself told Augustin Hamon, the anarchist social psychologist, that a friend had told him that his individualistic aesthetic convictions could only be complete if he acquired "an integral conception of life," and in simple phrases explained anarchy to him.[52] Letters by Maurice Barrès and André Veidaux in response to an article he wrote for *La Plume* in February 1893 also influenced the young poet. Rebutting an article that had appeared in *L'Ermitage* the preceding November, Retté denied that an anarchist writer must serve the people by words and actions and said that art and sociology must remain distinct. He attacked Zola and Naturalism for cheapening art's ideals and pandering to bourgeois tastes, and even warned artists that their reward for uplifting the proletariat would be a revolutionary regime that would allow only useful art. In February 1893 he was at most the "theoretical anarchist" who foresaw the era of socialist realism with as much loathing as he had for contemporary capitalism. In September he lauded Jean Grave's *La Société mourante et l'anarchie* in *La Plume,* and in November he wrote again on the role of poets, this time defining them as the paradigm of the free being, whose social role lay more in being a model for less liberated humanity than in producing useful works. Summoning images of Hercules killing the monster of Authority, and of Prometheus struggling to free himself, Retté remained in the Romantic genre that corresponded to the heroic anarchism of the early 1890s.[53]

Retté was briefly imprisoned in January 1894 in the general antianarchist campaign, and information on him was sent by the police to the Ministry of the Interior on August 29, 1894.[54] In his *Reflections on Anarchy* of that year, reprinted as *Promenades subversives* in 1896, he distinguished himself from the young men who thought it fashionable to assume a subversive demeanor but who were "made more prudent by 'certain noisy incidents'" and who returned to the superior world of art.[55] For Retté there was no return. In 1893 the Naturalist/Symbolist opposition between the popular and pure work of art still defined the boundary between the socialist art of the masses and the anarchist art of the individual. Retté's 1894 critique of political dilettantism marked his rupture with his old artistic milieu. Wary of ideological adherence to a political philosophy, he determined to live rather than discuss the Rousseauistic creed that he called the development of the integral man. In the autumn of 1894 he retreated into the forest of Guermantes; the poetry he produced over the next two years was vastly different from his Symbolist efforts and would be marked by the dual influences of his anarchism and return to nature. Accompanying this poetry was a long series of articles that appeared in *La Plume* in 1896, which provided the critical justification for his rejection of Symbolism. The most notorious feature of these articles was a heated attack on his former preceptor Mallarmé, which had more shock value among his fellow poets than any political diatribe could have had. He caricatured Mallarmé as the decadent who produced a small amount of sterile poetry that nobody but himself could understand but which everybody therefore believed was of profound significance. Mallarmé was the chief mystagogue of the religion of art that had been erected on the dogma of symbolic correspondences and the synaesthesia of genres, described by Retté as "that confusion of one art with another, that hypertrophy of the sense of correspondence [in which] is found all decadence."[56] He similarly decried the art for art's sake detachment of the poet who sought the ideal in an atmosphere of "poignant solitude," as Vielé-Griffin described it.[57]

Retté's rejection of Symbolism was almost subsumed by his anticlerical and pantheist rejection of all religious attitudes that repressed the human self and will. Summarizing the conflict between the spiritual and "integral" (we might say "organic" or "humanist") individual, Retté wrote:

The situation is very clear. On one side there are those that Christianity still poisons under the bastard form of a troubled spiritualism. The love of the sterile dream, the disdain for life, the hatred of science and of realities entrain them in the night—they perish there.

On the other hand, those who return to nature, those whom the

Great Pan possesses work in the light. Robust and sane, they are no longer men of letters; they are integral men—the future belongs to them.[58]

Retté was attacking the Symbolists not simply for being asocial, but also for being unnatural and therefore decadent. The biological metaphors applied to the Symbolists' passive ennui, their cerebral anemia, reminiscent of Max Nordau's argument that *degeneration* was a feature common to artists, anarchists, and criminals, reflected Retté's own version of positivist faith in nature and science. For example, when he attacked Mallarmé's "personal syntax," he compared the grammatical order of the French language to the laws governing evolution and spoke ingenuously of "the natural laws of his art." Mallarmé's violation of natural law could then be dismissed as "a moment of literary aberration, the extreme decadence of a period of art."[59] This critique by the anarchist-Naturist was not very different from that by the Catholic apologist of a decade later.

Retté's first collection of poetry to appear after his anarchist-Naturist conversion was the 1895 *L'Archipel en fleurs.* The combative poet could not present his poems without a lengthy preface in which he defined the poet's role by the Rabelaisian motto "tu feras ce que tu voudras" (do what you like). He counseled the reader to "seek your rhythm among the profound empires of your soul," far from the "well-made" things invented by the masters.[60] The day that Rimbaud made the first upside-down sonnet was the moment when "the first bomb exploded in the temple of the Rule" (p. 8). The poetic prologue, dedicated to Stuart Merrill, announced Retté's self-image as the "Voyager in space and time" (p. 26), seeking new ideologies beyond those offered by the chorus of voices. Poems such as "Maison des fous" (Madhouse), describing a place where lies and dreams came and went like so many madmen, were composed of short lines of six and seven syllables with an occasional longer line. There was much alliteration and repetition of sound, in phrases such as "Les Songes et les Mensonges" (Dreams and Lies) or "Penchés vers les dalles des salles / en quête de perles pales" (Stooping toward the floor of rooms / in quest of pale pearls) (pp. 42, 43). In two poems Retté looked back to his arch-Symbolist book of 1892, remembering "Thulé des Brumes par tes grèves / C'est un Pauvre qui chante et rêve" (Thulé of the

Mists by your shores / It's a Poor Man who sings and dreams). Each stanza ended, "La Folle des chemins perdus" (The Madness of lost roads), referring to the lost roads of Symbolism. In the epilogue, Retté returned to the Adventurer motif of the prologue and rejected the dream-world so often referred to in his Symbolist period. Shipwrecked on Thulé, he tasted Circe's drunken kisses, swam off to sea "along with my pride, alone in the immensity, finally washed ashore on an island where there are no kings, no merchants with false weights" (pp. 119–26). The poem "Triomphale," dedicated to Jean Grave, was written in declamatory alexandrines despite the ideological brunt of the preface, and it described how the simple folk would rise up when they saw through the lies and laws of the Princes of error (pp. 115, 116). Retté varied the meter of his poems according to their particular message, and he kept that message simple and clear.

Simplicity became all-important to Retté as the sign of his increasing distance from the values of Symbolism. In the poetic morality tale that Retté wrote at Guermantes in the spring of 1895, called *Similitudes,* an ignorant wanderer named Guillaume told tales of the land beyond the dawn where there were no kings or police to take one's produce. A wind blew the king's portrait off the wall where Guillaume was staying, and it shattered. He addressed the grape pickers and miners until he was hauled off by the authorities. An "alienist" declared him a victim of hallucinations and "ecstatic monomania," and Guillaume was finally stoned to death for saying "there is no country; there is only the earth." Guillaume, the *Pauvre* of whom Retté wrote "my heart always beats in unison with those of all the Poor," was buried at a crossroads at which four men met to tell of the revolution rising in all directions, as the miners, grape pickers, factory workers, and intellectuals all arose against Authority.[61] The parable ended as nightingales sang that the country of the sunrise announced by Guillaume was not some distant land, but their own.

Retté made a conscious decision to write popular and propagandistic works in the service of the revolution, texts that increasingly shed their poetic form in expressing the dual theme of natural simplicity allied with revolt against authority. This tendency toward simplification culminated in 1896 with *Le Forêt bruissante,* which was divided into a prologue called "the tale of the black shepherd" and an epilogue, "Arcadia," between which were eight songs that formed an epic in free verse. The protagonist, now called Jacques Simple, was lured by a poet who offered visions of pastoral beauty, when a suffering old hag came forth and called the poet a prostitute who sold his rhythms and beauty to kings. Jacques chose suffering over beauty and together with the hag had plunged into the forest on the road to Arcadia. A place of refuge from the corrupt city but still an ominous realm of illusion and fear, the rustling forest was a transitional place between silence and noise, between solitude and revolution. When this forest-purgatory burned down one apocalyptic night, Christ came down from his cross of suffering and declared the new dawn. Jacques invited him to the new paradise on earth but Christ refused, saying, "The last of the gods can die / To sacrifice himself to the salvation of other worlds."[62] Retté the Naturist decided that the forest was not an end in itself but only a passage to revolution. An old man told the shepherd, "The word of the Forest is necessary for you to find / You alone—and by yourself you can be saved" (p. 18). In summarizing all poetic art with the phrase, "go, with simple heart, to nature," Retté strived to make his work self-effacing rather than self-focusing, to use free and epic verse to make poetry appear as naturally speechlike as possible. The same desire to collapse distinctions between art and life, to escape linguistic arbitrariness for some absolute, inspired his pantheism, his anarchism, and later his Catholicism, as first he denigrated culture and then renounced nature for an elusive ideal.

For all of his efforts, Retté's Naturist poetry reached no more of an audience than had his Symbolist work. It was not until his next great shift that he found his literary market. His 1906 book *Du Diable à Dieu* (From the Devil to God), which recounted his spiritual passage from anarchist to fervent Catholic, went into several editions and translations and even converted his own mother. With the conversion that signaled his renunciation of anarchism came a concomitant rejection of all avant-garde literary pursuits. He symbolically accepted poetic orthodoxy by seeking spiritual advice from François Coppée, the surviving Parnassian academician whom he had lambasted a decade earlier. As a literary strategy, it was his most successful conversion, at least in terms of popular appeal. Having relegated his anarchism and his avant-gardism to his egotistic and antagonistic youth, Retté spent the remaining quarter-century of his life composing works of Catholic piety, none of which had quite the impact of the conversion experience of which he wrote in 1906.

In this act of supreme humiliation, Retté collapsed the literary, political, and religious fields into a composite experience in which the basic drama of his life was enacted. The fundamental opposition determining his successive conversions (as Symbolist, as anarchist-Naturist, and as Catholic) was that between rebellion and its attendant critical consciousness, on the one hand, and acceptance and faith on the other. Elements of rebellion and faith were mutually operative in Retté's earlier ideological and symbolic positions, and his poetry of the 1890s was full of Christian imagery despite his fierce anticlericalism. Only in 1906, the same year that Barrès was elected to the Academy, did he renounce the principle of doubt itself, in attempting to escape from the poet's pariah status. Retté's case demonstrates the relevance of the literary field in determining an artist's ideological choices, and also highlights the semiotic overtones of this analysis. Retté's conversion was a sign bearing greater significance than its overt religious referents indicated. Its meaning lay in a network of relations ensconced in the differences and oppositions within the cultural system to which he belonged. His meeting with Coppée explicitly connected his new religious adherence with the renunciation of old literary heresies. Political, religious, and literary avant-gardism and orthodoxy were homologous. What might be interpreted as an individual and idiosyncratic decision (based on Retté's advancing age, his lifelong search for faith or for a surrogate father, and so on) actually encapsulated a whole series of systemic relations. Retté described his leap of faith as taking place in the solitude of the forest, but his decision was really made only upon returning to Paris, where its meaning was clarified in the context of his old literary and political environment.

Interpreting a writer's political choices in terms of his career pattern requires one to span decades rather than to restrict one's vision to a few short years. The politicization of the aesthetes of the 1890s can not fully be understood without reference to the relative lack of activism in the preceding decades, and even to earlier literary generations' hopes to join in the decision-making process. The subsequent careers of the anarchist aesthetes of the 1890s also shed light on the rationale behind their early political positions. The diachronic reinforces the synchronic perspective. The Naturist search for roots in the late 1890s is strongly reminiscent of Maurice Barrès's quest for "the earth and the dead" in *Les Déracinés*. Adolphe Retté's decisions of 1906 are unintelligible without reference to his earlier anarchism, but the specific choice of religious orthodoxy as the means by which he recanted his former apostasy also reflected the Catholic revival that affected many intellectuals in the decade before World War I.[64] One of several former anarchists who later turned to religion, Retté's transformation from political activism to pious quietism reproduced the trajectory taken by other apocalyptic revolutionaries (see chapter 10).

Anarchism meanwhile had also evolved, but in a very different direction from the route taken by Retté. Next to direct action, the demand for autonomy from all political parties, particularly from the socialists, was the rallying cry voiced most often by the anarcho-syndicalists in the years preceding the war. The autonomy of the economic and political fields demanded by the anarcho-syndicalists bears comparison with the autonomy of the literary and political fields demanded by the artistic avant-garde. The anarcho-syndicalists did not renounce their dreams of political and social change, but wanted to accomplish these goals through the revolutionary general strike, that is, by acting on their own terrain. So the artistic avant-garde wished to preserve their artistic integrity without disregarding the political turmoil around them. The literary field was autonomous, but only relatively so. What made the artistic anarchism of the 1890s both remarkable and complex was the anarchistic valuation of autonomy and independence. Not only did rebellion against aesthetic orthodoxy within the literary field have political connotations, but the autonomy of the field itself was homologous with the anarchists' own fiercely maintained independence. This autonomy created a tension within literary anarchism between the claims of formalist and socially conscious art, as the avant-garde writers, especially poets, realized that their works were inaccessible to the public. Faced with this disjunction between signification and communication, the Naturists rejected the obscurity they identified with Symbolist aesthetic experiments, and instead used local traditions and everyday diction to broaden their appeal. Anarchist militants and proponents of "social art" such as Fernand Pelloutier and Bernard Lazare also doubted the political efficacy of Symbolist art. Ironically, the demand for anarcho-syndicalist autonomy from political parties did not make the anarcho-syndicalists more receptive to the artistic autonomy of the Symbolists, who were attacked for being ivory tower aesthetes. Despite their hostility toward the masses (who were associated with the degrading popular art of Naturalism), for a few years the Symbolists pioneered in exploring the political potential of literary modernism. In doing so, they exercised a uniquely aesthetic influence on fin de siècle anarchism.

Literary Anarchism:
The Aestheticization of Politics

Eight

The Symbolists came down from their ivory tower in order to change the world—aesthetically. The tower itself remained standing, surmounted by a beacon—their aesthetic ideal—which they hoped would light the way to the new society. Although the Symbolists followed their Romantic literary forebears Victor Hugo and Alphonse de Lamartine in wanting to play a role in society, they were much more alienated from the political process, which is why anarchism suited their temperaments. Their political response was ambivalent; they were more willing to aestheticize their politics than to commit themselves wholeheartedly to the political fray. Aesthetes as well as artists, they perceived all of life in essentially aesthetic terms, as a continuous process of seeking meaning and form in phenomena. The preceding chapter looked at what made writers anarchists; this chapter will focus on these writers' search for an appropriate anarchist poetics.

The tensions within the literary field that predisposed the second generation of Symbolists, those who came to maturity around 1885–90, to maintain an antagonistic attitude toward their poetic elders and toward those they considered vulgarizers of art were exacerbated by the publishing crisis that surfaced around 1890. An overcrowded field with a glutted market made literary newcomers more prone to radical solutions. This social malaise was matched by what might be termed a semiotic crisis in the production, role, and value of signs.[1] Though the Symbolists largely accepted the Parnassian belief in the purity of art and its supremacy over nonaesthetic considerations, they questioned the syntactic rules upon which French poetry was based; that is, the formal relationship between signs, the semantic relations between the poem and the world it designated, and the pragmatic relations existing between signs and their social interpretation.[2] Despite the individualistic rhetoric which seemed to sanction solitariness, the Symbolists pursued a new system of relations at all semiotic levels. Just as they sought correspondences between the phenomenal and noumenal realms, they also wished to integrate the social and aesthetic aspects of poetry that had formerly been divorced. When contemporary Symbolist critics such as Rémy de Gourmont virtually defined Symbolism as anarchist poetics, they were referring not to the level of engagement but to the degree to which the poets' semiotic project at formal, semantic, and pragmatic levels was congruent with anarchist ideals. Symbolist experiments with free verse, with the sounds of words and the internal rhythms of the poem, together with their concern for densely symbolic, multilayered levels of meaning, brought frequent charges of hermeticism. Rather than reducing complex poems to simple programmatic statements, a writer's political activism added a new context in which to interpret the work.

"The latter half of the nineteenth century," according to one linguist, was "a period of sudden, violent inflation of linguistic signs."[3] As poets detached themselves from normal social intercourse, their work became increasingly self-referential to the point where meaning was deemed secondary to the sound of the words, or else the subject of the poem was the poetic process itself. Charles Maurras was criticizing this linguistic inflation when he characterized the poetry of Mallarmé by its astoundingly free play of signifiers (in this case the words) totally removed from any recognizable signifieds (the content to which the word refers). Mallarmé was instrumental in redefining poetry as being freedom in language. By allowing his poetic signifiers an unlimited autonomy from simple, referential meaning, he was free to explore the possibilities of sound, rhythm, and multivalent meaning. The liberation of poetic language was acquired, however, at the cost of normal intelligibility. He bequeathed to his many disciples a sense that poetry demanded testing the limits of order, rules, and constraints.[4] Mallarmé recognized the anarchistic implications of signifying freedom through poetic discourse, and he clearly believed that poetry should not be a didactic political instrument but rather should embody anarchist ideals. A poem that shocked bourgeois sensibilities was akin to revolution; one that achieved freedom from prior constraints was a metaphor of utopia. Poems would exemplify, not lead to, social change.

The extreme disjunction between signifiers and their referential and informational functions caused a reaction among second-generation Symbolists such as Stuart Merrill, Adolphe Retté, Ferdinand Hérold, and Saint-Pol Roux, who did not want to deflate the importance of the sign, but tried to re-encode it in the larger cultural system. They did not deny the artist's priestly role as manipulator of symbols, but their renewed Romantic stress on the poem as spiritual instrument and on the creative process led them away from the isolated perfection of the passively contemplated, self-sufficient poetic object. Their opponents pointed out derisively that all art demanded symbolization, but by calling attention to the symbolic process, the Symbolists emphasized poetry's semiotic mission to give meaning to the world by establishing unexpected relations between discrete phenomena. The young poets who elaborated an anarchist poetics within Symbolism did not require more social content, but rather the socialized codification of the creative process, so that the esoteric language of initiates would have more public resonance. Signs derive their meaning within the context of a particular culture, and those meanings are generally ensconced in social codes of behavior. In describing Symbolism's task as "the work of inscribing a dogma in a symbol," Paul Adam hoped to link clearly signifier to signified.[5] The Symbolism of the 1890s evolved from the idiolectal privacy of the symbol to the contextual world of the sign.

The process of establishing links between phenomena and between the sacred and profane had been known as the doctrine of correspondences since Baudelaire's famous poem by that name. As elucidated by Georges Vanor in his 1889 L'Art symboliste, finding correspondences was fundamental to Symbolism, "the literature of metaphors and analogies; it seeks the possible affinities among heterogeneous phenomena and appearances. Hence those frequent expressions over which artless persons are amazed and which evoke the sound of a color, the color of a note, the fragrance of a thought."[6] If the symbol was the expression of a synesthetic perception, why limit such analogies to sensory phenomena or even to the vertical relation between the real and the ideal? One might extend the tendency to interrelate discrete phenomena (as Paul Adam and Camille Mauclair described it) to epistemological metaphors as well, so that one order of experience might stand for another. In enlarging the artistic mission beyond the confines of aestheticism, the young Symbolists sought not only engagement but a new unity between aesthetic, spiritual, social, and political experience. The desire for unity that underlay the doctrine of correspondences was parallel to the anarchists' wish to regain the prelapsarian state of innocence and spontaneity from which corrupt society had strayed.

Because they scorned didactic art, the Symbolists generally did not write overtly about anarchism. Poetic propaganda would have falsified the very nature of Symbolist poetry, in reducing its symbolic multivalence to a single referent and focusing it outside the structure of the poem itself. Closely approximating the linguistic definition of the poem as an ambiguous and self-focusing message, Symbolist poetry was scarcely the ideal medium for rabble-rousing.[7] Such reticence has led a modern commentator to conclude that anarchism and Symbolism had little in common between their mutual avant-gardism.[8] Such an evaluation ignores the metacommunicative function of Symbolist art. The prefix *meta* signifies the commentary on the rules or code underlying the object of discourse, so that metacommunication is dialogue about the process of communication rather than the communicated message. With their vaunted indirectness, the Symbolists were notoriously shy about making simple programmatic statements; instead they would establish parallels between aesthetic and political practice. Aesthetic modernism and radicalism would stand for social change. Not only their literary politics but also the formal liberties they took with their texts metacommunicated to the social sphere such values as the free play of creativity. Their metasemiotic project to change the codes governing French poetry generated new signals to the political field which in turn tended to restructure the codes.[9] Retté's literary career furnishes one clear-cut example of the dialectic between political message and aesthetic code. When Paul Adam wrote that "social dissonance outrages those who love the beautiful," and perceived the postrevolutionary society as a work of art to be constructed by skilled utopianists, he was extrapolating from artistic to social practice.[10] The Symbolists tended to aestheticize politics as they would a poem, to treat it as a consummatory rather than an instrumental activity, sometimes echoing Bakunin's adage that destruction was a creative act. Despite the ambiguity of the content of their work, the Symbolists' political message was clear to their contemporaries: not just words but deeds could be beautiful, if carried out with style.

Art helped define the central anarchist issue of liberty. The anarchist idea of freedom differed from the Marxist in exactly the same way that their emphasis on revolutionary will diverged from the "scientific" theory of economic determinism.[11] Whereas Marx conceived of freedom as resulting from people's increased control over their environment, specifically over the means of production, the anarchists regarded skeptically the complex technocratic state such control required. Nature was not so much to be controlled through the reason as listened to from the heart, which encouraged irrational and spontaneous modes of behavior. Human beings would experience freedom less in work than in play. The aesthetic sense, a means of transcending purposefulness, functioned best in a realm of total freedom from the constraint of economic considerations. The appreciation of beauty and contrast of art with an ugly society was also seen as a radicalizing factor, but the aesthetic sensibility was not confined to the beautiful.[12] More important, it suggested the triumph of form over function, of the gratuitous and the contingent over the necessary. Beauty was appreciated for its own sake; art for art's sake should not be cast down, but rather extended as a model for all activities. The practical corollary of this aestheticized position was that any reduction of artistic purity and integrity, any sign of a functional element displacing the delight in pure form, compromised the autonomy of the poetic model.

Amid the noise of Ravachol's bombs, Pierre Quillard could write, "Good literature is an eminent form of propaganda by the deed," not by its propaganda value but by its very existence. He argued that simply by contrasting itself with the sordid reality of society, a beautiful work of art constituted an act of revolt. Quillard cited Plato's banishment of poets from the Republic as evidence of poets' enduring subversive potential. The novels of Zola, by dwelling on contemporary society, inevitably affirmed the status quo; in contrast, every Symbolist poem was a tiny utopia, an experiment in the absolute. Quillard sanctioned the interpretation of art as the presence of an absence, a simultaneous statement of what was and what was not. The work of art embodied its own negation, whose dialectical trace was the society in which it existed.[13] The Symbolists had no thought of their works' social relevance until the era of literary anarchism presented them with their mirror opposite, their social reflection, the crucial absence from their poetry that broke forth in such unexpected places as Mallarmé's notes to the unwritten *Le*

Livre. Their aesthetic idealism was placed in relief by their political involvement, which presented them with the option of writing didactic poetry, an alternative they largely rejected in favor of more purely connotative interpretations like Quillard's.

As a complex response to contemporary intellectual and political currents by a cosmopolitan cultural elite, French literary anarchism must be situated within the broader context of European culture. If anarchist cultural politics were simply a matter of writers adopting the ideas of Bakunin or Kropotkin in their works, such a comparative literary focus would be unnecessary. Yet the Symbolists were more likely to be influenced by Tolstoy, Nietzsche, and Ibsen than by anarchist ideologues. The question of influence is still more complex in that in cases where the writings of such thinkers as Nietzsche, Kant, and even Hegel were given an anarchist interpretation, the interpreters were clearly imposing their own readings onto their texts. Thus within the domain of elite culture there was generated not only anarchist ideas but an anarchist criticism that was preoccupied with individualism, autonomy, violence, martyrdom and self-sacrifice, and other characteristically anarchist themes.

More cosmopolitan than any previous French literary generation, the Symbolists scoured the literature and philosophy of Germany, Russia, and Scandinavia, thereby provoking accusations of being un-French from chauvinist critics. The Parnassian poet José-Maria de Hérédia, who himself was foreign-born, spoke of the malign influence of Germanic and Norse literature on Latin culture, and Charles Maurras accused the Jewish *littérateurs* surrounding *La Revue Blanche* of having imported the works of August Strindberg, Hauptmann, Wilde, and Georg Brandès into France, replacing French with "European literature."[14] There was considerable interest during the fin de siècle in promoting international languages such as Volapük and Esperanto, and it was easy to ascribe political motives to movements toward pan-European fraternity, not only by hostile critics but by police watching for signs of international anarchist conspiracies.[15] One cosmopolitan figure on the French literary scene was Alexandre Cohen, a Dutch writer who translated the works of Hugo von Hofmannsthal and other Germanic writers into French. He was first deported and later tried in absentia in the Procès de Trente. The

Symbolists did in fact draw radical political conclusions from many of these foreign works, undeservedly in some cases. In an era when nationalism was becoming the province of the right, the foreign and exotic were readily associated with the subversive.

The cult that formed around Richard Wagner received just such an anarchist interpretation. In the 1880s, Edouard Dujardin's *La Revue wagnerienne* had championed the cause of the master of Bayreuth at a time when it was nearly impossible to hear his works in anti-German France. By the 1890s, *Tristan and Isolde* was playing at the Opéra to appreciative audiences, while the anarchists prepared propaganda claiming Wagner for themselves. A leaflet seized by the police told how Wagner, living in poverty in 1840s Paris, sold his dog to buy an opera ticket, and asked the opera-goers why those who lacked money should be deprived of spiritual cultivation: "Supreme derision. This Wagner, of whom your admiration makes a sort of demigod, was condemned to death in 1848 as a revolutionary, while his friend Bakunin was the first to formulate anarchist theories, and by this fact is seen to be a predecessor of Ravachol."[16] Wagner's *Art and Revolution* was first translated into French under the aegis of Jean Grave's *Les Temps Nouveaux* in 1895. The young Wagner foreshadowed Kropotkin's dream of a collective as well as total work of art produced cooperatively in the anonymous manner of medieval art.[17]

German philosophy as well as German music strongly influenced the young Symbolists' thought. The greatest spokesman for German idealism among the Symbolists was the critic and novelist Rémy de Gourmont. In his 1891 interview with Jules Huret for the *Enquête sur l'evolution littéraire,* he very nearly equated idealism and anarchism. As opposed to the subject matter of Naturalism, Symbolist idealism conceived the dream, fantasy, and the unconscious to be the true reality; such subjects lent themselves to "unlimited liberty in the domain of artistic creation, literary anarchy. This is the present state of literature as well. It is the most enviable. We defend ourselves from rule-makers; we accept no formula; we deliver ourselves to our temperaments, to be and remain free."[18] A year later in an article entitled "Idéalisme," de Gourmont called idealism "an immoral and desperate doctrine; antisocial and antihuman—and for that idealism is a very commendable doctrine in a time concerned not with conserving, but with destroying."

The idealist was resigned to remaining imprisoned in the ego and was uninterested in the relativities of morality, the nation, tradition, family, or procreation, all notions banished to the practical domain. "An individual is a world . . . the idealist will admit only one type of government, an-archy."[19] One might seek traces of Kant's classical individualism and of Stirner's egoism as underlying this denial of all abstractions beyond the self. Yet de Gourmont placed himself between the pessimistic idealism of Schopenhauer, which he said ended in despotism, and the optimistic idealism of Hegel, whose result was, surprisingly, anarchy. Notwithstanding his equation of Symbolist creativity and anarchy, de Gourmont held with Schopenhauer that in the absence of laws, superior men would dominate. If idealism did not remain asocial, it would lead immorally to anarchism and despotism. Rémy de Gourmont considered Symbolism to be the aesthetic manifestation of philosophical idealism's stress on personal intellectual development. Symbolism "translates literally by the word liberty and, for the violent ones, by the word Anarchy."[20] Pushed to anarchic individual extremes, this subjective art tended to be incomprehensible and therefore had to fix its meaning in eternal and ultimate truths while scorning all ephemeral rules. Rémy de Gourmont's individualist and libertarian discourse demonstrated how anarchist terminology had influenced his aesthetic theories.

If the Germans dominated French avant-garde philosophical attention and the Scandinavians the theatrical scene, it was the Russian novel that provided greatest alternative to contemporary Naturalist models. The novels of Dostoyevsky and Tolstoy were first translated into French in 1885–86, and Melchior de Vögüé's influential *Le Roman russe* of 1886 stressed the religion of suffering and compassion as a respectable alternative to sordid and cynical Naturalism.[21] The image of the passionate and tortured Russian soul that fed into fin de siècle spiritualism was one part of the reaction against the confident positivism of the generation of Zola, Eiffel, and Thomas Edison.

By the 1890s Tolstoy had renounced the role of novelist for that of saint. His moralistic approach to art, his rejection of the creative potential of the isolated artist and his preference for the artisanal productions of the folk, were remote from the aspirations of most Symbolists. As Adolphe Retté wrote, "Morality is one thing and literature is another. If one wants to marry them, one runs the risk of having abortions." In contrast to moral didacticism, Retté cited Paul Adam's *Le Mystère des foules* for its "aesthetic which only considers moral values from the viewpoint of their intensity, corroborating a unitary and pantheist philosophy."[22] Tolstoy and Adam both based their dreams of social harmony on an altruistic moral code. Other French anarchists were attracted to Tolstoy's evangelical Christianity and pacifism, which he expressed in a number of essays translated into French between 1885 and 1903. Tolstoy's influence was sufficient to warrant a study on *Le Tolstoïsme et l'anarchie* that was presented to the International Revolutionary Workers' Congress of 1900. It concluded that Tolstoy was an excellent Christian of the primitive church but a poor anarchist and revolutionary.[23] Though Tolstoy's rejection of the state, law, and militarism was admired, his pious nonviolence sat poorly with activists and even with intellectuals such as Kropotkin, who might have reservations about individual acts of terrorism but who would not go so far as to elevate nonviolence to a principle of action. Retté disliked Tolstoy's monastic asceticism and believed that humanity must evolve between the poles of the altruism of Tolstoy and the "frenzied individualism" of Friedrich Nietzsche. "Such is, in substance, the conception of the Symbolists."[24]

Though Retté had already fallen out with the Symbolists when he wrote this last statement, he was correct in linking the names of Tolstoy and Nietzsche as the alternative extremes influencing the social and political thought of the Symbolists. In 1895, one of the French Nietzscheans, Hugues Rebell, praised the German master's philosophy as a cure for Tolstoyan sentimental humanitarianism, and other early disciples saw in Nietzsche the antidote for all the recent Nordic influences: Ibsenism, Schopenhauerian and Wagnerian pessimism, the cult of pity and death. Nietzsche was put into a social and political framework by the newly politicized writers, who perceived an aristocratic moral that was the opposite of the socialist egalitarian ideal. Despite its German origins, this new philosophy stood for pure individualism, Latin vitality, and paganism, against the social and sentimental importations from the north. While Mauclair perceived anarchist echoes in Nietzsche, Henri Mazel of *L'Ermitage* saw a return to order and aristocracy. Geneviève Bianquis describes the Nietzschean cult in France among the generation following Nietzsche's own, those born between 1865 and 1885, as "the generation of intellectualist and pragmatist Nietzscheans, of authoritarian and anarchist Nietzscheans ... royalists and syndicalists, skeptics or dionysians, solitary immoralists or imperialists of action."[25] Nietzsche's abundant flaws as a social thinker were matched by the ambivalence of the Symbolists toward the range of available political positions, and their mutual mistrust of the democratic and moralistic sentiments of the masses was expressed in a very similar pose of aristocratic individualism. Nietzsche's antipolitics was more likely to attract Rémy de Gourmont and the *L'Ermitage* staff than the more *engagé* writers associated with *La Revue Blanche* and *La Plume*. Despite a common antidemocratic and anti-Romantic bias, Nietzscheanism could not be assimilated to the doctrines of Charles Maurras, for whom individualism represented the essence of the Romantic and social malaise.

Nietzsche's works were first becoming known to the French intelligentsia in 1892 and 1893, at the height of literary anarchism.[26] Nietzsche was incompletely understood in the early 1890s, and his image merged with that of Zarathustra, the lone prophet reviled and uncomprehended by society, a rebel against all conventional morality and sociability who recognized heroic creators alone as capable of rising above the herd instinct, over the abyss of nihilism to affirm life. He was perceived as an opponent of the ivory tower of aestheticism, whose call for energy and virility was echoed by the Naturist reaction to Symbolist idealism. Nietzsche's most important contribution to the literary anarchists was the combination of extreme individualism with his all-encompassing critique of contemporary morés. The dialectic of egoism and altruism represented by Nietzsche and Tolstoy, mediated by Ibsen's social realism, was not merely the expression of a literary and philosophical vogue, but was at the heart of both the Symbolist and anarchist dilemmas, and as such was one of the most essential linkages between the creative revolutionaries and the revolutionary creators.

The Symbolists' relation to anarchism was doubly determined by their perception of formal homologies between their art and elements of anarchist ideology, and by the sense of opposition they felt between their transcendental pretentions and the anarchists' social concerns. The Symbolists were as notoriously ambiguous about their political participation as were the anarchists themselves. They were attracted to the anarchist ideal, but like Kropotkin, Reclus, and Grave, their own idealism often precluded a mundane view of the necessities of political compromise, of the realities entailed by social change. When Walter Benjamin later wrote about the Paris of Baudelaire, he emphasized the poet's ambiguous relation to modern society: "Modernity is a main accent in his [Baudelaire's] poetry. He shatters the ideal as spleen. But it is precisely modernity that is always quoting primeval history. This happens here through the ambiguity attending the social relationships and products of this epoch. Ambiguity is the pictorial image of dialectics, the law of dialectics seen at a standstill. This standstill is utopia, and the dialectic image therefore a dream image."[27] The Symbolists were less attuned to modernity and more idealistic than Baudelaire had been. Ambiguity and transcendental idealism brought them closer to the anarchist utopia than to the social reality acknowledged by Baudelaire.

The disorder in the streets, the noise of bombs and meetings ill-accorded with the priestly mien of Mallarmé and his acolytes. Mallarmé's comparison of the book and the bomb, occasioned by the notoriety of the propaganda by the deed, made explicit the analogy between differing forms of symbolic discourse. In saying that the most powerful bomb was actually the book, the poet implied a contrast between the noisy acts of the bomb thrower and the silent words of the writer, distancing himself from political activity even while acknowledging it.[28] Reflecting the ambiguity of their political thought, the Symbolists' fascination for silence can only be understood in relation to their social and political environment. The more insistent the demands of the noisy outer world, the more the artist was tempted by the otherworldly vow of silence that would confirm the artist's superiority over the masses, the artist's renunciation of the social for the spiritual realm.[29]

Paul Adam, who was moved to write a eulogy for Ravachol, was enchanted by the thought of "the moral power of SILENCE," and explained his dream of the silent and ineluctable multitude: "It is my most striking childhood memory of having seen pass by on the boulevards on September 4, 1870, the Blue People [presumably the workers marching out of their neighborhoods after the collapse of Emperor Napoleon III's army at Sedan and the proclamation in Paris of the Third French Republic] descending from the faubourg St.-Antoine and marching in absolute silence, grandiose, eternal, with the symbolic appearance of the

Race. . . . an immutable, frightful silence evoking in the crowd the divine sovereignty of the Race which gives birth to a phase of its social rhythm: and success will follow."[30] Not just quiet but "absolute silence" transformed the masses demanding a new republic into the symbolic manifestation of the onward march of the people. Silence, like revolution, cut through the mundane noise and rhythm of daily urban life. Camille Mauclair described a tripartite contrast between urban noise, silence, and the specter of revolution, as his poet-character André de Neuze walked around the Butte of Montmartre late one night:

Little by little the noise subsides. . . . The sole, strange noise of the millions of beings who still speak, in their bedrooms or in the last open cafés. Then it dies. . . . This was the mysterious and bizarre hour when Paris was silent. Barely an hour before the people who arose at dawn began again to parody the sea; the hour when the colossus slept without dreams, without breath. The sensation of this unparalleled silence is more frightening and more majestic than the tocsin of revolutions. André de Neuze tasted the great horror.[31]

The noise of steps disturbed his reflections: it was Roche (Paul Adam) and the anarchist Passat, who entreated de Neuze to leave behind his love problems and join the cause. Elsewhere in the novel Mauclair declared that "the credo of the modern artist is silence," and despite Calixte Armel's brilliant conversation, one felt in this Mallarmé-figure "the habit of silence."[32]

Silence therefore distinguished the "modern" artist from loquacious but traditional peers as well as from the clamoring masses. Silence existed in the white interstices between the words that became increasingly noticeable in the late poetry of Mallarmé, an absence first made possible by free verse that encouraged one to read between the lines. Free verse was silent verse, designed to be followed by the eye across the page on which it appeared as an object with a distinctive topological configuration. Free verse exploited the print medium more fully, thus purging poetry of its rhymed similarity to the song, this despite the Symbolists' fondness for modeling their art on music. This paradox of the musically minded Symbolists creating a visual art of silence was reinforced by their new stress on rhythm as a formal element that would replace rhyme, a concept that also had its musical analogies.[33]

The meditative and priestly virtue of silence initiated the artist into some higher mystery. The artist took refuge in the silence of the cloister; it was like a religious vow to sanctify and separate one's art from the profane world. As poetry was stripped of its linguistic and communicative elements, its semantic value pared down, it became totally inner-directed.[34] Even Adam's silent marchers announced their unshakable unity and identity, their collective being, rather than their particular grievance or cause. Although in the later form of Gandhian nonviolence such a tactic could be an effective political tool, satyagraha was as distant from the reality of struggle in the Third Republic as India was from France. This extreme poetic tendency, the dialectical opposite of social ferment and of propaganda stripped of its syntactic value, was one element figuring in Retté's critique of Symbolist introversion and other-worldliness. If silence demarcated art from society, it could also set one off from the bombast of political oratory. Recently ousted from the Chamber of Deputies, Maurice Barrès made this his theme in "Le Grand Empire du Silence," a phrase he borrowed from Carlyle to contrast the provincial silent majority with the vocal Parisians.[35] The sound of bombs, of marching feet, of political speeches reminded writers that total silence existed only in the stillness of death, an absolute that the most hermetic poems could only approach. In fact, their silence was always relative to words and to deeds, protesting against a society that silenced its bards.

If not deathlike, Mallarmé's poetic universe was widely known for its private, inaccessible character. In his response to Huret's *Enquête,* Mallarmé compared the poetic process to the devious means by which the psyche spoke in dreams, suggesting but never naming the object of its desires. Poetry "is the perfect usage of that mystery which constitutes the symbol—to evoke an object little by little in order to reveal a state of soul by a series of decodings (*déchiffrements*)."[36] As the editor of *La Plume,* Léon Deschamps, wrote in "L'Esthétique," Symbolism only provided the palace which the reader was free to furnish. Symbols must be subtle and indecisive, a condition allowing for obscurity but also for freedom of interpretation, an elitist but nondominative relationship to the reader.[37] Silence was only the outer limit of the Symbolists' general valuation of signification over communication. Though Mallarmé was sometimes accused of being too silent, that is, of not producing enough poetry to justify his position of high esteem, more often his critics pointed to his impenetrable poetic shell that frustrated potential readers' efforts at comprehension.

After he had left the Symbolist fold, Adolphe Retté lambasted Symbolist obscurity for its solipsistic concern with the poem's internal relations over its semantic and pragmatic uses. "Le Décadent," as he termed Mallarmé, invented "a personal syntax, to accept unusual words in order to confuse the vulgar. But the vulgar, in his sense, is a priori everyone. . . . He dreams of a poem summed up in a strophe, of a strophe condensed in a line, of a line compressed in a word—that he would repeat to infinity and whose melody, appreciated only by himself, plunges him in an inexpressible ecstasy."[38] Implicit in this Symbolist mystagogy, Retté was saying, was valuation of the word itself, detached from all social context or even from relations with other signs. The cult of the symbol decontextualized signs, stripped them of their signification and focused instead on their "intrinsic musical virtue which permits them to cohere, finally obtaining sonorities to which, by a phenomena of singular self-suggestion, he [Mallarmé] discovers a literary sense."[39] Retté defined decadence as the poetic reproduction of the social isolation of the writer, with the artist bent on producing incomprehensible poems that nobody would read. The Symbolists' "poignant solitude" was really the erection of an artistic idiolect, a private language whose cosmic pretensions masked the social alienation of the artist.[40]

Despite the elements of caricature, Retté's articles had the merit of distinguishing the poet's public responsibility from the private pursuit of sonority or meaning. However much an idiolect might connote individualism, rebellion, or originality, the poet's reluctance to communicate detached him from the anarchist dialectic between individual and social pursuits. To the degree that it really had shed its common relations, oppositions, and referents, Mallarmé's deification of the symbol led to its detachment from the semiotic context, and thereby to its impotence as a sign. An idiolect such as Mallarmé's, as a radically individual construction challenging conventional aesthetic codes, could conceivably revise artistic norms. By departing from standard systems of signification, the personal idiolectal style, reflected ideologically in the jargon of individualism, called attention to the artistic codes themselves.[41] Though Retté correctly singled out some of the metaphysical presumptions of the Symbolists, their confusion of mysticism and mystification that sometimes led them to purposeful obscurity, one suspects that his single-minded attack on Mallarmé as the chief decadent of art for art's sake was done for reasons of literary politics. Even in his most anarchistic phase, when he tried to broaden the communicative range of his poetry through simplification of language and themes, Retté did not forget that radical art could serve as a model as well as a vehicle for social change; that its formal properties metacommunicated the artist's own freedom from convention and the artist's awareness of social codes. While railing against aestheticism, he did not reject Symbolist techniques such as free verse.

The noted critic Albert Thibaudet has written of the three revolutions of Symbolist poetry: the first was the liberation of verse, the second the purification of poetry (the Mallarméan aspects discussed earlier), and third its revolution of revolution, by which the critic meant its persistent avant-gardism. "Symbolism accustomed literature to the idea of an indefinite revolution, an artistic Blanquism."[42] The creation and encouragement of *vers libre* was the chief aesthetic means of abetting this revolution. Free verse was the privileged medium for translating one's idiolect into harmonious and communicative self-expression, as the spontaneous anarchist revolution would lead the individual to the realm of social harmony. In June 1892, the important article by Mallarmé, "Vers et musique en France," appeared to lend the master's assent to the young poets' project. Mallarmé cited Jean Moréas, Kahn, Vielé-Griffin, Charles Morice, Verhaeren, Dujardin, Maeterlinck, and Albert Mockel as practitioners of free verse. Among these writers, those whose responses were reported in the *L'Ermitage* questionnaire of 1893 all sided with the partisans of liberty, and Verhaeren in particular was an outspoken leftist. They had escaped the "rigid and puerile mechanism of the alexandrine for the polymorphous tonality of the value of words. . . . A new literary liberty is acquired."[43] Mallarmé emphasized the open-endedness of this poetic form, which made possible as much interpretation on the part of the reader as it did individual freedom of expression. This suggestive, indeterminate quality was not a major element in the frequent literary anarchist accolades paid to the liberation of versification. Although poetic liberty was acclaimed, such lack of direct expression meant that the poem's meaning was open to question. Although poetic overdetermination was often rejected on grounds of obscurity, free verse extended the creative process from a single act of inspiration to each successive reading of the work. Mallarmé, who spoke as a character witness for Félix Fénéon at the Procès de Trente and was far from oblivious to the social currents of the 1890s, possessed a more democratic poetic vision than many of his younger and more *engagé* compatriots.

The straightforwardly anarchistic use of free verse can be seen in the *Hurles de haine et d'amour* (Howls of Hate and Love), which the young writer Manuel Devaldès (a pseudonym for Ernest Lohy) published in 1897. Devaldès called poetry "the exteriorization of an individual's feelings, a spontaneous gushing of the soul, a chant, a cry" for which free verse could be the only appropriate form. The liberation from poetic rules was equated with the individual's freedom of expression. In spite of this, the anarchist's poems were entirely rhymed, but he varied the line length dramatically, rhyming three-syllable with twelve-syllable lines. The conclusion of the poem "Défaillance" (Swoon) was typical of his personal rhythmic quality, as of the quality of his poetry in general:

> **Toute dernier est mon heure**
> **et musicale monte la plainte**
>
> **des fleurs**
> **qui pleurent**
> **et meurent.**
>
> **(The hour is late**
> **and the plaint rises musically**
>
> **of the flowers**
> **that cry**
> **and die.)**[44]

The theory of rhythm replacing rhyme constantly accompanied Adolphe Retté's championing of the cause of free verse. As early as 1893, the anarchist *littérateur* Jean Carrère reviewed Retté's *Une belle dame passa* in terms of the individual quality of Retté's free verse, so distinct from that of Henri de Regnier or Moréas or Vielé-Griffin. "There is no other code to free verse than the special sense that the poet has of Harmony." Retté replied the following month, "Art is rhythm and rhythm is life itself."[45] Rhyme schemes, the alternation of masculine and feminine rhymed words, fixed meters, and length of stanzas were forms placed upon the poem to ensure its poeticity. Retté and Carrère maintained that this special poetic sensibility came from within, and was only stifled by uniform stylistic encodings. Retté's vitalist belief that the rhythm of free verse was the means by which life was transmuted to art was echoed by Paul Adam in a review of the poetry of Francis Vielé-Griffin. Adam found a wonderful correspondence between the poet's philosophy of man as "a state of cosmic energy" and the movement of his strophes, "which reflects and contains marvelously the total rhythm of Forces."[46]

If carried to its logical conclusion, where Retté did in fact take it, the doctrine of rhythm suggested that poetry was neither a métier to be practiced and honed nor a uniquely God-given gift of genius, but merely a way of expressing the wellsprings of the self. In the article "Sur le rhythme des vers," in which Retté expanded his brief comment on Carrère's review, he brings to mind Wordsworth in his comparison of the poet to the simple child, a specialist in instincts rather than in polished verse. This rejection of complexity and craft was further than most Symbolists would go, and it led Retté to Naturism, which accorded well with anarchist Rousseauistic tendencies. For Retté, the technique of free verse became indistinguishable from his primitivist pantheism, the personal and natural means of expression that surged forth from close contact with nature. He described the process by which one's sense of rhythm operated as if it were some supraindividual force that depended on one's being in the proper state of receptivity: "A rhythm draws itself, obsesses you, to which you unknowingly conform your steps. The rhythm becomes precise, some words precipitate in a crowd that forces entry. Then a hundred accessory images launch themselves as rockets (*fusées*) of your Unconscious and attempt to associate themselves to the premature image."[47] Later one could polish the poem, but only nature could awaken it in the poet.

Anarchism was too complex to be reduced to individual spontaneity, as Retté's later poetry would have had it; it also contained an element of conspiracy, of cryptic messages, subterfuge, and evasion that was closer to the Symbolist poetic practice. Symbolist delight in rare words and neologisms, in impenetrable poems and poses, and even in the doctrine of correspondences which linked the immediate with the ineffable, were all analogous to the *argotique* element of the anarchist underworld which made a similar virtue of mystification. There was no question of accepting a previous generation's or society's rules, but were they best toppled by the cunning revolutionary who triply coded his messages, or by the naïf who rejected all codes other than those embodied in nature? As with so many conflicts of the period, this too was unresolved. This irresolution should serve as a warning that Retté's desire to abolish the conflict between art and life and devote his poetry to the social cause could not lay a better claim to being the privileged anarchist aesthetic than Symbolist doctrine that maintained and even dramatized such conflicts. Though Retté could argue that his populist aesthetic was more useful, it was not necessarily the position most homologous to the anarchist cause. His doctrine sounds suspiciously like Romantic nature poetry, shorn of the hyperawareness of technique that differentiated late Romantics such as the Symbolists from less-alienated predecessors such as Hugo and Lamartine. The anarchism of Kropotkin and Bakunin was not the Young Europe of Giuseppe Mazzini and Lajos Kossuth, and Retté was no Byron, though one may imagine his willingness to have been thrust in such an affirmative and active role in support of revolution.

The Symbolists' most effective means of expressing literary values without compromising their art was by means of critical articles published in the Symbolist reviews. Though *Le Mercure de France,* with which Rémy de Gourmont was closely associated, was less overtly anarchistic than *Le Revue Blanche* or *La Plume,* it was nonetheless pervaded by the ubiquitous Symbolist/anarchist rhetoric of the year 1893, which encoded an anarchist value system whatever the content of the message. The poet was portrayed as *l'homme libre* and was advised to seek his true self as if that were some holy grail. Camille Mauclair began a review of Maurice Beaubourg's *Nouvelles passionées* with this delirious passage: "I keep a violent taste for exceptional natures, events which will not recur, attitudes that differ from the conventional, gestures deliberately thrusting outside the rhythm of custom; for isolated and singular souls, dreams without analogies and prophets without traditions." His review of Beaubourg's stories rang with phrases such as "Our independence consists in submitting only to ourselves," and "I believe he touches true originality, true autonomy."[48] Two months later in the same journal, the Symbolist critic Charles Morice reviewed the opening of Paul Gauguin's first exhibition of paintings since his recent return from Tahiti, but his language could have applied to Beaubourg's stories or Ibsen's plays. He did in fact suggest the latter comparison; he found it significant that *Enemy of the People* opened the same day as Gauguin's exhibition: "At the Oeuvre and at Durand-Ruel [Gallery], the same play was enacted," which he expressed as "accepting the total independence which is the first right of the painter as of the poet."[49] To Morice, Gauguin and his followers stood for the untrammeled freedom of the imagination, for the triumph of mind and feeling over nature. Individuality did not guarantee great art, but it was its necessary precondition.

The series of parallels and oppositions traced in these essays encoded the proposition "Symbolism is equivalent to anarchism, and both are opposed to the current social structure." Each comparison between Symbolism and anarchism was accompanied by an opposition between artistic and social values. Thus the artists' common belief in individualism was opposed to social conformism; artistic and anarchistic concern for autonomy and independence similarly implied mistrust of the dogmatism of parties and sects; Symbolist idealism was equated with social utopianism and was opposed to materialism and the acceptance of the status quo; beauty was likened to the dream of a harmonious society and opposed to current ugliness. The parallel antagonisms of anarchism placed the artists' normative values in a political context.

The equivalence between Symbolism and anarchism in part simply expressed the doctrine of the dual avant-gardes of art and politics. Though literary anarchists surely transferred their aesthetic radicalism to the social sphere, anarchist ideals and deeds influenced their critical discourse as well, reinforcing their sense of antagonism toward the poetic status quo of Parnassianism. Camille Mauclair succinctly expressed the perceived parallel between poetics and politics in his 1898 novel of literary anarchism, *Le Soleil des morts* (Sun of the Dead). Calixte Armel clearly represented Mallarmé, Claude Passat possibly the anarchist Charles Malato:

At one end of society, Calixte Armel prepared that which at the other end Claude Passat utilized: both prophets and excommunicated, they summed up the antinomy which activated the decomposition of the

century, both had the same mysterious influence, the same individual magnetism. The intellectual isolation preached by the poet necessitated the absolute individualism of the anarchist. . . . The heroic and mad attempt of Claude Passat in Italy was neither more heroic nor otherwise crazy than that of Calixte Armel creating in modern Paris a Charterhouse of scoffed-at artists. But Passat no longer believed in such romanticism; he worked now in secret, disappearing before acting.[50]

Though the young follower of Armel in the novel was impatient with the limitations of aestheticism and wished to act on and in the world, the primary role of the artist remained that of symbolizing the ideal sought by all people, the free play of creativity. Their art and their artistry served as a model of a future human society based on aesthetics rather than on economics, that is, on a nonutilitarian, nonexploitative framework in which all acts were self-fulfilling.

While many fin de siècle poets gravitated toward anarchism, the anarchists themselves were sometimes described as being poets and dreamers. In 1892, Emile Zola typified the anarchist *compagnon* by exclaiming "C'est un poète!" The journalist who interviewed him expanded the comparison: "He dreams an enormous poem, of which the first song opens in profound gloom [of the corrupt present]. . . . He dreams. The poet is born. . . . He dreams of the happiness of peoples, union, love, universal fraternity. . . . The poet who is the anarchist has a horror of blood, of dynamite. He knows he must fight to reverse bourgeois society, but he hopes that this bloodshed will be the last. After that will be the golden age."[51] Anarchists and poets struck Zola as hopeless idealists, negators of social reality who were temperamentally fated to be revolutionaries.

Zola was not alone in his appraisal of the anarchists. At the 1895 trial of Léon Bouteilhe, who had placed an apparently harmless bomb under Rothschild's porch, his lawyer claimed that "he is not an anarchist, but a dreamer, whose feeble brain only conceived an inoffensive demonstration," and read a letter from the defendant repudiating violence.[52] A similar statement was made on Jean Grave's behalf at his trial for his book *La Société mourante et l'anarchie*. His counsel, Maître Saint-Auban, declared, "Leave it go, leave the liberty to the dream, gentlemen of the jury who are today our judges thanks to the emancipation of a former dream."[53] In these political contexts, dream was used synonymously with ideal. The word *rêve* (dream) was also among the most frequently used terms in the poetry and even the prose of the Symbolists. Nearly always used in this spiritual sense, *rêve* also indicated the artistic vocation itself as an alternative access to a higher reality, a chaste and pure devotion that represented the poet's freedom from sordid earthly concerns. Despite the Symbolist interest in the subconscious, and despite the density and overdetermination of their symbols and the difficulty in decoding their poems, all characteristics suggestive of dreams themselves, one finds little in their use of the term *rêve* to justify a psychological interpretation.[54] Their frequent allusions to smoke and mist, their desire to suggest rather than state, indicate a dreamlike quality that is undercut by the distinctly pre-Freudian and spiritualized context of *rêve* in their works. The domination of the ideal over the libidinal in these last of the Romantics reveals a vast gulf between them and the Surrealists of the interwar era. It also made the term less problematic by suggesting pure ideals rather than unpredictable inner drives. Dreams were opposed either to reality or to action, which posed a very different sort of ambivalence in terms of political activity than if they had been seen as irrational subverters of the authoritarian personality. Literary anarchists had difficulty in deciding whether Symbolist dreamlike purity corresponded to the dream of an anarchist future or sapped the energy of current struggle.

At its most politicized, the dream was equated with the future anarchist utopia, as in the traditionally rhymed poem by Théodore Jean that Jean Grave printed in the literary supplement to *Les Temps Nouveaux* in 1895. The last stanza of "Anathème" read:

> **What matters that vanquished we fall without having**
> **Contemplated the sublime City of our dreams.**
> **Eternity doesn't take count of our brief hours.**
> **Our sons will see the Time that our eyes could not see.**[55]

In Retté's *L'Archipel en fleurs* (The Archipelago of Flowers) of the same year, despite his renunciation of Symbolism, one finds many such references. In the poem called "Songe" (Dream), one is led to "this fabulous country that my dream has dreamed," to which he has fled from the madness of the city. Yet this dreamland was the palace of Circe, from whose embrace he awoke at dawn to arm himself, ready to fight for "the Idea / for the free battle and the free epoch."[56] The dream itself was not political, but it did not hinder his fight. The poet was inevitably caught between the dream and reality, certain of his taste for action but unsure whether idealism was a drug clouding his vision or providing the necessary perception of the future. Paul Adam had no such difficulty in deciding that poets were separated from all other artists by their capacity to dream evanescent and unrealizable dreams. In a provocative story called "Grandeur future de l'avare" (Future Grandeur of the Miser), Adam envisioned a future utopia where technology rendered all dreams immediately realizable, thus making it a difficult place for poets to dream. "Art will efface itself therefore at the same time as these forms of intelligence, if there does not remain in this time an unrealizable wish by essence: the desire to desire."[57] In this society of plenitude lacking the pathos of the unrealizable dream, Adam postulated a new quasi artist, the miser who hoarded gratuitous wealth, and whom artists would praise as a hero. Poets were not perceived to be technicians of the word, but dreamers impelled by a strange metadesire to pursue a Quix-otic quest. Four decades later, the old anarchist historian Max Nettlau, caught up in ther fervor of the hopeful days of the Spanish Civil War, wrote that Don Quixote was the best friend of the anarchists, indeed one of their own kind, whose skill at toppling windmills they would try to equal.[58]

Many writers who were sympathetic to anarchism were equivocal about dreams: In the novel by Eugène Morel, *Terre promise,* published by *La Revue Blanche* in 1898, the word *dream* appeared roughly twice a page, but the author struggled between his adherence to the dream of the Promised Lane and his desire to live for the present. "No, the dream does not assuage that life, it poisons it. Promised Land . . . Revolution. . . . One day . . . perhaps! It is not one day. . . . It's right now that I want."[59] As the defense lawyers tried to ease the juries' fears by saying that their clients were mere dreamers, so writers had mixed feelings about the salutary effects of dreaming. In his memoirs, Camille Mauclair remembered with scorn the Montmartre *flâneurs* who did little else but fantasize: "The Dream is the negation of militant, lucid, creative Thought. The Dream, it was their cocaine."[60] The sequel to Mauclair's novel about literary anarchism, *Le Soleil des morts,* left no doubt where he stood. *L'Ennemi des rêves* (1900) described an aesthete who left behind his narrow egoism for the moral altruism of the social activist. In the novel's preface, Mauclair seized the issue of the social role of dreams as the central conflict of the decade in terms of writers' political involvement:

The story of Maxime Hersent is that of a soul warped by dreams and struggling against a soul magnified by accepted realities: the opposition of the injurious dream, which lies to itself for fear of life, and of the dream identified with prayer, which is the contemplation of realities taken from a higher viewpoint; the confrontation of the cult of self with the courage to live and the devotion to love. . . .

We have doubtlessly come to recognize that the dream and the cult of self, in perverting both the energy and imagination of the epoch, have become direct hindrances to all happiness, and the sure adjuncts to pessimism.[61]

In the aftermath of the Dreyfus Affair when this book was written, the idealism of the 1890s and its limited tangible results appeared questionable, as did the *culte du moi* whose chief proponent, Maurice Barrès, had now swung over to the right. Though Mauclair was reluctant to castigate the devotional aspects of the dream, he now wished that "the superior logical role of love in a society of free energy" would deliver artists from their aesthetic dreams.[62] In opposing instinct to intellect, society to self, the dream to sexual energy, Mauclair confirmed the idealistic and pre-Freudian connotations of this literary image.

The dream was the dominant metaphor of Symbolism because it signified the autonomy of the literary field and the purity and refuge of art, as well as the idealism of young artists that made them overstep the bounds of art in an attempt to make society conform to their dreams. This effort to harmonize the aesthetic and the social dream was sure to lead to the disillusionment and pessimism condemned by Mauclair and underlined by the short-lived anarchist involvement of most *littérateurs*. Mauclair was not opposed to the social activism of artists, but wished it to issue from a moral rather than an aesthetic viewpoint. Though his own doctrines of love and energy were equally aestheticized approaches to politics as the *culte du moi* or the *beau geste* had been in the early 1890s, it signified to Mauclair the escape from the artificial world of aestheticism, *le soleil des morts,* and the return to a social world that was lived rather than dreamed. The intercession of the dream in the Symbolists' comprehension of society was one aspect of the aestheticization of politics that typified literary anarchism.

The most widely reported incident of aestheticized politics was that timely phrase uttered by Laurent Tailhade at the Soirée de la Plume the evening of Vaillant's bombing of the Chamber of Deputies. When the enterprising journalist Jules Huret asked the anarchist poet his opinion of the bombing, Tailhade grandiloquently asserted, "What do the victims matter if the gesture is beautiful? What does the death of some unidentified persons matter if, by it, the individual is affirmed?" In a letter to *Le Temps* several days later, Tailhade clarified his statement: "For us, contemplatives, disasters of this sort offer no interest beyond the Beauty which sometimes emanates from them."[63] Tailhade's epigram, which was immediately perceived as epitomizing the aesthetes' relation to politics, clearly subordinated ethical to aesthetic values. Retté later compared Tailhade's phrase to Oscar Wilde's suggestion that old people be suppressed "because they are ugly"; Zo d'Axa wrote in 1891 that a hunchback who committed a crime would probably displease him more than some lovable old offender.[64] Although his statement of clarification appeared to be restricting the artist to the aesthetic elements of political and social life, Tailhade was actually extending art to include all aspects of life in which one perceived the pursuit of pure form to predominate over the utility of an action. This was not essentially different from the dandy's application of aesthetic principles to his presentation of self, erecting a cult of the studied gesture and the nonutilitarian act. A very different creed of the aestheticized political act was that of Zo d'Axa, who editorialized in *L'Endehors* that "we fight for the joy of battles and without dreaming of a better future . . . it is for the instant, immediate, that we want to be left alone to our pities, our passions, our sadnesses, our rages, our instincts—with the pride of being oneself."[65] As with Tailhade, Zo d'Axa saw politics as an outlet for personal expression, so personal that he even refused to enroll himself under the anarchist banner. Activism for its own sake could never arouse the pathos that Vaillant achieved by his perfect alternation between terror and pity. The writers admired the expressive force of the terrorist's gesture, but their narcissistic interpretation of such deeds failed to evoke their terrible beauty, the pure outrage that would tear the veil covering the social malaise.

Paul Adam, among the most politicized writers of his generation, wrote an extended critique of aestheticized politics in *La Revue Blanche*. First quoting Francis Vielé-Griffin's hyperbole that "if the people knew how much their sadness haunts us, they would massacre us out of respect for capitalism" as evidence of literary anarchism, Adam proceeded to identify the cause of this concern for suffering:

In effect, the literary infatuation for active altruism is born out of purely aesthetic considerations. The disharmony of the moral world shocks as a fault of art. The extreme disquietude of some obese people and the suffering that writers believe is common to the laboring multitude outrages the writers as an architectural disproportion, an unpleasant opposition of tonalities, an orchestral cacophony. This judgment is apparent in those whose critique of art praises compositions founded on the bases of synthesis to the detriment of the old-fashioned canvases lending their prestige to the theory of contrasts.[66]

As the senses and the arts were synesthetically interrelated by artists who theorized that each vowel possessed an equivalent color, each poem an appropriate rhythm, so artists pushed the pursuit of aesthetic harmony to include different levels of social experience. Art and artistry were models for society in an era when many artists expressed the desire to totalize the artistic calling beyond the confines of the limited work of art. That the aesthetic mode, whether in its dissociation of form from function, its denial of purposefulness, or its pursuit of the synthetic and harmonious whole, should serve as an epistemological metaphor for the regulation of social affairs, seemed a dubious and dangerous prospect to writers such as Adam and Lazare. On the one hand, they suspected the authenticity of such aesthetically defined involvement (Adam also wrote a scathing critique of literary anarchist snobbism), and they doubted the social efficacy of such a purely expressive and symbolic political approach, on the other. Thus, after subjecting socialism to the usual accusation of Caesarism and overcentralization, Adam went on to say that "anarchy can not sustain itself integrally. It gives, at most, a gracious and touching aesthetic idea." Declaring that what was needed was "a new idea of social freedom entirely free of principles of bourgeois organization," he offered internationalism, the autonomy of free communes, and the like, suggestions that were very close to the anarchist ideal. In wanting to create "beyond all parties, a league against human sorrow," Adam proved himself no more realistic than the aesthetes whose politics he criticized.[67] Too Darwinian to believe in mutualism as a way of life, still skeptical of the divisiveness of individualism, Adam sought a third way.

Yet between the mainline alternatives of capitalism and socialism, anarchism was that other way, hanging in uneasy balance between the claims of the individual and the collective, between self and society. Anarchism embodied the great refusal of the power politics of European nations and parties in the late nineteenth century, as aestheticism signified the rejection of the mercantile values of the bourgeoisie from whose ranks most artists were drawn. Avant-garde artists shared the anarchists' aversion to contemporary society, and the dreams of a utopia that was meant to replace it. Above all they shared an outsider position, a critical and often hostile relation to the society in which they lived. "The aesthetic function, by virtue of its being the dialectical negation of any practical function, always and everywhere takes on the character of the function to which it is opposed."[68] In cultifying art's perfect uselessness, the Symbolists dialectically asserted that its true purpose was to offer an aesthetic alternative to social reality.

Nine

The period from 1892 to 1894 is chiefly remembered in the literature of French anarchism as the "era of *attentats*," when the continual incitements to violence by the anarchist press of the 1880s and the occasional responses to this chorus of encouragement suddenly escalated into a series of terrorist acts that were unprecedented in the history of the Third Republic. In these years a handful of men perpetrated thirteen attacks on the institutions and symbols of authority, most of them accomplished with the use of a relatively new weapon, the dynamite invented by Alfred Nobel in 1868 (though two of the terrorists resorted to the time-honored tool of the assassin, the dagger, none used guns). Ten people were killed by anarchist assailants, from café proprietors and patrons to the president of the Republic. In return, five anarchists were condemned to death, and the three others sentenced to life imprisonment did not live much beyond their sentencing.[1] Another blew himself up in an attempt to destroy the Church of the Madeleine. Bombs exploded in the Chamber of Deputies, army barracks, judges' homes, restaurants, and cafés. The bombs and daggers made a great deal of noise both on their own and in the press, but succeeded in changing only the name of the man sitting in the Elysée palace.

The noise of bombs that had some Parisians singing "La Ravachole" and others afraid to visit fashionable restaurants for fear of attack has similarly occupied most historical attention, to the detriment of the cultural anarchism that flourished in the same period.[2] Bombings and assassinations are sensational events that draw attention to themselves and seem to constitute a movement when a number of attacks occur in a short space of time. Though one attack did in fact provoke others in the 1890s, the chain reaction occurred spontaneously rather than conspiratorially, undertaken by individuals who took it upon themselves to avenge the prosecution of their fellows. This very lack of direction might be taken as evidence of the deep-rooted appeal of terrorism within the anarchist rank and file, and the *attentats* did succeed in capturing the popular imagination, although there were never more than a handful of desperate idealists who were willing to engage in terror. Rather than focusing on the spectacular deeds to the exclusion of the social context that produced them, these *attentats* should direct our attention to the social and especially the cultural contexts that made such acts both possible and meaningful. Lacking the organizing principle of party directives from the top or conspiracies from underground, the terrorists were dependent upon anarchist culture both for inspiration and approbation of their deeds. They in turn influenced both intellectuals and *compagnons.* Terrorists may have resented the more elite practitioners of anarchist culture, but they also relied upon them. The inchoate act of the bomb thrower demanded interpretation by purveyors of words, ideas, and images, and the dissemination of these interpretations in various forms of media. Terrorists needed intellectuals, intellectuals fawned on terrorists; this symbiotic, highly symbolic form of activity typified fin de siècle anarchism.

Putative connections between anarchist intellectuals and terrorists fascinated journalists and magistrates alike. Contemporary social critics would frequently divide the movement into the *impulsifs* and *contemplatifs,* the activists and theoreticians. The government unsuccessfully tried to link the two segments of the anarchist world in a grand conspiracy between the cunning propagandists and publicists of the deed and the easily manipulated individuals who carried it out. The activities of anarchist intellectuals and terrorists were indeed related, but not in the way that the government thought. The failure of conspiracy theory in the abortive Procès de Trente reveals the fallacy of trying to link directly the hand that penned the call to arms and the hand that threw the bomb, for underlying this failure was the false distinction between passive and active anarchists. Unlike the Russian precedent of the Narodnaya Volya a decade earlier, no one in France pulled the strings of a vast conspiracy, nor were the intellectuals in control of the "hit men." A more accurate contemporary distinction than that of activists and theorists was that between various kinds of propaganda: by the deed, by the song, by the written word, by oral discourse, by example.

Contrasting the public gestures of Ravachol and his successors with the anarchist terrorism of other decades highlights the purely symbolic and nonutilitarian nature of 1890s violence. Earlier attempts at *la reprise individuelle* focused on theft for the cause, in the name of restitution to the people of the bourgeois' ill-gotten gains. The interface between criminality and radical politics, which existed on a real level within the lower-class anarchist milieu, had been championed by Bakunin some decades earlier. Bakunin considered the thief a sincere revolutionary devoid of rhetorical flourishes, and he had favored a revolution that would be a peasants' revolt merged with an uprising by the underworld and *déclassés*.[3] In the late 1880s, Kropotkin regretted that one young anarchist thief, Pini, had thrown away his life for several thousand francs that he had stolen for the cause. While Sebastien Faure proclaimed theft a revolutionary act, Jean Grave wrote three articles in 1891 condemning theft as a characteristic of the society that they wanted to destroy.[4] The pattern of illegality resurfaced with the clever thief Marius Jacob in the first decade of the twentieth century and continued in spectacular fashion on the eve of World War I with the Bonnot Gang, the first terrorists to make use of getaway cars in the course of their crimes.[5] Such banditry, though not unknown in the 1890s, played no part in the much-publicized throwing of bombs, and conversely such pure acts of terrorism during the Third French Republic appear to have characterized only this brief period, though Charles Gallo's attack on the Paris Bourse in 1886 was a precursor of later symbolic attacks. Although Ravachol had engaged in theft earlier in his career, his *attentats* had no personal motivation; they simply avenged the anarchists who he adjudged were too harshly condemned for their role in the May Day disturbances of 1891. One could not calculate, as Kropotkin had done with Pini, whether a terrorist act was worth risking the punishment that would follow, unless one tried to determine an act's potential propaganda value. Theft had instrumental motives and its risk was therefore quantifiable, but terrorism was purely expressive, accrued nothing to the individual involved, and even increased in effectiveness if the perpetrator was allowed to stand trial, expose his views, and then expiate his deed. It thrilled society and led to the sainthood of the terrorists within the anarchist cultural milieu because of the pure and selfless nature of a deed that appeared to speak to society as if through the voice of divine retribution. Criminals could become popular heroes, but fanatic terrorists had the chance to become martyrs.

The meager results gained in three years of violence emphasizes that throwing a bomb was not a functional but a symbolic act, one designed not to bring down the government but to fan the ardor of the *compagnons*. The bomb was a sort of magical device that would explode the myth of bourgeois invincibility, an indispensable part of the ritual drama of heroic self-sacrifice.[6] In fact the deed itself was less significant than that the terrorist-turned-martyr set an example for others of self-abnegation and personal devotion. How he died was more important than whom he killed, and each execution was widely reported in the press. The symbolic force of his bomb, though potent, was less powerful than the exchange of his life for the cause. The terrorists generally accepted death stoically, expecting that they would be avenged, which was in fact a major cause of the series of bombings in 1892 and 1894. But they did not really expect their bombs to start a chain of events that would lead to the revolution. Rather, they collapsed the revolutionary process into one act that metaphorically stood for the whole. Each bomb warned the bourgeoisie of the coming *Grand Soir,* when society would be overturned in a night of violent redemption and be reborn in the New Dawn.

Both the paradigmatic act and the ritual exchange of the present individual life for the ideal future society were intuitively grasped by the artists, more than one of whom proclaimed the bombs of Ravachol to be the dawn of a new era. Others were less moved by the terrorists' pleas for a just society than by the beauty of their gesture of disdain for social conventions, a gesture that magnified and encapsulated the poets' own attitudes. Still others who were fascinated by the symbolic violence and sacrificial spirit were shocked into condemnation of the *attentats* by the implacable logic by which Emile Henry justified his ruthless deeds. Nevertheless, the decisive violent act held an undeniable fascination for young poets weary of being confined to the sterile inactivity of their dreams. The revolution symbolized by a single explosion perfectly paralleled the relation of their own poems to the apocalypse to come. The bomb was not just a symbol of revolution but, for the anarchist writers, a metasymbol that revealed how the idea and the act could be united, which demonstrated that the disjunction between art and life which was the essence of decadence would be transcended through symbolic action. This was not an activist generation in the sense of Hemingway or Malraux, but one that wished to extend the range of symbol creation from narrowly literary pursuits to the larger social sphere.

A number of contemporary commentators perceived that the symbolic nature of the terrorists' acts differentiated them from ordinary crimes, even those of a political nature. At the 1892 trial of those accused of stealing dynamite, a defense lawyer tried to attenuate the evil imputed to Ravachol's bombs which were made from this dynamite. When the judge asked whether the accused had prepared any explosions, the lawyer replied, "They were perhaps symbolic explosions which frighten and kill no one." An accused thief announced, "The fact is that it's truly time to frighten the bourgeoisie." The judge queried, "You want . . . especially to make noise?" to which the defendant carelessly replied, "Noise and other things! In the churches, for example, where the priests stupefy the people."[7] The lawyer was obviously hoping to diminish the impact of the bombs by implying that they were closer to loud firecrackers than to weapons of destruction, a point made more credible by the fact that neither Ravachol's nor Vaillant's bombs killed anyone (Ravachol did commit murder by other means). Augustin Hamon reiterated the point that the bombs were making a social statement: "The explosions of these anarchists, as M. Humbert said justly in *L'Eclair,* are purely symbolic: they strike men of all types or buildings in order to strike at the institutions of landlords, the magistrature, the police, etc."[8] Zo d'Axa protested what he termed the incomprehension of the press toward the terrorists, which could only see destruction being unleashed upon society: "They believe they have seen furious vengeance at work . . . it is something else . . . a primitive propagandist of Anarchy has wanted to force their attention by the brutality of the act. Behind this deed is the faith, so often denied, on which he led the fruitful discussion. It is an Idea that the dynamiter deploys."[9]

As a more sophisticated person would offer an article to a journal to expound his or her views, the terrorist offered his bomb. Yet elsewhere Zo d'Axa gave vent to more characteristic invective in which he recommended the cathartic value of violence not for the Idea but for its own sake. In January 1893, he foretold the bombing of the Chamber of Deputies later that year and declared that all institutions of authority were threatened:

In truth, it is not necessary to feel oneself an anarchist to be seduced by the ensemble of the next demolitions. All those that society whips in the intimacy of their being instinctively want violent revenge.

A thousand institutions of the old world are marked with a fatal sign. The affiliates of the plot have no need to hope for distant better futures, they know a sure means of plucking the joy immediately: Destroy passionately![10]

Zo d'Axa was the most nihilistic apostle of the therapeutic uses of violence, ready to sever the means from the elusive goal if he felt the process affirmed one's individuality. At a time when most writers were devoted to the ideal expressed through the word, Zo d'Axa professed faith in whatever heightened the sense of the existential moment. Whether he interpreted bomb throwing as a symbol or as a pure act shattering the complacency of a meaningless world, Zo d'Axa did not mistake it for an instrumental means of bringing on the revolution, a goal to which he was no more devoted than to any other.

The most coherent contemporary assessment of the series of *attentats* was possibly that by the committed anarchist and aesthete Félix Fénéon, who approved of the terrorists because they "awaken our contemporaries from their torpor." On December 26, 1894, Paul Signac noted in his diary the remarks that Fénéon had made to him on the subject of propaganda by the deed:

Félix remarked at Thévenot that the anarchist *attentats* have done much more for propaganda than the twenty years of Kropotkin's and Reclus's brochures. He shows the logic of the diverse *attentats* which attack with Gallo the Bourse, with Ravachol the magistrature and the army, with Vaillant the deputies, with Henry the voters, with Caserio the representatives of power. Henry's *attentat,* addressed to the voters, perhaps more guilty than the elected, since the latter are forced by the former to engage in this trade in deputies, seems to him the most anarchistic.[11]

This rare record of a private conversation of the time reveals the clarity with which a writer perceived the underlying pattern behind the unorchestrated attacks by various individuals. All the commentators knew that a particular judge or deputy was not being singled out except as a symbol of authority, which was particularly clear in Léauthier's random attack on a foreign plenipotentiary or the Belgian anarchist Jean Pauwel's attempt to blow up the Madeleine. It was least clear in the case of Henry, since the voters, as Fénéon described the café patrons who received Henry's bomb, were not very visible authority figures. His act seemed the least symbolic and most purely and randomly terrorist, and thus received the least sympathy among the populace and the artists.

Ironically, after anarchist leaders such as Kropotkin and Grave had called for propaganda by the deed throughout the 1880s, the most intense period of such activity came in the 1890s, when these same leaders had lost faith in the efficacy of individual deeds divorced from collective action. Why did the series of *attentats* that gripped public attention in these years surface when they did? Ravachol's decision to take personal vengeance for what he conceived to be injustice toward his fellows began a cycle of revenge for each successive *compagnon* who fell under executioner Deibler's blade. Each martyrdom encouraged another lone anarchist to come forward and sacrifice himself for the cause. In the course of Ravachol's trial a bomb blew up the restaurant (and its proprietor) where Ravachol had been denounced. Emile Henry expressly committed his assault in memory of Vaillant a week after the latter's execution, and Santo Caserio declared after he assassinated Carnot that Ravachol had been avenged. The "collective psychosis of the *attentat*" activated by the press coverage of the bombings, trials, and executions magnified the escalatory feedback system.[12] This coverage included not only *Le Père Peinard, L'Endehors,* and the Symbolist reviews, but also the Parisian daily press, which commonly carried regular columns entitled "Les Anarchistes," and also published eyewitness accounts of public executions such as the one that Barrès wrote on the death of Henry for *Le Journal.* The fear of dynamite ran high, and the police medical staff reported a doubling of cases of emotionally disturbed people suffering from persecution mania occasioned by the explosions and police searches.[13]

The culmination of this epoch of symbolic violence, the assassination of the head of state, might seem to have shown the ease with which figures of authority could be toppled and therefore to have led to many more such acts. Yet no one avenged the execution of the young Italian anarchist who stabbed Carnot in Lyons on June 24, 1894, perhaps because he was not a compatriot known to the Parisians. Shortly afterward, the acquittal of those tried in the Procès de Trente defused tensions, and President Faure's amnesty of February 1895 further pacified the *enragés*. The effect of the police repression of 1894 on continuing terrorist acts is hard to gauge. It did not hinder Henry or Caserio in committing their deeds, but it did greatly cut back on the anarchist press and made the literary anarchists much more careful about inciting violence or glorifying terrorists. Thus during and after Carnot's assassination the anarchist propagandistic infrastructure was seriously disrupted, as the authorities concentrated on suppressing the anarchist press which provided the only apparent link between the attacks. Because individual deeds were notoriously hard to prevent, the police concentrated instead on denying the anarchists the means of publicizing further acts (although of course in a society with a relatively free press the assassination of Carnot received ample publicity in the nonanarchist press). The new current of anarcho-syndicalism after 1894 shifted the militants' attention from individual to collective activity.[14]

In seeking the etiology of the violence of this era, one can not discount the literary and intellectual influences on the terrorists. Among their literary sources of inspiration, the Symbolists did not play a prominent part. In his memoirs dictated while in prison, Ravachol said that a youthful reading of Eugène Sue's *Le Juif errant* had turned him anticlerical.[15] Before his attack, Vaillant sent a letter to Elisée Reclus in Brussels in which he wrote, "What I am about to do is the logical outcome of my studies in Darwin, Buchner and Herbert Spencer."[16] Ironically, he meant the natural scientist Ludwig Buchner, not his revolutionary brother Georg, and apparently concluded from such reading that anarchism was a more highly evolved form of social organization that was destined to replace the capitalist order. Henry was by far the best educated of the terrorists, having excelled in his lycée studies before being accepted into the Ecole Polytechnique from which he voluntarily withdrew, and having assisted Zo d'Axa in the preparation of *L'Endehors*.

At his trial he referred to the character of Souvarine from Zola's novel *Germinal* and quoted his statement that "all arguments about the future are criminal because they hinder pure and simple destruction and hamper the march of revolution."[17] The newspaper *L'Eclair* reported that while awaiting trial, Henry read James Darmesteter's *Prophètes d'Israël,* Darnaudeau's *Les Nihilistes,* and *Germinal,* in which he had underlined the passage, "Begin then by letting me blow up the prison where you perish."[18] If Henry awaited prison to read these works, they are poor evidence of literary influence upon his deed. A better indication of the terrorist's literary orientation lies in the fact that Vaillant and Henry both wrote poetry, and that Henry's father was also an occasional poet, having written a philosophical piece called *Chaine des êtres.* One of Henry's poems contained many of the key words and themes of the Symbolists, speaking of the ideal, the soul, the dream, and, most remarkably for a thrower of bombs, of silence. Twice in the poem he referred to silence, when he wrote, "After these verses I will be quiet," and again "I will suffer silently."[19] His suffering may have been exacerbated by a personal love affair as well as by social conditions, but his poetic frustration was finally alleviated by the bombshells that ended his silence. One can easily imagine Henry as an aesthete who was psychologically pushed to more extreme measures than other young poets.

In Henry's anarchist terrorism was a large element of revenge not only on behalf of Vaillant but for his own father, who had been a Communard. Henry was born in Spain in 1872 during the period of exile, and thus bore witness to the most savage repression of a political movement meted out by the French government in the course of the nineteenth century. Both Henry and his brother became committed anarchists even though they could have found places in the French society to which they returned, full of bitterness, after the amnesty for the Communards. In the case of other terrorists, oedipal revenge against the authoritarian father figure of the state appears likely. Ravachol's father abandoned his family when the boy was eight, and he subsequently took his mother's maiden name as his own. Vaillant's father also left him and returned to Corsica. When his mother remarried, his stepfather refused to support him, and he was cast out on his own at the age of twelve. Santo Caserio's father died when he was young and he was raised by his mother.[20] All three bore antagonisms that reflected their personal distress at finding themselves without a male symbol of authority in the difficult period of adolescence, and who transferred their resentment against their own irresponsible fathers to the state. Henry had more direct reasons for opposing the Third Republic that had been created in blood and had sentenced his father to death in absentia. When Henry's mother first heard of his crime, she reputedly exclaimed, "He has avenged his father."[21]

"Dynamite, in 1894, played a great role in the social order as much as in the criminal order, as much in fantasy as in reality." Thus did a deputy from the Ain speak of the rage of bombings that occurred not only in Paris but throughout France in 1893 and 1894.[22] Terrorism was nevertheless an urban phenomenon, as the terrorists desired to make a public impact and the more removed they were from the centers of publicity the less reportage and notoriety would ensue.[23] The deputy described how dynamite was used not only for anarchism but as a means of suicide, involved in a fraudulent scheme for collecting insurance, and even used for fireworks, and he implied that this expanded usage was due to its notoriety as a terrorist weapon. The prefect of the Dordogne reported to the minister of the interior in 1894 that the purveyor of a liquor called "Dynamite" who also subscribed to anarchist newspapers did so only out of curiosity and was not dangerous. The liquor had existed under the provocative name since 1888, "at a time when no one could foresee the abominable use which would be made of that explosive, [when] its inventor [would be] considered by the anarchists as one of their political co-religionists."[24] A publication smacking both of fantasy and anarchist terrorism was the very ephemeral newspaper called *La Dynamite,* which appeared on May Day, 1892. It listed the imprisoned Ravachol as its political director and, under "Our Program," spoke of dynamite as a form of discourse: "If the revolver is the American language, dynamite henceforth will be the language of the French. To what purpose is discussion now? Have we not found the most convincing argument: the explosive?" The familiar metaphor by which revolvers "speak" could apply to the French taste for a yet more vociferous form of expression (of course, dynamite was used in the United States too). The article concluded with a Futurist-style rendition of such a dialogue: "Poum! Pif! Paf! Patapoum! Crac!"[25] As politically ineffectual as terrorism might have been, it captured the popular imagination as no brochure or the most impassioned speech could have done, adding another element to the culture of anarchism. As Ravachol sang the blasphemous sixth stanza of the "Père Duchesne" on his way to the guillotine (which was then promptly reprinted in *Le Père Peinard*), so the anarchists soon intoned "La Ravachole," which was freely adapted from the French Revolutionary "Carmagnole" and used to best advantage that song's refrain, "Vive le son / D'l'explosion."[26]

The propaganda by the deed resounded forcefully within both working-class and bourgeois literary milieus, apparently having the effect that Félix Fénéon claimed for it of spreading the anarchist message to the masses. From the Belleville bar that he tended in the northwest corner of Paris during the height of the terrorist period, the writer Henri Leyret reported that when the workingmen learned of Vaillant's pariah existence they felt that he was one of their own, and his death created a martyrdom far more powerful than anarchist theories. No one doubted that he would be avenged, and sly smiles appeared after Henry's Café Terminus explosion. The people's love of mystery, Leyret said, convinced them that a vast secret society coordinated the bombings. After Henry's trial, Leyret wrote that there were "few workers, even among those whose socialist indoctrination makes them the determined adversaries of Anarchy, who had not read, reread, meditated on the Declaration of Emile Henry."[27] Some were upset by the killing of innocent people relaxing in a café, but they were generally pleased by Henry's erudition, as they had been moved by Vaillant's cry from the heart. One martyr was worth many thousands of words. The police reported an underground trade in Henry artifacts, and all unsigned articles in *La Révolte* were attributed to him. "Thus all make panegyrics to Emile Henry, whose name runs in Paris, the provinces, and in the English bars of Fitzroy Square, where they write articles and poetry in his honor."[28] In much the same way as the dispossessed and colonized peoples who would later lead bloody revolts against French domination in North Africa, Henry the boy-martyr (he was twenty-one when he killed and died) realized his manhood through a rite of violence, and through his act the denizens of Belleville's bars also felt manlier.[29]

Leyret claimed that the speech Henry delivered at his trial was eagerly studied by the workers of Belleville, but the police believed that it had an even more marked effect upon the anarchist sympathizers in the middle classes:

The declaration of Emile Henry, which is certainly the most learned produced up till now, is read less in the plebeian and alcoholic anarchist milieus than by the rebels of the liberal classes. The text has been cut from diverse papers, notably *Le Petit Temps,* which was the first to publish it in its entirety. And this text has been pocketed by lawyers, doctors, students, traveling salesmen (who suffer from the concurrence of the Jews), by painters, sculptors, etc. The *littérateurs,* young or old, who frequent *Le Revue Blanche.* . . .

The declaration was even circulated abroad, among "German, Austrian, Swedish *littérateurs,* to the admirers of Ibsen, who sent inflammatory letters from Berlin, Vienna, Stockholm, Budapest, etc."[30]

This popularity was due to Henry's eloquence as much as to his violence, which contrasted greatly with the inarticulate revolt of his predecessors. Reprinted in numerous Parisian newspapers, his speech constituted excellent propaganda for terrorist reprisals as an answer to governmental repression. Henry was probably the best interpreter of his own deeds:

The bomb at the Café Terminus is the response to all your violations of liberty, to your arrests, to your searches, to your laws on the press, to your mass expulsions of foreigners, to your guillotinings. But why, you say, go attack peaceful consumers who listen to music, who perhaps are neither magistrates nor deputies? Why?

The answer is simple. The bourgeoisie has made a bloc of the anarchists. A single man, Vaillant, threw a bomb; nine-tenths of the compatriots did not even know him. That meant nothing. They persecuted *en masse*; all who had some anarchist relations were tracked. Ah well, since you render a whole party responsible for an individual's acts and you strike in a bloc, we too strike in a bloc.

Police are simply hirelings of the bourgeoisie. All who applaud the present order, who make three or five hundred francs a month, are guilty.[31]

The Parisian anarchist press was no longer extant in April 1894, which partly explains the importance of international contacts. The notoriety of his deed assured Henry of press coverage from newspapers less vulnerable to police harassment. These included the liberal newspapers such as *L'Eclair, Le Journal,* and *Le Petit Temps,* and also the literary reviews, though these latter became more circumspect during the period of repression.

The phenomenon of the intellectual fellow traveler crossing class lines to identify and side with the oppressed stirred as much controversy as the attacks themselves. In July 1894, a writer for a rival literary journal accused Symbolist writers of having been sufficiently attracted to the anarchist *attentats* to have become "apostles of that propaganda by the deed, the preachers of anarchy and social disorganization," and found it ironic that the radicals were "just those whose tastes and conditions of life are the least anarchic, the most aristocratic, bourgeois. . . . The articles that they publish in the journals and reviews purvey a violence so much more dangerous as they are surrounded by a most careful literary form." He was mystified by the evident contradiction between their ideas and their social position, as between their claim that "art only exists by and for itself" and their political commitment. His suspicions about their sincerity increased his judgment that "the moral responsibilities of these *attentats* will weigh on them."[32] The pseudonymed journalists Flor O'Squarr went further in ascribing greater guilt for the *attentats* to the educated bourgeoisie than to the anarchists. Whereas anarchists proclaimed their solidarity with their fellows and dreamed of a better future, intellectuals were nihilists who felt isolated and vengeful for not finding the place they felt was due them in society. Shortly after the exploits of Ravachol, O'Squarr wrote that

in anarchy, some men are imbued with the nihilistic spirit, recommending propaganda by the deed, the use of explosives. These are the lettered, the diplomaed doctors, the scholars, the mathematicians of the party, those who, by their instruction and their community of interests, relate most to the pure nihilist element.

It is these who have conducted Ravachol under the knife of M. Deibler—this Ravachol who was assuredly guilty, but more yet a dupe and a victim.[33]

The untutored people were the pawns of an irresponsible educated elite who, unlike their Russian brethren, did not have the courage of their convictions.

Both the wave of violence and the repression that followed and which was largely directed at the press were as widely debated within the anarchist milieu as in French society as a whole. As was mentioned earlier, many anarchist leaders were unsympathetic toward individual acts that served no strategic purpose. Adolphe Retté recalled a luncheon he shared with Jean Grave, Elisée Reclus, and other anarchist friends at which Grave asked Reclus's advice, complaining that he had been lambasted for failing to endorse the terrorists. Reclus upheld Grave's position that they must be exemplars of the future society as well as the destroyers of the present one, and Retté agreed with the theoreticians.[34] Grave had a great deal to lose from such violence: as a result of *les lois scélérates* his paper was shut down and he spent a year in prison. In April 1894, the same police informer who reported on Emile Henry's popularity also noted

a very marked movement of hostility between the literary anarchists and the amateurs of the propaganda by the deed whom the former commonly call "the gang" (*la bande*). The *littérateurs* find the arrest of colleagues who can only be linked to criminals by acquaintance excessive. . . .

The *littérateurs* believe that they can only accomplish an anarchy-tinted work of renovation if one ceases to accuse them of complicity with dynamiters.

On the other hand, the Mirbeaus, the Paul Adams, the Ivanovs, the Lugné-Pöes, etc., suffer from believing themselves always persecuted by the police. They see a police agent at each neighboring café table.[35]

Many of the leading literary anarchists were prepared to flee the country, until the acquittal of the intellectuals tried in the Procès de Trente ended immediately fears of further arrests. The random terrorism of Henry especially caused dissension in anarchist ranks, as did the article of Octave Mirbeau that appeared in *Le Journal* on February 19, 1894, which unhesitatingly condemned the bombing of the Café Terminus. Mirbeau wrote that a mortal enemy of anarchism could not have done more harm to their cause than Henry when he threw his bomb into a room filled with tranquil and anonymous persons, and regretted that each party had its share of criminals and madmen.[36]

The terrorists also found their literary defenders. A month after Mirbeau's article, Henri Ribeyre tried to explain Emile Henry's motivation if not to justify his crime. He remembered the Commune, that bloody event that shook the preceding generation and whose children were just coming of age after a lifetime of vituperation from an unforgiving bourgeoisie. It was logical that this "anarchist occultist and poet, a sort of seeker of the absolute" would avenge himself not on the symbols of power but on the pitiless bourgeoisie. The critic tried to link the escalating violence with the government's wholesale repression of the theorists of anarchism: "If in the eyes of opinion, moral revolt is already as criminal as real violence, why hesitate before the revolutionary act? And the persecution of ideas having effaced the nuances of culpability between thought and act, why is it astonishing that some naive and impulsive souls will immediately choose the most energetic translation of their latent indignation? One multiplies criminals in insulting pacific adversaries."[37]

While cautiously avoiding any overt incitement to violence (one can imagine the careful editing that must have preceded such articles' publication in 1894), *La Revue Blanche*'s critic argued that blind governmental force would inevitably arouse violence among the oppressed. Though he was probably thinking of Henry as the first of the intellectual terrorists, in fact no other educated proponent of anarchism seems to have followed his lead. According to contemporary terminology, the terrorists were *impulsifs* and *illuminés* but not *intellectuels* in marked contrast to the Russian terrorists of the Narodnaya Volya whose activities between 1878 and 1881 culminated in the assassination of the czar. The pattern of systematic Russian terrorism carried out by children of the middle classes contrasts sharply with French autonomous attacks by mostly lower-class *compagnons*. Lenin's statement made in reference to his brother, that terrorism "was and remains a specific kind of struggle practiced by the intelligentsia," may have been valid for Russia and for much of modern European and American terrorism, but did not hold true for anarchist or national separatist movements (such as the Irish Republican Brotherhood or the Fenians).[38]

Among the writers fascinated by the cycle of violence and retribution being played out by the anarchists, Maurice Barrès attended Henry's early morning execution and was moved by the proud mien of the martyr grafted onto the body of a boy. Barrès apparently considered Henry's *attentat* to be as epochal an event as had Paul Adam in the case of Ravachol two years before. As reported by Ribeyre, Barrès termed the era that he felt was coming to an end "Balzacian." Typically viewing French history through literary lenses, Barrès summed up the old century in Balzac's character Rastignac, whose avidity for money and power would always preclude any true revolutionary fervor. Henry, by contrast, represented the much more dangerous zeal of contemporary youth, who would destroy the world in order to save it. Ribeyre saw in Barrès himself the best example of Rastignac's opportunistic approach to social change.[39]

While Barrès was moved and frightened by the contrast between his own literary detachedness and Henry's last bold words on the scaffold, "Courage camarades, Vive l'Anarchie!" Paul Adam continued to approve of propaganda by the deed despite his fears for his own safety. He later wrote that "we excused Ravachol, Vaillant, and that Emile Henry who, striking the consumers of the Café Terminus, attacked the stupidity of the voting citizen, sole guilty party." Rather than deploring the activists, he recalled his dismay with the anarchists who talked endlessly in the cafés but refused to risk serious struggle or even to arm themselves. It was the ideological discussion rather than the violence that calmed the writers' anarchist fervor, according to Adam.[40]

Violence clearly fascinated young writers. Novels of the period displayed the taste for action that drew young literary anarchists who had lost faith in the sufficiency of words or the satisfactions of silence. Camille Mauclair described the terrible fever that reigned in the Paris of the *attentats*: "Now there is public murder. . . . The mystery of souls, dispossessed, cedes to blood. Action is inaugurated. The desire to live is revealed by death. I read this morning the story of the explosion at the Bank. . . . Five victims." Mauclair's autobiographical character, the anarchist *littérateur* de Neuze, declared that writers would not go to such extremes, for "their will to action is only an expansion of their literary desires." The Mallarmé-figure Calixte Armel replied that "one does not continue literature in life: one must choose. . . . If the intellectuals . . . declare themselves separated from thought, they can only distract themselves in tensing their muscles. . . . Boredom or blood, it is the dilemma of the epoch." Armel was certain that thought itself was the supreme action, but younger men were drawn to bolder deeds, as "the pale face of Blanqui haunted the faubourgs."[41]

Intellectuals such as Mauclair fell prey to the anarchist vision of an apocalyptic night of violence that would sweep the old world clean. Bloodletting possessed the mystique of a supernatural force that seized *compagnons* and common criminals and transformed them into *illuminés*. Mauclair sometimes resorted to surgical metaphors of violence, with the gangrenous limbs of society cauterized to purify it of its rot. Violence was no more cruel than the "eternal therapeutic that nature coldly adapts for itself," the purging of unhealthy parts of the body politic so that the rest could survive. Like revolution, terrorism too was equated with an irresistible force of nature that swallowed individuals in its imperious necessity:

Anarchism, troubling the crowd while remaining mute on its theories and purely individual, appeared to the public as an unseizable divinity, illogical, terrible, and imbecilic, a force of nature against which reasonings and habitual justifications served nothing. The real promoters of destruction allowed the bewildered gazetteers to preach the most utopian programs, but never disclosed their true thoughts. From being struck without knowing why, bourgeois society was demoralized, passed from the most savage revolt to the frightened offer of compensations, of transactions with the invisible enemy. . . . The somber prestige of the vague, indiscernible terror, borrowing from natural calamities something of their anonymous fatalism, grew even by reason of its imprecision.[42]

Equating anarchist terror with natural calamities reinforced the sense of the blind inevitability of acts that were in fact the consciously willed deeds of individuals.

Although terrorist acts created the need for articulate representatives, the bombs' main appeal lay in their unmediated directness. In this sense the symbolic deed was closer to the pictorial or literary image than to more discursive forms of anarchist propaganda. Art and violence were more powerful than ideology because they acted on the sensibility rather than on the intellect. Paul Adam agreed with Fénéon and Zo d'Axa that violence could be a more powerful form of propaganda than speeches and writings. In his 1895 novel *Le Mystère des foules,* Adam wrote that only the "discourse of madmen" could sway the crowd. His anarchist character, Bérat, affirmed the same disgust with the theoreticians of anarchy as did Adam in the preface to *Lettres de malaisie.* In order to impress upon the people the seriousness of one's purpose, "One must warn them by terrible examples. The nihilists were right. One must strike the imagination first, and when they see men seize the hand of justice and undertake the struggle, alone against the multitude, against nations, when they see these struck by death, and then run joyously to the martyrdom of the guillotine, the people will begin to reflect. The time for discourse is past. . . . Let individuals reveal themselves by acts."[43]

Elsewhere in the novel, a painter named Pascal declared "It is necessary to act. . . . The sole beauty is in action." When asked about the repressive laws that would arise from these actions, the painter affirmed that "the immediate goal of propaganda by the deed is to provoke that reaction," and called the anarchist mission "a holy war."[44] Paul Adam was a proponent of collective as well as individual violence, less for the sake of beauty (a position that Pascal spoke for in the novel in order to represent a characteristic attitude of contemporary aesthetes) than as the sole efficacious means of inducing social change. Adam also considered himself a political realist and could willingly embrace militarism and even imperialism in the service of the European working classes, while criticizing the idealistic antimilitarism of a figure like Jaurès. Thus in one of his 1893 articles collectively entitled *La Critique des moeurs,* Adam counseled that if the strikers at Fourmies had thrown "fifteen bombs 'Bons-Enfants' in the batallion of Commandant Chipus" (the reference is to the 1893 explosion of the police comissariat in the rue des Bons-Enfants, which killed five people, an attack that Emile Henry later claimed), they might have convinced the authorities of their seriousness, because force only understood force.[45]

Pragmatic interpretations of mass violence such as Adam's were the exception in an era seized by the exploits of lone impassioned men. To most writers, violence would either be employed once and for all in some future *Grand Soir,* or else it conveyed a symbolic condemnation of society by men who sacrificed themselves for the sake of future generations. In the latter case, the propagandists by the deed were heroicized by their literary admirers either as fellow aesthetes who created perfect gestures or as martyrs who gave themselves to the cause. As aesthetes they were considered supreme individuals, as martyrs the models of altruistic selflessness. The solitary challenge and the myth of a future order rested on an aesthetic judgment; the appeal of martyrdom was based more on a religious sensibility.

Behind the overt praise of the violent gesture lay Symbolist allusions to the functional similarity between the bomb and the work of art. In the month after Ravachol's bombs awakened Paris to the anarchist threat, Pierre Quillard, already committed to anarchism by more peaceful means, wrote of the "destructive power of the poem." Whereas a bomb's force was immediately dispersed and mainly provoked police reprisals, the action of literature was certain to continue its propagandistic effect:

There is no affirmation of individual liberty more heroic than this: to create, in view of eternity, mistrusting all reticence and all sacrifice to the preoccupations of transitory contingencies, a new form of beauty. . . .

Thus, consciously or not—but what does it matter—whoever communicates to his suffering brothers the secret splendor of his dream acts on ambient society as a dissolvant, and all who understand them become, often unbeknown to them, outlaws and rebels.[46]

Though Quillard was not glorifying violence, that immediately after the wave of terrorist attacks broke over Paris he perceived characteristics of explosive force to be common to both expressive mediums indicates the readiness of aesthetes to simultaneously politicize their art and aestheticize their politics. Mallarmé likewise commented after Vaillant's bombing, "I know of no other bomb but a book" and said of Fénéon's incarceration for possession of explosive devices, "Certainly there were not any better detonators for Fénéon than his articles. And I do not think that one can use a more effective weapon than literature." When a reporter asked Henri de Regnier if he would go so far as to recommend the use of bombs, the poet and future Academician replied, "Yes sir, and immediately."[47] The artistic praise of violence became a political issue after Vaillant's bombing of the Chamber of Deputies led the government to consider how it could suppress further attacks on the institutions of authority. In the debates that led up to the passage of *les lois scélérates* on December 16, 1893, the Guardian of the Seals Dubost read passages taken from *La Revue Anarchiste*, the Montmartre anarchist journal with which Charles Chatel replaced the defunct *L'Endehors*. The passages read by Dubost from the tribune were reproduced in the newspaper *Paris* on December 13, 1893, and had been written in response to Léon-Jules Léauthier's knife attack on the Serbian minister of the preceding month:

The act of this last [Léauthier] is particularly sound: *an immense beauty is revealed by the act in itself* **(sain:** *une beauté immense se dégage de l'acte en soi***) [emphasis in** *Paris***], from the conditions where it is elaborated and from the superb attitude of the avenger (***justicier***). . . . I esteem it very beautiful and very useful. Very beautiful, because it is a striking demonstration of revolt and growls in the depths of the laboring classes, because it is courageously independent; very useful, because it will perhaps make those who possess reflect, and inspire in them the terror of reprisals.**[48]**

The act in question was not a carefully planned assassination attempt as that which would kill Carnot the following year, but a random attack on an unlucky representative of the ruling class. The day before his attack, Léauthier wrote to Sebastien Faure, "I will not strike an innocent in striking the first-come bourgeois." Even more purposeless than Ravachol's earlier deeds and the explosion at the police commissariat the week before, the stabbing was a statement of revolt written in blood on the clean white napkin on a diner's chest.[49] The working-class youth's impulsive act was simply meant to strike fear into all the bourgeoisie. The reputed beauty of this act stemmed from its spontaneous, independent execution, but also from its purity of motive and symbolic force.

The author of the *Paris* article was not greatly concerned with the fate of the Serbian minister, who managed to survive the assault despite serious wounds; the author was not trying to say that art and violence were both amoral, but that they both embodied gratuitous beauty. It was left to Laurent Tailhade to epitomize the decadent's lack of concern for normal humanitarian sentiments in his contrast between the beautiful gesture that accompanied a bomb thrown in the face of society, and the suffering that might result from that deed. Tailhade was a good representative of the decadent strain in contemporary literature. Born in 1854 to a family of magistrates, Tailhade was a decade older than most of the anarchist writers, and came from a typically privileged social background. He was sent to law school in Toulouse but ended up in Paris, where he published his first book of poetry, *Le Jardin des rêves,* in 1880, with a preface by the Parnassian Théodore de Banville. Tailhade was known for his elegant, dandified manner and his rancorous wit, which revealed itself in his poems satirizing the pretensions of the bourgeoisie, *Au pays des mufles* (In the Land of the Cads). His caustic pen earned him a year in prison in 1901 for suggesting that someone might perform a useful service by assassinating the czar on his impending visit to Paris. Though his commitment to anarchism was of longer duration than that of most of his fellow poets, it has often been asserted that his anarchism was purely a reflection of his outrageous individualism, and that he cared for nothing outside of style.[50] Nevertheless, his failure to renounce the movement even after he had lost an eye in the unsolved bombing of the Restaurant Foyot in April 1894, his contributions to *La Revue Rouge* and other anarchist journals after the heroic years of anarchism ended, and his jail sentence of 1901, all speak for the political commitment, if not the utter seriousness, of this most Parnassian of the poets enamored of anarchism.

Tailhade's notorious statement—made at the Soirée de la Plume the evening of Vaillant's bombing of the Chamber of the Deputies, "What do the victims matter if the gesture is beautiful? What does the death of some unidentified persons (*des vagues humanités*) matter if, by it, the individual is affirmed?"—enraged the bourgeoisie because it conferred aesthetic standards of behavior upon the terrorist that seemed to give him license to ignore the normal moral restraints placed upon other members of society.[51] The gesture was deemed aesthetically satisfying by virtue of its beauty and individuality, but both traits were actually defined by the bohemian standard of disregard for ordinary mores. The epigram was infused with elitism and certainly diverged from Vaillant's own motivations, but both artist and anarchist were aware that throwing a bomb was a gesture symbolizing discontent with the status quo and one man's willingness not so much to assert himself as to sacrifice himself for the benefit of others. In fact no victims emerged from the bombing except for Vaillant and the anarchist press, and Vaillant disclaimed ever having wanted to kill, so that symbolism and morality were not even at odds in this particular case. The anarchist had fashioned a nonlethal bomb containing nails rather than bullets for projectiles, and the weapon was therefore designed to attract attention to his cause rather than to kill some "vagues humanités." Especially after Vaillant's trial and execution, statements such as Tailhade's were swept aside in the rush to martyrology, though the poet's own martyrdom in a bomb attack some months later returned his words to the front page amid many self-satisfied smirks in the *bien-pensant* press.

Tailhade's mixture of egoism and amorality echoed a common refrain in fin de siècle aesthetic circles, where proponents of the *culte du moi* subsumed everything to the heightening of their own sensibilities, and where the first Nietzscheans proclaimed the master's undemocratic appeals to superior men who could transcend the morality of the herd. The specifically antihumanist tone of Tailhade's statement reflected the elevation of technique over experience and feeling that separated the writers of the late nineteenth century from their Romantic predecessors and which turned poets into aesthetes. The Parnassians' excessive concern for style was mirrored in Tailhade's acceptance of terrorism as a political technique not essentially different from other forms of radical propaganda, and one whose form immediately conveyed its message. The individual's gesture, symbolically exploding on the public stage in restaurants, barracks, the streets, in the Chamber, was a powerful element of propaganda that appealed to those artists who wished that their own voices might be heard above the din. One may surmise that the artists also perceived bomb throwers as a metaphor for their own hostile and destructive relationship with their bourgeois audience, upon whom they were dependent and yet toward whom they were filled with rancor.

The humanitarian outrage at Vaillant's bombing and Tailhade's *bon mot* was mocked in a satirical sketch that appeared in *La Revue Blanche* in the month following the explosion. The writer and boulevard wit Tristan Bernard satirized the president of the Chamber Charles Dupuy's widely publicized declaration made to the hall shortly after the smoke had cleared and some order had been reestablished: "Messieurs, la séance continue" (Gentlemen, the meeting will continue). In the parody, "Le Gros Dupuy" was talking when a servant spilled sauce on a woman seated at the same table. Nobly he announced, "le repas con- tinue" (the meal will continue). Later during the meal a noise was heard and a domestic rushed in to announce that a factory boiler explosion had just killed 200 workers. Dupuy proclaimed calmly, "The sage must consider with the same serenity the unhappiness of those he does not know as the misfortunes of his friends. (Heroically) I'll have some more of that excellent *foie gras*."[52]

Though some artists like Tailhade perceived terrorism as a means of heroic self-affirmation of the individual, many others focused not on the deed but on the cycle of vengeance, retribution, sacrifice, and redemp- tion in the ranks of anarchist martyrs. The hero became the saint. If Tailhade perceived the *beau geste* with an aesthete's eye, writers such as Paul Adam, filled with the mystical religiosity that equally characterized the fin de siècle, canonized the terrorist. In his "Eloge à Ravachol," published the month of the anarchist's death, Adam exposed his religious bent in commemorating the first French anarchist martyr: "Ravachol remains the propagator of the great idea of ancient religions which extol the seeking of individual death for the Good of the world, the abnegation of self, of life and of reknown for the exaltation of the poor, the humble. He is definitively the renovator of essential Sacrifice." Adam thought Ravachol's most deeply symbolic act was his attempt to steal jewels from a cadaver locked in a crypt in order to feed a starving family, to pluck life from death. This act which Adam found so appealing received a consider- able share of horrified attention from the prosecuting attorneys and the press. Adam also advised artists to "trace in pious triptych the life of the Saint, and his passage to death," a call heeded by Charles Maurin, whose woodcut of Ravachol's bust framed by the guillotine appeared not only in *L'Almanach du Père Peinard* but also in *Le Figaro,* where it was repro- duced at the end of Félix Dubois's "Le Péril anarchiste" with the caption "Le Ravachol Symbolique."[53] Dubois described how a cult of Ravachol had arisen, and how the terrorist had become "the assassin, the violator of the sepulcher, the dynamiter, the guillotined—*symbolique.*"[54] His execution even more than his bombings had stimulated the search for a logical pattern among his diverse criminal and political deeds, for in the light of his death, all his acts appeared sacrificial and altruistic. Whereas Tailhade was content to see in the heroic gesture the affirmation of self against the world, Adam felt compelled to trace the progressive disregard for the self for the sake first of others, then for the Idea. Each event in Ravachol's life was symbolically reinterpreted so that nothing was random; even his age at the time of his death was deemed significant. Thus in another eulogy to the terrorist published in July 1892 in *L'Endehors*, Victor Barrucand called him "a sort of violent Christ," and noted that both martyrs were delivered to the executioner at the age of thirty-three. He further identified one of Ravachol's partners, Chaumartin, as the Judas who betrayed him to the authorities. Not content to sanctify Ravachol, Barrucand also wished to make of Jesus an anarchist forebear.[55] Three years later, in his adaptation of the Indian play *Le Chariot de terre cuite,* he similarly interpreted the Buddha as an antiauthoritarian iconoclast.

The sacrificial motif that turned acts of terrorism into deeds of Christian piety reappeared in several of the stories that composed Paul Adam's *Critique des moeurs* of 1893, a collection in which the eulogy to Ravachol was reprinted. "La Charité suprême" portrayed a woman who, amid jeers and catcalls, was selling a Christian newspaper on the streets, when she learned of the plight of a man who needed to raise money quickly to avoid going to jail. She promptly decided to sell her body to raise the necessary funds, and then mysteriously died from the loss of blood pouring from her virgin body, modestly covering the puddles of blood with her skirt as "an ineffable smile" lit her face.[56] This brief story, practically a pastiche of favorite literary themes of the time, was full of classic ironies: the prostitute-despite-herself, who gave herself for the sake of others, victim of a heartless society, who retained her purity despite the corruption around her, compelled to commit a reprehensible act but redeemed by her unselfish motives and ultimately by her own bloodshed. Her smile showed that she knew she had not betrayed her ideals despite her ostensible immorality. The terrorist too was a victim rather than a victimizer, forced by social injustice to compromise his humanity but then redeemed by the ritual exchange of his own life for those of his victims.

The story of "Invectives au mendiant" was a yet more incendiary plea for violence and the inevitable sacrifice that followed. Adam passionately incited a beggar to commit a bold deed, writing "Do you not know the courage of murder" and "You must kill"; for while a lone attacker was called a murderer by society and a group was termed a riot, thousands engaged in the same act could make a revolution. From terrorism to revolution was a quantifiable leap. It was far better to kill and then sacrifice one's life than to die in poverty or commit suicide: "Be a martyr, up till the end, oh beggar my brother! . . . Be magnificent in your blood," though not in Adam's blood. His deed accomplished, the beggar could present himself before God, his hands black with powder, as the symbol of Human Sadness.[57] This piece of invective was the fitting companion piece to the eulogy to Ravachol that immediately followed it. Adam's call for a holy war of beggars and criminals reveals the distance between anarchist and Marxian models of revolution.

The stress on the nobility of sacrifice meant that the manner by which the anarchists met their death was very important. The courage, the bearing, and the last words of each terrorist who ascended the scaffold were widely reported. Ravachol aroused a great deal of praise by his blasphemous insouciance in singing the "Père Duchesne" as he walked to the guillotine, and the lyrics that suggested that priests ought to be cut in two and proprietors hanged did not seem to faze religiously minded literary sympathizers, most of whom practiced their spiritualism without benefit of clergy. Vaillant and Henry also owed much of their martyrdom to their stoic attitudes in the face of death, and only Santo Caserio betrayed fear in his last moments. In contrast, Léauthier was sent to prison rather than executed (though he survived less than a year in the notorious Iles du Salut), and was therefore relatively forgotten by the *compagnons*. The Italian criminologist Cesare Lombroso opposed capital punishment for the terrorists because he reasoned that the death penalty, far from deterring further attacks, might actually encourage individuals with suicidal tendencies to come forward.[58] The sacrificial motif so central to Catholic theology retained its hold over mass psychology. A novel in the form of a diary which appeared in 1895 revealed the fascination with death that accompanied the most outwardly irreligious sentiments. The *Journal d'un anarchiste,* supposedly found by a prison archivist in the year 2002, related the story of an anarchist condemned to die for an *attentat* committed at a Paris restaurant back in the late nineteenth century. The diary ended just before he was taken to the scaffold, and the anarchist maintained his *sang-froid* till the end, dying without religion and believing in nothing, in this case devoid even of faith in the social revolution.[59]

The heroic gesture bathed in blood and certified by death aroused the same aesthetic curiosity as that stimulated by the violent act. What the aesthetic appreciation of violence failed to convey was the sense of belief and commitment sought by the spiritualists of politics. Maurice Barrès, who wrote a newspaper article after witnessing Emile Henry's execution, was sufficiently moved by the boy-terrorist to feel that the "Balzacian era" was threatened by an unprecedented passion for destruction, but he remained personally remote from such a sacred fury. In a similar spirit, Barrès also published *Du sang, de la volupté et de la mort* (Blood, Passion and Death) that same year. Among other topics dealing with his travels in Latin Europe he recounted his impressions of bullfighting, an art that could appeal to Barrès without deeply involving him in its sacrificial religious overtones. Whereas Adam identified with the new era of altruism that he foresaw originating with the death of Ravachol, Barrès was clearly a man of the past, less an aesthete than a dilettante imbued with the Renanian skepticism that tarnished all his commitments. This spirit of inauthenticity and detachment had been attacked by Paul Adam in his critique of aestheticized politics in *La Revue Blanche* in May 1893. Tailhade's anarchism was frequently discounted as an aesthete's pastime, and Jean Grave characterized Barrès's anarchism, as revealed in his novel *L'Ennemi des lois,* as suitable only for millionaires who could afford to indulge their independence and search for meaning. The aestheticized violence focusing on the unique gesture of a defiant individual, whether throwing a bomb or approaching the guillotine, was surpassed in the 1890s by the religious valuation of the terrorists' self-sacrifice as a ritual recapitulation and expiation of the cycle of suffering bound up with the social order. Whereas the detached aesthetic judgment had endowed the artists with a critical perspective on social affairs, the religious attitude that clung to anarchist hopes for the purification of society and the redemption of humanity expressed a deeper seriousness and commitment to those goals. Sanctification invested a political movement with a persuasive authority denied to art.

Anarchism, Religion, and Religiosity:
From *Politique* to *Mystique*

Ten

Throughout history, the secular order has been buttressed by the sacred order, the king by the priest. The more absolute the monarch, the more likely he has been to claim divine sanction of his power. In nineteenth-century France, the parties of conservatism or reaction generally favored close ties between church and state, whereas progressive forces wished to wrest the Republic from papal and priestly influence. On the extreme left, socialists and anarchists opposed not only the secular power of religious institutions but also their doctrines, especially the promise of an afterlife that blunted the efforts of reformers to improve conditions on earth. Every anarchist thinker from Godwin and Stirner to Proudhon, Bakunin, and Kropotkin believed that people must be freed from religious enslavement before they would be capable of overthrowing the authority of the state.

The anarchists' hostility toward all religious dogmas and institutions was ironically accompanied by a persistent idealism which generated a quasi-religious faith in the purifying power of revolutionary violence to sweep away the old world and usher in the society of natural harmony. The rebellious and nihilistic passion for destruction served a spiritual end. The most noticeable manifestation of the anarchists' religious sensibility, their apotheosis of the terrorists as martyrs, was only one aspect of the tendency to turn a political movement into an all-embracing system of rituals and beliefs. Criticizing all aspects of contemporary society rather than just the governing polity, the anarchists required some sort of syncretistic alternative to the reigning truisms and values buttressing bourgeois society. The same inclination to relate all fields of experience in a total critique of bourgeois culture led them to fulfill religious as well as cultural needs from within the anarchist frame of reference. Although intellectually rooted in the tradition of eighteenth-century rationalism and antagonistic to the mystification of social realities practiced by religion and government alike, late nineteenth-century anarchist politics evolved its own mystique by which to exalt and transcend the daily struggle.

The anarchists' ideological attitude toward religion in the late nineteenth century was best represented by that lengthy fragment found among Bakunin's writings by Elisée Reclus and Carlo Cafiero, and published by them in pamphlet form in Geneva in 1882, under the title *God and the State.* The unfinished text was actually a segment of a larger work on which Bakunin had labored between 1870 and 1872. First published in French, *God and the State* was soon widely circulated in many other languages.[1] Its initial appearance in Geneva under Reclus's aegis certified it as the quasi-official doctrine of the theoretical leaders of French anarchism grouped around the newspaper *La Révolte,* which was still based in Geneva in 1882 (under the title *Le Révolté*). Despite his rambling, discursive style, Bakunin's thesis was simple: God and the state, priest and king, were allied authorities, with the secular relying on the sacred authorities for sanctification of their power and for the submissive acceptance of the status quo by the people in return for the solace of a promised afterlife. His thoroughgoing materialism showed little originality over the arguments laid out by Ludwig Feuerbach, whom he cited in the text, or by Marx, whom he did not. All metaphysical ideas were reducible to psychological needs; all appeals to divinity inherently diminished one's humanity by reifying one's own qualities into an external authority. The creation of an omnipotent God automatically impoverished and enslaved humankind. The anarchist critique focused on Christianity's support of the state and on the theological negation of human liberty; Roman Catholicism was therefore Bakunin's pure type of the religious potential to subvert humanity's free will and rebellious instincts.

According to Bakunin, the essence of religion was the sacrifice of human beings to God: "All religions are cruel, all founded on blood; for all rest principally on the idea of sacrifice—that is, on the perpetual immolation of humanity to the insatiable vengeance of divinity. In this bloody mystery man is always the victim, and the priest—a man also, but a man privileged by grace—is the divine executioner."[2] All priests had a cruel and sanguinary element in their hearts, however humane they might appear. Bakunin would not have been surprised to discover the same blood-lust existing in the ruling class, as it executed the terrorists whose methods he had avidly championed in the 1860s and 1870s. But could he have foretold that twenty years after he wrote these words anarchist intellectuals would write that anarchism also rested on the idea of sacrifice of man to the Idea, that giving one's life for the movement was a most exemplary act of altruism and one which had great propagandistic value? Since his own years spent in prison greatly enhanced Bakunin's popularity, perhaps he would have recognized something of the martyr's appeal, but he undoubtedly would have condemned the martyrology, the Idealism, the millennialism, and all the other spiritual trappings that clothed cultural anarchism in the 1890s. The spirit of sacrifice, the appeal of blood shed for the cause, was the most popular aspect of this religious impulse within the movement, but in a more profound sense all of anarchism played upon the desire to escape from historical time in a moment of apocalyptic revolutionary fury and to enter the future paradise that would cyclically return men and women to their primal innocence and goodness. Bakunin's dialectic of idealism and materialism, in which the most idealistic nations, such as Germany, produced the most materialistic society, could have been useful in predicting that the ideology of materialism and atheism would lead to proclamations of *l'anarchriste* and mystic cults. An earlier dialectician, William Blake, had already had the foresight to query, "Are not Religion and Politics the Same Thing?"[3]

Inverting Voltaire's famous dictum declaring that if God did not exist it would be necessary to invent Him, Bakunin said that "if God really existed, it would be necessary to abolish Him."[4] In his eagerness to destroy the concept of divinity, Bakunin failed to notice the secularized idealism that replaced it. A more thoroughgoing critique of religion as a subset of abstract idealism was carried out by the German philosopher Max Stirner, whose egoistic denial of all spiritual essences and moral abstractions surpassed Bakunin's substitution of the human for the divine. Stirner felt that the abstraction "humanity" was as likely to enlist people under its banners as was some true faith. All ideals greater than the individual were potentially hostile to one's integrity and autonomy, and bespoke one's alienation.[5] This forerunner of the *culte du moi* would obviously have made a poor revolutionary, as his only cause was his own existence. The thoroughness of Stirner's critique of Hegelian idealism highlights the incompleteness of Bakunin's rejection of God, and the continuing imprint of Bakunin's own youthful Hegelian enthusiasm. Whereas Bakunin willed the immediate embodiment of freedom in revolution, Hegel (and Kant and Johann Fichte before him) was responsible for the spiritual and idealistic concept of freedom as a motive for the world-historical process.

Anarchist utopianism and insurrectionary ardor ultimately negated the ideology of materialism preached by Bakunin. Anarchist commitment to social welfare was never as strong as the commitment to the insurrection that would beget the era of liberty and harmony. It called for the abolition not merely of the present social order, but the end of the very conception of the human being as *homo economicus,* whose behavior was reducible to the satisfaction of his or her material needs. The anarchists' goal was not to satisfy these needs, but to free everyone from the constraints upon their freedom such necessity entailed. A psychological reevaluation of human nature underlay any prescription for physical well-being. The reigning conception of humanity epitomized by Benthamite utilitarianism considered individuals as interchangeable bundles of needs capable of being economically satisfied and calculated; and capitalism enshrined this quantifiable behaviorist image into a system declaring each person's value to be that of a commodity on the labor exchange market. Money created only relative not absolute differences between people. The anarchists believed that the socialists challenged not the supremacy of economic relations in society, but only the unequal distribution of wealth. Without fundamentally altering the materialistic model, the socialists would only increase people's uniformity. In promoting an image of the human being as *homo faber* rather than *homo economicus,* the anarchists stressed each individual's unique creative capacities which were irreducible to some common denominator. In the present system of social relations only a few fortunate individuals, chiefly artists and artisans, were able to express their essences, but after the revolution all would be freed to engage in self-expression. The future utopia was to be qualitatively different from the present, yet the transition to such a state would not be difficult because of the anarchists' rationalist faith in humanity's essential goodness, once liberated from the corrupting effects of authority, hierarchy, and economic exploitation. Here too the anarchists expressed a strong belief in an innate human essence, as against the infinitely plastic concept of human nature upheld by Benthamites and socialists alike. In protesting their exploitation, their solution was not to devise a more just rearrangement of the economy, but to revise the standards by which status and hierarchy were determined. Not an economic but a spiritual revolution was tendered.

The anarchists' antimaterialism was also expressed in the rejection of Marxian economic stages of development which led unalterably to the final upheaval. For this theory of historical change the anarchists substituted no real theory of their own, save for the faith that revolutions could be made by a tremendous effort of will, that they would occur spontaneously, in a dynamic liberation of energies presaging the era of absolute freedom to follow. The revolution was a cataclysm rather than a rational, instrumental tool for social change, a purifying orgy of destruction that would create the conditions for the eventual era of harmony. One rarely encounters anarchist discussions of revolutionary strategy or the likely conditions or time-frame that would accommodate such total violence. Instead, the revolution was prefigured in each individual act of violence which, as Paul Adam wrote, differed from the mass insurrection only in the number of participants willing to dedicate themselves to the cause. When, after sufficient propagandistic preparation, the masses expressed their will as spontaneously as individuals did at present (one is reminded of Rousseau's general will), the revolution would be an accomplished fact. Lenin adjudged the difference between communists and anarchists to be that the latter thought about the future without understanding the present, by which he meant that their utopianism mixed with chronic insurrectionism impeded their critical understanding of social realities.[6] Unlike Lenin, who possessed a firmly historical time-sense, the anarchists often confused the immediate means with the long-awaited end. The *attentats,* which exploded into contemporary consciousness and made anarchism a word on everyone's lips, prefigured the cataclysm that would really shake society's foundations. The phrase of Charles Malato that inspired Paul Signac's painting *Au temps d'harmonie,* "the golden age is not in the past but in the future," summarized the utopian faith of the anarchists which lay behind their appeals to future generations to redeem their deaths.

Anarchism, with its insurrectionism combined with longing for a paradisaical golden age, has frequently been compared to the chiliastic social-religious movements of the late Middle Ages, and there is considerable justification for believing that the anarchists' social idealism found a religious outlet of the millennial and prophetic variety.[7] Norman Cohn concludes his work on medieval and early modern millenarian movements with a definition that closely approximates the social makeup and psychological appeal of anarchism: "A boundless, millennial promise made with boundless, prophet-like conviction to a number of rootless and desperate men in the midst of a society where traditional norms and relationships are disintegrating."[8] Karl Mannheim was more specific about the social composition of the chiliasts. He called it a mental structure characteristic of the lowest strata of society: "oppressed peasants, journeymen, an incipient *Lumpenproletariat,* fanatically emotional preachers, etc." In a footnote he referred to evidence that the lower classes were joined in some cases by the "intellectuals" of the period, who gradually withdrew their support as the movement became more radical.[9] These are the same social groups in the same tumultuous period which Marcel Schwob described in his portrayal of the first bands of argot-speaking outcasts floundering amid the social and economic disarray following the Hundred Years' War (see chapter 4). Coquillards and chiliasts comprised two different responses to the same psychosocial pressures: the formation of secret societies of outlaws, or the more radical declaration of war upon the whole status quo in the name of spiritual salvation and the Kingdom of God at hand. The twin options of secret societies or mass insurrection still faced the anarchists of four centuries later, as they were continually reminded of the necessity of surviving in the present even while dreaming of the future. Their most fertile soil for propaganda came from those groups that conformed least to the economic model of behavior fostered by industrial capitalism: handcraftspeople and artisans, printers, artists, and intellectuals, and all those whose mode of economic production was based on traditional methods of small-scale production. Because these groups could frequently remember better times, they tended to conceive of future social change in terms of a restoration of an earlier state of affairs. The pressures brought to bear on marginal economic groups, in this case brought to the fore not only by industrialization but by the long depression of 1873–96 that increased demands for economic rationalization, resulted in the anarchists voicing chiliastic hopes for redemption by apocalyptic means.

The people who were attracted to anarchism, then, were experiencing relative deprivation. This does not mean starvation, but rather a gap between expectations and possible achievements, between the model of society with which they were socialized and that which was validated by peer consensus and daily reality. The best examples of populational response to relative deprivation come from the ethnographic literature on the American Indians: the movements of Washakie, Handsome Lake, and Black Elk, and the Ghost Dance and Peyote movements.[10] One such movement having a profound if short-lived effect on popular social participation and political consciousness was exactly contemporaneous with the anarchists, though probably unknown to them. Spiritual leaders had arisen among a dispirited Lakota Indian people on the reservations of South Dakota and preached that by means of the Ghost Dance their bodies would become invulnerable to bullets. Aided by their ancestors arisen from the dead, they could therefore rise up against the white men and reclaim their ancestral lands and way of life. The Ghost Dance religion succeeded in mobilizing the Indian nation but did not protect them from the massacre at Wounded Knee.[11] In general, such revitalistic movements are large-scale responses to secular pressures by nonsecular means that are found among populations in times of stress. Though the cognitive structure is mystical and often millenarian, such movements function to mobilize the population to meet concrete material needs. Anarchism had much in common with these movements.

Except for a few fringe sects the anarchists did not guarantee their members everlasting life and certainly did not guarantee invulnerability, but they did hold forth the promise of redemption in a future earthly paradise where oppression and exploitation would cease. The promise was of sufficient magnitude to encourage martyrs to feel certain that their deaths would be avenged and their lives immortalized. They themselves were avenging not only their imprisoned or executed comrades but the generation of their fathers who had been slaughtered in the Commune, whose extinction had paved the way for the establishment of the Third Republic, and who presented examples of heroic behavior to be emulated. The violent revenge of Emile Henry was most explicitly carried out in this context, but the whole younger generation of anarchists who had grown up in the shadow of the Commune could accept the revenge meted out to the bourgeoisie and could identify themselves as successors to the Communards. They would create the harmonious and just community envisioned by their fathers and crushed by Adolphe Thiers, head of the government centered at Versailles. Anarchism afforded them the comradeship and communion of the *compagnons,* with their *soirées familiales,* strong in-group sense, and hatred of informers, while also enhancing their individuality. To individuals beset by the anomie of the rapidly developing urban landscape (not only in Paris but in Lyon, Marseille, and other anarchist strongholds) and the pressures of large-scale industrialization, the socialist call to join the collective mass of humanity provided little psychological solace. Anarchism, on the other hand, not only ideologically supported individualism, but presented models of heroic individual action in behalf of the revolution. One did not have to wait for the eventual triumph of the proletariat, meanwhile voting for socialist deputies; one could act. The fervent revitalistic call for sacrifice and redemption enhanced the supports of the individual identity and the sense of community fostered by the cultural anarchism of the period.

Like the Ghost Dance, anarchism promised an indefinite, potentially imminent apocalypse. The anarchist utopia existed in a radically other place outside of history, capable at any moment of establishing itself in the present. The chiliastic mentality which Mannheim believed typified revolutionary anarchism existed in the absolute present, and could therefore conceptualize only insurrectionary immediacy rather than liberal continuity or Marxist teleology.[12] Mannheim's criterion of absolute presentness, which he considered the one true test of the applicability of the chiliastic model to a particular social movement, does not conflict with Lenin's critique of anarchist inability to deal with the present. Mannheim himself accused anarchists such as Gustave Landauer of blindness toward the present. By reducing the complexity of history to the overriding antithesis between authoritarian and libertarian social systems, all present forms of society were indiscriminately lumped together.[13] If freedom only existed in the anarchist utopia, then all of contemporary society must be enslaved, despite the fact that French anarchists could take refuge in liberal England but certainly not in czarist Russia.

A glance at the terrorist tactics prevailing in 1890s anarchism should clarify any possible confusion between acting on the present and the chiliastic immediacy that characterized the *attentats*. The terrorist acts perfectly symbolized "heroic anarchism" because of their passionate but ineffectual aim to destroy present reality rather than analyze or alter it. They were not functional but metaphorical acts, microcosms of the coming revolution that were more effective as sacrificial rituals than as mechanisms of social change. Only with syndicalism did the anarchists devise a realistic way of acting on the present, still retaining their faith in the cataclysmic, one-time break with the present through the medium of the general strike. Sorel's apotheosis of the general strike as a moral purification of the world, as an end in itself, typifies the chiliastic attitude, though it did not necessarily represent the attitude of the syndicalist rank and file. That terrorists such as Emile Henry realized that their act would not immediately precipitate the social revolution, that the golden age did not only lie in a sacred space but also in a future time, however unspecified, revealed the degree of abstract idealism that accompanied their chiliastic fervor. However immediate the prospect of salutary violence, the anarchist utopia was clothed in the golden glow of a distant, once-and-future time; much of the ambivalence of a movement that attracted disciples of Tolstoy and Bakunin lay in the heady mixture of idealism and exaltation that could lead to pacifism or violence. The chiliastic religious mentality was expressed in the presumptuous use of violence and in the expectation of a utopia that justified such forays of adventurism. Both the practice of violence and the belief in an imminent millennium rested on faith rather than on a critical evaluation of the weaknesses of contemporary society and their own possibilities of success.

Though anarchist religiosity may be considered to have undermined its political effectiveness by its unwillingness to grapple with social reality (as Mannheim believed), the spiritualization of politics was not entirely dysfunctional. The appeal to the sanctity of martyrs, to a revolutionary apocalypse and an anarchist millennium may all have served to impart an aura of meaningfulness to acts and ideologies that were difficult to rationally explain. The execution of Ravachol might have seemed to indicate the triumph of the state if his sacrifice was not equated with that of Christ. The future revolution would have appeared to be a distant and dubious prospect if not for the imagery of the *Grand*

Soir, closely followed by the New Dawn. Symbolic imagery functioned to concretize ideological abstractions; sanctity lent it the reliability of transcendent authority. Because there were no authorities as such in anarchism capable of compelling norms of behavior or certifying the orthodoxy of a particular doctrine, the quasi sanctification of such doctrines formed a surrogate authority that ensured faith in the cause. As demonstrated most strikingly in the case of the martyrs, sanctity may have been an alternative to real political power, but it also served to guarantee belief in a movement heavily dependent upon the reception and spread of propaganda. The weaker the leadership, the more recourse one had to spiritual sanctification as an alternate source of authority.[14] The anarchists' spiritual mission also spurred recruitment of new members and increased group cohesion.

The critique of the religious spirit underlying anarchism did not await later sociologists and historians. Contemporary critics with positivist or anticlerical leanings charged anarchism with religious fanaticism and irrationalism in order to discredit it. As early as 1886, *Le Journal de Genève* published a diatribe against the blind and contagious force that, because of its associations with Russian princes and nihilists, was called an "asiatic virus" spread by Mongols. Kropotkin was called the anarchist pontiff preaching the millennium in a movement described as "that religion, at once atheist and mystical, [which] has its loyal followers, as convinced, as sincere as one can be, its levites, its martyrs, ready to suffer all for their negative faith."[15] A decade after Bakunin's death, when anarchism was still thought of as a Russian import rather than an indigenous Latin movement, the paradox of religious exaltation being expressed in a resolutely secular form was already a journalistic commonplace. The point received great emphasis by the French deputy who published his attack on anarchism in 1897, when "the anarchist madness is perhaps definitely passed; but mysticism, which bore it, has been, is and will be always; only this mysticism will transform itself following the centuries; religious in the Middle Ages, it has shown itself anarchist in our *fin de siècle*; what form will it take in future ages?" Not the solid working class but the failures, the idlers, and artists had fallen prey to the lure of the bomb, that "spice for blasé senses." He characterized the anarchists as poets (citing the poetry of Emile Henry as evidence), but they were above all religious mystics. Henry's mother, he reported, told journalists that her son considered Saint Louis to be his patron saint and carried his picture in his pocket. "Emile Henry is a mystic by his origins, his dreams, the vagueness of his aspirations, even by the fashion in which he envisaged his death."[16] To the deputy, poets and mystics were distinguished only by the greater fanatic zeal of the latter. The charge of mysticism allowed the deputy to detach the anarchists from the legions of the progressive left and situate them among the atavistic cults common to social outcasts; the terrorists were throwbacks to the religious regicides of the sixteenth and seventeenth centuries, rather than harbingers of the future society.

The most realistic and successful element of early 1890s anarchism, the desire to turn every deed and personal encounter into an occasion for propaganda for the cause, was seen as attesting to the evangelical fervor of its adherents. The *compagnons* were portrayed as monomaniacal propagandists who resorted to all the means at their disposal, as they traveled along the rural routes to spread the word. Each anarchist was a missionary who must convert the world. Even in prison, Ravachol's first thought was to convert his prison guards. (His terrorist predecessor, Bakunin's one-time associate Sergei Nechaiev, succeeded in radicalizing his guards, though his eight years in the czar's prison afforded him a more leisurely opportunity to expound his views than the few months granted to Ravachol.) Augustin Hamon called the spirit of proselytism one of the basic traits common to all anarchists and linked it with the thirst for knowledge that characterized even the working-class members.[17] The raising of political consciousness was very important to the anarchists, as no ironclad laws of economics were going to bring about the revolution, but only the human will. Proselytism was the responsibility not only of trained missionaries like the one-time Jesuit seminarian Sebastien Faure, but of each *compagnon*.

Hamon acknowledged the religious impulse behind this spirit, but he carefully limited its extent to that of devotion to the cause: "Pantheist or atheist, the anarchist has for his ideal a sort of cult. His love for that which he conceives true is really religious. The anarchist-socialist has a religion, but it is without rites; it is purely intellectual and its object is his conception of Truth, Justice, Beauty."[18] Hamon maintained that the anarchist intellectual was like a deist who was willing to admit a distant godlike ideal but disavowed the panoply of saints and rituals that formed the exoteric religious superstructure. Anarchism to Hamon was a pure ideal, not a vulgar practice or a millenarian ecstasy. The sociologist was less prone than the artists to recognize the importance of symbols and the analogic reasoning they implied. An article appearing in *Le Figaro* shortly after Vaillant's execution sharply contradicted Hamon's contention that anarchism was without rites. The Parisian did not generally believe in God, the writer said, but was very susceptible to the cult of saints and relics in which he incarnated his desires, his passions, and his bitterness. He had the same need of amulets and fetishes as the Negroes of Guinea, and over the years the white crosses of Saint Bartholomew had given way to "more dangerous idols: the guillotine and the goddess Reason in 1793, the Ravachols and Vaillants today." In the outpouring of sympathy for Vaillant, the journalist feared the "false sensitivity . . . which has created the atmosphere where the religion of the bomb becomes possible."[19]

The alacrity with which deputies and journalists described anarchism as a religious effusion should not be lightly glossed over. In contrast to Hamon's sympathetic portrayal of anarchist idealism, the *Figaro*'s journalist equated anarchists with superstitious, "primitive" peoples in order to reduce their ideology to mere irrationalism. The anarchists' socialist rivals on the left were and are equally likely to write off anarchism as being fundamentally mystical, while priding themselves on being scientific—which has not prevented other commentators from noting the messianic implications of Marxism itself.[20] To perceive the importance of secular religions does not necessarily discredit these movements, but rather recognizes the continued hold of symbols, rituals, and appeals to transcendence on the human spirit. It does require jettisoning the positivist evolutionary model that maintains that humankind has evolved from a theological to a metaphysical to a scientific world view. The typology of increasing secularization may be at fault, not the revolutionaries who seek meaning in unorthodox ways.

Some of these ways were more unorthodox and peripheral than others. The popular appeal of saints and rituals led to more esoteric spiritualist offshoots than imagined either by Hamon or the *Figaro* journalist. In the southern coastal city of Toulon in 1895 was born the cult of Universellism (which the practitioners took pains to distinguish orthographically from Universalism), whose brief history on the physical but longer tenure on the "astral plane" was recorded by its founder, Marie de Saint-Rémy, in an 1899 volume entitled *Les Dieux des anarchistes*. This cult, which arose on the fringes of popular anarchism, apparently had its origins in the police repression of 1894. Marie Andrieux, as she was then known, was arrested in Marseille and spent three months in prison. Her husband had died in 1890, and her twenty-year-old painter son Raphael perished shortly after her release (according to Marie out of grief at his mother's imprisonment). The next year the anarchist Christ appeared to her in Toulon, and thereafter she had many communications with deceased political figures. In her book she reproduced letters sent in by Ravachol, Léon Gambetta, Boulanger, and others, and described conversations between Carnot and Ravachol. Vaillant ascended into the assemblage of saints two years after his decapitation. She also edited a newspaper called *Le Christ Anarchiste* from 1895 through 1897. It was joined by another Universellist publication in 1897, this one called *L'Antéchrist*.[21]

In the same year that her own work appeared in print, Marie de Saint-Rémy wrote the preface to the book *Anarchie et Spiritualisme: Réponse d'un anarchiste spiritualiste à ses camarades materialistes,* written by one of her disciples, a young Italian named Antonio de Nocera. Again de Saint-Rémy's obsession with martyrdom was evident, as she wrote that the materialist anarchists' time of trials was past; now the spiritualists were just beginning "the bloody calvary of persecution." She for one was ready to die and be reborn as a "libertaire réincarnationniste." De Nocera summarized his beliefs as "Reincarnationist, Philosophically. Libertarian, Politically. Anti-Capitalist, Economically." The belief in reincarnation was an ingenious spiritual concomitant to the anarchist critique of the endlessly repeating cycle of authority, by which, after each successive revolution a new regime imposed itself that was no less tyrannical than the previous one. By accumulating good karma, anarchist martyrs were reborn higher on the chain, and would eventually free themselves entirely from the wheel, whereas the bourgeois would suffer for eons before they vanquished their authoritarian and egoistic spirit and rose to join the higher collective mind [*Pensée*] which controlled and united all individual thoughts. The material and spiritual anarchist goal was freedom from the wheel of existence, the cycle that the socialists would only perpetuate. The struggle for liberty did not end at death: "the need of all Libertarians is to think, to will, to act with the same force and energy in the beyond as here."[22] As the Naturist element of anarchism extended the critique of the state to that of civilization, the spiritualists pushed libertarianism to the liberation of the individual from life itself. The metapolitical tendencies of anarchism merged with the metaphysical, as the vision of an order of natural harmony and of absolute liberty militated against limitations on the grandeur of its own conception. Anarchism's political and social critique was imaginatively escalated to assume increasingly broad ramifications. The tendency to interpret the social malaise as a totality rather than as discrete issues led to the anarchist penchant for ultimate solutions, from the insurrectionary to the theosophical.

Symptomatic though this spiritualization of politics was, theosophical anarchism was clearly on the fringe of the anarchist movement. Much more representative of anarchist beliefs were the four issues of *Les Crimes de Dieu* (The Crimes of God) that also appeared in the south of France in 1897 to publicize the anticlerical lectures of Sebastien Faure.[23] Did this "official" doctrine correspond to the beliefs of the "typical" working-class anarchist? Some useful testimony about French working-class attitudes toward religion comes from a worker named Henry Steele, of French and English parentage, who lived in Paris and worked in a factory at the turn of the century. In 1904, Steele published *The Working Classes in France: A Social Study* in order to enlighten the parochial English about everyday life across the channel. Early in his sojourn, Steele became engaged in a discussion with a priest while out on a stroll. Initially amazed at this boldness, the priest discovered that Steele was English, and assured him that a French worker would never be seen conversing with a priest in public. Such temerity would warrant immediate ostracism by his fellows, since it was considered tantamount to collaborating with the class enemy. Steele confirmed this after spending more time in the working-class milieu: "Most of the workmen I met . . . look upon the priesthood as a sort of police in the employers' interests, and as the organizers of all attempts to destroy their movements, and to bring back more hated forms of government." He also noted that the forms of religion remained long after the beliefs had evaporated, and that most people received communion and a Christian burial largely because of the women's attachment to the church.[24] Steele's working-class acquaintances belonged to a variety of left-wing organizations, principally socialist, but it is safe to assume that most working-class anarchists shared this extreme anticlericalism, and were probably even less likely to accede to the outward forms of Catholic practice. Yet relations between the church and anarchism were more complex than these generalizations would suggest. One must distinguish between hostility toward the church and toward religious belief: anarchists were undoubtedly anticlerical, but with normal religious channels closed to them, they were more likely to look elsewhere to satisfy questions of ultimate meaning.

Anarchist flirtations with religion reached their most ecstatic level with spiritualists such as Marie de Saint-Rémy; nevertheless, although esotericists estimated optimistically that there were 300,000 practicing French Buddhists in the early 1890s, religion in France still by and large meant Catholicism, and spiritual metaphors for politics were mostly drawn from Catholic sources.[25] Anarchism's relations with the church ranged from the members' own religious backgrounds through contemporary attempts by the church at conversion and infiltration of the movement, to future conversions by disillusioned anarchists. Alexandre Bérard eagerly pointed out that Ravachol and Vaillant had had religious upbringings, that a condemned activist of the 1880s, A. Cyvoct, had been part of a Catholic circle in Lyon, and that Henry was devoted to Saint Francis. The director of Sebastien Faure's newspaper *Le Libertaire* came from an ultraclerical background, having been employed by the Catholic paper *Le Monde* and serving as an aide to the devout abbé Finot. Bérard's favorite example of the tendency to transfer religious devotion to the political sphere was Faure himself, who came from a bourgeois, royalist family in Saint-Etienne, was raised religiously, and went to a Jesuit seminary before family financial reverses sent him out in the world, where he was first attracted to socialism and then became the chief orator for anarchism.[26] Adolphe Retté claimed that Jean Grave's coeditor Martin was also an old seminarian who had become a speaker at workers' meetings. Retté wrote, "Despite his apostasy, Martin retained something clerical in attitude and discourse. One day . . . he made this declaration to me: 'We are the fathers of the anarchist church and we promulgate dogmas.'" Upon hearing this, Jean Grave, himself referred to as the movement's pope for his ideological orthodoxy, upbraided his co-worker: "Have you finished posing as sovereign pontiff, you defrocked priest?"[27]

The involvement of legitimate priests with the anarchists of the early 1890s reflected the new liberalism of Rome and the doctrine of social Catholicism promulgated by Pope Leo XIII in 1891. In the papal encyclical *Rerum Novarum* of May 15, 1891, the pope denounced the exploitation of labor by capital, recognized the right of workers to equitable treatment and even to a minimum wage, and recommended the reestablishment of guilds. The following year, the pope declared that the church was not opposed to any particular form of government, thereby sanctioning clerical republicanism. This was of course a far cry from the anarchist credo that opposed all forms of government, but it did allow liberal Catholics like Marc Sangnier to speak out in favor of social democracy. A certain number of French priests now felt encouraged to take the cause of the working class, in order both to improve their lot and to wean them away from atheistic socialism. The abbés Théodore Garnier, Naudet, Dabry, and Lemire tried to enroll workers in Christian unions, and in the *cercles d'ouvriers* that preached workers' self-help.[28] They went so far as to justify their efforts as fulfilling the biblical promise of a kingdom of God on earth, which at least had a millenarian ring to it. The Christian democrats were most active in the early and mid-1890s, before the Dreyfus Affair alienated the church from the Republic and led to the formal separation of church and state in the aftermath of the affair. The activities of these priests exhibited more social conscience than millenarianism, yet the congruence of religious and social objectives preached by the *abbés démocrates* paralleled the "secular religions" of socialism and anarchism (and even Dreyfusism) that flourished in this epoch, if not ideologically then psychologically.[29] In an era of ferment and incertitude, in the last years of a generation-long economic depression matched by inexorable urbanization and social dislocations, the demand for faith accompanied that for justice. In secularizing their religion or in spiritualizing their politics, both Christians and anarchists broadened their appeal.

The speeches of the abbés Garnier and Jouet sounded progressive, but the anarchists suspected them of seeking converts, if not of actually wanting to subvert the movement. Thus at a meeting held on July 27, 1891, the police informer reported, the abbé Jouet "invited the workers to unionize to struggle against the exploiters: the great thieves known under the names of capitalists and bankers." The priests Jouet, Garnier, and Monfort were invited to speak at another meeting but were shouted down by many among the several hundred anarchists who attended the large gathering, and Michel Zévaco warned the anarchists that the "superstitious idea" was disseminated by priests whose object was always conversion.[30] Zo d'Axa reported on the well-publicized conversion of a revolutionary in *L'Endehors,* but doubted the sincerity of the *compagnon* in question. He could understand that "sometimes the most frankly libertarian temperaments are impassioned by a high mysticism," but not how one could revoke the dream of liberty for "the puerilities of a ready-made religion." He was convinced that self-interest rather than piety led anarchists to the church.[31]

The greatest public uproar about priestly collusion with the anarchists came not from attempts at conversion but from fears of conspiracy. During the police roundup of anarchists under *les lois scélérates,* a man named Marius Tournadre was arrested in March 1894 and was found with letters on his person from priests who had contributed funds to the anarchists. The priests had requested funds from the duchesse d'Uzès and had sent transfers of funds to London groups for the purpose of fomenting new bombings. Marcel Schwob wrote of this event on March 6 and 9, 1894, and believed that clerical support of anarchist violence had clarified matters for those socialists who had hitherto believed that all attacks against establishing society abetted their cause: "They [the socialists] sing another tune now. The documents found on Marius Tournadre have inspired some wise reflections. They have understood that these violent attacks, disunited and isolated, could be calculated to lead to a reaction rather than a revolution."[32] Schwob immediately suspected a radical rightist conspiracy to use the anarchists to help topple republicanism, and thereafter to install a conservative, proclerical regime. Instead, the position of the French church vis-à-vis the state was to worsen over the course of the next decade.

Schwob deduced that the clergy and the royalists supported the extreme left in order to undermine the republic; meanwhile the police, usually quick to jump at any conspiracy theory, believed that the anarchists were merely using the gullible abbé Théodore Garnier in order to raise funds. They "come to him for moral consultations . . . and demands of money," and Garnier sent lists of their names to the publication *Peuple Français* thinking he had converted them. On April 15, 1894, the police report claimed that the abbé's close relations with the anarchists were due to his desire for converts and theirs for money, but two weeks later "Legrand's" emphasis had changed: "The abbé Garnier wants to play the role of mediator between the church and anarchy. The aristocrats and clergy whom he knows feel protected by him against attacks. And certain of them show him their sympathies and their pocketbooks." Another report, dating from February 1894, was more equivocal about the political implications of clerical support, noting only that "many people believe that the anarchists are subsidized by the clerics and the Orléanists. It is a legend which tends to spread in the masses."[33] But two days later, an informer noted the rumors among the small shopkeepers and the working classes that the bombings were a government ploy to discredit the newly powerful socialists, so such talk only proved the populace's own taste for conspiracies.[34]

If anarchism functioned as an alternate focus of inspiration for lapsed Catholics such as Faure, one might expect that when the lure of revolution waned and especially as the *compagnons* aged and the millennium remained as distant as ever, they might just as readily turn to more traditional sources of faith. The shift from chiliastic to pietistic forms of spiritual devotion is a well-known feature of failed millenarian movements, when inner freedom is substituted for social radicalism.[35] Whereas pietism retained a potentially subversive autonomy from state control and social norms, conversion to Catholicism represented the capitulation of one's individuality in return for the certitude of faith. Former anarchists joined a number of literati who returned to the church in the decade from 1905 to the war. Among the younger generation that matured during and after the Dreyfus Affair, the return to spiritual faith after the era of positivism and freethinking was accompanied by respect for authority and the eventual embrace of nationalism and militarism.[36]

Two books published in the decade before World War I witnessed the political implications of this shift toward traditional Catholicism on the part of former anarchists. H. Tricot was a mechanic who first gave his allegiance to revolutionary socialism, then to anarchism after 1882. He left his job in 1885 and turned to selling thread and cloth on the road, the better to spread anarchist ideas. *De l'anarchie à l'évangile*, published in 1910, confessed his youthful errors and announced his new peace in the bosom of the church. Three years before, Adolphe Retté had published *Du Diable à Dieu: Histoire d'une conversion,* which turned out to be his best-selling book, going into several editions and translations. Though these books appeared long after their authors' anarchist fervor had ended, their publication was not devoid of political significance, as the years from 1906 to 1910 witnessed the high point of revolutionary anarcho-syndicalism. The labor violence and calls for a general strike were far more threatening to the state than individual terrorism had ever been, and the conservative Catholic appeal was directed at this current threat. Grasping the church as an immutable rock in a sea of flux, Retté fervently renounced change and individuality. *Du Diable à Dieu* charted the passage from anarchy to order, whereas *La Maison en ordre* championed the monarchism of the Action Française, thereby completing his political evolution from left to right and confirming the political implications of his conversion.

While he was an anarchist, Adolphe Retté had ostensibly accepted fully the movement's extreme anticlericalism; nevertheless, Christian imagery abounded in his Naturist poetry and revolutionary tracts of 1895–96. Guillaume in *Similitudes,* Jacques Simple in *Le Forêt bruissante,* were approximations of the humble Christ-figure who sacrificed himself for the sake of the poor and oppressed, who then took his cause and proclaimed him their messiah against the authority of Rome. Well before this, anarchists had compared Ravachol and Jesus, and an article entitled "L'Anarchrist" that appeared in *La Plume* shortly after Ravachol's execution went so far as to include the Jesuits in the ranks of anarchist predecessors for preaching disobedience to unjust kings and even for inciting regicide. Though Retté was not a great proponent of terrorism, he did call the bomb throwers heroes "in the absolute sense," and "martyrs who sacrificed themselves for the Idea."[37] More typical was Retté's evocation of primitive Christianity before its institutionalization, expressing his longing for a pure faith and also for a return to an era of natural simplicity and goodness such as Jesus represented. In an illuminating interview that Augustin Hamon conducted with Retté, probably in 1894, the religious appeal of anarchism was clear:

I can add that before being an anarchist, I had tossed about between a hundred philosophical systems; today Hegelian, tomorrow pessimist,

then Catholic, what do I know? I was like a shuttlecock between the rackets of these ghosts which would amuse me among the ruins. Since I have understood, since I no longer believe, since I am an anarchist, in a word, I have acquired the interior light, the inextinguishable conviction, serenity. Every day I meditate on the Idea, every day it is with a new joy; every day the horizon enlarges and the human future appears to me more beautiful, because I see that Anarchy can not not realize itself effectively, because I see that it is virtually realized, because we carry it in us. Recently I made acts of faith and mistrusted my adversaries. Now I reason and I pity those in the shadows.[38]

Even though Retté claimed he had exchanged faith for the power of reason, his terminology was replete with religious imagery: "interior light," "serenity," "meditate on the Idea," "inextinguishable conviction." That Retté seemingly equated anarchism with unbelief did not diminish the fact that this was one more "philosophical system," one more act of faith.

Retté's search for order led him to the church, but many radical rightists were attracted by the satanic and supernatural. Léon Daudet and Charles Maurras of the Action Française, Edouard Drumont and his city editor Gaston Méry, were all enticed by magic, mediums, and clairvoyants. If satanism and mysticism reflected the conspiratorial world view of anti-Semites and nationalists, such cults had no less appeal for writers attracted to anarchism in the same period.[39] The extreme left and right shared a common taste for the irrational and the cult of action, and a similar disdain for the materialist rationalism of the socialists and Radicals.

Mysticism played at least as great a role in intellectual circles as it did in the popular milieu of Marie de Saint-Rémy and friends. Some writers were motivated by authentic spiritual disquietude—such as Villiers de l'Isle Adam, Paul Claudel, and Léon Bloy—others sought mysterious veils in much the same way as they draped themselves in the black flag of revolution. Paul Adam, one of the most passionately mystical of anarchist writers, parodied these religious *poseurs* in "Le Nouvel Anarchiste." Montmartre, where Sacré-Coeur was rising in pious expiation of the sins of the Communards, was called the "new Calvary of the new Jerusalem," where Rothschild would be crucified among a myriad popu-

lation of soothsayers and Rosicrucians. Adam characterized the religiously inclined anarchist as one whose

religion will depend on his imaginative and sumptuous temperament; he will be a magi, will make some vegetarian withdrawals for forty days, carry in his breast pocket a *pentacle* **of lead against the malign influence of Saturn and will evoke salamanders in the vermillion of spoonfuls of sherbet.**

Meditative and passionate, he will be a Buddhist, will leaf through the celestial poems of the Orient in the dust of libraries and will burn sticks of sandalwood before gilded dragons.

Intuitive and valorous, he will proclaim himself a Catholic, explain the symbols of dogma, their esoteric and social meaning forgotten by the ignorance of orthodox contemporaries.[40]

Spiritual trappings played as great a part as pietistic introversion in the popular mysticism which Adam linked to the snobbism of self-professed revolutionaries. Religion and politics were both capable of being aes-theticized, and in either case Adam impugned the authenticity of the commitment. Center of fashion and style, Paris consumed cultural vogues as readily as the products of the *haute couturiers.* For a serious spiritualist such as Adam, the embellishments of occultism were like gaudy costume jewelry that cheapened the real article.

Mystics, artists, and revolutionaries were interrelated in the thought of Paul Adam. He wrote in *Le Mercure de France* in December 1894, that as the eighteenth century had Count Cagliostro and Franz Mesmer along with Abbé Sièyes and the count de Mirabeau, so in the late nineteenth century the occultists Stanislaus de Guaita and Jules Bois stood alongside Proudhon, Fourier, Marx, Bakunin, and Reclus. In a typical rhetorical burst of enthusiasm, Adam wrote that the individual must "extend himself in the universe, to make an effort to embrace the universal harmony, and unify himself with the all."[41] In an essay called "The Origins of Socialism," Adam tried to show that religion and social-ism should not be opposed. He defended the medieval church as the protector of the poor, and argued that "Christian socialism is therefore not utopian, as deluded men are fond of saying, but the sole form of socialism that has fully known realization." He saw atheism as intri-cately linked to the eighteenth-century philosophes and the bourgeoisie of the French Revolution who attacked religion instead of property and social inequality. The Third Estate withdrew the peasants' sole spiritual sustenance in return for promises of happiness on earth. Anticlericalism was the great false issue of the Radical bourgeoisie.[42]

A decade later, another philosophical anarchist, Georges Sorel, did not call for a *rapprochement* between religion and radical politics, as Adam did, but did draw parallels between the symbolic force of Christianity and socialism. In "The Religious Character of Socialism" (1906), Sorel denied that socialism was a science based on laws of social development, but manifested instead the need for faith and meaning, a secularized search for public morality.[43] Where Adam attributed an altruistic and therefore moral motive to the individual acts of propaganda by the deed, Sorel apotheosized the mass rising of the workers in the general strike. For both men, anarchism provided a political outlet for the turn-of-the-century rejection of positivism and parliamentary democracy, and the search for vitalist alternatives of social and moral regeneration. Adam was more Christian than Sorel in believing that expiation and sacrifice rather than violence would purify the spirit, but both men considered anarchism to be a holy war fought for the people's salvation as much as for their liberation.

The Symbolist ideal of escaping from the religion of art by making an art of religion led in some cases to a superficial religiosity, but others went beyond mysticism and incense to envision in anarchism the social reflection of their own quest for the absolute. The decade of the 1890s was primarily a decade not of aestheticism but of commitment to a higher purpose which recalled the Romanticism of an earlier age. The deepening religious awareness stood for this commitment, over and against the detachment, passivity, and even voyeurism associated with the "decadence" of the preceding decade. Where aestheticism led to an attitude of ironic indifference to social problems, the Symbolists' spirituality implied a greater sense of social involvement. The Symbolists desired the transformation of the world as the material counterpart of their goal of spiritual transcendence.

The passionate urge for destruction expressed a religious desire to transcend the temporal flow of history, to effect a great break out of which a new millennium would emerge. The vision of the anarchist apocalypse incited Laurent Tailhade to resort to biblical images of prophets of doom. In 1901, Tailhade wrote the preface to a book of poems by Emile Bans called *Ballades rouges,* just around the time of his imprisonment for inciting violence against the czar. He wrote that anarchism "proclaims its hatred and its irreducible hope . . . with the unchained fury, the infamous invective of Juvenal or of the Nabis of Israel. Thus before the Assyrian princes, before the Egyptian Pharaohs, rose the execration of the prophets."[44] Bans's poetry justified Tailhade's impassioned preface, epitomizing the revolutionary fin de siècle conception of the engulfing cataclysm that would purify the world. Though Bans was extremely anticlerical, he could not resist linking *Christ* and *Anarchiste* in his rhyme-scheme, and the poetic imagery incorporated a spiritual motif almost despite the wishes of the author. Written in cadenced and flowing lines shorn of any trace of Symbolist aestheticism, the effective poetic style retained a regular rhyme-scheme while approaching the natural rhythm of prose. His fervor was terroristic as well as prophetic: "If tomorrow I could have in my hands the bomb, the supreme bomb that could blow up everything, I would set the fire to destroy the world." His prose-poems told the story of the final days brought on by the general strike that by 1901 was accepted anarchist policy. His chapter titles read "the Strike, Humanity, Solidarity, the War, Rebellion, Revenge, Revolt." There was much *Grand Soir* apocalyptic imagery to accompany these forbidding headings. A typical passage read: "The great red night will engulf the evils of society in the dark of which numberless beings across the ages have suffered too long, and the new dawn in gilding the infinity on a better world will pour out its light, benevolent Anarchy will awaken in the desired city of happiness, of harmony."[45]

Bans's use of traditional religious imagery in a political context was typical of the late nineteenth and early twentieth centuries. References to the *Grand Jour* of the revolutionary day of judgment had dominated radical poetic discourse earlier in the nineteenth century, but had given way to a more vengeful spirit during the Paris Commune; after 1871 matters were to be settled on the eve of the Judgment Day under cover of night. A good example of the nonviolent appeal to a New Dawn, flooded with the light of truth and justice, is the conclusion of John Henry McKay's novel *The Anarchists,* which first appeared in German in 1890 and was published in English the following year. It presented social change in a most utopian light:

The wanderer walks alone. But he does not feel lonely. The chaste freshness of nature communicates itself to him.

He feels: it is the morning of a new day.

Then he meets another wanderer. And another. And they understand each other by their looks as they pass each other.

The light rises and rises.

And the early morning walker opens wide his arms and salutes it with the liberating cry of joy. . . .

After a long night of error and illusion, he walked through a morning of light.[46]

D. Steenhuyse finds the first overt reference to the *Grand Soir* in an 1882 trial of anarchists at Montceau-les-Mines, where the image was noticed by Albert Bataille, the judicial reporter for *Le Figaro*. He finds the first trace of this image in anarchist poetry when Jean Carrère used it in the poems he published in the May 1893 anarchy issue of *La Plume*.[47] Actually both his and Théodore Jean's contributions to that journal were filled with such imagery, and it seems unlikely that Carrère, the "student prince" of the Latin Quarter, would have originated this motif in 1893, a year after the deeds of Ravachol had given rise to a host of references to a violent Christ who would redeem his people through sacrifice and bloodshed. The same images were found in the poems of Adolphe Retté around 1895 and 1896, in *Similitudes* and *Le Forêt bruissante,* in which the night-time violence was promptly followed by the New Dawn (see chapter 7). Steenhuyse claims that the discourse of the *Grand Soir* appeared in the milieu of writers, poets, and journalists before it entered the anarchist movement itself, and although Camille Mauclair could write of "Les Snobs du Grand Soir," it was not until Adolphe Retté contributed some works to *Le Libertaire* in 1898–99 that the term gained currency among the rank and file, where it remained popular from 1900 to about 1920. If this chronology is valid, it would appear that the literary anarchists had considerable influence on revolutionary symbology.

The "soir du monde" spoken of by Carrère evoked a typical fin de siècle literary motif that became incorporated in anarchism as foretelling the end of the social order. The millenarian element in this call for the apocalypse is most evident in the gap between the continual exhortations to insurrection by poet-prophets and the lack of concrete plans to achieve it, at least in the presyndicalist years. The revolution was imminent but not specifically situated in historical time; it would be a total cleansing of the body politic; the new society would emerge immediately upon the ashes of the old, and the whole spontaneous affair would have the effect of a supernatural transformation. Perhaps the reason for the gap between poetic and popular usage of the *Grand Soir* image was that the movement's ideologues did not take the call for wholesale destruction more seriously than they did any other effusive poetic fantasy and so did not promote its spread. Though the *Grand Soir* may not have been commonly applied to anarchist insurrectionism before the era of literary anarchism, the writers who used it were appealing to a discourse as old as the book of Saint John, part of a cultural heritage that they shared with the people of all classes. The nexus of revolution/revelation was grasped least by the resolutely anticlerical ideologues, and yet this potent connection linked the poets directly to the people. The Symbolists' sense of the "sacred ritual" of poetry and their own incantatory power encouraged them to pursue the role of prophet of the movement of revitalization, so that by their magic words and the suffering of martyrs the social order would mysteriously be reborn, albeit after a brief violent interlude. The *Grand Soir* would be the final reenactment of the ritual violence of each *attentat*.

Each cycle of symbolic attack, trial, and courageous death of the martyred terrorist, followed by vengeance for his death by another selfless hero, metaphorically prefigured the total cataclysm of the future. The impact was sufficiently strong to give Paul Adam and Maurice Barrès the sensation that the execution of a particular anarchist signaled the end of one era and the beginning of another. Due to the sacred aura that surrounded the expiatory death, the sacrifice marked a boundary between ordinary secular time and a newly ambiguous social state, a metaphysical shift in which all worldly events were henceforth held in suspense until the final redemption, much like the Christian doctrine of the Second Coming that had repeatedly been prophesied as imminent by numerous charismatic leaders in times of social unrest. Now the Revolution rather than Christ would deliver the people. Because bureaucratic organization and charismatic leaders were specifically eschewed by the movement, there was little real possibility of taking power, and the sanctity and martyrdom of the terrorist served as an alternative to real power. The martyr's death reciprocated his own act of murder, except in the case of Vaillant, who died without having killed and whose execution therefore violated sacrificial reciprocity. Whereas Ravachol's execution was followed by a great deal of commentary but no more bombings for over a year, Vaillant's brought on the bombing of the Café Terminus a week later, because immediate revenge was needed to restore the symbolic balance.[48] It was in this spirit that Schwob had soberly written of the weight on Carnot's shoulders for having failed to commute the sentence of the first Frenchman in many decades to have been executed without having committed a murder. Schwob was not alone in sensing that Carnot too would pay for Vaillant's death.

The poems of Carrère, Jean, Bans, and Retté which symbolically or explicitly told the story of the final days also served as paradigms of revolt, but as individual artistic expressions they lacked the religious element of sacrifice and selflessness, the pathos of *propagande par l'exemple* that raised amoral acts to heroic proportions. Though the religious tone applied to the human sacrifice for the Revolution infused the grimmest suffering with hope, occasionally a nihilistic note intruded in the dream of redemption. In the suggestively named novel *Terre promise,* Eugène Morel tried to place himself in the shoes of the condemned man mulling over the promised land as he awaited the guillotine. Certainly based on the example of Ravachol who sang the "Père Duchesne" on the way to the scaffold, Morel's martyr recited bits of songs—"Dynamitons, Dansons"—as the anarchist dream turned into his personal nightmare. In an inspired prose-poem Morel gave way to revolutionary despair:

> **And there is nothing, alas! and there will be nothing.**
> **There were some revolutions, and the Barbarians.**
> **There were some elections, and hopes.**
> **There were some tyrants, dreamers, *arriveurs*.**
> **There were some religions. One adored beasts, men,**
> **things, spirits, words, flags, republics.**
> **There were some anarchists.**
> **And there will be nothing more.[49]**

The imminent promise receded in the face of death. The antireligious ideology seemed to triumph over the chiliastic illusion of the approaching apocalypse. One must concede that the religious sensibility opiated the anarchists against their own despair or the prospect of a useless death. Faith compensated them for their powerlessness and lack of a coherent revolutionary program. The ever-present possiblity of sudden revolution would substantiate anarchist ideology and the mode of organization derived from it, and therefore kept them chained to social poetry rather than encouraging analysis of political realities.[50] But ritual regulation helped fill the organizational vacuum that the anarchist press was only partly able to handle. Sanctification increased the authority of the movement by turning political into religious acts which could not be discredited by rational argumentation. The ritualized sacrifice of individuals for the sake of a future ideal functioned to bind the anarchists together around a symbolic figure and invested them with a sense of mission. Where the press communicated the anarchist message, the religious function signified that that message was worth pursuing.[51]

The ultimate truth-value of such rituals was certified chiefly by the spiritually inclined anarchist writers rather than by the atheist theoreticians. The artists seized the nonlinguistic symbolic statement of the bomb and the guillotine as an extension of their own desire to transcend the compromising limitations of language. Like the aesthetic ideal of silence expressed in the white spaces around Mallarme's words, the ineffable immediacy of the ritually pure act arrested the flow of historical time.[52] In the twenty-minute gap between Vaillant's bomb and Dupuy's declaration that the show must go on, a hiatus had briefly been opened in the normal course of affairs. The silence following the drop of the guillotine blade was pregnant with meaning and invariably exorcised all the anarchist's human failings. The ultimate mystery of the beyond, heavenly or terrestrial, was implied in the fact of his death. Propaganda by example was even more potent than propaganda by the deed; silence spoke louder than words or deeds. Anarchist millennialism may have been compensatory, but sacred authority was only summoned to fill the gap left by secular incoherence. Both art and religion manifested the cultural need for order-creating mechanisms. In their passion to liberate themselves from cultural constraints and to approximate the spontaneous and inherent order of nature, the anarchists merely substituted aesthetic and religious norms for political and economic ones. The cultic tendencies only took shape when the crisis faced by the members of the sect was unresolvable by ordinary means.[53]

Anarchy or Decadence?

Conclusion

All anarchists agreed that France needed another revolution, yet many revolutions had come and gone in the previous century, and France seemed no closer to the anarchist idea of utopia. It was enough to dampen the ardor of the most dedicated revolutionary. How would the next revolution be different? Although some anarchists were tempted to conspire among themselves or with other groups on the extreme left or right, many renounced secrecy and conspiracy altogether and preferred a more spontaneous strategy, either of the individual terrorist or mass insurrectionist variety. Diverging from such nineteenth-century revolutionary forebears as F. Buonarroti and Blanqui, the anarchists distrusted the elitist practice of a revolutionary vanguard, whose eternal plotting in ill-lit garrets seemed to enact a contrived scenario of the revolution. The anarchists hoped not merely to tear down society but to regenerate it. The revolution would break over existing society like a tidal wave, washing all before it in a vast rising of popular discontent. Metaphors drawn from nature were more appropriate to convey the anarchists' apocalyptic dream than was the rational language of conspiratorial planning employed by vanguard revolutionaries from Buonarroti to Lenin. The anarchists' language was poetic, even magical, while the conspirators' was prosaic and functional.

Given the overt anarchist tendency, from Peter Kropotkin to Paul Paillette, to appeal to the realm of nature for models of civilized behavior, it is not difficult to see the fundamental distinction between nature and culture as underlying the antithesis between revolutionary spontaneity and conspiracy. Few anarchists would go as far as the editors of *L'Etat Naturel* in totally rejecting modern industrial civilization, but many *compagnons* harbored an image of the ideal society that was simpler, more personal, and somehow more "natural" than contemporary urban society. Thus in the *Almanach du Père Peinard* for 1897 there appeared an article about a recently discovered tribe (the Moïs) living in Cochin China (now Vietnam) with little apparent social or spiritual organization. "Decisions are made by an assembly in which the whole tribe takes part. . . . Individual property does not exist." Emile Pouget carefully refrained from making the Naturist assumption that anarchism implied regressing to a more primitive state. Rather, he concluded that "in the worst conditions (the Moïs are the proof) one lives more morally under the communist libertarian regime than in the best civilized conditions," yet how much better it would be if all the accumulated wealth of modern society could be shared.[1] Laws and government, not wealth and technology, were at fault. Both anarchist practice and utopian ideals were governed by the notion that corrupt society could only be overthrown by a movement that was guided by the pure hand of nature.

No term in intellectual history has been more elusive and transient than *nature,* as Arthur O. Lovejoy made clear many years ago. The anarchists' conception of nature was largely derived from the Romantics' revaluation of the term, although as Lovejoy pointed out, aesthetic primitivism developed gradually from neoclassical ideals. Lovejoy defined the artistic practice seen as most natural by the Romantics as the "disregard of rules and precedents, free self-expression of the artist," often identified with "naïveté, unsophistication, likeness to the primitive."[2] Nature conceived as naturalness implied both freedom from convention and rules, and freedom from premeditation, aesthetic values with clear political corollaries to anarchist praxis. To the anarchists, appealing to nature appeared to sanction the rejection of established authority and the freedom to ignore conventional moral norms. In a larger sense nature was identified as the realm of freedom, civilization as constraint. To behave naturally rather than as society dictated was equated with living freely. When combined with the injunction against premeditation or excessive rationality, this also suggested the liberation of the instincts from religious and moral strictures, as well as the liberation of the revolution itself from premeditated control by an elite. The similarity of these positions to Maurice Barrès's ideals as expressed in *L'Ennemi des lois* was due both to the writer's flirtation with anarchism and to his status as an unreformed Romantic.

The anarchists' faith that one's natural self should be expressed because it was essentially good, and that given a return to a system approximating the state of nature men and women could be expected to behave rationally and altruistically toward their fellows, was based less on a Romantic than an Enlightenment attitude toward human nature, as expressed in William Godwin's 1793 essay *Enquiry Concerning Political Justice*. The most important anarchist thinker of the fin de siècle, Peter Kropotkin, was situated directly in this optimistic tradition. He recorded his conception of a beneficent and sociable natural universe in a series of articles written between 1890 and 1896 for *Nineteenth Century* and eventually published in book form in 1902. *Mutual Aid* was written to counter Julian Huxley's *Struggle for Existence and its Bearing on Man* (1888), in which "Darwin's bulldog" popularized the grimly competitive vision of natural law known as Social Darwinism. Instead of competition, Kropotkin sought examples of natural sociability not only among such members of the animal world as ants and bees, but among primitive peoples who organized themselves into tribes and redistributed their wealth in the potlatch. The instincts of community and self-sacrifice were frustrated by the imposition of complicated theologies and autocracies upon society. Kropotkin traced the evolution of the natural impulse toward community to its apex in the free medieval town, before it was destroyed by the dual power of kings and lawyers in the sixteenth century and later.[3] Both Kropotkin and the Darwinians saw human culture as continuing rather than opposing the promptings of natural law, yet implicit in Kropotkin's scheme was a critique of contemporary society for straying from nature's ways.

Outside of anarchist circles, the popular way of saying that modern society was unnatural was to accuse it of decadence. The term *decadence*, derived from the Latin *decadere*, suggests a falling away from some ideal normative state. A society can only be considered decadent relative to an earlier era or to an external norm. Perhaps in all times but certainly in its late nineteenth-century formulation, the ultimate norm was nature, deviation from which was manifested in delight in the artificial and the perverse, and in dedication to an urban way of life. Just as the doctrines of Social Darwinism or Mutual Aid were based on natural history, so decadence can not be divorced from its biological implications. Decadence was not merely artificial but unhealthy, not merely febrile but unfecund. The duke Jean des Esseintes, hero of that breviary of literary decadence, Joris-Karl Huysman's 1884 novel *A rebours*, was the scion of an ancient and dying lineage, who gave a feast to commemorate the loss of his virility.

Frenchmen of the era could have felt justified in doing the same. After a century-long decline, population growth had nearly stopped in the Third Republic; in five of the last ten years of the century, deaths actually outnumbered births.[4] One reason for the decline may have been the generation-long depression of 1873–96 (the depression of the 1930s similarly would cause an already-low birth rate to drop still lower), but whatever the cause, French social critics were all too aware of being surpassed both in population and in economic production by Great Britain and Germany, while the vocal *revanchistes* reminded Frenchmen of their humiliating defeat by the Prussians in 1870. Other nations were far more politically in eclipse than France, yet Spain, Turkey, or China were not simultaneously undergoing rapid industrialization. Perhaps only Austria was equally aware of its decadence vis-à-vis the Northern European countries, as it too faced modernization together with political decline and the rise of nationalism.[5] Beyond these political connotations, the term *decadence* conjured up the biological metaphor of an aging civilization that had lost its vigor, an image that lent itself to racial theories of decadent Latins being overtaken by the virile Anglo-Saxons and Teutons of America, Britain, and Germany. The last refuge of such a loss of national faith was within the palely aristocratic ivory tower of Culture. If the old civilizations faced a new onslaught of Nordic barbarians (or alternately of the socialist-inspired masses), one could encase oneself in walls of art, secure in the knowledge of one's aesthetic superiority. The antitheses of the dynamic, productive, mass society of Europe, aesthetes such as Oscar Wilde proudly proclaimed their own uselessness as well as their profound individualism.

Both critics of decadence distressed at the waning power and prestige of France, and the heirs of Baudelaire who accepted the derisive label *decadent* as an apt description of their cultural condition, defined decadence as anarchic individualism. The promoters of state power decried the substitution of private interests for the good of the whole and felt that the unity and moral force of *la patrie* was threatened by the self-seeking proponents of the *culte du moi*. A decadent society was one that had lost its raison d'être, one whose citizens then turned toward private satisfaction rather than to civic virtue. An adjective that formerly had been applied only to society as a whole now became a noun applied to individuals within that society who typified decadent characteristics. It never occurred to Baudelaire to call himself a decadent, but after his death Théophile Gautier began to apply the term to the poet to define a constellation of traits supposedly revealed in *Les Fleurs du mal*.

Even before Huysmans's novel and the self-styled decadent literary movement made the term famous in the mid-1880s, Paul Bourget wrote a brief "Théorie de la décadence" in 1881, in the course of an article on Baudelaire, in which he itemized and perhaps influenced most of the associations subsequently attached to the term. Comparing society to an organism in which the various cells serve the whole being, Bourget defined social decadence as the inverse of societal health, when the individuals in that society no longer subordinated their energies to the good of the whole but instead pursued their private interests. Bourget called this state of social decadence anarchy and clearly used the term in a pejorative sense. A healthy society produced many children and many soldiers; "decadent" Rome and modern France produced neither and so would lose out in the struggle between races. Bourget believed that the same criterion of decadence could be applied to literature, so that a decadent work lacked unity and tended toward the independence of the page, of the sentence, and finally of the word. Yet what was socially unhealthy could be literarily and psychologically productive; a society composed of bad citizens or workers could produce great artists from the very tendency to look inward and explore the recesses of the soul.[6] In the same year that young Maurice Barrès arrived in Paris from Lorraine, the justification for the *culte du moi* was established by the leader of the psychological school of novelists.

Bourget and his fellow *psychologues* were not radicals and certainly not anarchists, and they generally opposed the Dreyfusards in 1898. Though Bourget could associate anarchic individualism with aesthetic modernism, he maintained and even strengthened the art for art's sake separation between literature and society, in that the flourishing of art was a sort of spiritual consolation for a state of social decay. Yet it was not long before those writers who identified themselves as decadents also gave a positive valuation to anarchy. As a term synonymous with the avant-garde and modernism, decadence came to standard for a culture of negation, that is, a conscious disregard for all the dominant social norms. Political radicalism increased the shock effect that the decadents wished to achieve, yet anarchism was also the perfect political outlet for their aesthetic tendencies and social nonconformism. That Bourget epitomized Edmond de Goncourt as a decadent writer and applied the term to himself as well indicates that decadent aestheticism need not lead to political radicalism; on the other hand, England's chief decadent writer, Oscar Wilde, wrote an anarchist-sounding utopian tract and Anatole Baju, editor of *Le Décadent,* moved directly from literature to radical politics in about 1890. As the aesthetic 1880s gave way to the politicized 1890s, the "style favorable to the unrestricted manifestation of aesthetic individualism, a style that has done away with traditional authoritarian requirements such as unity, hierarchy, objectivity," could not fail to express itself in political terms.[7]

The vogue of literary decadence appeared short-lived, for in 1886, the same year that Baju's *Le Décadent* appeared, Jean Moréas issued his Symbolist manifesto, and by 1890 most of the poetic avant-garde had accepted the Symbolist rubric. Of the new reviews that arose to champion the movement, the longest-lasting and most closely identified with Symbolism was probably the *Mercure de France,* whose guiding intellectual light was Rémy de Gourmont. Though de Gourmont rejected the term *decadent* as a slur applied by traditional and imitative writers to those like Mallarmé who were most innovative, his definition of Symbolism as "the expression of individualism in art" was fundamentally the same as Bourget's definition of decadence a decade earlier.[8] Symbolism continued and even heightened the emphasis on aesthetic individualism, as well as the self-conscious acceptance of the avant-garde's role as a culture of negation. If the aesthetes no longer identified themselves as decadents, that does not mean that the term suddenly dropped out of the cultural lexicon. To conservative critics, the decadent tendencies of the 1880s increased along with the fin de siècle. Not only excessive individualism, called ego-mania by Max Nordau in *Degeneration* (1893), but the Symbolist desire to merge all the arts seemed ample proof of decadence even without cataloging the thriving cults of satanic mysticism, perverse sexuality, and the association of eroticism and death in the image of the femme fatale, all popular literary and artistic preoccupations of the era.

While literary elitists such as Paul Bourget positively transvalued decadence as aesthetic individualism, as a bastion of taste and refinement against the incursions of mass democracy, Baju's *Le Décadent* paradoxically identified decadence with the most modern avant-garde sensibility. Far from being symptomatic of decline, decadence was progressive, at least in cultural terms. Baju readily applied his literary avant-gardism to its political corollaries, running as a socialist in the 1889 legislative elections before turning toward anarchism in the 1890s. Conservative critics concurred that aesthetic modernism was decadent; the aesthete typified for them the loss of vigor and moral fiber that endangered the health of the social whole. If that aesthete was also a socialist or an anarchist eager to tear down the social edifice, that confirmed their worst fears about the profoundly asocial temperament of these offenders of public morality. Both conservative and socialist critics of the 1890s would have agreed that decadents were inimical to the collective well-being, be it defined as proletariat or *patrie*. The charge of decadence was leveled at the Symbolists from the left by proponents of *l'art social* such as Bernard Lazare, and from the right by critics such as Charles Maurras, whose articles in *La Revue Bleue* of 1894 attacking the Symbolists were joined by a host of works by lesser authors bearing titles such as *L'Anarchie dans l'art* and *L'Anarchie littéraire*. All agreed with Lazare that the Symbolists' vaunted individualism reproduced the general social chaos, but their hunger for order lent their works a desperate tone lacking in Lazare's confident acceptance of revolutionary change. As if in direct response to the prevailing spirit of decadence, a new political philosophy called solidarism arose to emphasize each individual's debt to the social whole.[9] Emile Durkheim elaborated his theory of anomie as the malaise responsible for the majority of suicides in the political context of an era in which republicans such as himself wished to preserve France from the internal forces of anarchy which they feared were dissolving the social fabric.

Forty years after Max Nordau's diatribe, the Nazis, with equal fervor and much more effect, would label modern art as degenerate and unfit for the virtuous *Ubermensch* of the fascist state. In the twentieth century, fascists and communists alike have been notoriously hostile to aesthetic modernism, which has usually been attacked as hyperindividualistic bourgeois formalism or, in short, as decadent. Only anarchism appeared to tolerate and even encourage the individual expression which the literary avant-garde considered to be the basis of artistic creativity. Unlike the Marxist G. Plekhanov, whose definition of bourgeois decadence led directly to the counterdefinition of socialist realism, the anarchists never elaborated a theory of decadence, or at least not in the 1890s.[10] The term in fact found no place in their rhetoric, probably because as social criticism it had been appropriated by the right, and for a culture of negation it was too close to their own antagonistic position. Until Georges Sorel, the anarchists' relations to decadence were far too ambiguous to be dealt with ideologically.

Anarchism was the ideal political outlet for individualistic, antisocial aesthetes, many of whom had already been labeled decadent. Yet anarchism was a vigorously antidecadent movement that intended to regenerate a corrupt and unnatural social order. The cultural elite was attracted to a movement that was suspicious of contemporary culture and had a strong tendency to idealize a simple pastoral existence. Even though one might suspect that intellectuals such as Barrès were attracted to anarchism simply because it was an escape from the decadent hothouse of aestheticism, it has been argued that anarchism satisfied the most decadent tendencies of fin de siècle littérateurs.[11] Not only did it outrage public morality by its libertarian attitudes toward such institutions as marriage, the church, and the family as well as the state, but it encouraged individuals to destroy the social status quo. The aestheticized crime violated social norms and symbolized the superiority of the artist-rebel to humanitarian values. This violence had to be perpetrated by a lone individual; the aesthetes would never have identified to the same degree with the mass violence created by a labor dispute. Those violent angels, the propagandists by the deed, were applauded and sanctified not only for the imputed beauty of their acts but even more for the nobility of their deaths. The erotically ritualistic cult of death and martyrdom would seem to implicate the violent and nihilistic side of anarchism with decadence especially by Barrèsian voyeurs who watched the childlike Emile Henry's execution with a certain joyous pathos. When the terrorist perished on the scaffold, the artist felt that he too had suffered and sacrificed for his ideal.

Just as anarchist violence occurred simultaneously with the idealism of Kropotkin and Reclus, so in Montmartre the decadent and natural elements of anarchism coexisted, the pastoral village of sinuous cobble-stone streets and the licentious nightlife, E. Gravelle's L'Etat Naturel and Lisbonne's Taverne du Bagne. Among the artists, many of whom resided on the Butte during the anarchist heyday, the Impressionist Camille Pissarro and the Post-Impressionist Paul Signac were both anarchists and landscapists, and Maximilien Luce bathed both industrial scenes and landscapes in a natural light, displaying his drawings of workers in *La Révolte* before being arrested during the repression of 1894. Diverging sharply from the nature-oriented Impressionists, Henri de Toulouse-Lautrec and Charles Maurin eschewed natural settings and together with a host of Montmartrois illustrators preferred to record the vulgarity of urban life. While Signac set his anarchistic *Au temps d'harmonie* in an idyllic outdoor setting, Lautrec revealed the corruption and hypocrisy of Parisian nightlife. Epitomizing the decadent perversity of the epoch, Lautrec's acerbic commentary did not imply blithe acceptance of his milieu any more than had Baudelaire's several decades before, yet both painter and poet did accept modernity as the necessary precondition of their work. Signac and the Naturist Retté represent one element of anarchist culture; Lautrec and, perhaps, Laurent Tailhade may stand for the other. Decadents and Naturists were linked not only by their anarchism but by their mutual opinion that modern society was corrupt and decadent. They differed in that decadents took a perverse pleasure in that corruption, aware perhaps that as products of that society they necessarily embodied what they condemned. To accept the epithet *decadent,* to revel in a society fallen from grace, necessitated a love-hate relation with that society that was more equivocal than the simple Naturist rejection of modernity. Perhaps unredeemed decadents could not give themselves fully to anarchism, for their cynical acceptance of the sordid present would preclude harboring faith in a future golden age. For some decadents, such as Lautrec, alliance with anarchists resulted from their hostility toward the dominant culture; for others, such as Barrès, anarchism also represented an escape to the ideal of natural harmony. Both antagonistic and escapist, anarchist ambivalence toward modernity was matched by decadent rejection and transvaluation of dominant social mores and humanitarian values. The critical difference between them was that decadence was a dead-end that cultivated a passively hopeless attitude toward life, whereas anarchism maintained a millenarian faith in a better society emerging from the inevitable cataclysm. Decadents agreed that society was on a downward course toward *Götterdämmerung* or in French parlance, *le Grand Soir*; anarchists had a vision of life rising from the ashes. Decadents were merely perverse, anarchists dialectical in embodying both the depths of depravity (in violence, criminality, and hyperindividualism, all of which coalesced in the propagandists by the deed) and its cure (return to the bosom of nature).

The relation between Symbolism and anarchism was also dialectical, in that each movement generated needs that the other fulfilled. The aesthetes bequeathed to the anarchists a model of aesthetic individualism that could serve as a blueprint for the anarchist utopian image of liberated humanity; the anarchists gave the aesthetes a passage out of the ivory tower. Political commitment was an alternative to decadent lassitude, and revolution was the ultimate vitalist challenge to "Les Déliquescences d'Adoré Floupette," as an 1886 decadent parody was called. The antinomy of literary decadence and anarchist revolution emerged clearly in Camille Mauclair's fin de siècle novel *Le Soleil des morts*. The poet-seeker was encouraged by the femme fatale Lucienne Lestrange to leave behind his aesthetic existence, symbolized by the dying sun of the book's title, and to express instead "a powerful anger, a dizziness of brutal and primitive beauty which ignores your minutiae and which, I am sure, is the true life, the life of stings, of eloquence, of the tragic, of the great sun necessary to beings like me."[12] The young poet wavered between the Mallarméan hermitage of pure art and the vitality of life and action, chose the latter, and was wandering amid the carnage of a failed revolution at the novel's close. The same condemnation of aesthetic lifelessness was represented in Mauclair's next book as *le rêve*, the all-consuming dream that never manifested itself in life.[13]

The pursuit of energy as a way out of the ivory tower; the rejection of the dilettante's self-immersion for pursuit of a more inclusive ideal, frequently expressed in organicist terms as the fatherland; identification with the masses as a great irrational force in human destiny: all spelled the growing fascination with vitalism and action that marked the reaction against decadence. Works as dissimilar as André Gide's *Les Nourritures terrestres* (The Fruits of the Earth) and Maurice Barrès's *Les Déracinés*, first volume of his trilogy *Le Roman de l'energie nationale*, broadcast the same longing for a life of passion and intensity. Barrès's great teachers of the 1880s were Taine and Renan; the generation coming to maturity after 1895 looked to Nietzsche and Henri Bergson, who rather than sophisticated skepticism preached a doctrine of the *élan vital,* albeit without drawing the political corollaries that their students would find. Anarchism's cultural vogue was an early symptom of the disaffection that intellectuals felt not only toward society but for their limited social role and the self-limiting, overly formalist conception of a writer's role that had predominated in literary circles for half a century. That self-conception was largely a defensive response to the frustrations attached to the anomalous position of being a nonproductive member of a capitalist society. Anarchist politics were an ideal outlet for the frustrations of the young literary avant-garde, yet anarchism was not overtly antidecadent in the same sense that nationalist movements of the right might claim to be. The social whole that the anarchists wished to substitute for contemporary social chaos lay in the future, beyond the purifying revolution; thus one had to accept both negation and affirmation rather than the uncritical acceptance of the traditional institutions of church, army, and nation.

While nationalist and monarchist sentiments were on the rise in the years preceding World War I, the affiliation of intellectuals such as Georges Sorel and Hugh Lagardelle with anarcho-syndicalism testifies that heroic vitalism continued to appeal to both ends of the political spectrum. From Paul Bourget's acceptance of decadence as the hallmark of the aesthetic modernist in 1881, to the anarchists' rejection of the elitism inherent in purely aesthetic individualism and their cult of the natural and spontaneous (which nevertheless coexisted with a lingering fondness for conspiracy and the aura of mystery surrounding the individual deed), to the abstractions of nation or proletariat that intellectuals after 1898 championed as great life-endowing forces, one can trace a continuum from decadence and individualism to their opposites, to vitalism and collective regeneration. It has been argued that a critique of decadence was implicit in fin de siècle anarchism, but that critique awaited Georges Sorel to become an explicit and even central element of anarchist ideology. His seminal *Reflections on Violence* was first published in 1906 and was addressed to the revolutionary anarcho-syndicalist movement; Sorel's thought is thus not directly relevant to a study of 1890s anarchism. Yet Sorel illustrates perfectly the political ramifications of intellectual vitalism. Sorel was as profoundly convinced as any ultraconservative that France was decadent. He devoted one entire book, *The Illusions of Progress,* to refuting the optimistic and ameliorative social vision that he ascribed to liberals and parliamentary socialists, and his more famous *Reflections on Violence* included a chapter entitled "Violence and the Decadence of the Middle Classes." Sorel believed and feared that the French bourgeoisie, unlike their robber baron counterparts in America, were growing decadent, that is, that they were less fiercely competitive in the spirit of laissez-faire capitalism and more prone to heed the enticing idealism of Jean Jaurès and to try to buy off the working class with social welfare legislation. Sorel equated decadence with humanitarianism and proposed salutary proletarian violence in the form of class warfare as the cure for soft-minded sentimentalism. The 1890s aesthetes tended to aestheticize politics; Sorel made violence a moral imperative, designed to revivify the sagging fiber of society and, more particularly, to increase class tensions. His equation of class violence and moral vigor was not very different from F. T. Marinetti and the Italian Futurists' praise of war; class and national warfare were both seen as heroic antidotes to pacifist cowardice and bourgeois material satisfaction. In his 1895 novel *Le Mystère des foules,* Paul Adam had shown a similar vitalist tendency to epitomize war as the ultimate manifestation of collective energy. Adam, Barrès, Marinetti, and above all Sorel, in whose minds radical social forces were to be commandeered for the aesthetic or moral purpose of extirpating decadence—identified with the stifling normalcy of daily life—reveal the political ambiguity inherent in the apocalyptic politics of vitalism. In the highly individualistic 1890s, such a blanket condemnation of decadence was not readily voiced by anarchist thinkers. That critique awaited the strident fervency of a more collectivist and bellicose epoch, a century whose mass-based and institutionalized violence would make the era of propaganda by the deed and decapitated anarchist martyrs seem, in retrospect, like an age of innocence.

Notes

I have used the following abbreviations for archival sources:
AN—Archives Nationales, Paris
APP—Archives de la Préfecture de Police, Paris
IFHS—L'Institut Français d'Histoire Sociale, Paris

INTRODUCTION

1. See Joseph Conrad, *The Secret Agent* (1908), Henry James, *The Princess Cassamassima* (1910), G. K. Chesterton, *The Man Who Was Thursday* (1908), and Emile Zola, *Paris* (1898).

2. *L'Histoire des mentalités* translates somewhat awkwardly as the history of mentalities. Robert Darnton suggests "the new cultural history" instead, which differs from the old in emphasizing how ordinary people interpreted their world, especially those "elemental passages of life" such as birth, marriage, and death. *Mentalités* thus embodies a much more anthropological conception of culture than does the traditional high culture historical approach, which was generally limited to the beliefs and artistic expression of social elites, or of the artists who served them. For recent accounts in English of this largely French-influenced historical trend, see Patrick H. Hutton, "The History of Mentalities: The New Map of Cultural History," *History and Theory* 20, 3 (1981): 237–59; also Robert Darnton, *The Great Cat Massacre and other Episodes in French Cultural History* (New York: Basic Books, 1984), introduction. Darnton provides a good list of important French contributions to this school on 282, 283.

3. Darnton, *Cat Massacre*, 3.

4. Postman, *Teaching as a Conserving Activity*, 52, 53.

5. Reszler, *L'Esthétique anarchiste,* 75, argues that anarchists value the experience of revolution perhaps more than the goal of the revolution. I agree that anarchists tend to be experientially oriented, but I believe that the concept of analogic information more accurately reflects anarchistic epistemology.

6. See Garraud, *L'Anarchie et la répression.*

7. See Geertz, *The Interpretation of Cultures,* 312.

8. See Carroll, *Break-Out from the Crystal Palace.*

9. Reszler, *L'Esthétique anarchiste,* 104.

10. See Joll, *The Anarchists,* 167, 168; Maitron, *Mouvement anarchiste,* 1:480; Aubery, "L'Anarchie des littérateurs au temps du symbolisme," 21–34; Monférier, "Symbolisme et l'anarchie," 233–38.

11. In *The Artist and Social Reform,* Eugenia Herbert offers a synoptic account of a whole generation of writers and painters, including Naturalists and Realists as well as Symbolists, with a chapter dealing with the visual arts as well. Her attempt to chart the repoliticization of artists after several decades of residence in the ivory tower of aestheticism is useful, but the term "social reform" that appears in the book's title is sufficiently vague to allow Herbert to beg the question of more specific relations between politics and the arts beyond mere *engagement.* For instance, nothing Herbert tells us allows us to distinguish a uniquely anarchist from a socialist aesthetic. Furthermore, her conception of politicized art is limited almost entirely to the level of content, and she believes that the Symbolists' avant-garde aesthetic simply diminished their political impact by widening "the gulf between themselves and any public, whether middle class or proletarian" (179). Finding little of an overt political nature in their art, she generalizes that what minor contribution the Symbolists made to anarchism "found expression preeminently in noncreative, journalistic writing" (179), unlike the more *engagé* art of the Realists and Naturalists. I will attempt to rebut these arguments in chapter 8, while focusing in much greater detail and with a different theoretical emphasis on the rationale underlying their *engagement* in chapters 6 and 7.

12. Maitron, *Mouvement anarchiste,* 1:225.

1. Joll, *The Anarchists,* 77. Joll provides an excellent short history of European anarchism, and I have drawn many of my general comments from his account. George Woodcock's *Anarchism* (Harmondsworth: Penguin, 1963) is another standard account; Maitron's *Mouvement anarchiste* is by far the most detailed account of French anarchism. Unless otherwise noted, all translations are my own.

2. Joll, *The Anarchists,* 107, 108.

3. Ibid., 95.

4. Maitron, *Mouvement anarchiste,* 1:113–15.

5. Terrou, "L'Evolution du droit de la presse de 1881 à 1940."

6. Lethève, *Le Caricature et la presse,* 46.

7. Leyret, *De Waldeck-Rousseau à la C.G.T.*; Thomson, *Democracy in France since 1870,* 46.

8. *Le Révolté* 11 (September 13–26, 1885), quoted in Maitron, *Mouvement anarchiste,* 1:118; the name change is explained on 144.

9. Evidence that most anarchists of this period were young comes from police reports and arrest records, which list a great many individuals still in their teens who were rounded up in the wave of arrests in the winter of 1894. Also, Augustin Hamon, writing *Psychologie de l'anarchiste-socialiste* in 1895, called anarchism a movement of youth, which he qualified as including those under forty years of age.

10. Maitron, *Mouvement anarchiste,* 1:146, note 140.

11. APP B/a 77, "Bulletin de quinzaine," November 5, 1891.

12. Photograph in IFHS, 14 AS 52.

13. Zo d'Axa, *Endehors,* preface, 12.

14. Ponton, "Le Champ littéraire en France, de 1865 à 1905," 115.

15. Durand, "L'Evolution littéraire dans *Les Entretiens Politiques et Littéraires,* 1890–1893," ii.

16. IFHS, 14 AS 184a, D., 327, November 30, 1894.

17. IFHS, 14 AS 184b, M., 1098, undated.

18. Thadée Natanson's notes are in the Mme. Fénéon archives on the Procès de Trente, Bibliothèque Jacques Doucet, Paris.

19. Pouget, *Almanach du Père Peinard,* 1896, 64.

20. APP B/a 1508, April 19, 1898. For his distrust of intellectuals, see Emile Pouget, "Philosophes et chieurs d'encre," *Le Père Peinard,* November 1, 1896, 322, 323.

21. Moss, *The Origins of the French Labor Movement,* 147.

22. Terrou, "Presse," 25.

23. Maitron, *Mouvement anarchiste,* 1:251, 252, note 1.

24. AN F7, 12508, *Journal Official,* January 28, 1894, 106, 114, 115.

25. APP B/a 79, "Legrand," April 10, 1894; no date, but around April 1894; July 11, 1894; "Bouchon," July 18, 1894.

26. Garraud, *L'Anarchie et la répression,* 11.

27. Varennes, *De Ravachol à Caserio,* 286.

28. Fénéon, *Oeuvres,* xix, citing police report of April 28, 1894. See also *Le Journal des Débats,* April 27, 1894.

29. *Gazette des Tribuneaux,* August 9, 1894. See also Fénéon, *Oeuvres,* xx ff., and Maitron, *Mouvement anarchiste,* 1:255, for a description of these and other remarks.

30. Though violence abated in France, it continued elsewhere. In the next seven years, Premier Antonio Canovas of Spain, Empress Elizabeth of Austria, King Umberto of Italy, and President William McKinley of the United States all lost their lives to anarchist assailants.

31. Maitron, *Mouvement anarchiste,* 1:268–69.

32. Ridley, *Revolutionary Syndicalism in France,* 30, 67–71.

33. Manuel Devaldès et al., "Declaration," *L'Action d'Art* 1, 1 (February 15, 1913). See also André Colomer, "De Bergson à Bonnot: Aux sources de l'heroïsme individualiste, M. Bergson et les 'Jeunes Gens d'aujourd'hui,' " *L'Action d'Art* 1, 2 (March 1, 1913). For the Futurists' involvement in anarchism, see Shapiro, *Painters and Politics,* 31–32, 184–85. Shapiro cites Carlo Carrà, Umberto Boccioni, Giacomo Balla, and Gino Severini as active in leftist politics, and even claims that Marinetti favored "an uncompromising anarchism and idealism" as late as 1922. For the influence of the journal *L'Action d'art* on André Breton and surrealism, see Siegel, *Bohemian Paris,* 370. Maitron, *Mouvement anarchiste,* 1:275, 277, 420–35, and Georges Lefranc, *Le Syndicalisme en France* (Paris: Presses Universitaires de France, 1953), 23, discuss the cur-

rents of individualist anarchism that opposed syndicalism after 1895.

34. Gérard Jacquemet, *Belleville au XIXe Siècle*, 371.
35. Berlanstein, *The Working People of Paris*, 8.
36. Retté, *Promenades subversives*, 35, 36; first published as *Reflections on Anarchy* in 1894. The impact of the repression of 1894 on the anarchist literati is also discussed in Jean Pierrot, *The Decadent Imagination*, trans. Derek Coltman (Chicago: University of Chicago Press, 1981), 253. Pierrot claims that "as soon as repressive measures began to be taken, the majority of them [writers] abandoned the movement entirely in alarm," but the only evidence he cites for this conclusion is Retté. Retté himself abandoned Paris but not anarchism in 1894, yet by the late 1890s his anarchist enthusiasm had waned, suggesting to me that changes within the anarchist movement were at least as important as the government crackdown in separating intellectuals and militants.
37. Maitron, *Mouvement anarchiste,* 1:379–81.

CHAPTER TWO

1. See Sternhell, "Barrès et la gauche." See also Sternhell's *Maurice Barrès et le nationalisme francais* and *Droite,* and Soucy, *Fascism in France.*
2. Sternhell, *Droite,* 52, 53, 59.
3. Sebastien Faure made this distinction between natural laws and forces, preferring the latter term as more appropriate to extralegal anarchists. Faure was a leading figure in the anarchist movement in the 1890s, and would remain active until his death a half-century later. He was a renowned orator and editor of *Le Libertaire.* See Maitron, *Mouvement anarchiste,* 1:132 ff.
4. Sternhell, *Droite,* 44, note 2, mentions that as late as the eve of World War I, Alfred Naquet and C. A. Laissant, another leading Boulangist-turned-anarchist, were active in the defense committee of the Spanish anarchist Francisco Ferrer and became the bêtes noires of the royalist Action Française.
5. Soucy, *Fascism in France,* 196.
6. See Sternhell, *Droite,* 52, 53, for sources of Boulangist support.

7. APP B/a 76, January 13, 1889.

8. APP B/a 76, January 26, 1889.

9. APP B/a 76, January 16, 1889; "Jean," October 7, 1889. Evidence of the continuity between Boulangism and anarchism also appeared in the form of a letter written by a political prisoner banished to French Guiana addressed to the minister of the interior. Writing in October 1892, the prisoner recounted the temporary alliance in 1888–89 between Boulangists and anarchists to overthrow the government. Boulanger himself remained aloof from the union of revolutionaries, while some of his lieutenants, such as Henri de Rochefort, encouraged anarchist support. See AN F7, 12504, letter of Pierre Alexandre Armand de Kerdrell from Cayenne, Guiana, October 1892.

10. APP B/a 76, "Auger," November 4, 1889, asserted that Drumont and the anarchists were undertaking a violent campaign against high finance. APP B/a 76, *Le Nation,* clipping of April 30, 1890. According to *Le Paris* of May 5, 1890, de Morès was freed along with Gabriel Cabot, head of the anarchist printing operation, in the wake of the celebration.

11. APP B/a 76, April 16, 1890.

12. AN F7, 12506, Chambre des Députés meeting of May 21, 1892.

13. Sternhell, *Droite,* 40.

14. APP B/a 77, December 12, 1892.

15. APP B/a 78, January 6, 1893.

16. APP B/a 79, March 17, 1894.

17. AN F7, 12504, undated but probably between December 16, 1893, and early 1894.

18. APP B/a 79, probably March 1894.

19. APP B/A 79, May 21, 1894.

20. APP B/a 79, May 21, 1894.

21. APP B/a 79, June 13, 1894.

22. APP B/a 79, September 10, 1894.

23. Sternhell, *Droite,* 207, 208.

24. Nevertheless, later French revolutionary, or at least insurrectionary, movements appeared to have followed the anarchist rather than rightist model of bourgeois revolutions. The May 1968 stu-

dent revolt that temporarily allied students and workers was certainly closer politically to the anarchists than to the Action Française.

25. Bataille, *Causes criminelles et mondaines de 1892,* 4.

26. Sternhell, *Droite,* chapter 4, "L'Antisémitisme de gauche," 177–214.

27. O'Squarr, *Les Coulisses de l'anarchie,* 86.

28. APP B/a 76, April 22, 1890.

29. APP B/a 77, "z-3," December 24, 1892.

30. APP B/a 79, "Legrand," May 9, 1894.

31. APP B/a 79, April 10, 1894.

32. AN F7, 12517, August 27, 1895. On Adam, see Sternhell, *Droite,* 203.

33. Emile Pouget, "Youtre et Jésuite," *Le Père Peinard,* April 20, 1890. The Grave caricature was mentioned by Adolphe Retté in *La Maison en ordre,* 175.

34. See de Goustine, *Pouget: Les Matins noirs de syndicalisme,* 123, 124.

35. APP B/a 1502, October 23, 1892; APP B/a 79, August 22, 1894.

36. A. B. Jackson, *La Revue Blanche,* 42.

37. APP B/a 79, August 22, 1894.

38. See Lethève, *Le Caricature et la presse,* 106.

CHAPTER THREE

1. Benjamin, "Paris, Capital of the Nineteenth Century," in *Reflections,* 146–49.

2. See Maitron, "Bibliographie du mouvement anarchiste en France, 1880–fin 1972," in *Mouvement anarchiste,* 2:211–342.

3. Joll, *The Anarchists,* 169.

4. APP B/a 79, April 4, 1894.

5. Ibid.

6. APP B/a 79, April 4, 1894; "L'Anarchie lettrée," n.d., probably March 1894.

7. Cited in Billy, *L'Epoque 1900,* 422.

8. "La Vie et littérature," *Le Gaulois,* October 7, 1898, cited in Caras-

sus, *Le Snobisme et les lettres françaises,* 362. On 601, Carassus calls the 1890–1905 era the high point of snobbism as a social factor.

9. APP B/a 79, "Bouchon," January 20, 1894.
10. Cited in Rudorff, *La Belle Epoque,* 149.
11. APP B/a 78, July 4–9, 1894.
12. Maitron, *Mouvement anarchiste,* 1:245, 250, 254.
13. AN F7, 12506, "Contre l'anarchie," *Le Matin,* March 9, 1894.
14. Leyret, *En plein faubourg,* 10.
15. Ibid., 206, 213.
16. Ibid., 249–50.
17. Ibid., 24.
18. APP B/a 79, "Jean," November 15, 1889. For the Musée du Soir, see Gustave Geffroy, *La Musée du Soir aux quartiers ouvriers.*
19. Lesourd, *Montmartre,* 396.
20. Jullian, *Montmartre,* 33, 34; Rudorff, *La Belle Epoque,* 45.
21. Ariès, *Histoire des populations françaises,* 290.
22. Quoted in Sanborn, *Paris and the Social Revolution,* 273.
23. Jean, *Les Bas-Fonds du crime et de la prostitution,* 158, 159.
24. Jullian, *Montmartre,* 63–69. Jerrold Siegel, in his exhaustive and perceptive *Bohemian Paris,* discusses the genesis of the Chat Noir in detail in chapter 8, "Publicity and Fantasy: The World of the Cabarets," 215–41. Much less analytical but well illustrated is Oberthur, *Cafés and Cabarets of Montmartre.* Lisa Appignanesi, *The Cabaret* (London: Studio Vista, 1975), explores cabaret life across Europe.
25. Artus, "Presse montmartroise," 316.
26. APP B/a 1157, July 9, 1894.
27. "Maxime Lisbonne," *Dictionnaire biographique du mouvement ouvrier français,* 7:172.
28. APP B/a 1157, June 6, 1892.
29. Cerf, *Le d'Artagnan de la commune,* 192.
30. Ibid., 175.
31. APP B/a 1157, March 23, 1892; April 11, 1892. The following year, Lisbonne wrote a light-hearted proposal to the prefect of police on how to empty the streets of anarchist demonstrators during the May Day season: "Fifty anarchists are presently behind bars. Could

you not install them at St. Pelagie in the Pavilion of Princes? Lunch and dinner with champagne. Our prettiest mondaines of the Casino, Moulin Rouge and Elysée-Montmartre would be authorized to console these unhappy prisoners. The next year two hundred anarchists would solicit their internment. In five years all Paris would be anarchistic from April 20 to May 2. . . . could you not then assure tranquility?" APP B/a 1157, April 23, 1893.

32. APP B/a 1157, July 28, 1895.
33. APP B/a 76, July 20, 1889; August 15, 1889.
34. For a discussion of the dramaturgical aspects of the epoch, see Roger Shattuck, *The Banquet Years,* 6: "Paris was a stage where the excitement of performance gave every deed the double significance of private gesture and public action. Doctor and ragpicker alike performed their professional flourishes, and the *crime passionel* was practiced as a fine art." Siegel, in *Bohemian Paris,* 215–41, does not discuss Lisbonne, but emphasizes Montmartre bohemia's capacity for self-advertisement.
35. APP B/a 79, "Les Anarchistes," approximately March 1, 1894.
36. APP B/a 79, April 30, 1894.
37. One Lagrange was singled out by the police for his political associations, having helped to organize and recruit "Le groupe d'études sociales des artistes de la Seine." Lagrange was known at the Maison du Peuple and in the workers' party committees, and was familiar with Jean Allemane on the extreme left wing of the Socialist party. Ibid., September 10, 1894; APP B/a 1157, July 9, 1894; October 17, 1894.
38. Sarrazin, *Souvenirs de Montmartre et du Quartier Latin,* 208; Shapiro, *Painters and Politics,* 51; Carco, *La Belle Epoque au temps du Bruant,* 49.
39. Adam, *Le Mystère,* 2:25, 30.
40. On the etymology of "revolution," see Hannah Arendt, *On Revolution* (New York: Viking Press, 1965), 34 ff.
41. These communiqués are collected in a file on censorship of cabarets during the Third Republic. AN F21, 1338. The correspondence dated April 25, year uncertain but probably 1872, judging from the report that follows, is signed by the directors of Les Ambassadeurs, Alcazar d'été, Gaîté-Montparnasse, and so on.

42. Laurent Tailhade, "La Pudeur à Montmartre," *La Revue Rouge* (March 1896), 7.

43. AN F21, 1338.

44. AN F21, 1338, April 16, 1892.

45. AN F21, 1338, May 4, 1886.

46. AN F21, 1338, March 11, 1897.

47. AN F21, 1338, probably 1897.

48. Ibid.

49. AN F21, 1338, letters of May 23 and May 29, 1897.

50. Robichez, *Lugné-Pöe,* 128.

51. Ibid., 101.

52. Tailhade repeated his performance for the same play at the Oeuvre six years later, and the quotation is taken from the published 1899 version. The brunt of his remarks had a very Nietzschean ring, and it is possible that they altered between 1893 and 1899. *L'Ennemi du peuple* par Henrik Ibsen, Conférence donné au Théâtre de l'Oeuvre, le samedi, 18 fevrier 1899 par Laurent Tailhade (Paris: Société Libre d'Editions des Gens des Lettres, 1900), 11.

53. Jourdain, *Né en 76,* 197, 198, 201–3.

54. Robichez, *Lugné-Pöe,* 129; A. Dikka Rique, Trois Auteurs Scandinaves, 137, cited by Jasper, *Adventure in the Theater,* 127.

55. Antoine, *Mes souvenirs sur le Théâtre-Libre,* 301, January 15, 1894, notation.

56. See Shattuck, *The Banquet Years,* 206–11.

57. APP B/a 79, May 25, 1894.

58. Alfred Jarry, "Questions de théâtre," *La Revue Blanche* 12 (January 1897): 17.

59. Shattuck, *The Banquet Years,* 210, quoting Mendès in *Le Journal,* December 10, 1896.

60. Rudorff, *La Belle Epoque,* 184, quoting Henry Fouquier in *Le Figaro,* December 1896.

61. Robichez, *Lugné-Pöe,* 94. On Jarry's 'pataphysics, see Siegel, *Bohemian Paris,* 312.

62. Description of the theater performance in APP B/a 76, December 20, 1890; copy of "Germinal" found in AN F7, 12518, April 7, 1894.

63. Artus, "Presse montmartroise," 316.

64. See de Goustine, *Pouget: Les Matins Noirs de Syndicalisme,* 26.
65. Artus, "Presse montmartroise," 329. Artus described *La Sociale* merely as "Journal politique illustré" when in fact it was Pouget's first journalistic effort after returning from exile in London. It appeared from May 1895 until October 1896, when it was supplanted by the second series of *Le Père Peinard,* which came out regularly until April 1899. Nor was the anarchist sentiment of two other 1895 papers, *L'Etat Naturel* and *Le Libertaire,* mentioned by Artus, who reserved the most detailed coverage for the cabaret and artistic journals that were more germane to Montmartre's cultural reputation.
66. I will have more to say on this deflation of cultural activity in my discussion of Lautrec's tenure in Montmartre. See chapter 6.
67. APP B/a 79, "La Sentinelle de Montmartre," November 15, 1889.
68. APP B/a 1507, Affiche, November 2, 1889.
69. APP B/a 1507, November 3, 1889.
70. APP B/a 76, November 5, 1889.
71. APP B/a 79, May 17, 1894.
72. APP B/a 1507, June 17, 1893.
73. APP B/a 76, November 12, 1890.
74. APP B/a 79, January 1, May 22, May 23, 1894.
75. APP B/a 79, July 11, 1894.
76. APP B/a 79, July 27, 1894.
77. APP B/a 76, July 16, 1894.
78. APP B/a 1507, March 5, 1897; *Le Libertaire,* November 13–19, 1896, in Musée de Montmartre, Paris, Box 2; APP B/a 1507, *Le Libertaire,* November 5, 1897.
79. A seminal work on the role of festivals in French popular culture of the Renaissance is Mikhail Bakhtin's *Rabelais and His World* (Cambridge, Mass.: M.I.T. Press, 1968), written in 1940 and first published in Moscow in 1965. More recently, Emmanuel Le Roy Ladurie, *Carnival at Romans,* trans. Mary Feeney (New York: Braziller, 1979); Mona Ozouf, "Space and Time in the Festivals of the French Revolution," *Comparative Studies in Society and History* 17 (July 1975): 372–84, and *La Fête révolutionnaire, 1789–99* (Paris: Gallimard, 1976); Natalie Z. Davis, "The Reasons of Misrule," *Society and Culture in Early Modern France* (Stanford:

Stanford University Press, 1975); Lynn Hunt, *Politics, Culture, and Class in the French Revolution* (Berkeley: University of California Press, 1984); and Charles Rearick, *Festivals of the Belle Epoque* (New Haven: Yale University Press, 1985), have written on the *fête* in a French context.

80. The phrase is Jean Duvignaud's, quoted by Rearick, "Festivals in Modern France," 437. For a discussion of the contemporary relevance of the feast of fools, see Harvey Cox, *The Feast of Fools* (New York: Harper, 1969).

81. The phrase is Jacques Rougerie's, "Recherche sur le Paris populaire. Espace populaire et espace révolutionnaire: Paris, 1870–71," *Recherches et Travaux* 5 (January 1977).

82. See Rearick, "Festivals in Modern France," 451.

83. AN F7, 12518, Le Groupe de l'Avant-Garde de Londres, "Fête du 14 Juillet," July 19, 1892; APP B/a 1507, July 18, year unknown; Zo d'Axa, *Endehors*, "14 juillet sanglant," July 10, 1892.

84. Barrows, *Distorting Mirrors*, 34. Barrows gives a good brief analysis of the first May Days on 24–35. For more detailed information, see Maurice Dommanget, *L'Histoire du premier mai* (Paris: Editions de la Tête de Feuilles, 1972), and Claude Willard, *La Fusillade de Fourmies* (Paris: Editions Sociales, 1957).

85. AN F7, 12518, May 1, 1893, "An Anarchist Group," bilingual English-French leaflet.

86. Herbert, *La Chanson à Montmartre*, 309, 310.

87. Quoted in ibid., 88.

88. Sanborn, *Paris and the Social Revolution*, 274, 275, 309.

89. Herbert, *La Chanson à Montmartre*, 82, 83. Salis received 82 votes out of 5,480 cast.

90. Quoted in ibid., 412.

CHAPTER FOUR

1. Argot differs from the more familiar term "slang," which is spoken mainly by adolescents.

2. The Sapir-Whorf hypothesis is the classic statement of the way in which language influences cognition. See Whorf, *Language, Thought and Reality: Selected Writings of Benjamin Lee Whorf,*

esp. the essay "The Relation of Habitual Thought and Behavior to Language."

3. Whorf himself lumped the Indo-European languages into one overall category that he called Standard Average European, which he contrasted with the radically different structure of Hopi. Yet modern sociolinguists such as Basil Bernstein do make substantial claims for the cognitive impact of class-stratified speech. See Bernstein, *Class, Codes and Control,* 50; also Mueller, *The Politics of Communication,* 53–55.

4. Guiraud, *L'Argot,* 11.

5. See Sainéan, *Le Langage parisien*; Niceforo, *Le Génie de l'Argot*; Joly, *Le Crime, étude social.*

6. Sainéan, *Le Langage parisien,* 482.

7. Delesalle, *Dictionnaire,* xxii.

8. The submergence of picturesque crime into lower-class poverty in the rapidly growing Paris of 1800–1850 is a major theme of Louis Chevalier in his *Laboring Classes and Dangerous Classes,* though he does not specifically refer to the parallel linguistic trend.

9. See for example the works of the Italian sociologist and socio-linguist Alfredo Niceforo, *Les Classes pauvres* and *Le Génie de l'argot.*

10. The terms "public," "restricted," "formal," and "elaborated" are Basil Bernstein's. For a discussion of a number of sociolinguistic studies that seem to confirm Bernstein's conclusions, see Mueller, *The Politics of Communication,* 53–57.

11. Maitron, *Mouvement anarchiste,* 1:146.

12. Le Père Peinard 35 (October 20, 1889): 13, cited in Sainéan, *Le Langage parisien,* 485.

13. APP B/a 76, report of agent "X no. 1," May 15, 1890.

14. See APP B/a 1502. The final letter in the file, dated May 13, 1906, was an inquiry from one O. Boisson, who said he had heard that the anarchists were using Esperanto to relay messages, and offered his services as a translator to the police. No response to the offer was included in the file.

15. *Le Père Peinard* 53 (March 16, 1890): 11, 12.

16. Trudgill, in *Sociolinguistics,* 108, notes that conservative French political parties tend to use the formal *vous,* leftists the informal

tu. See Roger Brown and Albert Gilman, "The Pronouns of Power and Solidarity," in Sebeok, ed., *Style in Language,* 253–76, for a detailed analysis of the political implications of using singular and plural pronouns.

17. Bernstein, *Class, Codes and Control,* 47.
18. "As the structure of a public language reinforces a strong inclusive relationship, the individual will exhibit through a range of activities a powerful sense of allegiance and loyalty to the group, its forms and its aspirations, at the cost of exclusion and perhaps conflict with other social groups which possess a different linguistic form which symbolizes their social relationships." Ibid., 47–48.
19. Sainéan, *Le Langage parisien,* appendix A, 481, cites six such dictionaries, two of them unfamiliar to me, and neglects one that I found in the Bibliotheque Nationale, Lermina and Levêque's *Dictionnaire thématique français-argot* (1897).
20. For lexicalization, see Trudgill, *Sociolinguistics,* 29. The four argot dictionaries consulted are Bruant, *Dictionnaire français-argot* (1901); Delesalle, *Dictionnaire argot-français* (1896); Lermina and Levêque, *Dictionnaire thématique français-argot* (1897); and Rossignol, *Dictionnaire d'argot* (1901). In order to see how representative my categories actually were, I did a random sampling of one more dictionary, Charles Virmaître's *Dictionnaire d'argot fin de siècle.* I recorded the argot words on every tenth page of Virmaître's dictionary, categorized these terms, and then compared these categories with my own. This tabulation revealed a number of important nonpolitical categories, such as those referring to bodily functions, often of an excremental nature, and to sexual differentiation. Important categories I had not considered referred to money, religion, death, and more generally to a wide variety of behavioral traits and attitudes. Nevertheless, overall I found a high degree of correlation between Virmaître's terms and the categories I had elaborated, with a great many words designating legal authorities, places of incarceration and types of punishment, criminality, social class, and prostitution. The greatest number of terms referred to theft (23 words), prostitutes (15), prisons (14), parts of the body (16), bodily functions (13), and types of persons (17). Virmaître also indicated the social origin of the terms, attributing the creation of argot words to soldiers, artists, laundresses, and so on.

Some 177 words were simply attributed to "the people"; another 107 issued from the thieves' milieu, clearly implying that these were now in general circulation among the argot-speaking populace. The other significant argot-creating groups were pimps and prostitutes (9) and printers (5); the rest were responsibile for one or two terms each. For a complete numerical breakdown, see Sonn, "French Anarchism as Cultural Politics in the 1890s," appendix 3, pp. 455–81.

21. "The so-called dangerous classes—criminals, scoundrels, hoodlums, pimps, etc.—have exercised a considerable influence on the vocabulary of the popular Parisian of our days. They have furnished it with its most abundant and original contingent." Sainéan, *Le Langage parisien,* 209. Sainéan also cites regional patois as a third, more minor ingredient in the formation of late nineteenth-century Parisian.

22. Sainéan, *Le Langage Parisien,* 337, discusses the archaic fund of words preserved in argot. The criminal expropriation of goods and assault on persons is reminiscent of the "primitive rebels" that Eric Hobsbawm describes rising up in inchoate revolt against the elements of social change revamping their familiar world. See *Primitive Rebels* (New York: Norton, 1959).

23. Tilly and Tilly, *The Rebellious Century,* 78.

24. Delesalle, *Dictionnaire,* 82.

25. Alain Corbin, *Les Filles de noce,* 179; Servais, Laurend, *Histoire et dossier de la prostitution,* 210, 217.

26. Commenge, *La Prostitution clandestine à Paris,* 314–16, 325, 336. Many prostitutes preferred to reside in the ninth arrondissement, just below Montmartre, but very few were born there. The leading arrondissement of origin was the eleventh, faubourg du Temple, followed by the eighteenth, Montmartre, the twentieth, Belleville, and the nineteenth, La Villette, with the rest of Paris far behind. The most arrests for illicit prostitution in the 1880s took place along the boulevard Sébastopol.

CHAPTER FIVE

1. So claimed Henry Steele in his 1904 study of Parisian working-class life, *The Working Classes in France,* 8, 83.

2. The issue of whether literacy stimulates rebelliousness or habits of obedience and conformity is raised by Robert Pattison, *On Literacy: The Politics of the Word from Homer to the Age of Rock* (New York: Oxford University Press, 1982), 128, 129. In England, literacy among the lower classes was sometimes feared as tending to incite popular radicalism. See Tom Laqueur, "Toward a Cultural Ecology of Literacy in England, 1600–1850," in Daniel Resnick, ed., *Literacy in Historical Perspective* (Washington, D.C.: Library of Congress, 1983), 44, 53. Richard Altick, *The English Common Reader* (Chicago: University of Chicago Press, 1957), 324, 325, expressly refers to the English workers' penchant for reading radical journals such as Cobbett's aloud, and to the government's threats of revoking publicans' licenses if the practice continued, in the years just after the end of the Napoleonic wars. The French government during the early years of the Third Republic had very similar fears and also tried to suppress the practice of reading opposition papers aloud in cafés, according to a personal communication from Susanna Barrows, University of California, Berkeley, December 1984. As for the anarchists' distrust of literate culture, Maitron reports that the anarchist thief announced that "whoever signs [their names to] a book or a journal article cannot be an anarchist." See *Mouvement anarchiste*, 1:187.

3. Cipolla, *Literacy and Development in the West*, 12, 76, 94, 119, 127, 129.

4. See Francois Furet and Jacques Ozouf, "Three Centuries of Cultural Cross-Fertilization: France," in Graff, ed., *Literacy and Social Development in the West: A Reader.* Among the working classes in England, oral and local traditions are said to have persisted despite the pervasive mass media as late as the 1950s. See Richard Hoggart, *The Uses of Literacy: Changing Patterns in English Mass Culture* (Fair Lawn, N.J.: Essential Books, 1957), 27. Frequently heard suggestions that over half of American high school graduates are functionally illiterate also may warn us that obligatory school attendance does not necessarily guarantee an educated reading public, though the Third French Republic did substantially improve the general level of education.

5. It is interesting to speculate on why Russian nobles—Bakunin, Kropotkin, Tolstoy—contributed so much to anarchism. Although

they themselves were literate, their contact with a largely oral culture may have led them to support anarchism rather than the more theoretical, Western-oriented Marxist socialism.

6. Ong, *Orality and Literacy,* 45.

7. Mazisi Kunene, *Emperor Shaka the Great* (London: Heinemann, 1979).

8. Leyret, *En plein faubourg,* 24.

9. Mannheim, *Ideology and Utopia,* 215–18, 243–44.

10. Ong, *Orality and Literacy,* 44.

11. Maitron, *Mouvement anarchiste,* 1:135, 132, note 85.

12. Steele, *Working Classes,* 88, 89.

13. For the role of song in French culture, see Pierre Barbier and France Vernillat, *Histoire de France par les chansons,* Vol. 8, *La Troisième république de 1871 à 1918 (Paris: Gallimard, 1961),* and Brochon, *La Chanson sociale de Béranger à Brassens.* For music in 1890s Montmartre, see Herbert, *La Chanson à Montmartre.* Herbert focuses almost entirely on the performers and cabarets rather than on the audience. For Agent "Jean's" report, see APP B/a 76, October 21, 1889. The text of "Faut plus de gouvernement" was quoted in "Muse rouge," *L'Eclair,* December 18, 1893, APP B/a 78. Here is a typical stanza: "Le gouvernement d'Ferry / Est un système pourri; / Ceux d'Floquet, de Constans / Sont aussi Dégoutants; / Carnot ni Boulanger / Ne pourront rien changer. / Pour être heureux vraiment / Faut plus d'gouvernement" (The government of Ferry / Is a rotten system; / Those of Floquet and Constans / Are also disgusting; / Neither Carnot nor Boulanger / Can change anything / To be truly happy / No more government).

14. APP B/a 78, *L'Eclair,* December 18, 1893.

15. Mourey, "La Chanson politique et sociale," 150–54.

16. O'Squarr, *Les Coulisses de l'anarchie,* 187, 188.

17. See *Les Chants du peuple.*

18. Leyret, *En plein faubourg,* 95, 96.

19. Ponton, "Le Champ littéraire de 1865 à 1902," 85, has found only one singer from a "cultured" background, whereas three came from the lower classes and most were of petit bourgeois origin.

20. Herbert, *La Chanson à Montmartre,* 222, 223.

21. Boukay, *Chansons rouges.*

22. Jehan Rictus, "Espoir," *Les Soliloques du pauvre,* 49.

23. Yon Lug, "Les Lanternes, Aventure rouge," quoted in Bercy, *Montmartre et ses chansons.*

24. In her study of the political songs of the Third Republic, Michele Mourey notes a great turning point in class consciousness after 1889, with the rupture of the early republican spirit of consensus. "The years 1890 to 1894 appear to be the years of mutation" as singers denounced the treason of the bourgeoisie and indicted parliamentarianism in particular ("Le Chanson politique et sociale," 168).

25. Tailhade, *Platres et marbres,* 40.

26. Alexandre Zévaès, *Aristide Bruant* (Paris: La Nouvelle Critique, 1943), 48.

27. Ibid., 111. Bruant did everything to encourage the comparison between himself and Villon, so it is not too surprising that such a linkage was frequently made. His dictionary *L'Argot au XXe Siècle,* which appeared in 1901 after his retirement from cabaret life, contrasted the iconography of turn-of-the-century Montmartre with images of fifteenth-century Paris. The cover of the book, illustrated by Borgex in a more romantic and generally inferior manner compared to his predecessors Toulouse-Lautrec and Steinlen, showed a silhouette of Montmartre over which were juxtaposed two heads, one in archaic feathered cap, the other in workingman's soft visored cap. Thereafter the book interspersed fifteenth- and nineteenth-century images, often those of the authorities and underworld characters.

28. Special issue on Bruant, *La Plume* 43 (February 1, 1891): 41.

29. Bercy, *Montmartre et ses chansons,* 49, 64.

30. See Soucy, *Fascism in France*; and Sternhell, *Maurice Barrès et le nationalisme francais.* See also chapter 2 of this book. Siegel, *Bohemian Paris,* 236–39, basing himself on Zévaès, also concludes that Bruant was more a *poseur* than a man of the left, but comments that his brand of populist nationalism would have fared better a decade earlier during the Boulangist period than in 1898, when socialism was more firmly established in France. Such a judgment ignores the growth of the radical right during the 1890s.

31. Tailhade, *Platres et marbres,* 40.
32. Jourdain and Adhémar, *Toulouse-Lautrec,* 32.
33. Byvanck, *Un Hollandais à Paris en 1891,* quoting Marcel Schwob, 40.
34. Ibid., 46.
35. Giard, "Les Elections à Paris sous la IIIe République," tome II, cartes, map 14, entitled "Nombre d'ouvriers pour 1,000 parisiens, années 1880–1884"; map 13, "Nombre d'employés pour 1,000 parisiens, années 1880–1884."
36. Ibid., map 87, "La Gauche, 20 Aout 1893"; map 75, "Boulanger, 27 Janvier 1889."
37. Bercy, *Montmartre et ses chansons,* 91, 93; APP B/a 76, November 15, 1889.
38. Herbert, *La Chanson à Montmartre,* 115.
39. René-Louis Doyon, *Jehan Rictus* (Paris: La Connaissance, 1943), 44, citing Tailhade in *La Dépêche de Toulouse,* September 21, 1897. See also Léon Bloy, "Le Dernier Poète Catholique, Jehan Rictus," *Mercure de France* 47 (July 1903): 13; and Herbert, *La Chanson à Montmartre,* 239.
40. Bloy, "Jehan Rictus," 12.
41. Doyon, *Jehan Rictus,* 28.
42. Bloy, "Jehan Rictus," 10.
43. Herbert, *Montmartre et ses chansons,* 240. "L'Hiver" apparently was the work with which Rictus premiered on the stage, as the opening word of that poem, "Merd'," was known to be the first word that he uttered on stage. This was the same year that Jarry performed the identical feat with *Ubu Roi,* by adding the suffix "*-re*" where Rictus had dropped the final "*e*." See Rictus, *Les Soliloques du pauvre,* 17.
44. Doyon, *Jehan Rictus,* 51, 52.
45. Sainéan, *Le Langage parisien,* 485, 486.
46. Ong, *Orality and Literacy,* 136.

CHAPTER SIX

1. Francis Haskell, "Enemies of Modern Art," *New York Review of Books* 30, 11 (June 30, 1983): 25.

2. Shapiro, *Painters and Politics,* 7.

3. Cachin, *Paul Signac,* 21.

4. Courbet's art and ideology have been ably discussed by Clark in *The Absolute Bourgeois.*

5. Proudhon, *Du Principe de l'art et de sa destination sociale,* 14, 294, 376.

6. Le Bot, *Le Peinture et la machinisme,* 86; Manuel Devaldès, "D'Art Constantin Meunier," *La Revue Rouge* (March 1896): 19.

7. Jean Sutter, "Maximilien Luce," in Sutter, ed., *The Neo-Impressionists,* 156, 159.

8. IFHS, Grave Correspondence, 14 AS 184.

9. Paul Yaki, *Le Montmartre des nos vingt ans* (Paris: Tallandier, 1933), 93, 94; Carlo Quintavelle, "The Development of Poster Art," in Max Gallo, *The Poster in History* (New York: New American Library, 1974), 302; Egbert, *Social Radicalism,* 265.

10. IFHS, Grave Correspondence, 14 AS 184.

11. Egbert, *Social Radicalism,* 241.

12. Cachin, *Paul Signac,* 69.

13. Ibid., 23, 33, 65. The painting was given by Signac's widow shortly after the artist's death in 1935 to the city hall of Montreuil, a Communist-party-run suburb east of Paris.

14. Ibid., 77.

15. Egbert, *Social Radicalism,* 240.

16. Signac, *D'Eugene Delacroix au néo-impressionisme,* 58–60, 66, 75.

17. Ibid., 71, 72.

18. Ibid., 48, 58, 73.

19. See Herbert, *The Artist and Social Reform*; Herbert and Herbert, "Artists and Anarchism"; and Egbert, *Social Radicalism,* 238–65.

20. Huisman and Dortu, *Lautrec par Lautrec,* 48, letter of February 10, 1883. See also Toulouse-Lautrec, *Lettres,* and Jourdain and Adhémar, *Toulouse-Lautrec,* 46.

21. Perruchot, *Toulouse-Lautrec,* 108; Stuckey and Maurer, *Toulouse-Lautrec,* 107.

22. The drawing entitled *La Blanchisseuse* was published in the July 1888 issue of *Paris Illustré,* but some dispute surrounds the exact dating of the painting by the same name. Although most French

authorities, following Lautrec's friend Maurice Joyant, date it as 1889 (see Huisman and Dortu, *Lautrec par Lautrec,* 52, or Jacques Lassaigne, *Toulouse-Lautrec* [Paris: Hyperion, 1939]), the curators of the exhibition of Lautrec's paintings at the Art Institute of Chicago date it as late 1886 or early 1887. They base their argument on stylistic grounds, especially on the somber colors employed, and on the model, Carmen Gaudin, whom Lautrec had met in 1885 and painted regularly for the next few years. In either case, the relatively naturalistic, open-air setting of the drawing becomes less typical of Lautrec's work in the 1890s.

23. Cachin, *Paul Signac,* 46–48.

24. Marcel Schwob, *Les Vies imaginaires* (Paris: Mercure de France, 1896), iii. Schwob's biographer described the writer's japoniste furnishings and bibelots of the late 1890s. See Pierre Champion, *Marcel Schwob et son temps* (Paris: Bernard Grasset, 1927), 139, 210.

25. Ives, *The Great Wave,* 108.

26. Smith, *Japan: A History in Art,* 191, 218. For Buncho's story, see Rosenfeld, "Japanese Printing and Graphic Arts of the Edo Period," 475.

27. Bella, ed., *A Collection of Posters,* 10: "Lautrec stands pre-eminent for tremendous force . . . ruthlessness . . . Satanic power. . . ."

28. Gauzi, *Lautrec et son temps,* 53. One may imagine the impact on his career had Lautrec journeyed to Japan in the company of his friend Fénéon. But by the time of their association, the Sino-Japanese War may have tarnished the japoniste ideal. Gauzi mentioned a reproduction of a lacquered samurai helmet among the bibelots in Lautrec's studio (116), and from photographs we know there were others, including Japanese prints.

29. Duret, *Lautrec,* 81.

30. Novotny, *Toulouse-Lautrec,* 27.

31. Rouchon, *L'Appel des ombres,* 45, citing *Le Courrier du Soir,* September 20, 1885; Perruchot, *Toulouse-Lautrec,* 195; Natanson, *Peints à leur tour,* 167, 168.

32. Rouchon, *L'Appel des ombres,* 47, 48, 50.

33. Fénéon, *Oeuvres plus que complètes,* 217; *L'Endehors,* February 12, 1893.

34. Perruchot, *Toulouse-Lautrec,* 182.

35. It is included by Halperin in Fénéon's *Oeuvres plus que complètes,* 229–31.

36. Ibid., 229. There was indeed a mania for collecting posters, if not on the part of the workers then certainly among the bourgeoisie. See Douglas Cooper, *Toulouse-Lautrec* (New York: Abrams, n.d.), 38.

37. Halperin includes it in Fénéon's *Oeuvres*; the respected critic Francis Jourdain also certified it as being from Fénéon's hand.

38. Fénéon, *Oeuvres plus que complètes,* "Ballade chez les Artisses Indépendents," 227, 228.

39. See Abraham Moles, *L'affiche dans le société urbaine* (Paris: Dunod, 1970), 11, 12, for a general discussion of these properties of the modern poster.

40. See Gordon Wright, *Between the Guillotine and Liberty: Two Centuries of the Crime Problem in France* (New York: Oxford University Press, 1983), chapter 7, "Vagrants, Workers, Executioners (1880–1914)."

41. Heppenstall, *A Little Pattern of French Crime,* 26, surmises about why Vaillant bombed the Chamber of Deputies. "In a popular almanac he had seen a picture of Ravachol's head framed between the upright posts of the guillotine. . . . He dreamed of surpassing his predecessor."

42. Jourdain and Adhémar, *Toulouse-Lautrec,* 68.

43. Ibid., 20.

44. Ibid., 22; see also Duret, *Lautrec,* 93; Perruchot also claimed that Lautrec "detests that one speaks of politics (he is nevertheless a royalist, considers the monarchy as a means of reducing the hold of functionaries on the daily life of citizens)," *Toulouse-Lautrec,* 212. Perhaps the distinction between monarchist and anarchist is less drastic than it would seem to be, judging from the December 15, 1978, Parisian press conference at which Salvador Dali described himself as a partisan of anarchy and monarchy.

45. Jourdain and Adhémar, *Toulouse-Lautrec,* 46. In March 1892, the sixteen-year-old Jourdain sent Jean Grave some essays and sketches he wished to have published in *La Révolte,* and asked to be sent a brochure of Kropotkin's. IFHS, Grave Correspondence, 14 AS 184a, 1504.

46. APP B/a 79, July 27, 1894. Jourdain and Adhémar, *Toulouse-Lautrec,* 69; Fénéon, *Oeuvres plus que complètes,* xxii.
47. Egbert, *Social Radicalism,* 261, notes *L'Escarmouche's* anarchist orientation; Delteil, *Toulouse-Lautrec,* has complete drawings and lithographs in twenty volumes. See plate LD 50.
48. Fénéon, *Oeuvres plus que complètes,* letter to Saint-Clair, plate V.
49. Natanson, *Peints à leur tour,* 159, 160; Lassaigne, *Toulouse-Lautrec,* 82; Delteil, *Toulouse-Lautrec,* plate LD 195-4.
50. Toulouse-Lautrec, *Lettres,* 208, 209.
51. Perruchot, *Toulouse-Lautrec,* 233; Delteil, *Toulouse-Lautrec,* plates LL 77-2, LD 14-2.
52. Mauclair, *Le Soleil des morts,* 118.
53. The other artist was probably Luce, as Steinlen issued from a Swiss family and Signac had bourgeois origins; Luce was of humble origins and had painted in a style bordering on Post-Impressionism.
54. Perruchot, *Toulouse-Lautrec,* 224.
55. Herbert and Herbert, "Artists and Anarchism," 481.
56. Lautrec and his friends were avid photographers, which accounts for the many photographs of the artist at work and at play.

CHAPTER SEVEN

1. Anatole Baju, "La Littérature de demain," *L'Evenement,* April 13, 1891.
2. Sutter, "Maximilien Luce," in Sutter, ed., *The Neo-Impressionists,* 153, 156; Adam, "De la révolte," *La Critique des moeurs,* 282, 283.
3. Raynaud, *Souvenirs de police au temps de Ravachol,* 52, 53.
4. Mauclair, *Servitudes et grandeurs littéraires,* 118; Théodore Randal, "Si Kropotkine voulait," *Les Entretiens Politiques et Littéraires* 5, 33 (December 1892): 260; Henri Bordeaux, "Les Temps dérisoires: Les petites socialistes," *Les Entretiens Politiques et Littéraires* 7, 56 (December 1893): 498, 499.
5. Quoted in Roman, *Paris fin de siècle,* 48.
6. APP B/a 77, "Les Anarchistes: Bulletin de quinzaine," November 5, 1891.
7. Séverine, *En marche . . . ,* 112, 113; Salmon, *La Terreur noire,* 270, 271. Salmon cynically noted that the intellectuals chose their

charity carefully, giving money to anarchists' wives rather than for a clandestine printing press, explosives, or similarly compromising items. Where the money really went perhaps diverged from the stated purpose, but if so it was better not to publicize the fact. Salmon also considered the painters to have been more serious anarchists than the writers, as most of these latter—he listed Adam, Kahn, de Regnier, Merrill, and Retté—later renounced anarchism. Salmon published the following list of twenty-seven names, which included painters (the Pissarros, Henri Gabriel Ibels, Signac, van Rysselberghe) as well as literary figures, and one singer (Randon, whose stage name was Jehan Rictus). Coolus, Muhlfeld, Fénéon, and Bernard were all associated with *La Revue Blanche*:

B. Lazare	**5 francs**	**Zo D'Axa**	**5 francs**
L. Descaves	**5**	**H. G. Ibels**	**1**
R. Coolus	**5**	**Jules Huret**	**5**
L. Muhlfeld	**5**	**Saint-Pol Roux**	**1**
O. Mirbeau	**20**	**T. Van Rysselberghe**	**5**
P. Quillard	**6**	**P. Signac**	**5**
F. Fénéon	**5**	**P. V. Stock**	**20**
Gérault-Richard	**2**	**G. Charpentier**	**1**
A. F. Hérold	**5**	**E. Verhaeren**	**2**
M. Zévaco	**5**	**Tristan Bernard**	**20**
C. de Saint-Croix	**5**	**L. Cladel**	**2**
H. de Regnier	**5**	**L. Pissarro**	**20**
C. Pissarro	**20**	**Gabriel Randon**	**.50**
Severine	**20**		

8. Varennes, *De Ravachol à Caserio.*
9. APP B/a 79, October 1 and 3, 1894.
10. AN F7, 12506, no date but probably 1894. Some of the names, including the majority of artists, were accompanied by blue crosses, whose meaning remains mysterious. Mallarmé and *La Plume* had crosses next to their names; Severine, Sarcey, and *La Revue Blanche* did not. Could they be check marks made by some other researcher?
11. AN F7, 12506, November 19, 1894, with an undated list in the same file; Ponton, "Le Champ littéraire," 139.

12. "Referendum Artistique et Social," *L'Ermitage* 4, 7 (July 1893).

13. Ibid., 13.

14. Ibid., Stuart Merrill, "Chroniques," 50.

15. Ibid., 6, 3.

16. APP B/a 77, "Jules," September 29, 1892.

17. Hamon, *Psychologie,* 51, 66, 67, 124.

18. Kropotkin, *Paroles d'un révolté,* 66.

19. Quoted in Reszler, *L'Esthétique anarchiste,* 49.

20. Elisée Reclus, "Aux compagnons des *Entretiens," Les Entretiens Politiques et Littéraires* 5, 28 (July 1892): 3, 4.

21. For Verlaine's comment, see "Constrainte et liberté," *L'Ermitage* 4, 11 (November 1893): 264; Toutain, *La Population de la France de 1700 à 1959,* 38; Mauclair, *Servitudes et grandeurs littéraires,* 121.

22. Charles, "Groupes littéraires," 50; Hamon, *Psychologie.*

23. Ponton, *Champ littéraire,* 33, 42; Charles, "Groupes littéraires," 38.

24. Ponton, *Champ littéraire,* 36, 50, 139, 140.

25. Ibid., 66. Ponton explains the trend as resulting from the progressive legitimization of the novel genre among the middle classes, especially as practiced by Bourget, Barrès, and the other *psychologues,* which led young bourgeois writers away from poetry.

26. Charles, "Groupes littéraires," 31, records that the decade 1876–85 registered an overall gain of 76 percent in number of titles published over the 1840–75 base period. The years 1886–90 showed a lesser increase of 36.9 percent, with publication of novels up 27 percent, poetry up 65 percent, theater up 46 percent. In the decade of the 1890s, the production of novels dropped 38.4 percent from the earlier period. Poetry was up a scant 2 percent, theater up 12 percent, the total down 20.2 percent.

27. Ibid., 60. Charles cites Robert F. Byrnes, *Antisemitism in Modern France* (New Brunswick, N.J.: Rutgers University Press, 1950), for the figures on sales of novels.

28. Charles, "Groupes littéraires," 81.

29. Emile Durkheim, "L'Individualisme et les intellectuels," *La Revue Bleue* 10, series 4 (July 2, 1898): 7–13.

30. Lagarde de Cardelus, "Discours sur l'education scientifique à don-

ner au peuple," 1894, cited by Idt, "L'Intellectuel avant L'affaire Dreyfus," 43.

31. APP B/a 79, September 29, 1894. The informer called the group "Les Intelectuels," but he also misspelled Retté's name, so his slip provides dubious evidence of the newness of the term.

32. Victor de Champvans, "L'Anarchie intellectuelle," *Revue de l'Est* 4, 1 (May 15–31, 1894).

33. Maurice Barrès, "La Question des 'Intellectuels,'" *La Cocarde*, September 20, 1894; only five months later he used the term again in the title of an article, this time without apostrophes. See "L'Intellectual et la politique," *La Cocarde*, February 24, 1895; Camille Mauclair, "Sensibilité du sceptique: À propos du Maurice Barrès," *Mercure de France* 12 (December 1894): 360.

34. André de Seipse [A. Suarès], *Lettre d'un solitaire sur les maux du temps*, "Premier lettre, Barrès," (Paris: Ollendorff, 1899), 10.

35. André Gide, "A Propos des déracinés du Maurice Barrès," *L'Ermitage* 9 (February 1898).

36. Charles, "Champ littéraire et champ du pouvoir."

37. Pierre Bourdieu, "Le Marché des biens symboliques," 15.

38. Francis Vielé-Griffin, "Entretiens sur le mouvement poétique," *Les Entretiens Politiques et Littéraires* 6, 42 (May 1893): 535.

39. Quoted in Billy, *L'Epoque 1900*, 433.

40. Réberioux, "Avant-garde esthétique et avant-garde politique," 78.

41. Wilde, *The Soul of Man Under Socialism*, 46, 48, 50, 51, 54, 82.

42. Emile Goudreau, "L'Individualisme," *Les Entretiens Politiques et Littéraires* 1 (July 1890): 141; "Notes et Notules," *Les Entretiens Politiques et Littéraires* 31 (October 1892): 198; Gourmont, "Qu'est-ce que c'est le Symbolisme," *Le Livre des masques*, vol. 1.

43. Mallarmé, quoted in Huret, *Enquête sur l'evolution littéraire*, 56, 57.

44. *La Revue Socialiste*, August 1893, quoted in Madeleine Réberioux, "critique littéraire et socialisme au tournant du siècle," *Le Mouvement Social* 59 (April–June 1967): 19.

45. Scoffham-Peufly, *Les Problèmes de l'art social à travers les revues politico-littéraires*.

46. Bernard Lazare, "Les Livres," *Les Entretiens Politiques et Littéraires* 6, 43 (May 25, 1893); Lazare, *L'Ecrivain et l'art social*,

lecture given at Salle Cardinet, April 4, 1896 (Paris: Bibliothèque de l'Art Social, 1896), 19, 25. In the opinion of his contemporaries and the police, Lazare figured prominently in the anarchist milieu of the early 1890s, frequently acting as go-between for the literary elite and the militants.

47. Maitron, *Mouvement anarchiste,* 1:298, 299; Reszler, *L'Esthétique anarchiste,* 56.

48. Poinsot, *La Littérature sociale,* 56.

49. Bernard Lazare, review of Adolphe Retté's *Thulé des brumes, Les Entretiens Politiques et Littéraires* 4, 23 (February 1892): 85.

50. Adolphe Retté, "Stéphane Mallarmé," *L'Ermitage* 4 (January 1893): 7.

51. William K. Cornell, *Adolphe Retté (1863–1930)* (New Haven: Yale University Press, 1942), 59–61.

52. Hamon, *Psychologie,* 107. Retté also cited his hospitalization for a foot ailment which in true Symbolist fashion made him aware of suffering humanity, as changing him from a theoretical to a militant anarchist. See Hamon, 257.

53. Adolphe Retté, "Sur le rôle des poètes," *La Plume* 109 (November 1, 1893).

54. APP B/a 79, September 29, 1894. Paul Verlaine's name appeared on the police list after Retté's, with the notation *non anarchiste* alongside it.

55. Retté, *Promenades subversives,* 35, 36.

56. Adolphe Retté, "Aspects XV," *La Plume* 181 (November 1–15, 1896): 657.

57. Retté's critique of Symbolist aesthetic pretensions was neatly condensed into a parody entitled "Veillée de Noël," originally published in *La Plume* and reprinted in a volume called *Aspects,* 210, 211. In a grove sacred to the Muses, a bust of Puvis de Chavannes seemed to cry at the homage being paid to him. A "road to the Absolute" led the visitor to a group of men crouched on all fours, "of which several had Jewish noses," admiring an upside-down statue which they claimed was made of marble, but which was actually snow, as a little later they were admiring a puddle of water. They were led by "the president of the Republic of Letters," also known as the "Master of Mysteries." When the visitor mistook an eye for a

toe of the statue he was told, "an eye, you hear, where reside the most decisive fragrances of the symbol," and was asked to leave, for "you intensify the ellipse of null being."

As a small minority of Symbolist poets were Jewish, one suspects that Retté's rejection of the city, artifice, and cosmopolitanism was translated into a peasant's anti-Semitism. This also may have been a reference to the owners and staff of *La Revue Blanche*. The bulk of the article satirized the Symbolists' mystagogic vocabulary.

58. Retté, "Aspects," 658.

59. Ibid., 656.

60. Retté, *L'Archipel en fleurs,* 18, 19.

61. Retté, *Similitudes,* 8.

62. Retté, *Le Forêt bruissante,* 137.

63. Adolphe Retté, "Sur le rhythme des vers," in *Le Symbolisme,* 264, 265.

64. See Weber, *The Nationalist Revival in France.*

CHAPTER EIGHT

1. Even this fundamental semiological distinction was being challenged at the turn of the century, as poets struggled against the inherent arbitrariness of words, either by seeking synesthetic correspondences between letters and colors or words and sounds, or else by ideogrammatic words and poems. Painters of course moved in the opposite direction, toward greater abstraction, thus reducing their paintings' iconicity.

2. These three dimensions of semiotics are defined by Morris, "Foundations of a Theory of Signs."

3. Roman Jakobson, "What Is Poetry?" in Matejka and Titunik, eds., *Semiotics of Art,* 173.

4. Maurras, *Les Poètes.*

5. Adam, *Mystère,* 1:xxxiii.

6. Quoted and translated by Boon, *From Symbolism to Structuralism,* 29.

7. Roman Jakobson, "Closing Statement: Linguistics and Poetics," in Sebeok, ed., *Style in Language,* 173.

8. See Herbert, *The Artist and Social Reform.*

9. For a theoretical discussion of the dialectic between message and code, see Eco, *Theory of Semiotics,* esp. chapter 3, "A Theory of Sign Production."

10. Adam, *Mystère,* I:xxix.

11. See Thomas, *Karl Marx and the Anarchists.*

12. The definition of art as antipurposeful activity was made by Gregory Bateson, cited by Roy Rappaport, "Sanctity and Adaptation"; Theda Shapiro defines an "aesthetic attitude to the world," in *Painters and Politics,* 223.

13. Pierre Quillard, "L'Anarchie par la littérature," *Les Entretiens Politiques et Littéraires* 4, 25 (April 1892): 150. I have borrowed the notion of the "trace," that perception of the sign as a structure of differences implying an absence or opposition as well as denoting a positive and particular image, from Jacques Derrida, *Of Grammatology,* trans. G. C. Spivak (Baltimore: Johns Hopkins University Press, 1974, 1976). See the translator's preface, xvii, for a concise definition of the trace and Derrida's representation of it by his technique of putting terms "under erasure" to indicate the term and its inverse simultaneously.

14. Charles Maurras, "Les Jeunes Revues," *La Revue Bleue* 31, 4 (January 27, 1894): 118.

15. Georges Saint-Mleux, "La Socialisation du langage," *Les Entretiens Politiques et Littéraires* 4, 24 (March 1892).

16. AN F7, 12518, "A Propos de Tristan et Yseult," March 29, 1894.

17. Reszler, *L'Esthétique anarchiste,* 42.

18. Huret, *Enquête sur l'evolution littéraire,* 138, 139.

19. Rémy de Gourmont, "Idéalisme," *Les Entretiens Politiques et Littéraires* 4, 25 (April 1892), 145.

20. Rémy de Gourmont, "Le Symbolisme," *La Revue Blanche* 6 (June 1892): 322.

21. Hemmings, *Culture and Society in France.*

22. Retté, *Le Symbolisme,* 237, 239.

23. Maitron, *Mouvement anarchiste,* 2:183, 184, note 53.

24. Retté, *Le Symbolisme,* 237. Joll, *The Anarchists,* 154, compares the views of these two Russian nobles.

25. Bianquis, *Nietzsche en France,* 111. See also 12–14, 47.

26. Bianquis cites the 1892 translation of *The Wagner Case* as the first available work of Nietzsche in France. She also mentions some fragments of Nietzsche's works published in *L'Ermitage* in 1894, in *La Revue Blanche* in 1897, and in *Le Mercure de France* only in 1898, the year that *Thus Spake Zarathustra* and *Beyond Good and Evil* were finally translated. In fact, *L'Ermitage* published a long extract of *Thus Spake Zarathustra* in April 1893, introduced and translated by Hugues Rebell, and entitled "De l'homme supérieur." This text was preceded by articles devoted to Nietzsche in the January and February issues of the journal, written by Henri Mazel and Marcel Schwob.

27. Walter Benjamin, "Paris, Capital of the Nineteenth Century," in *Reflections*, 157.

28. Lewis, *The Aesthetics of Stéphane Mallarmé in Relation to His Public*, 78. In Mallarmé's article "La Musique et les lettres," literary action was described as "the presentation, as an explosion, of a very pure concept of society."

29. See Sontag, "The Aesthetics of Silence," *Styles of Radical Will*, 50–71, for a provocative appraisal of the dialectical implications of silence in terms of the artist's social relations.

30. Paul Adam, "De la révolte," in *La Critique des moeurs*, 282, 283.

31. Mauclair, *Le Soleil des morts*, 160.

32. Ibid., 24, 28.

33. For a discussion of the visual and spatial qualities of free verse, see Longrée, "Le Vers libre et l'avenir de la poésie."

34. Silence as initiation is a theme raised by Steiner, *Language and Silence*.

35. Maurice Barrès, "Le Grand Empire du silence," *La Cocarde*, January 2, 1895.

36. Huret, *Enquête sur l'evolution littéraire*, 60.

37. Léon Deschamp, "L'Esthétique moderne," *La Plume* 33 (September 1, 1890).

38. Retté, "Le Décadent," *Aspects*, 55, 56.

39. Ibid., "Esthétiques divergents," 164.

40. The irony of Retté's vituperative critique was that in these last years of Mallarmé's life he was taking a greater interest in the social life of the people. He admired the simplicity of their daily activities and saw them as the future hope of society. He even wrote

some "Chansons Bas" which sang of cobblers, women selling garlic and onions, newspaper vendors, and so on. See *Mallarmé,* ed. and trans. Anthony Hartley, 75–79.

41. See Eco, *Theory of Semiotics,* 272, 310.

42. Thibaudet, *French Literature,* 429.

43. Stéphane Mallarmé, "Vers et musique en France," *Les Entretiens Politiques et Littéraires* 4, 27 (June 1892).

44. Devaldès, *Hurles de haine et d'amour,* 26, 27.

45. Jean Carrère, "Adolphe Retté, *Une belle dame passa,*" *La Plume* 101 (July 1, 1893): 289, followed by Retté, *La Plume* 104 (August 15, 1893): 355.

46. Adam, "De la critique," *La Critique des Moeurs,* 7.

47. Retté, "Sur le rhythme des vers," *Le Symbolisme,* 256.

48. Camille Mauclair, "Maurice Beaubourg," *Mercure de France* 9 (October 1893): 139.

49. Charles Morice, "Paul Gauguin," *Mercure de France* 9 (December 1893): 289, 290.

50. Mauclair, *Le Soleil des morts,* 137, 138.

51. O'Squarr, *Les Coulisses de l'anarchie,* 30, 31, 35, 36.

52. Bataille, *Causes criminelles et mondaines de 1895,* 357.

53. Varennes, *De Ravachol à Caserio,* 163.

54. For a comparison between the operation of poetry and drama, see Defontaine and Defontaine, "Figure, langage et réprésentation," 130.

55. Théodore Jean, "Anathème," *Les Temps Nouveaux* 1, 2 (1895): 12.

56. Retté, *L'Archipel en fleurs.*

57. Adam, "Grandeur future de l'avare, *La Critique des moeurs,* 316.

58. Nettlau, *Histoire de l'anarchie,* 10.

59. Morel, *Terre promise,* 30; dots between words were included in the original text to suggest stream of consciousness.

60. Mauclair, *Servitudes et grandeurs littéraires,* 20.

61. Mauclair, *L'Ennemi des rêves,* xiv–xvi.

62. Ibid., xxiv.

63. Billy, *L'Epoque 1900,* 424. See also chapter 9 for a discussion of the apotheosis of acts of violence.

64. Retté, *La Maison en ordre,* 169; Zo d'Axa, "Nous," *L'Endehors* 1, 34 (December 27, 1891).

65. Zo d'Axa, "Nous."

66. Paul Adam, "Critique de socialisme et de l'anarchie," *La Revue Blanche* 5 (May 19, 1893): 371.

67. Ibid., 375, 376.

68. Jan Mukarovsky, "Art as Semiotic Fact" (1936), in Matejka and Titunik, eds., *Semiotics of Art,* 159.

CHAPTER NINE

1. Maitron, *Mouvement anarchiste,* 1:214–17, narrates that Léauthier and also Ravachol's accomplice Simon were killed during a prison revolt in 1894.

2. Maitron for example devotes a forty-six-page chapter to "L'ère des attentats," but deals with literary anarchism almost as an afterthought in the last two pages of volume one. In his chapter on the *attentats* he does refer to the eulogies written by the Symbolists for the anarchist martyrs. Most other histories of the movement are heavily weighted toward accounts of the terrorist activity, including Maitron's own *Ravachol et les anarchistes.*

3. Laqueur, *Terrorism,* 28.

4. Maitron, *Mouvement anarchiste,* 1:193.

5. Both Jacob and the Bande à Bonnot were sufficiently romantic criminals to inspire artistic treatment, the former becoming the model for the literary character Arsène Lupin, the creation of Maurice Le Blanc, the latter appearing in a film called *Le Bande à Bonnot.*

6. Iviansky, "Individual Terror: Concept and Typology," 46, 61.

7. Bataille, *Causes criminelles et mondaines de 1892,* 74.

8. Hamon, *Les Hommes et les théories de l'anarchie,* 31.

9. Zo d'Axa, "Articles de Paris," *Endehors,* 232, 233.

10. Ibid., "Notre Complot," originally published 1893.

11. Quoted by Joan Halperin in the preface to Fénéon, *Oeuvres plus que complètes,* lxv.

12. Maitron, *Mouvement anarchiste,* 1:258.

13. Marcel Schwob reported this fact in his "Lettres parisiennes" of March 13, 1894. Collected in Schwob, *Oeuvres,* 8:27, 28.

14. Maitron, *Mouvement anarchiste,* 1:259–61.

15. Maitron, *Ravachol et les anarchistes,* 105.

16. Heppenstall, *A Little Pattern of French Crime,* 25.

17. Maitron, *Ravachol et les anarchistes,* 105.

18. APP B/a 1500, "Les Anarchistes," *L'Eclair,* March 17, 1894.

19. Bérard, "Les Mystiques de l'anarchie," *Sur l'anarchie,* 15. Bérard quotes a poem of Henry's that is worth reproducing:

> Je vois autour de moi les anges
> Et les déeses de l'amour
> Accourir tous et, tour à tour,
> Venir me chanter ses louanges.
>
> Mais tous ils murmurent: "Espère"
> Et moi qui sais qu'ils sont trompeurs
> Je sens raviver mes douleurs
> Car ils se rient de la misère.
>
> Je ne puis avoir d'espérance.
> Apres ces vers je me tairai;
> Mais toujours je vous aimerai
> Et je bénirai ma souffrance.
>
> Je souffrirai silencieux
> Et vous serez toujours ma dame
> Le bel ideal de mon âme
> Rêvant d'amour sous les grands cieux.
>
> (I see around me the angels
> And goddesses of love
> All running up and, each in turn,
> Coming to sing me their praises.
>
> But they all murmur: "Hope"
> And I, who know they are liars
> Feel my sorrows revive
> Because they laugh at my misery.
>
> I can not have hope
> After these verses I will be quiet;
> But always I will love you
> And I will consecrate my suffering.

I will suffer silently
And you will always be my lady
The beautiful ideal of my soul
Dreaming of love under the high heavens.)

20. "Les Anarchistes," *Le Journal de la France* 73 (September 15, 1970).
21. Reported by Henri Ribeyre, "Chronique politique," *La Revue Blanche* 6 (March 1894).
22. Bérard, *Sur l'anarchie*, 8. In *Causes criminelles et mondaines de 1895*, Bataille referred for instance to the trial of the Dynamiters of Liège, who had bombed a theater and the residences of the mayor and a doctor in the spring of 1894.
23. See Laqueur, *Terrorism*, 109, who sharply distinguishes between the urban terrorist and the rural guerrilla.
24. AN F7, 12506, March 21, 1894.
25. First page of *Le Dynamite*, reproduced in Blond, *La Grande Armée du drapeau noir*.
26. Maitron, *Mouvement anarchiste*, 1:219, 223.
27. Leyret, *En plein faubourg*, 262.
28. APP B/a 79, "Legrand," May 11, 1894.
29. See Frantz Fanon, *The Wretched of the Earth* (New York: Grove Press, 1965), on violence as a necessary element in the colonized male's coming of age.
30. APP B/a 79, May 9, 1894.
31. "Declaration d'Emile Henry," *L'Echo de Paris*, April 30, 1894, in Fénéon Archives, Bibliothèque Jacques Doucet, MS 6920.33.
32. Leonard Rivière, "Anarchistes en chambre," *La Revue Moderne* 11, 45 (July 1894): 1–3.
33. O'Squarr, *Les Coulisses de l'anarchie*, 40, 41.
34. Retté, *La Maison en ordre*, also described the more violent attitude of a friend named Milo who was also present at the luncheon.
35. APP B/a 79, "Legrand," April 10, 1894.
36. APP B/a 79, February 20, 1894, reports the furor caused by Mirbeau's article; text of Mirbeau's article partially quoted in Maitron, *Mouvement anarchiste*, 1:246, 247.
37. Ribeyre, "Chronique politique," 278.
38. Quoted in Laqueur, *Terrorism*, 66.

39. For Emile Henry, see the Barrès article in *Le Journal,* May 22, 1894; Ribeyre, "Chronique politique," 278.

40. Adam, preface to the second edition of *Lettres de malaisie,* v, vi.

41. Mauclair, *Le Soleil des morts,* 181–83, 217.

42. Ibid., 223, 224.

43. Adam, *Le Mystère,* 2:143.

44. Ibid., 2:147–49. The desirability of provoking a strong public reaction, even a negative one, was and is a controversial issue surrounding the use of terror. Whereas the anarchist writer Octave Mirbeau condemned Emile Henry's bombing of the Café Terminus as publically discrediting anarchism, Paul Adam seemed to favor polarizing opinion in the interest of hastening a revolutionary confrontation. At its most extreme, leftist eagerness to weaken the democratic center would lead to complicity with the radical right, encouraging Boulangism in the 1880s, fascism in the 1930s.

45. Adam, "De la grève," *La Critique des moeurs,* 215.

46. Pierre Quillard, "L'Anarchie par la littérature," *Les Entretiens Politiques et Littéraires* 4, 25 (April 1892): 151.

47. Mallarmé referred to literary activity as a "bomb" in *Le Livre.* See Lewis, *The Aesthetics of Stéphane Mallarmé in Relation to His Public,* 78, 79; Henri de Regnier quoted in Carassus, *Le Snobisme et les lettres françaises,* 376.

48. APP B/a 78, *Paris,* December 13, 1893.

49. Letter to Sebastien Faure, November 12, 1893, cited by Maitron, *Mouvement anarchiste,* 1:229. Although Vaillant also had notified an anarchist leader of his intentions on the eve of his *attentat,* there is no evidence that the leaders played any role in instigating the attacks. Including the revenge bombing of the Restaurant Véry and the attack on the Restaurant Foyot, it was one of a series of attacks on eating establishments that brings to mind the December 1977 bombing of Fauchon, the luxury food market in the place de la Madeleine that readily symbolized the necessities of life being elevated to luxuries that few could afford.

50. This is the judgment of Billy, *L'Epoque 1900,* 426. Jean Moréas commented on Tailhade's political involvement that actions carried on in the social milieu were only pretexts for his songs. See Ernest Raynaud, *En marge de la melée symboliste,* 127.

51. "Qu'importe les victimes si le geste est beau? Qu'importe la mort

des vagues humanités si, par elle, s'affirme l'individu?" Maitron, *Mouvement anarchiste,* 1:236, note 114.

52. Tristan Bernard, "Monsieur Dupuy, ou le courage civique," in "Le Chasseur de Chevelures, moniteur du possible," supplement to *La Revue Blanche* 6 (January 1894): 94.

53. Paul Adam, "Eloge à Ravachol," *Les Entretiens Politiques et Lit-téraires* 5, 28 (July 1892): 28, 30.

54. Félix Dubois, "Le Péril anarchiste," *Le Figaro,* January 27, 1894.

55. Victor Barrucand, *L'Endehors* 64 (July 24, 1892), cited by Maitron, *Mouvement anarchiste,* 1:224, note 72.

56. Adam, "La Charité suprême," *La Critique des moeurs,* 294.

57. Ibid., "Invectives au mendiant," 296–304.

58. Cited in Laqueur, *Terrorism,* 134, 135.

59. Leger, *Journal d'un anarchiste.*

CHAPTER TEN

1. Introduction by Paul Avrich to Michael Bakunin, *God and the State* (New York: Dover, 1970), viii, ix.

2. Ibid., 25, 26.

3. William Blake, "Jerusalem," in *Complete Writings,* ed. Geoffrey Keynes (Oxford: Oxford University Press, 1969), chapter 3, plate 57, 689.

4. Bakunin, *God and the State,* 28.

5. For a good summation of Stirner's philosophy, see Carroll, *Break-Out From the Crystal Palace.*

6. Joll, *The Anarchists,* 174.

7. See Joll, *The Anarchists*; Cohn, *Millennium*; and Mannheim, *Ideology and Utopia.*

8. Cohn, *Millennium,* 319.

9. Mannheim, *Ideology and Utopia,* 226–28.

10. See La Barre, *The Ghost Dance*; James Mooney, *The Ghost-Dance Religion and the Sioux Outbreak of 1890* (Washington, D.C.: Bureau of American Ethnology, Fourteenth Annual Report, 1896); David Aberle, *The Peyote Religion Among the Navaho* (Chicago: Aldine, 1966); Wallace, *Religion*; and Anthony F. C. Wallace, *The Death and Rebirth of the Seneca* (New York: Knopf, 1970).

11. See La Barre and Mooney, cited in note 10, for detailed accounts of the Sioux or Lakota uprising.

12. Mannheim, *Ideology and Utopia*, 215, 225–26.

13. Ibid., 197.

14. See Rappaport, "Ritual and Regulation of Ecological Systems," *Pigs for the Ancestors*, esp. 236, 237; also Rappaport, "Sanctity and Adaptation."

15. AN F7, 12504, "Bulletin," *Le Journal de Genève*, February 27, 1886.

16. Bérard, "Les Mystiques de l'anarchie," *Sur l'anarchie*, 21, 36.

17. Hamon, *Psychologie*, 270.

18. Ibid., 313, 314.

19. *Le Figaro*, February 14, 1894.

20. For a lengthy survey of the religious and messianic implications of modern revolutionary movements, see James H. Billington, *Fire in the Minds of Men: Origins of the Revolutionary Faith* (New York: Basic Books, 1980). For a recent example of a Marxist critique of anarchist millenarian tendencies as a reflection of their fundamental ineffectuality and utopianism, see Eric Hobsbawm, *Revolutionaries* (New York: New American Library, 1975). By contrast, in *Anarchists of Andalusia* (Berkeley and Los Angeles: University of California Press, 1976), Temma Kaplan denies that Spanish anarchists at the turn of the century were fundamentally millenarian, and maintains that they had a firm grasp of social realities.

21. Saint-Rémy, *Les Dieux des anarchistes*; Maitron, *Mouvement anarchiste*, 2:256, 260.

22. Nocera, *Anarchie et spiritualisme*, preface by Marie de Saint-Rémy, iii, 32.

23. Maitron, *Mouvement anarchiste*, 2:260.

24. Steele, *The Working Classes in France*, 8, 68. Gordon Wright, *France in Modern Times* (New York: Norton, 1981), 268, notes that even that was changing. In the Limoges region, for example, the proportion of nonbaptized children rose from 2 to 40 percent between 1899 and 1914, and the number of civil marriages rose from 14 to 60 percent.

25. Emile Cère, "Le Bréviaire du Bouddhiste," *Les Entretiens Politiques et Littéraires* 7 (August 10, 1893): 113. The figure he cites of 300,000 Buddhists is almost certainly exaggerated.

26. Bérard, *Sur l'anarchie,* 18–36.

27. Retté, *La Maison en ordre,* 176.

28. Phillips, *The Church in France, 1848–1907,* 226, 227.

29. See Montuclard, *Conscience réligieuse et démocratie,* 7, 13, for a discussion of this conjunction.

30. APP B/a 77, August 4, 1891.

31. Zo d'Axa, "Le Néophyte Cacolet," reprinted in *Endehors,* 98.

32. Marcel Schwob, "Lettres Parisiennes," March 9, 1894, in *Oeuvres,* 8:26.

33. APP B/a 79: April 28, 1894, "Alexandre," February 22, 1894.

34. See Maitron, *Mouvement anarchiste,* 1:236–38. It is indeed possible that Vaillant's harmless bomb was supplied to him by a police agent to give the government the necessary authority to persecute the anarchists in earnest; the police had been watching his activities only days before the deed. For evidence of collusion between the royalists, the anti-Semitic right, and the anarchists, see chapter 2. Marcel Schwob may have been right in believing that the clergy was involved in such intrigues.

35. See Mannheim, *Ideology and Utopia,* 237–39.

36. Cornell, *Adolphe Retté,* includes Verlaine, Huysmans, Coppée, Brunetiere, and Paul Bourget among the earlier, fin de siècle converts to Catholicism. In 1905, Francis Jammes followed the advice of Paul Claudel, and shortly afterward Charles Guerin, Jacques Maritain, and Louis Bertrand converted. In 1908 it was Péguy's turn; in 1910 a host of *littérateurs* declared their faith, including Lotte, Thorel, Lafou, Fleury, and Morice; in 1913 Psichari and Massis converted. See also Hughes, *Consciousness and Society,* 342, 344; Weber, *The Nationalist Revival in France.*

37. Retté, "Des Morts," *Aspects.*

38. Hamon, *Psychologie,* 196.

39. See Weber and Rogger, eds., *The European Right,* 92.

40. Adam, *Le Nouvel anarchiste," La Critique des moeurs,* 258.

41. Paul Adam, "Un Philosophe nouveau," *Mercure de France* 12 (December 1894): 370.

42. Paul Adam, "Les Origines du socialismes," *La Critique des moeurs.*

43. See Hughes, *Consciousness and Society,* 96.

44. Laurent Tailhade, preface to Emile Bans, *Ballades Rouges* (Paris: Edition Libre de l'Auteur, 1903), v, vi.

45. Ibid., 47, 48. 14.

46. MacKay, *The Anarchists,* 293.

47. Steenhuyse, "Quelques jalons dans l'étude du thème du 'Grand Soir,' jusqu'en 1900."

48. For a discussion of sacrificial reciprocity and ritual performances, see Leach, *Culture and Communication,* 50 ff.

49. Morel, *Terre promise.*

50. See Debord, *Society of the Spectacle,* paragraph 74.

51. See C. H. Waddington's discussion in Sol Tax, ed., *Issues in Evolution* (Chicago: University of Chicago Press, 1960), 3:171–73; and Rappaport, "Sanctity and Adaptation."

52. The blank page was visually expressed in Mallarmé's poem "Un coup de dés jamais n'abolira le hasard," and was alluded to in the final stanza of "Salut": "Solitude, récif, etoile / à n'importe ce que valut / Le blanc souci de notre toile." *Mallarmé,* ed. Hartley, 7.

53. See La Barre, *The Ghost Dance,* for a complete discussion of crisis cults. Whereas La Barre stresses the irrational foundations of millennial movements, I have emphasized the functional, order-giving elements of religion.

CONCLUSION

1. Pouget, "Au pays des moïs," *Almanach du Père Peinard,* 1897, 63.

2. See Lovejoy, " 'Nature' as Aesthetic Norm," *Essays in the History of Ideas* (essay originally published 1927), 77, also 72, 74.

3. Kropotkin, *Mutual Aid.*

4. See J. J. Spengler, *France Faces Depopulation* (Durham, N.C.: Duke University Press, 1938).

5. This is the thesis of Swart in *The Sense of Decadence in Nineteenth-Century France,* 253–62.

6. Bourget, "Charles Baudelaire, théorie de la décadence," *Essais de psychologie contemporaine,* 1:19–26.

7. See Calinescu, *Faces of Modernity,* 171.

8. Rémy de Gourmont, "Stéphane Mallarmé and the Idea of Decadence," from *La Culture des idees* (1898), in *Rémy de Gourmont,*

Selected Writings, 67–77; quotation from the preface to *Le Livre des masques* (1896), 1:182.

9. See Theodore Zeldin, *France, 1848–1945: Politics and Anger* (Oxford: Oxford University Press, 1979), chapter 8, "Solidarism."

10. See Calinescu, *Faces of Modernity,* 198–202.

11. See Weingarten, *Writers and Revolution,* chapter 14, "Literary decadence and revolutionary anarchism," 213–28.

12. Mauclair, *Le Soleil des morts,* 149, 150.

13. See Mauclair, *L'Ennemi des rêves.*

Bibliography

The research for this book was carried out at Doe Library, University of California at Berkeley, and at the following Parisian schools, libraries, and archives:

Archives Nationales
Archives de la Préfecture de Police
Bibliothèque de l'Arsenal
Bibliothèque des Arts Décoratifs
Bibliothèque de l'Histoire de la Ville de Paris
Bibliothèque Jacques Doucet
Bibliothèque Nationale
L'Ecole des Hautes Etudes en Sciences Sociales
L'Institut Français d'Histoire Social
La Musée de Montmartre
La Musée Social

The Archives Nationale F7 Series (*Police générale*) was a moderately useful source of police and Ministry of the Interior reports on anarchist activity; the F21 series provided information on censorship in the Third Republic. I relied more heavily on the detailed reports in the police archives, as my notes reveal. The Institut Français d'Histoire Social was chiefly useful for the Jean Grave Correspondence.

Principal anarchist journals consulted were *L'Endehors, Le Père Peinard, La Révolte,* and *La Revue Rouge.* The major Symbolist reviews were *Les Entretiens Politiques et Littéraires, L'Ermitage, Le Mercure de France, La Plume,* and *La Revue Blanche.* I read Maurice Barrès's *La Cocarde* in microfilm in the periodicals room of the Bibliothèque Nationale. Primary source articles cited in full in the notes have not been included in the bibliography.

Adam, Paul. *La Critique des moeurs.* Paris: Kolb, 1893.

———. *Les Imperialismes et la morale des peuples.* Paris: Boivin, 1908.

———. *Lettres de malaisie.* 2d ed. Paris: Crès, 1922.

———. *Le Mystère des foules.* 2 vols. Paris: Ollendorff, 1895.

Adam, Paul, and Gabriel Mourey. *L'Automne.* Paris: Kolb, 1893.

Antoine, André. *Mes souvenirs sur le Théâtre-Libre.* Paris: Fayard, 1921.

Ariès, Philippe. *Histoire des populations françaises.* Paris: Self, 1948.

Artus, Maurice. "Essai de bibliographie de la presse montmartroise: Journaux et carnards." *Le Vieux Montmartre* 49–50 (July 1905).

Aubery, Pierre. "L'Anarchisme des littérateurs au temps du symbolisme." *Mouvement Social* 69 (1969): 21–34.

Barrès, Maurice. *L'Ennemi des lois.* Paris: Perrin, 1893.

———. *Examen de trois idéologies.* Paris: Perrin, 1892.

———. *Une Journée parlémentaire.* Paris: Charpentier, 1894.

———. *Un Rénovateur de l'occultisme: Stanislaus de Guaita (1861–98).* Paris: Chamuel, 1898.

Barrows, Susanna. *Distorting Mirrors: Visions of the Crowd in Late Nineteenth-Century France.* New Haven: Yale University Press, 1981.

Barthes, Roland. *L'Empire des signes.* Geneva: Skira, 1970.

Bataille, Albert. *Causes criminelles et mondaines de 1892.* Paris: E. Dentu, 1893.

———. *Causes criminelles et mondaines de 1895.* Paris: E. Dentu, 1896.

Bateson, Gregory. *Steps to an Ecology of Mind.* New York: Chandler, 1972.

Beachboard, Robert. *The Montmartre Colony.* Santa Barbara: University of California Press, 1963.

Beaubourg, Maurice. *Contes pour les assassins.* Paris: Perrin, 1890.

Bella, Edward. *A Collection of Posters.* London: Royal Aquarium, 1894–95.

Bellah, Robert. *Beyond Belief.* New York: Harper & Row, 1970.

Benjamin, Walter. *Illuminations.* Trans. Harry Zohn. New York: Harcourt, Brace and World, 1968.

———. *Reflections.* New York: Harcourt, Brace, Jovanovich, 1978.

Bérard, Alexandre. *Sur l'anarchie.* Lyon: A. H. Storck, 1897.

Bercy, Léon de. *Montmartre et ses chansons.* Paris: H. Daragon, 1902.

Berlanstein, Lenard. *The Working People of Paris, 1871–1914.* Baltimore: Johns Hopkins University Press, 1984.

Bernstein, Basil. *Class, Codes and Control.* New York: Schocken, 1975.

Bianquis, Geneviève. *Nietzsche en France.* Paris: Félix Alcan, 1929.

Billy, André. *L'Epoque 1900: 1885–1905.* Paris: Jules Tallandier, 1951.

Blond, Georges. *La Grande Armée du drapeau noir.* Paris: Presses de la Cité, 1972.

Boon, James A. *From Symbolism to Structuralism.* New York: Harper & Row, 1972.

Boukay, Maurice. *Chansons rouges.* Paris: Flammarion, 1897.

Bourdieu, Pierre. "Champ du pouvoir, champ intellectuel, et habitus de classe." *Scolies* 1 (1971).

———. "Le Marché des biens symboliques." *L'Année Sociologique* 22 (1971).

———. "Le Pouvoir symbolique." *Annales: Economies, Sociétés, Civilizations* 32 (May–June 1977).

Bourget, Paul. *Essais de psychologie contemporaine,* vol. 1. Paris: Plon, 1883.

Brochon, Pierre. *La Chanson sociale de Béranger à Brassens.* Paris: Les Editions Ouvrières, 1961.

Bruant, Aristide. *Dans la rue.* 2 vols. Paris: Aristide Bruant, 1889, 1895.

———. *Dictionnaire français-argot: L'Argot de xxᵉ siècle.* Paris: Flammarion, 1901.

Byvanck, W. G. C. *Un Hollandais à Paris en 1891.* Paris: Perrin, 1892.

Cachin, Françoise. *Paul Signac.* Paris: Bibliothèque des Arts, 1971.

Calinescu, Matei. *Faces of Modernity.* Bloomington: University of Indiana Press, 1977.

Carassus, Emilien. *Barrès et sa fortune littéraire.* Bordeaux: Ducros, 1970.

———. *Le Snobisme et les lettres françaises.* Paris: Armand Colin, 1966.

Carco, Francis. *La Belle Epoque au temps du Bruant.* Paris: Gallimard, 1954.

Carroll, John. *Break-Out from the Crystal Palace: The Anarcho-Psychological Critique: Stirner, Nietzsche, Dostoyevsky.* London: Routledge and Kegan Paul, 1974.

Cerf, Marcel. *Le d'Artagnan de la commune.* Paris: Le Pavillon, 1967.

Les Chants du peuple. Paris: Les Temps Nouveaux, n.d.

Charles, Christophe. "Champ littéraire et champ du pouvoir: Les écrivains et l'affaire Dreyfus." *Annales: Economies, Sociétés, Civilizations* 32, 2 (March–April 1977).

————. "Histoire sociale des groupes littéraires de 1865 à 1902 environ." Doctorat du troisième cycle. Ecole des Hautes Etudes en Sciences Sociales, Paris, 1975.

Chevalier, Louis. *Laboring Classes and Dangerous Classes.* Trans. Frank Jellinek. Princeton, N.J.: Princeton University Press, 1973.

Cipolla, Carlo. *Literacy and Development in the West.* Harmondsworth: Penguin, 1969.

Clark, Thomas J. *The Absolute Bourgeois.* London: Thames and Hudson, 1973.

Clark, William C. "Camille Mauclair and the Religion of Art." Ph.D. dissertation. University of California at Berkeley, 1976.

Cohn, Norman. *The Pursuit of the Millennium.* New York: Harper & Brothers, 1961.

Commenge, O. *La Prostitution clandestine à Paris.* Paris: Schleicher Frères, 1897.

Corbin, Alain. *Les Filles du noce: Misère sexuelle et prostitution (19e et 20e siècles).* Paris: Aubier Montaigne, 1978.

Cornell, William K. *Adolphe Retté (1863–1930).* New Haven: Yale University Press, 1942.

Culler, Jonathan. *Structuralist Poetics.* Ithaca, N.Y.: Cornell University Press, 1975.

Debord, Guy. *Society of the Spectacle.* Detroit: Black and Red, 1977.

Defontaine, B., and J. Defontaine. "Figure, langage et répresentation." *Annales: Economies, Sociétés, Civilizations* 28, 1 (January–February 1973).

Delesalle, Georges. *Dictionnaire argot-français et français-argot.* Paris: Ollendorff, 1896.

Delteil, Loys. *Toulouse-Lautrec.* 20 vols. Paris: published privately, 1920.

Devaldès, Manuel. *Hurles de haine et d'amour*. Paris: F. Clerget, 1897.

Doty, C. Stewart. *From Cultural Rebellion to Counterrevolution: The Politics of Maurice Barrès*. Athens: Ohio University Press, 1976.

Duncan, J. Ann. *Les Romans de Paul Adam*. Berne: Peter Lang, 1977.

Durand, Xavier. "L'Evolution littéraire dans *Les Entretiens Politiques et Littéraires*, 1890–1893." Maîtrise de lettres classiques. Université de Paris, 1968.

Duret, Théodore. *Lautrec*. Paris: Bernheim-Jeune, 1920.

Eco, Umberto. *A Theory of Semiotics*. Bloomington: Indiana University Press, 1976.

Egbert, Donald. *Social Radicalism and the Arts*. New York: Knopf, 1970.

Fénéon, Félix. *Oeuvres plus que complètes*. Ed. Joan Halperin. Geneva: Droz, 1970.

Garraud, R. *L'Anarchie et la repression*. Paris: L. Larose, 1895.

Gauzi, François. *Lautrec et son temps*. Paris: Perret, 1954.

Geertz, Clifford. *The Interpretation of Cultures*. New York: Basic Books, 1973.

Geffroy, Gustave. *La Musée du Soir aux quartiers ouvriers*. Paris: André Marty, n.d. [1895].

———. *La Vie artistique*, 1er series. Paris: E. Dentu, 1892.

Giard, Louis. "Les Elections à Paris sous la IIIe République." Ph.D. dissertation. Université de Dakar, 1966–68.

Gourmont, Rémy de. *Le Livre des masques*. 2 vols. Paris: Mercure de France, 1896, 1898.

———. *Rémy de Gourmont, Selected Writings*. Trans. and ed. Glenn S. Burne. Ann Arbor: University of Michigan Press, 1966.

Goustine, Christian de. *Pouget: Les Matins noirs du syndicalisme*. Paris: Ed. de la Tête des Feuilles, 1972.

Graff, Harvey, ed. *Literacy and Social Development in the West: A Reader*. Cambridge: Cambridge University Press, 1981.

Guiraud, Pierre. *L'Argot*. Paris: Presses Universitaires de France, 1956.

———. "Chronique de l'Argot, 'Pier,' 'Argot.' " *Cahiers de Lexicologie* 12, 1 (1968).

Hamon, Augustin. *Les Hommes et les théories de l'anarchie*. Paris: La Révolte, 1893.

———. *Psychologie de l'anarchiste-socialiste*. Paris: Stock, 1895.

Hemmings, F. W. J. *Culture and Society in France.* New York: Charles Scribner's Sons, 1971.

Heppenstall, Rayner. *A Little Pattern of French Crime.* London: Hamish Hamilton, 1969.

Herbert, Eugenia. *The Artist and Social Reform, France and Belgium, 1885–1898.* New Haven: Yale University Press, 1961.

Herbert, Eugenia, and Robert Herbert. "Artists and Anarchism: Unpublished Letters of Pissarro, Signac and others." *Burlington Magazine* (November 1960).

Herbert, Michel. *La Chanson à Montmartre.* Paris: La Table Ronde, 1967.

Horowitz, Irving L., ed. *The Anarchists.* New York: Dell, 1964.

Hughes, H. Stuart. *Consciousness and Society.* New York: Vintage, 1958.

Huisman, Philippe, and M. G. Dortu. *Lautrec par Lautrec.* Paris: Ed. Lausanne, 1964.

Huret, Jules. *Enquête sur l'evolution littéraire.* Paris: Charpentier, 1894.

Idt, G. "L'Intellectuel avant L'affaire Dreyfus." *Cahiers de Lexicologie* 15, 2 (1969).

Ives, Colta Feller. *The Great Wave.* New York: Metropolitan Museum of Art, 1974.

Iviansky, Ze'ev. "Individual Terror: Concept and Typology." *Journal of Contemporary History* 12 (1977).

Jackson, A. B. *La Revue Blanche.* Paris: Lettres Modernes, 1960.

Jacquemet, Gérard. *Belleville au XIXe siecle: Du faubourg à la ville.* Paris: Ecole des Hautes Etudes, Jean Touzot, 1984.

Jasper, Gertrude R. *Adventure in the Theater.* New Brunswick, N.J.: Rutgers University Press, 1947.

Jean, "Monsieur." *Les Bas-Fonds du crime et de la prostitution.* Paris: Bibliothèque du Journal Fin de Siècle, 1899.

Jourdain, Francis. *Né en 76.* Paris: Pavillon, 1951.

Jourdain, Francis, and Jean Adhémar. *Toulouse-Lautrec.* Paris: Perre Tisne, 1954.

Joll, James, *The Anarchists.* New York: Grosset and Dunlap, 1964.

Joly, Henri. *Le Crime, étude social.* Paris: Léopold Cerf, 1888.

Josephson, Matthew. *Zola and His Time.* New York: Garden City Pub. Co., 1928.

Julien, Edouard. *Lautrec.* New York: Crown, 1976.

Jullian, Philippe. *Montmartre.* Trans. Anne Carter. Oxford: Phaidon, 1977.

Julliard, Jacques. "Fernand Pelloutier et les origines du syndicalisme d'action directe." *Le Mouvement Social* 75 (April–June 1971).

Kropotkin, Peter. *Mutual Aid.* London: Heinemann, 1915.

————. *Paroles d'un révolté.* Paris: Marpon et Flammarion, 1885.

La Barre, Weston. *The Ghost Dance: The Origins of Religion.* New York: Delta, 1970.

Laqueur, Walter. *Terrorism.* Boston: Little, Brown, 1977.

Lazare, Bernard. *L'Ecrivain et l'art social.* Paris: Bibliothèque de l'Art Social, 1896.

Leach, Edmund. *Culture and Communication.* Cambridge: Cambridge University Press, 1976.

Le Bon, Gustave. *The Psychology of Peoples.* New York: Macmillan, 1898.

Le Bot, Marc. *Le Peinture et la machinisme.* Paris: Klingseick, 1973.

Leger, Augustin. *Journal d'une anarchiste.* Paris: Albert Savine, 1895.

Lermina, Jules, and Henri Levêque. *Dictionnaire thématique français-argot.* Paris: Chacornac, 1897.

Lesourd, Paul. *Montmartre.* Paris: France-Empire, 1973.

Lethève, Jacques. *La Caricature et la presse sous le Troisième République.* Paris: Armand Colin, 1961.

Lewis, Paula Gilbert. *The Aesthetics of Stéphane Mallarmé in Relation to His Public.* Cranbury, N.J.: Associated Presses, 1976.

Leyret, Henri. *De Waldeck-Rousseau à la C.G.T.: La société et les syndicats.* Paris: E. de la Sirène, 1921.

————. *En plein faubourg.* Paris: Charpentier, 1895.

Longrée, Georges. "Le Vers libre et l'avenir de la poésie." *Il y a des poètes partout, Revue Esthétique,* no. 3–4 (18 October 1975).

Lovejoy, Arthur O. " 'Nature' as Aesthetic Norm." *Essays in the History of Ideas.* New York: G. P. Putnam's Sons, 1960.

MacKay, John Henry. *The Anarchists: A Picture of Civilization at the Close of the Nineteenth Century.* Trans. George Schumm. Boston: Benjamin Tucker, 1891.

Maitron, Jean. *Dictionnaire biographique du mouvement ouvrière française.* 15 vols. Paris: Les Editions Ouvrières, 1973.

―――. *Le Mouvement anarchiste en France.* 2 vols. Paris: Maspero, 1975.

―――. *Ravachol et les anarchistes.* Paris: Julliard, 1964.

Mallarmé, Stéphane. *Mallarmé.* Ed. and prose trans. Anthony Hartley. Harmondsworth: Penguin, 1965.

Mancini, Jean-Gabriel. *Prostitution et proxénetisme.* Paris: Universitaires de France, 1962.

Mannheim, Karl. *Ideology and Utopia.* New York: Harcourt, Brace and World, 1961.

Matejka, Ladislav, and Irwin Titunik, eds. *Semiotics of Art: Prague School Contributions.* Cambridge, Mass: M.I.T. Press, 1976.

Mauclair, Camille. *L'Art en silence.* Paris: Société d'Editions Littéraires et Artistiques, 1901.

―――. *L'Ennemi des rêves.* Paris: Ollendorff, 1900.

―――. *Servitudes et grandeurs littéraires.* Paris: Ollendorff, 1922.

―――. *Le Soleil des morts.* Paris: Ollendorff, 1898.

Maurer, Charles B. *Call to Revolution: The Mystical Anarchism of Gustav Landauer.* Detroit: Wayne State University, 1971.

Maurras, Charles. *Les Poètes.* Paris: Le Divan, 1924.

―――. *Romantisme et revolution.* Versailles: Bibliothèque des Politiques, 1928.

Mitchell, Bonner. *Les Manifestes littéraires de la belle epoque.* Paris: Seghers, 1966.

Moles, Abraham. *L'Affiche dans la société urbaine.* Paris: Dunod, 1970.

Monférier, Jacques. "Symbolisme et l'anarchie." *Revue d'Histoire Littéraire de la France* 65 (April–June 1965).

Montuclard, Maurice. *Conscience réligieuse et démocratie.* Paris: Seuil, 1965.

Morel, Emile. *Les Gueules noires.* Paris: Sansot, 1907.

Morel, Eugène. *Terre promise.* Paris: La Revue Blanche, 1898.

Morris, Charles W. "Foundations of a Theory of Signs." *International Encyclopedia of Unified Science,* 1, no. 2 (1938).

Moss, Bernard. *The Origins of the French Labor Movement, 1830–1914: The Socialism of Skilled Workers.* Berkeley and Los Angeles: University of California Press, 1976.

Mourey, Michele. "La Chanson politique et sociale de 1871 à 1906:

Etude d'une source." Mémoire de maîtrise. Université de Paris, 1970.

Mueller, Claus. *The Politics of Communication.* New York: Oxford University Press, 1973.

Natanson, Thadée. *Peints à leur tour.* Paris: Albin Michel, 1948.

Nettlau, Max. *Histoire de l'anarchie.* Trans. Martin Zemlich. Paris: Ed. du Circle, 1971.

Niceforo, Alfredo. *Les Classes pauvres.* Paris: Giard et Brière, 1905.

———. *Le Génie de l'argot.* Paris: Mercure de France, 1912.

Nietzsche, Friedrich. *The Portable Nietzsche.* Trans. and ed. Walter Kaufmann. New York: Viking, 1968.

Nocera, Antonio de. *Anarchie et spiritualisme.* Paris: H. Durville, 1899.

Nordau, Max. *Degeneration.* New York: Howard Fertig, 1968.

Novotny, F. *Toulouse-Lautrec.* London: Phaidon, 1969.

Oberthur, Mariel. *Cafés and Cabarets of Montmartre.* Trans. Sheila Azoulai. Salt Lake City: Gibbs M. Smith, 1984.

Ong, Walter. *Orality and Literacy.* New York: Methuen, 1982.

O'Squarr, Flor [pseud.]. *Les Coulisses de l'anarchie.* Paris: Albert Savine, 1892.

Paillette, Paul. *Tablettes d'un lézard.* Paris: Librairie Nouvelle, 1892.

Perruchot, Henri. *La Vie de Toulouse-Lautrec.* Paris: Hachette, 1958.

Phillips, C. S. *The Church in France, 1848–1907.* London: Society for Promoting Christian Knowledge, 1936.

Poggioli, Renato. *The Theory of the Avant-Garde.* New York: Harper & Row, 1968, 1971.

Poinsot, M.-C. *La Littérature sociale.* Paris: Bibliothèque Générale d'Edition, 1907.

Ponton, Remy. "Le Champ littéraire en France, de 1865 à 1905." Doctorat du troisième cycle. Ecole des Hautes Etudes en Sciences Sociales, Paris, 1977.

———. "Programme esthétique et accumulation de capital symbolique: L'example de Parnasse." *Revue Française Sociologique* 14 (1973).

Postman, Neil. *Teaching as a Conserving Activity.* New York: Delacorte Press, 1979.

Pouget, Emile. *Almanach du Père Peinard*. Paris: Le Père Peinard, 1893, 1896, 1897.

———. *Le Père Peinard*. Ed. Roger Langlois. Paris: Ed. Galilée, 1976.

Proudhon, P. J. *Du principe de l'art et de se destination sociale*. Paris: Garnier Frères, 1865.

Rappaport, Roy. *Pigs for the Ancestors: Ritual in the Ecology of a New Guinea People*. New Haven: Yale University Press, 1968.

———. "Sanctity and Adaptation." *Coevolution Quarterly* 1, 2 (Summer 1974).

Raynaud, Ernest. *En marge de la melée symboliste*. Paris: Mercure de France, 1936.

———. *Souvenirs de Police au temps de Ravachol*. Paris: Payot, 1923.

Rearick, Charles. "Festivals in Modern France: The Experience of the Third Republic." *Journal of Contemporary History* 12 (1977).

Réberioux, Madeleine. "Avant-garde esthétique et avant-garde politique: Le Socialisme français entre 1890 et 1914." *Raison Présente* 6 (April–June 1967).

Reszler, André. *L'Esthétique anarchiste*. Paris: Presses Universitaires de France, Collection SUP, 1973.

Retté, Adolphe. *L'Archipel en fleurs*. Paris: Bibliothèque Artistique et Littéraire, 1895.

———. *Aspects*. Paris: Bibliothèque Artistique et Littéraire, 1897.

———. *Le Forêt bruissante*. Paris: Bibliothèque Artistique et Littéraire, 1896.

———. *La Maison en ordre: Comment un révolutionnaire devint royaliste*. Paris: Nouvelle Librairie Nationale, 1923.

———. *Promenades subversives*. Paris: Bibliothèque Artistique et Littéraire, 1896.

———. *Similitudes*. Paris: Bibliothèque Artistique et Littéraire, 1895.

———. *Le Symbolisme*. Paris: Vanier, 1903.

Richard, Emile, *La Prostitution à Paris*. Paris: Baillière, 1890.

Rictus, Jehan [Gabriel Randon]. *Les Soliloques du pauvre*. Paris: published privately, 1896.

Ridley, F. F. *Revolutionary Syndicalism in France: The Direct Action of Its Time*. Cambridge: Cambridge University Press, 1970.

Robichez, Jacques. *Lugné-Pöe*. Paris: L'Arche, 1955.

Roman, Jean. *Paris fin de siècle*. Paris: Robert Delpire, 1958.

Rosenfeld, John M. "Japanese Printing and Graphic Arts of the Edo Period." *Apollo* 107 (June 1978).

Rossignol. *Dictionnaire d'argot*. Paris: Ollendorff, 1901.

Rouchon, Ulysse. *L'Appel des ombres*. Le-Puy-en-Velay: Ed. de la Société Académique, 1931.

Rudorff, Raymond. *La Belle Epoque, Paris in the Nineties*. London: Hamish Hamilton, 1972.

Sainéan, Lazare. *Le Langage parisien au XIXe siècle*. Paris: E. de Bocard, 1920.

———. *Les Sources de l'argot ancien*. Paris: H. and E. Champion, 1912.

Saint-Rémy, Marie de [Marie Andrieux]. *Les Dieux des anarchistes*. Paris: H. Durville, 1899.

Salmon, André. *La Terreur noire*. Paris: J. J. Pauvert, 1959.

Sanborn, Alvan. *Paris and the Social Revolution*. Boston: Small, Maynard and Co., 1905.

Sarrazin, Jehan. *Souvenirs de Montmartre et du Quartier Latin*. Paris: published privately, 1895.

Schwob, Marcel. *Les Oeuvres complètes*. Ed. Pierre Champion. 10 vols. Paris: F. Bernouard, 1927–30.

Schwob, Marcel, and Georges Guieysse. *Etude sur l'argot français*. Paris: Emile Bouillon, 1889.

Scoffham-Peufly, Françoise. "Les Problemes de l'art social à travers les revues politico-littéraires et les groupes d'avant-garde politique en France, 1890–96." Mémoire de maîtrise. Université de Paris VIII, Vincennes, 1970.

Sebeok, Thomas ed. *Approaches to Semiotics*. Paris: Mouton, 1971.

———. ed. *Style in Language*. Cambridge, Mass.: M.I.T. Press, 1960.

Seipse, André de [A. Suarès]. *Lettres d'un solitaire sur les maux du temps*. Paris: Ollendorff, 1899.

Servais, J. J., and J. P. Laurend. *Histoire et dossier de la prostitution*. Paris: L'Encyclopédie Contemporain, n.d.

Séverine. *En marche*. . . . Paris: H. Simonis Empis, 1896.

Shapiro, Theda. *Painters and Politics: The European Avant-Garde and Society, 1900–1925*. New York: Elsevier, 1976.

Shattuck, Roger. *The Banquet Years*. New York: Vintage, 1958.

Siegel, Jerrold. *Bohemian Paris: Culture, Politics, and the Boundaries of Bourgeois Life, 1830–1930*. New York: Viking, 1986.

Signac, Paul. *D'Eugène Delacroix au néo-impressionisme*. Paris: La Revue Blanche, 1899.

Smith, Bradley. *Japan: A History in Art*. Garden City, N.Y.: Doubleday, 1964.

Société des Gens de Lettres. Livre d'hommage des lettres françaises à Emile Zola. Paris: Société libre d'Edition des Gens de Lettres, 1898.

Sontag, Susan. "The Aesthetics of Silence." *Styles of Radical Will*. New York: Farrar, Straus and Giroux, 1969.

Sorel, Georges. *The Illusions of Progress*. Trans. John and Charlotte Stanley. Berkeley and Los Angeles: University of California Press, 1969.

——. *Reflections on Violence*. Trans. T. E. Hulme. London: Collier-Macmillan, 1950, 1961.

Soucy, Robert. *Fascism in France: The Case of Maurice Barrès*. Berkeley and Los Angeles: University of California Press, 1972.

Steele, Henry. *The Working Classes in France: A Social Study*. London: Twentieth Century Press, 1904.

Steenhuyse, D. "Quelques jalons dans l'étude du thème du 'Grand Soir,' jusqu'en 1900." *Le Mouvement Social* 75 (April–June 1971).

Steiner, George. *Language and Silence*. New York: Atheneum, 1967.

Sternhell, Zeev. "Barrès et la gauche: Du boulangisme à *La Cocarde* (1889–1895)." *Le Mouvement Social* 75 (April–June 1971).

——. *La Droite révolutionnaire, 1885–1914: Les origines françaises du fascisme*. Paris, 1978.

——. *Maurice Barrès et le nationalisme français*. Paris: A. Colin, 1972.

Stuckey, Charles F., with Naomi E. Maurer. *Toulouse-Lautrec: Paintings*. Chicago: The Art Institute, 1978.

Sutter, Jean, ed. *The Neo-Impressionists*. Greenwich, Conn.: New York Graphic Society, 1970.

Swart, Konraad. *The Sense of Decadence in Nineteenth-Century France*. The Hague: Mouton, 1964.

Symons, Arthur. *The Symbolist Movement in Literature*. New York: E. P. Dutton, 1958.

Sypher, Wylie. *Literature and Technology: The Alien Vision.* New York: Vintage, 1968.

Tailhade, Laurent. *Au pays des mufles.* Paris: Bibliothèque Artistique et Littéraire, 1891.

———. *Platres et marbres.* Paris: Figuière, 1913.

Taube, Nils Evert. "Etude sur l'emploi de l'argot des malfaiteurs chez les auteurs romantiques." Thèse doctorat. University of Uppsala, 1917.

Terrou, Fernand. "L'Evolution du droit de la presse de 1881 à 1940." In Bellanger, Claude, et al., *Histoire générale de la presse française,* vol. 3: *1881 à 1940.* Paris: Presses Universitaires de France, 1969–76.

Thibaudet, Albert. *French Literature: From 1795 to Our Era.* Trans. C. C. Markman. New York: Funk and Wagnall, 1967 (orig. 1938).

———. *La Vie de Maurice Barrès.* Paris: Nouvelle Revue Française, 1921.

Thirion, Y. "Le Japonisme en France dans le seconde moitié du XIXe siècle." *Cahiers de l'Association International des Etudes Françaises* 13 (1961).

Thomas, Paul. *Karl Marx and the Anarchists.* London: Routledge and Kegan Paul, 1980.

Thomson, David. *Democracy in France since 1870.* Oxford: Oxford University Press, 1969.

Tilly, Charles, and Louise Tilly. *The Rebellious Century.* Cambridge, Mass.: Harvard University Press, 1975.

Toulouse-Lautrec, Henri de. *Lettres, 1871–1901.* Paris: Gallimard, 1972.

Toutain, J.-C. *La Population de la France de 1700 à 1959.* Paris: Cahiers de L'Institut de Science Economique Appliqué, 1963.

Trudgill, Peter. *Sociolinguistics: An Introduction.* Harmondsworth: Penguin, 1974.

Tuchman, Barbara. *The Proud Tower.* New York: Bantam, 1966.

Varennes, Henri. *De Ravachol à Caserio.* Paris: Garnier Frères, 1895.

Virmaître, Charles. *Dictionnaire d'argot fin-de-siècle.* Paris: A. Charles, 1894.

———. *Trottoirs et lupanars.* Paris: Henri Perrot, 1893.

Wallace, Anthony F. C. *Religion: An Anthropological View.* New York: Random House, 1966.

Weber, Eugen. *The Nationalist Revival in France.* Berkeley and Los Angeles: University of California Press, 1959.

Weber, Eugen, and Hans Rogger, eds. *The European Right.* Berkeley and Los Angeles: University of California Press, 1966.

Weingarten, Renee. *Writers and Revolution: The Fatal Lure of Action.* New York: New Viewpoints, 1974.

Whorf, Benjamin Lee. *Language, Thought and Reality: Selected Writings of Benjamin Lee Whorf.* Ed. John B. Carroll. New York: M.I.T. Press, 1956.

Wilde, Oscar. *The Soul of Man Under Socialism.* London: Humphreys, 1912.

Zo d'Axa [Charles Galland]. *Endehors.* Paris: Chamuel, 1896.

———. *Endehors.* Ed. Jean Pierre Courty. Paris: Champ Libre, 1974.

Zola, Emile. *L'Assommoir* [1876]. Trans. Leonard Tancock. Harmondsworth: Penguin, 1970.

———. *Paris.* Paris: Fasquelle, 1898.

Index

Prostitution, 59–60, 70, 78, 102, 109–13, 133–34, 136–37, 153, 162, 260, 316 n.20, 317 n.26

Protofascists. (*See* Fascist)

Proudhon, Pierre-Joseph, 5, 9–11, 17, 31–32, 81, 106, 144–45, 147–48, 201, 283

Psychological novelists, 294

Pujo, Maurice, 189–90

Puvis de Chavannes, Pierre, 149, 329 n.57

Quillard, Pierre, 186, 194, 200, 215–16, 255, 326 n.7

Ravachol, François-Claudius, 7, 15, 17, 24, 37, 43–44, 47, 66–67, 72, 76, 90, 94, 104, 114, 121, 124, 165–66, 173, 184, 189, 217, 221, 239–44, 252, 255–56, 259–62, 271, 273–75, 277, 281, 288

Realism, 5, 192

Rebell, Hugues, 188, 219

Reclus, Elisée, 15, 17, 20, 56, 190–91, 221, 242, 244, 250, 264, 283, 297

Regnier, Henri de, 226, 255, 326 n.7

Reincarnation, 275

Religion and religiosity, 194, 203–4, 207–8, 219, 263ff.

Renan, Ernest, 195, 300

Renard, George, 200

Retté, Adolphe, 15, 18, 21–22, 28, 56, 91, 186, 188–89, 194–95, 199, 202–9, 213–14, 218–19, 223–28, 231, 234, 250, 277, 281–82, 286, 288, 298, 307 n.36

Revitalistic movements, 269–71

Révolte, La, 3, 5, 8, 14–17, 20–21, 56, 78, 98, 114, 117, 147–48, 185–86, 247, 264, 298

Revue Anarchiste, La, 186, 256

Revue Blanche, La, 17–19, 21, 38, 40–43, 47–48, 55, 151, 154, 175–76, 185–86, 216, 220, 228, 232, 248, 250, 258, 262, 330 n.7

Revue Indépendante, La, 23, 143

Revue Socialiste, La, 198, 200

Revue Wagnerienne, La, 217

Richepin, Jean, 18, 129, 186

Rictus, Jehan (Gabriel Randon), 88, 128, 137–40, 326 n.7

Right Bank, 52

Rimbaud, Arthur, 205

Rochefort, Henri de, 37, 308 n.9

Romanticism, 114, 151, 179, 181, 197, 203, 211, 220, 228, 231, 258, 291

Rosny brothers, 182, 184, 200

Rothschild, Baron de, 44–46, 54, 230, 282

Rousseau, Jean-Jacques, 227, 267

Rousset, E., 185

Royalists and Royalism, 35–36, 39–43, 48, 279, 300, 324 n.44

Ruskin, John, 190

Rysselberghe, Théo van, 143, 326 n.7

Sacré-Coeur, 4, 50–51, 82, 92, 282

Sainéan, Lazare, 101–2, 139

Saint-Auban, Maître de, 230

Saint-Pol Roux, 21, 41, 191, 213, 326 n.7

Saint-Rémy, Marie de (Andrieux), 275, 277, 282

Salis, Rodolphe, 61–62, 73–74, 93, 154, 177

Salle, Gabriel de la, 54, 200

Sangnier, Marc, 278

Santo, Caserio, 26

Sarcey, Francisque, 186

Schopenhaur, Arthur, 218–19

Schwob, Marcel, 160, 191, 194, 268, 279, 288

Scoundrelly laws. *See* Les lois scélérates

Semiotics, 119, 208, 211–14, 224, 330 n.1